D0787456

PUBLIC DUTIES

Public Duties: The Moral Obligations of Government Officials

Edited by Joel L. Fleishman, Lance Liebman, Mark H. Moore

HARVARD UNIVERSITY PRESS

Cambridge, Massachusetts / London, England   1981

Library of Congress Cataloging in Publication Data
Main entry under title:

Public duties.

Contents: Realms of obligation and virtue / Mark H.
Moore — Hard choices, justifying bureaucratic deci-
sions / Douglas T. Yates, Jr. — Self-interest and political
integrity / Joel L. Fleishman — [etc.]
    1. Political ethics — Addresses, essays, lectures.
2. Administrative responsibility — United States —
Addresses, essays, lectures.   3. Public interest — United
States — Addresses, essays, lectures.   4. Corruption
(in politics) — United States — Addresses, essays, lec-
tures.   I. Fleishman, Joel L.   II. Liebman, Lance.
III. Moore, Mark Harrison.
JK468.E7P8   172'.2   81-6253
ISBN 0-674-72231-0   AACR2

For Don K. Price

Preface

In the last decade, America's traditional schizophrenia about government has taken on a new manifestation. From the beginning, the country existed in tension between a society of small landholders wishing to keep the state off their backs and a commercial class for which government could build roads, subsidize entrepreneurship, and establish profitable foreign relations. "Jeffersonian" and "Hamiltonian" are crude labels. Their ambiguity is visible in the contemporary Republican party, which is divided between an allegiance to small businessmen who want freedom from the regulatory state and an alliance with large capitalists who are comfortable with regulation and eager for government assistance abroad, for subsidies and bailouts, and for government-sponsored planning on something like a Japanese model. The same contradiction is exhibited by the suburban homeowner who demands freedom from government efforts to integrate the neighborhood and to control handguns, but active official action to bar abortion and pornography and to compel prayer in the public schools.

Representative democracy is a set of mechanisms for resolving disagreements about official policy that arise from differing values and situations. What seems new in recent years is not disagreement about appropriate exercises of official authority, but the generality and depth of the view that government is ineffective and inefficient at very nearly everything that it does. Monopoly power, absence of the profit standard, civil service combined with public employee unions, inattentive citizen oversight, lack of planning for the long run—each is part of the structural explanation for the failure of government to achieve noninflationary economic growth, to build housing, and to stamp out heroin. The result has been a general perception of unmade choices and unmet needs. At once, we have concluded that government does not work and adopted additional collective goals that only government can pursue for us.

The burden on contemporary governments is great, and government's inability to meet public expectations is not simply another frustration of consumer hopes — not just a short-lived light bulb, a balky carburetor, or an oversold movie. For government is not a company competing for our disposable income. Its services are life-and-death, present-versus-future. Its decisions are the dominant collective agreements of a diverse population. Its existence symbolizes identity and commands loyalty. In a secular postindustrial society, government assumes many of the roles of church, village, lord, company, and marketplace. If we give up on government, we do not have a ready substitute.

In this period of attention to government's failings, our reactions have combined moralism and proceduralism in a typically American ragout. We have believed that if only government officials were more honest, or if only the rules of government could keep them honest, government's performance would improve. This book considers these questions.

What does the idea of ethics mean in government? Americans are torn as was Machiavelli, who thought the successful state required a prince who was not a nice man, who indeed would forfeit his own chance for heaven by "immoral" pursuit of public aims that would allow other citizens to live "moral" (and prosperous) lives within the city's walls. We are trapped between a desire to constrain government to make it behave ethically (to assure ourselves that government's vast power is being exercised for legitimate goals and by accepted means) and our suspicion that effective government (achievement of the ends toward which government is a unique vehicle) requires suspension of private ethical standards and short-circuiting of procedural regularity.

A dominant theme in these essays is renunciation of the extreme version of legalism. The authors are dismayed to discover that ethical impulses, inevitably provoked by official errors and outrages, have led to procedural innovations that hinder and sometimes prevent effective governance. Making government true has been a reason for sunshine laws, sunset laws, individual rights to injunctions and damages, protection for whistleblowers, requirements for public hearings and reasoned explanations and mechanisms of coordination and consultation. At least some of the authors represented in the book are convinced that a consequence of procedural changes in reaction to less-than-ethical government performance has been to bring about, or at least provide excuses for, inaction and avoidance of responsibility by public officials. They see the resulting system of government as one less likely to do what is necessary, and less likely to allow the citizen to hold those elected responsible for the public policies that are implemented. The dominant tone of this book, then, is of government's capacity and responsibility to do good as well as to avoid doing evil, and of procedural arrangements that enable officials to act within an assigned (but broad) field of affairs.

There is, of course, a tension. These authors want action that pursues one or several public purposes and interests. They want officials to be encouraged—because they believe them to be ethically required—to convince themselves that they are pursuing public ends, and to state those ends, and the reasons they believe their policies will serve them, for inspection by those to whom they are responsible: bureaucratic supervisors, elected executives, legislators, voters. Yet isn't the progress toward a government of reasons just another procedural hurdle, one hostile to expedition and, worse, to the ambiguity of ends and means that assists compromise and coalition? Indeed, if, as for instance with Environmental Impact Statements, the requirement of written explanation is enforcable, isn't there inevitably a sharing of authority with judges, the public officials least capable of effective governance?

Only occasionally is this a book about the moral calculus of society's ends. It does not address the ethical arguments for a guaranteed minimum income, for the death penalty, or for privacy. There is some discussion of possible standards for appraising such important and difficult ethical issues. But overwhelmingly, the essays in this book address the structure of government in an era in which policy choices posing such ethical questions and presenting conflicts between compelling ethical commitments are bound to arise continuously. How can government be satisfactorily ethical when it faces so many difficult decisions, when these decisions provoke conflicting arguments that all have an ethical underpinning, and when the society has no habit of serious ethical discourse?

In part, the authors assert the point of view sketched above: that individual officials accept a responsibility to pursue the public interest, that they stop pretending decisions are made by others, that they explain and justify and take the consequences. In effect, the call is for a class of officials—permanent and temporary—with a new culture of responsibility, and a class of citizens newly vigilant and demanding. Our authors ask a great deal.

Some of the authors, however, confront narrower institutional questions. This book has no general assessment of the post-Vietnam, post-Watergate movement to reform government. But the book includes essays on selected institutional topics, showing the relationship between certain moral ends and schemes for seeking to advance them by procedure. What is so interesting when these particular chapters are assembled is the undeveloped state of the science of administrative procedure. We are not good at estimating, ahead of time or in retrospect, the consequences of different arrangements for doing the public's business. We can only set procedures in response to perceived failings; and we are certainly not equipped to reappraise with evidence the mechanisms we invent to combat abuse. Nevertheless, two related points stand out. First, while Alexander Bickel was wrong to say that the only morality is fair process, process and system and routine and method can have ethical content. Second, when values are in controversy and in conflict, procedural arrangements can advance or retard the way they are aired and discussed and struggled over. But the science of understanding the relationship between various procedural mechanisms and the ethical quality of the governmental actions they bring about is deprived, even by the standards of the social sciences.

Ultimately, then, there is a contradiction between the two themes that can be found in this book. Some of the authors imagine active, effective, moral officials using government for the public and taking personal responsibility for their choices. Other authors, more pessimistic about the issues and the personalities, struggle toward group processes that seem inevitably to require more constraints on even the welfare-seeking aggressions of the individual official who manages to place his hands on some lever of power. That the tension can be seen in the Federalist Papers, and in Machiavelli, and in Aristotle, does not make it any less a difficulty or a contradiction. It shows very well how little we have succeeded in solving the issues this book poses, and how much the book is an invitation to others to continue the inquiry. We will be happy if these essays, and the case studies that will appear in a forthcoming companion volume, provide fuel for the more powerful analytic engines that this work surely requires.

This volume is a product of two years of monthly seminars conducted by the Faculty Study Group on the Moral Obligations of Public Officials, under the auspices of the Institute of Politics of the John F. Kennedy School of Government, Harvard University. We are grateful to Jonathan Moore, director of the Institute, for his support and participation. We are also grateful to Joel Colton of the Rockefeller Foundation and to Charles Powers of the Cummins Engine Company for support and assistance.

Joel L. Fleishman
Lance Liebman
Mark H. Moore

Contents

I. Serving the Public Interest

Mark H. Moore

1. Realms of Obligation and Virtue

[handwritten annotation: lays out the ethical virtues of electrocity agency and the relationship to virtue pp 7-10]

THE LIMITATIONS OF PROCESS

Historically, this nation has been reluctant to place much faith in the moral character of its leaders.[1] Instead, we have relied on elaborate procedural and substantive rules to insure good governance by limiting official discretion. We have made officials accountable to us by forcing them to face electoral tests (or to be accountable to people who do). We have made them accountable to one another (and, therefore, to the diverse interests each represents) by dividing power among separate institutions. And we have made them accountable to our most fundamental traditions by subjecting governmental actions to constitutional limitations guarded by a powerful judiciary. Although this system made it difficult for wise and virtuous leaders to bless us with their statecraft, it also gave assurances that no evil men could ever torment us.

The heavy reliance on procedural and substantive rules diminished any sense of urgency about the moral character of public officials. To the extent we thought about it, the virtues of public officials seemed to lie in being respectful toward the rules that circumscribed their action, and in exemplifying upright personal conduct in their daily actions. To many who now consider the question of how public officials should conduct themselves this view still seems the most appropriate. We want nothing more than that officials dutifully satisfy obligations of the decisionmaking process in good faith. The last thing we want is an official who takes liberties with (or even operates aggressively within) the mesh of process obligations to pursue an independent view of what the public interest requires.

If one held this view, the questions of what virtues officials might pursue and what duties they are bound to honor would hold little interest. The questions could be answered with a simple list of formal rules guiding offi-

3

cial conduct. Several emergent characteristics of our governmental system suggest, however, that we will depend on the moral character of our officials much more in the future than we have in the past.

CORRUPTED STRUCTURES AND PROCESSES

For one thing, recent experience with procedural "checks and balances" has, to a degree, jaded our view of their value. Institutional structures and processes originally designed to facilitate widespread participation in public decisions, to focus attention on a limited number of issues, and to occasion choices in which some public values were advanced over others now shelter a horde of narrow and parochial interests attached like barnacles to shards of public power. Within Congress, for example, the specialized committee structure inevitably leads legislators to seek positions on those committees most influential in areas of concern to their constituents. Once ensconced, they use the influence of their office to serve constituency interests.[2] In the executive branch, institutional structures are created to give special attention to specific problems such as drug abuse, environmental protection, energy, and education, and they quickly become the channels through which advocates of particular interests exercise untoward influence over executive branch operations.[3] Similarly, government watchdog agencies (such as the Civil Service Commission, the General Accounting Office, and even the Office of Management and Budget) originally designed to promote accountability now elaborate their rules to such an extent that one suspects they are at least as interested in enlarging their own domains as in promoting effective administration. Since rules, processes, and structures can, therefore, be made to serve narrow purposes as well as broad, bad as well as good, their *general* claim on the allegiance of conscientious public officials may have weakened.

RESIDUAL OFFICIAL DISCRETION

Even if the moral claim of procedures were not weakening, however, it is apparent that the existing rules and procedures leave substantial discretion to senior public officials. Current case studies of the jobs of senior public officials consistently reveal wide discretion in using the legal authority and resources of the government lodged in their offices (for example, launching major programs to treat heroin addicts with an experimental and potentially dangerous drug, loosening visa restrictions, deciding on aggressive enforcement actions against municipal and industrial polluters, and so forth).[4] Sometimes the discretion is de jure — the system expressly delegates substantial discretion because it was unable (or, in many cases, unwilling) to resolve the difficult issues that would arise as a program began to operate.[5] More often, however, the discretion is de facto. The formal rules are simply silent on an important substantive or procedural issue. Alternatively, the guidance that officials receive from different authorizing positions may be conflicting.[6] Whatever the reasons, it seems clear that the dramatic expansion of the government's undertakings has left many pockets of discretionary authority lodged among individual public officials despite determined efforts to limit discretion with substantive and procedural rules.

THE OPPORTUNITY TO CONCEIVE AND PURSUE "THE PUBLIC INTEREST"

Finally, the governmental expansion has not only left substantial discretionary authority in specific positions, but also created significant competence and expertise. Inevitably, public officials in charge of specific public programs become expert in the substantive problems with which they deal, and the operating characteristics of the programs they direct. They will know whether the authority and resources entrusted to them are being used to greatest effect. And if not, they are well positioned to initiate corrections. This suggests that the nation has an interest in encouraging its officials to accept some responsibility for informing—even shaping—government programs in their areas of expertise. Otherwise a great deal of useful insight and information would be lost. One possible implication is that the duties of public officials are not simply to be passive instruments in policymaking but to work actively in establishing goals for public policy in their area, and in advocating those goals among the people who share their responsibility. In short, they have the opportunity and duty to conceive of and pursue the public interest.

Despite our best efforts, then, we have not succeeded in constructing a governmental system that is independent of the moral qualities of its leaders. This makes questions about the duties, obligations, and virtues of public officials more urgent than we suppose, and particularly so for those who teach in professional schools establishing professional standards for public officials. My purposes in this essay are two: first, to sketch three realms within which virtues may be pursued and obligations arise; second, to begin the analysis of where the paths of duty and virtue lie within each realm. Since the discussion risks becoming excessively abstract without specific examples, it is useful to begin with some actual cases.

THREE REALMS OF OFFICIAL OBLIGATION AND VIRTUE

Consider a few vignettes of official action:

Gordon Chase, the administrator of the Health Service Administration of New York City, launches a large-scale methadone maintenance program to combat an epidemic growth of the heroin problem in New York City. The program is a controversial one that holds substantial risks for patients and produces uncertain but apparently significant improvements in their lives. Chase is not directly responsible for addiction treatment programs in New York. Instead, the responsibility is lodged in the Addiction Service Agency, which is adamantly opposed to methadone maintenance programs. Chase seizes the initiative by assembling the program, assuming the necessary authority and resources will be available. Furthermore, to build momentum, Chase claims that he will be able to treat 15,000 addicts within a year—a claim that is demonstrably exaggerated.[7]

Orville Freeman, the secretary of agriculture, hears testimony that people are severely malnourished, even starving, in the rural south. He has the resources within his department to act to alleviate the hunger, but fears the wrath of congressional overseers who oppose such efforts. He is responsive to their views not only because they can affect the entire range of his department's programs, but also because President Johnson expressly cautioned him to avoid antagonizing the congressmen who head his authorizing and appropriating subcommittees. Although the demand for action comes from a congressional committee, it is *not* the committee that has jurisdiction over his agency's programs or funds. Consequently, Freeman takes no action except to send a few aides to the south who report that no emergency exists there.[8]

Dave Goldman, an official with "California Legal Services, Inc.," reports to the press and the officials who finance his program in Washington that he has *not* been representing a local farmworkers union or giving them legal advice. In fact, he has repeatedly met with the union leader to discuss both legal and political tactics. The terms of Goldman's contract with the federal agency prohibit California Legal Services from assisting the union.[9]

Caspar Weinberger, the newly appointed chairman of the Federal Trade Commission, encounters Representative Evins, the chairman of the FTC's appropriations subcommittee outside the hearing room just before his first appearance before the subcommittee. The congressman hands him a note with three names on it and asks Weinberger to "take care of these people." Weinberger, who has assumed responsibility for reforming the FTC and who believes that the core of the FTC's problems is its reliance on

patronage appointments, returns to his office and suggests that his personnel officer begin the process of terminating the employees whom Evins
named.[10]

These examples of official action are useful for our purposes because in
each instance the official acts in a way that violates widely shared notions
of officials' obligations. Chase cavalierly ignores a formal policymaking
process and launches a risky treatment program for heroin addicts. Freeman fails to meet a basic human need despite the availability of resources
to deal with the problem. Goldman lies to his superiors about his activities. Weinberger acts precipitately and perhaps unfairly toward his subordinates.

Interestingly, however, in each instance the official can present an excuse for his actions. Chase would argue that, on balance, methadone
maintenance programs were likely to produce more good than harm, and
since the mayor could have halted his activities at any time, his silence constituted approval. Freeman would point out that, of course, he would have
liked to respond to hungry people in Mississippi, but he received no in-
structions to do so from either the Congress or the president. In fact, he
received contrary messages. Besides, it was not clear that the problem was
as bad as alleged. Goldman would defend his actions by arguing that lying
was necessary to protect a fragile effort to redistribute political power.
Otherwise, the program would be crushed into irrelevance by those who
were then powerful. Besides, he suspected that his overseers in Washington
really wanted him to behave as he did. Weinberger would explain that his
actions were ordinary managerial tactics to rejuvenate and redirect a failing agency, and that the benefits of the energized agency far outweighed
any apparent unfairness to the employees.

The sins and excuses offered in these cases suggest the richness, ambiguities, and dilemmas of the moral life of public officials. Conscientious
officials ask themselves questions like the following: What substantive objectives should they pursue? What programmatic uses of governmental authority and resources are appropriate to consider in reaching those goals?
What process of consultation is required to legitimate a given policy decision? Can they take shortcuts in the process of consultation leading to
authorization? Can they manipulate procedures? Does it matter if their
opponents are manipulating procedures and expect them to do so as well?
What do officials owe to colleagues whose positions and personal relationships entitle them to frequent, familiar access to the officials? What do
they owe to subordinates whose careers depend on their stewardship? To

what extent should officials' personal interests play a role in the decisions they make?

To lend order to these questions, it is useful to think of obligations arising in three different realms. Officials are bound, first, by obligations to respect the processes that legitimate their actions. Typically, these processes require them to share their authority with others, and to subject proposed uses of government authority to the scrutiny of the public and their representatives. Second, they are obligated both by a general duty of beneficence and by their oath of office to serve the public interest—to use the powers of their offices to accomplish public purposes as effectively, efficiently, and decently as they can. Third, like all of us, on a more intimate and personal basis, they are obliged to treat their colleagues and subordinates—the individuals with whom they deal on a daily basis and who depend on them in important ways—with respect, honesty, and fairness.

While these realms of obligation usefully order the questions that officials might ask themselves, they also highlight two central difficulties. First, the nature of the obligations within each realm are often ambiguous. It is hard for an official like Chase or Freeman to know what the public interest requires of them in confronting heroin addiction or hunger. It is hard for Goldman to understand what programmatic activities are being authorized. And it is hard for Weinberger to know the extent of his responsibilities to the employees of FTC. Second, the obligations, once discerned, often conflict. Chase's, Freeman's, and Goldman's perceived duties to pursue the public interest conflict with the obligation to protect authorizing procedures. Similarly, Weinberger's duty to serve the public interest and pursue a reform mandate for the FTC conflicts with his duties to his employees.

Given ambiguity and conflicts, virtue in public officials lies in the skill and judgment they reveal in discerning the obligations and resolving conflicts among them. The rest of this essay seeks to help conscientious public officials (and those who would train them) pursue virtue by exploring the realms of obligation. I do not assume that the realms can be fully charted, nor that a complete chart could guarantee reliable navigation. In fact, my view is the opposite: that character and motivation to behave virtuously are much more important than concepts or technique. But given character and motivation, officials might still be aided by some discussion of the nature of their obligations. In any event, we will examine the nature of the obligations and virtues of public officials in pursuing the public interest, in protecting and authorizing processes, in preserving relationships with colleagues and friends, and, finally, in confronting their own conscience.

OBLIGATIONS TO PURSUE THE PUBLIC INTEREST

Public officials are obliged to pursue the public interest — to use the powers and resources of their offices to accomplish public purposes efficiently and effectively. In part, this duty derives from normal obligations that attach to administrative offices in which an agent works with the authority and resources of others to accomplish their purposes. But the duty also partakes of a general duty of beneficence — to do what one can to help others.

For private individuals, the duty of beneficence is a modest one, largely because the scope of plausibly effective private action (and hence the scope of moral responsibility) is comparatively small.[11] When, however, an individual assumes responsibility for broad public purposes, and has been granted discretionary command over the substantial powers and resources of the government, the duty of beneficence takes on a markedly different aspect. The difference is partly one of scale. Since the capacity to do things for people is so much greater for public officials than for private individuals, the relative importance of this general duty of beneficence must increase. But the difference seems to be based on the *public* character of the responsibility and the routine use of coercive power in pursuing the good as well. The hope of realizing broad public goals in which many take satisfaction and the concern about inflicting harm through clumsiness or a deliberate choice to sacrifice some interests to advance others make the duty of beneficence both more important and more difficult than in the private realm. The problem for a public official is to discern what the simple duty to "do good" requires in the complex undertakings of the public sector.

To argue that officials have an obligation to the public interest does not necessarily imply that they have either the duty or the right to develop their own conceptions of what the public interest requires in particular situations. One can argue, for example, that their purposes have already been established when they arrive. They can be discovered in explicit legislative mandates, inferred from prior policies, or guided by tacit understandings with the people who hire them. Moreover, if officials are in doubt about their mandate or want to change it, they can always seek explicit new authority by consulting with others who have authority or interests in their area. They need not, indeed *should* not, feel that they have to make all the decisions about purposes and programs themselves.

On the other hand, to argue that officials should take guidance from others in formulating and deciding matters of public policy does not relieve the officials of responsibility for taking some initiative in conceiving and proposing alternative uses of the powers vested in their office. After all, mandates are often quite ambiguous. Moreover, even when they are not, senior public officials are in an unusually good position to see new opportunities, or to discern the changing character of a given problem. Because they possess information and expertise, they are expected to play a special, but not necessarily dominant, role in making policy. Finally, on some occasions, when there is a compelling need that they can satisfy, and when there is reason to be distrustful of the process that would authorize action, officials may even be under some obligation to risk violating process obligations on behalf of an overriding obligation to serve the public interest. The point is that regardless of whether we consider the officials' role as discreet, neutral administrators giving operational content to well-established mandates, or as respectful advocates proposing changes in policy with full attention to authorizing procedures, or even as officials pursuing a public need at the moral risk of violating existing authorizing procedures, senior public officials must inevitably think about the purposes their current policies are serving.

In conceiving of the public interest in particular situations, conscientious officials must be careful to avoid some common pitfalls. Some concern the nature of their responsibilities for foreseeing the consequences of the policies they recommend. Others have to do with the way they size up or appraise the diverse effects they foresee.

FORESEEING CONSEQUENCES OF POLICIES

Intuitively, awareness of the consequences of one's actions seems a necessary if not sufficient condition for moral conduct. While this point is debated among philosophers with respect to private conduct, the principle seems beyond dispute for public officials deciding important policy issues. Officials have a duty to anticipate the important consequences of policies they advocate or implement.[12] This, in turn, requires them to conceive of categories of effect that would influence their judgment about the wisdom of pursuing given policies. Since these categories of effect become the terms in which old policies are evaluated and new policies advocated, they define the officials' moral vision of the social values at stake in their domain. The discerning sensibility officials reveal in developing these categories is, then, an important mark of their virtue. In actual practice, characteristic shortcomings occur.

Perhaps the most common pitfall is to miss entirely the importance of the activity. In a system that encourages public officials to avoid taking responsibility for advancing policies, it is all too easy for officials to shrink from the intellectually and politically demanding task of describing the important values that are at stake in their domain. Instead, they refer to terms established in legislative or policy mandates no matter how inadequate for describing actual effects, or to a few very broad goals which are commonly shared but are difficult to relate to the particular decisions at hand. They also commonly seek refuge by describing operational objectives that describe their activities well but do not connect easily with important social values. Worst of all, perhaps, they sometimes act as though the problem of developing a suitable accounting system was a technical matter best left to experts. Of course, it is not easy for officials to be aware of even the immediate effects of their actions. It is also difficult to connect the proximate effects of their programs with the ultimate effects envisioned somewhere further along elaborate chains of causation. And it is still more difficult to connect a wide variety of ultimate effects with a few overarching social values. But of such skills is discerning judgment made, and it is precisely these skills that are the virtues of responsible public officials.

A second common pitfall is to develop conceptions that are too narrow — that capture too few of the important effects of a given policy. Somewhat ironically, the narrowing can result from two radically different notions about the "proper" way to develop views of social values at stake in policy choices. Sometimes it occurs because officials become preoccupied with "quantifying" effects. They look primarily at those effects whose magnitudes can be reliably measured. Even worse, in a vain attempt to establish an "objective" measure of social value, they focus exclusively on effects that can be valued in terms of market prices. Alternatively, however, their vision may become improperly narrowed if they decide in advance that all policies will be ruled out if they produce harmful effects (however small) in areas that the officials regard as inviolable. In the end, of course, a principled stand basing a policy on one important effect may be seen as the proper choice since it was the only one that suitably honored an important social principle. But still, to refuse from the outset even to explore other consequences of the choice seems a moral luxury that cannot be afforded to public officials.[13] Public officials should have the discipline and detachment to see *all* the things at stake in their choices — even consequences that are "unthinkable."

It is not too difficult to resist these temptations to narrow one's vision, and expose one's sensibilities to a suitably far-ranging array of consequences. But even if officials free their minds to roam widely over the terrain of important effects, they are still likely to overlook or fail to accommodate an important class of consequences — namely, the long-run effects of given policies on institutions and institutional relationships in the society.[14] Such effects occur through several different mechanisms. Sometimes policies will create important precedents that give rise to new expectations or shape policy debates in other policy areas. Other times policies create new institutions whose future operations will importantly shape governmental actions in ways that are difficult to foresee. Perhaps the most common and important institutional effect, however, is the effect of each policy initiative on the authority, credibility, and prestige of government itself. Every policy claims for itself some of the government's prestige and some of the polity's attention. As our recent history makes clear, these are hardly inexhaustible resources. In fact, the recent sprawl of policy initiatives has shown just how quickly government credibility can be dissipated among a confused and increasingly disenchanted citizenry. It is not always true, of course, that a policy initiative saps the legitimacy of the government. When a policy initiative solves a salient public problem (such as polio or air pollution), or reaffirms an important public value (such as equal voting rights or equality of educational opportunity), the prestige of the government is enhanced, not reduced. The point, rather, is that it is insufficient for a public official to explore each policy exclusively in its own substantive terms — even when the terms have been expanded to accommodate many diverse effects, extended forward in causal systems to capture ultimate as well as proximate effects, and connected to broad social values. Beyond this, an official must assume the statesmanlike burdens of foreseeing the effects of policies on institutions, including, in particular, effects on the legitimacy of the government itself.

A third pitfall for public officials in foreseeing consequences is to mishandle the inevitable uncertainty in the choices they make. Perhaps the most common errors in this domain are to pretend that uncertainty does not exist or to try to exorcise it with the tools of science. Such temptations are an inevitable feature of a system in which officials take their responsibility to foresee consequences seriously. It is only natural for conscientious public officials to want to appear knowledgeable. And it is natural for them to reach out to experts and to science to bolster both the image and the reality of confident knowledge. On the whole, reaching out to science to provide certainty in the judgments they make is admirable. The problems arise only when the drive for certainty stands in the way of using current knowledge effectively.

This paradoxical result can occur in two different situations. First, when officials claim greater certainty than is warranted by current knowledge, major distortions can occur. By acting as though some consequences were certain, officials are, in effect, obscuring the possibility (perhaps even the probability) that some effects quite different from those they imagine could occur. In shrinking their conception of what might happen, some useful knowledge is lost. Second, officials can err by refusing to decide a question until science reduces all the major uncertainties to very low levels. For officials caught between an obligation to foresee consequences precisely and an apparent obligation to be conservative in using scientific information, it often seems desirable to delay choices until science reduces major uncertainties to very low levels. The problem with this, of course, is that delaying a decision is the same as deciding to live with the consequences of not deciding. Since some information about the consequences of failing to decide is often available, as well as some information about the possible consequences of different decisions, it is possible for officials to compare delay with some alternative choice. To the extent that officials fail to use this information and make the comparison, they leave us less well positioned against possible events than current knowledge would allow. Thus, the determined pursuit of confident knowledge can often drive out useful information.[15]

The alternative to the unrealistic drive for certain knowledge is simply to acknowledge the uncertainty in the choices that officials make. This has the enormous virtue of corresponding to the actual state of affairs. But it has the great liability of emphasizing the painful fact that, ordinarily, we do not know precisely what will happen as a consequence of policy choices. To say that we are uncertain is not the same as saying we know nothing, of course. We can imagine possible effects. We can usually even say that some effects are more probable than others. What we cannot say with a high degree of confidence is exactly what will happen. In this sense, then, officials are often "gambling" with the lives and fortunes of citizens. What standards should guide officials as they face these gambles?

Some activists hold the view that any uncertainty about the effects of a given policy should prevent the government from acting. The government simply should not gamble with the welfare of its citizens. The certain benefits of inexpensive electric power that could be guaranteed by the construction of nuclear power plants cannot offset the remote chance of a nuclear accident. Nor, presumably, can the uncertain benefits of prison reform or forced school integration justify the certain, immediate costs of these policies respectively to victims of crime and parents who want their children in neighborhood schools. It is simply wrong to expose people to risks of bad outcomes, or to try to justify certain losses in one area with uncertain gains in others. Unless the government can be sure of the consequences of a policy it should not act.

Other times we adopt a slightly less conservative stance: the government should not act if there is a chance (however small) of a very bad consequence. It is all right if there is uncertainty about potential benefits. It is even all right if there is a chance that there will be some small bad effects. The problem arises when there is a chance of a real catastrophe. Thus, the uncertain benefits of school integration could conceivably justify the imposition of certain costs if we think the likely benefits of school integration are sufficiently large, but subsidies to nuclear power plants could never be justified because some chance of a real disaster undeniably exists.

A third stance is less conservative still. It says that society should look at the relative likelihood of conceivable effects in all the relevant areas of potential impact and calculate the "expected magnitude" of a policy's effects in given areas. Of course, it could choose to weigh the possibility of very large bad effects disproportionately to other kinds of effects. But the mere possibility of very bad effects would not be an absolute bar to a policy. It would all depend on the probability of the very bad effect, and the other offsetting (or not quite offsetting) advantages of the policy.

My own view is that public officials should strike the third stance described above: they should look at the expected magnitude of the effects in given areas, and should count prospects of large losses much more heavily than other kinds of effects. I think the first stance, that the government should take no action if there is any uncertainty, is absurd. Since virtually all government actions, including the establishment of government itself, involve uncertain consequences, no government at all would be possible if we adhered to this rule. The second stance is more respectable, but still inappropriate since it rules out policy actions even where the chance of a bad effect is small, to the point of vanishing, and the potential benefits very large and quite certain. There seems to me no choice but to face up to the fact of uncertainty, explicitly assess the relative probabilities of different results in all areas of concern, and decide on the basis of some expected result appropriately weighted.

DISCERNING THE PUBLIC INTEREST

It is one thing to have the discipline, competence, and vision to foresee the diverse consequences of policies. It is quite another to discern the thread of the public interest in the tangle. Two broadly different concepts of the public interest or public welfare have been developed to help officials make the judgments with confidence and precision. One conception is the analysis of benefits and costs based on the logic of welfare economics. The second is the analysis of rights and responsibilities drawn from specific conceptions of justice. While specialists offer these conceptions as complete in themselves and antagonistic toward one another, I think it is more useful for public officials to know the strengths and limitations of each and to use both in searching for policies that move most surely in the direction of the commonweal.

The "benefit-cost" approach to discerning the public interest begins with the notion that the appropriate way to value the diverse effects of a given policy is to let their values be assigned by those who are affected.[16] Intuitively, this notion is extremely attractive. It reserves an important right — the right to say what is valuable and what costly, what dignified and what undignified, what virtuous and what contemptible — to individuals. In doing so, welfare economics honors the capacity to assign value as something fundamental to human existence. A practical problem soon appears, however: how to discover the value that affected individuals actually do assign to the imagined effects. For this problem, welfare economics proposes several solutions. Economic theory demonstrates, on the basis of a rigorous deductive logic, that in a world where consumers with stable, well-ordered preferences purchase goods in perfectly competitive markets populated by firms whose managers maximize profits by choosing efficient solutions to well-defined production problems, the set of prices one observes in the market will be pareto-efficient. At that set of prices, at the margins, individuals will be trading things of exactly equivalent value. If we go farther and assume that the initial distribution of rights and responsibilities in the society is fair, or that the current distribution of wealth and income is in some sense appropriate, then we can also say that the observed set of prices gives a fairly precise estimate of the *social* value attached to production and consumption of things traded on the market. Consequently, for things traded in markets, the observed prices provide a rough approximation of their social value. For things *not* traded in markets, welfare economics proposes a less elegant (and much more expensive) but still eminently practical solution: simply ask the individuals what they would be "willing to pay" to add additional units (or avoid losses) or whatever it is that is being affected by a policy. To the extent that we can observe market prices related to effects of policies or collect data on citizens' "willingness to pay" for given kinds of effects, we will have a convenient way of assigning social value to the diverse effects of a given policy.

The merits of this approach are formidable. It delegates to the affected individuals the right to assign value to the effects. In addition, it exploits some relatively inexpensive information (market prices) to suggest the value of alternative actions. Finally, and most important, the methods lead to results in which the value of diverse effects are all expressed in the same units. Thus, one can "add up" different effects, not only across different kinds of effects, but also across groups that are differentially affected. The sum of these values will represent the "net social value" of a given policy.

While these features commend the benefit-cost approach to our attention and make it prudent to gather information about the values that individuals attach to policy effects when convenient, several important limitations of the approach make it unwise to use this conception exclusively to fix a conception of the public interest in a particular situation. For one thing, information about prices and willingness to pay is likely to be distorted for technical reasons. Since actual market conditions rarely correspond to those required by the theory, observed market prices can be taken only as rough approximations of social value. Similarly, simple introspection suggests that it would be difficult to give meaningful responses to a survey of "willingness to pay." It is difficult to think of how much one would pay for a park, cleaner air, and national defense, to say nothing of more complicated effects such as integrated schools or a society in which satisfactory nutrition was guaranteed to everyone. Finally, both market prices and expressions of willingness to pay are dependent on the current distribution of wealth and income. If the current distribution is unfair, then these prices cannot be interpreted as appropriate expressions of social welfare. Since welfare economists have no theory that justifies a particular distribution of income, however, and since in any case their ability to gather information conveniently and inexpensively depends on accepting the current distribution of wealth and income, they are inclined to ignore the theoretical problem in order to get on with the practical task.

Second, although welfare economics accepts the relevance of distributional concerns in evaluating the outcomes of given policies, the theory handles these concerns quite cavalierly. The fundamental moral issue is whether losses to one group of citizens can be justified by "larger" gains for others. The welfare economist's answer to this question is that as long as the overall contribution to social welfare is positive, that is the gains to the gainers are "larger" than the losses to the losers, the policy should be adopted. The justification for this position is simply that the existence of a net social gain means that, in principle, the gainers from a policy decision could compensate the losers and both would be better off, in their own

view, than if the policy were not adopted.[17] The curious part of this solution, however, is that there is no requirement that the losers actually be compensated. That is treated as a different problem to be addressed at a different time. The crucial thing is that the compensation could, in principle, occur. Thus, although distributional issues arise both in estimating the values of specific effects and in determining whether a policy should be adopted, they are often ignored when actually evaluating a policy or deciding exactly how to execute it.

The standard of rights and responsibilities based on conceptions of justice starts from a much different premise. The idea is that with respect to some goods, activities, and conditions individual preferences should *not* be the basis for assigning social value. Instead, society as a whole should establish the value without reference to individual preferences. Far from being disinterested in the distribution of the socially valued goods, activities, and conditions, society takes responsibility for guaranteeing that the rights and responsibilities are distributed equally in the society. Thus, even in liberal societies we require everyone to attend school, to be immunized against some diseases, to accept the right to vote, to remain free from slavery, and to repress desires to attack their friends and neighbors, despite the fact that individuals would often be "better off" in their own eyes if they could exchange the rights for something they valued more, or escape an obligation by contributing something else. In effect, by requiring individuals to accept rights and duties, and by preventing exchanges in these areas, society forces individuals to act as though the rights and duties had infinite value.

Socially established rights and duties, then, are special things. They are established by collective decisions rather than individual preferences. They are distributed equally throughout the society. And citizens are not allowed to exchange them. Insofar as their creation overwhelms individual preferences and frustrates exchanges, the conception presents a stark challenge to the idea that social values should be nothing more than the sum of individual preferences. Insofar as we conceive of the exclusive purposes of the state as doing justice by guaranteeing these rights, an alternative conception of where the public interest lies is established.[18]

This conception of the public interest also has some enormously appealing features. While the conception of welfare economics celebrates our diversity, the conception of equal rights and responsibilities celebrates the idea that in some important areas we are (or should be) equal. If there are some areas in which we are the same, these must be the defining characteristics of being human. If they are the defining characteristics of being human, then they must be invested with a special significance: they represent minimal conceptions of human dignity which cannot be trespassed without making someone less than human. To establish such conceptions of human equality and dignity collectively, and to honor them reliably in public policy decisions is clearly consistent with an attractive notion of how officials might pursue the public interest.

Note that while part of the appeal of establishing conceptions of socially established rights is the sheer satisfaction of celebrating shared conceptions of human dignity and citizenship in a just society, the creation and maintenance of rights produce important individually consumed satisfactions as well. By allowing people to develop legitimate expectations that their rights will not be violated, they create a kind of wealth for individuals in the society. Some fears that might impoverish their lives can more or less safely be put aside. Similarly, the existence of rights creates a degree of equality in bargaining relationships because they give individuals enough security to withstand substantial economic or physical power. In fact, rights prevent individuals from yielding to temptations to abandon some virtues. So, the establishment of generally shared rights and duties meets individual and social needs to define the place of individuals in a collective enterprise — a need that has both expressive and instrumental value. Moreover, rights define the areas in which individuals will be powerful and autonomous, not only with respect to one another, but also with respect to the government.

But just as there are problematic aspects of the utilitarian standard of the welfare economists, difficulties also exist with this notion of rights and justice. One problem is that the strength of the obligation to protect a given right is often uncertain. Rights often conflict, and it is not usually obvious in advance which rights should take precedence in given situations. For example, do the rights of some citizens to equality of educational opportunity outweigh the rights of other citizens to attend schools in their own neighborhoods? Or, do the rights of citizens to accumulate wealth and pass it on to their children outweigh the rights of less advantaged people to have an "equal opportunity" to pursue their conception of virtue and satisfaction in their individual lives? Similarly, there are often good reasons to override specific rights in given situations as long as the rights are well defended by procedural safeguards and as long as some reasonable compensation is paid. So, like all contracts, establishing rights is not entirely free from uncertainty: apparently clear duties may not be honored. When this could or should occur will not always be clear to a public official who is seeking to protect the most important rights of citizens.

A second problem, related to the first, is that it is rarely clear which rights have been established within a society at a given moment. Academic justifications for different conceptions of justice always exist. They range from a notion that individual rights to life, liberty, and property are so far-reaching that almost any state action infringes on them significantly,[19] to a notion that rights leading to significant economic equality could be justified.[20] In the most commonly accepted formulations, rights are established primarily in civil and political areas. Rights to property in these schemes are only licenses to accumulate as much economic value as one can by using one's labor and enterprise in production and exchange. No guarantees are offered in the struggle with nature. More recently, however, as we have accumulated wealth, entitlements have been created that to some extent *do* provide guarantees in the struggle with nature. We now provide some levels of income, food, housing, jobs, and health care *almost* as a matter of right. Whether programs providing benefits in these areas represent extensions of rights to cover economic struggles that were previously left to chance, or whether these are simply charitable gifts that may be withdrawn by the rest of the society if economic conditions deteriorate or if the behavior of people accepting the entitlements departs from social expectations, is a major unresolved issue in our current politics.

While public officials weighing the consequences of policies should recognize effects on the current distribution of socially established rights, entitlements, and duties, which of these demand overriding allegiance is unclear. In many areas, recognition of relevant rights and entitlements may prove insufficient to guide the officials' judgment about whether and how to proceed with a given program. They may meet the objective of protecting all relevant rights, and still have some latitude about how to distribute additional costs and benefits of the proposed policy. So, as a practical matter in many areas the concept of justice turns out to be as ambiguous as the conception of maximizing individual satisfaction.

In my view, then, officials searching for the public interest must accommodate two fundamental problems. The first, discussed above, is the insufficiency of either the welfare standard or the justice standard when each is taken alone. The simple summation of individual preferences attached to effects fails to guide policy because it ignores legitimate *social*, as opposed to individual, values, and the distribution of gains and losses among individuals in different social positions. The assertion of a more or less limited number of absolute rights and inescapable duties is either inadequate in guiding policy (because it leaves many important effects of policies unvalued) or distorting (because it forces us to reject policies where rights are abridged even in situations where the rights are defended by elaborate procedures and suitable compensation can be arranged). The second problem for officials is that the specific content of both conceptions changes over time as a result of changing social conditions. Values that individuals assign to certain kinds of effects change with social conditions. So do the kinds of things that are called rights and duties.

To accommodate these difficulties, conscientious officials should make two broad commitments. The first is that in valuing the consequences of given policies they should adopt elements of both the welfare economics and the justice criteria. From the welfare economics criterion they should accept the responsibility to foresee the consequences of policies for individuals, and, when it is convenient, gather information about the values that individuals place on the diverse effects. But they should also go beyond the welfare economics criterion to see that the social interest in guaranteeing rights in some areas and promoting equality in others is reflected in the policy choice.

From the justice criterion, they should accept the notions that society as a whole has a legitimate interest in guaranteeing rights, even when individuals would abandon them and other individuals in the society would benefit from the abandonment. But, they should also understand that individual rights may be abridged when compelling reasons for doing so exist, and when the rights have been protected by procedures that force the state to establish compelling reasons, and, sometimes, arrange suitable compensation. Moreover, since rights and duties can change over time, and since governmental action in a just society inevitably creates precedents (since it always carries an expectation of equal treatment across individuals and over time), officials should consider how current policies affect the *future* structure of rights, entitlements, and duties. Moreover, they must realize that their actions are not only *reflecting* but also *shaping* these future rights and duties.

The second broad commitment of conscientious public officials is to accept responsibility for deciding issues and explaining their decisions in ways that strengthen the *process* of defining social and individual values. This commitment is important precisely because the domain and content of social values changes, and because the officials' actions affect these things. While the structure of the government frees officials to choose for all of us, and while they must do this as conscientiously as possible, they must ultimately acknowledge their subordination to social processes and their general obligation to make broad social processes work as well as possible. At the very least this means that in deciding on specific policies, they must give their reasons. They must explain which values are taking precedence, which are being subordinated, and why. At the most basic level these are obligations of the officials to themselves, otherwise how could they justify their own actions to themselves. But they are also their obligations to the rest of us. We need them to explain their actions partly so that they become accountable to us, and partly so that they can help our political choices become what they ought to be — a deliberate social weighing of relevant values in particular decisions against the backdrop of a changing context of individual preferences, rights, entitlements, and duties. Their justifications are part of the process of discovering what individual and social lives are possible at a given moment.

OBLIGATIONS TO AUTHORIZING
PROCESSES AND PROCEDURES

Beyond, and, as we have seen, part of, the obligation to explain and justify policy choices in terms of anticipated results, public officials have obligations to expose their views and judgments to elaborate mechanisms of consultation that legitimate their choices. This obligation can be derived both from a prima facie duty to respect and accommodate the interests of others whenever possible, buttressed by a long political tradition of solicitousness toward the interests of minorities,[21] and from a variety of utilitarian arguments that emphasize the instrumental values of consultation in making complex and controversial choices.[22]

At the heart of the prima facie duty is the notion that people should be asked to consent to actions that affect their interests. This presumption is very strong in situations where contemplated actions will produce adverse effects. It is also present, however, even when the expected results will be beneficial. No other posture is consistent with the notion that individuals or their representatives have independent capabilities to assign value and choose, and that in deciding on actions that affect us all, we confront one another as approximate equals. Of course, in the political realm, where the interests of many often stand in opposition to the interests of a few, we do not always insist on the strong condition that the consent of the few be secured (which would, in effect, grant veto power to the few). But we do often assume that a good-faith effort will be made to understand those interests, accommodate them as much as possible in the design of policies, and provide explanations, as well as occasional compensation, when those interests cannot be accommodated. Such actions are necessary to show respect for the equal status and legitimate interests of others in the society.

Three different utilitarian justifications for consultation can also be offered. One justification is based on technical considerations. Consultation is good because it develops better information on the likely consequences of policy choices and the preferences of affected parties than would be available without the elaborate machinery. Forced to confront interested parties, officials will see more clearly and vividly what is at stake in their policies and will make more informed decisions.[23] A second justification emphasizes the fact that the use of procedures granting "due process" will facilitate the execution of the ultimate choice. Parties whose interests are adversely affected will nonetheless accept the decision because they have been dealt with "fairly": they have been granted the expressive satisfaction of making their case as convincingly as they can, and they have been implicitly assured that their right to be heard in future decisions is intact. In fact, if they are gracious losers, they may legitimately think that their interests will attract greater solicitousness on the next decision.[24] A third justification is even more far-reaching. Processes of consultation, discussion, and negotiation are valuable because they teach people to be good democratic citizens. By confronting one another on an equal basis in situations where interests conflict, the parties learn skills in reaching compromises as well as an attitude of respect toward their opponents. These are extremely valuable for citizens in democratic societies.

Whichever justification appeals more strongly, good reasons for officials to feel generally obligated to consult extensively with affected parties clearly exist. In fact, the obligation cuts even more deeply because we all carry in the back of our minds a model of an "ideal" decision process. In this ideal, all parties interested in a choice are invited to participate. Their opportunities to participate are arranged to be more or less equal. Their aggressiveness in exploiting their opportunities reflects their degree of interest in the issues under consideration. They participate in the choice by emphasizing some values at the expense of others, by proposing alternative actions that seem well designed to achieve important values, and by presenting arguments and evidence that their proposals will produce attractive results that are consistent with common values or represent a fair distribution of costs and benefits. Because the participants expect to encounter others in the process who are more or less equally influential in the final choice, but have different interests and equal capabilities to make arguments, they are motivated to express their position in ways that show sympathy for the interests of the others, and to make truthful statements. Otherwise, their good faith can be questioned and, if it is, some increment of their influence in the final choice will be lost. Moreover, there is enough agreement within the group concerning appropriate values, institutional relationships, and concepts of justice and fairness that nothing offered as a reasonable proposal by one group sounds outrageous or beyond the pale to others. Finally, all parties feel motivated to confront the decision because no parties gain by the continuation of the status quo. (Or if they do, there is enough power among the others to force the other parties to negotiate.) In this situation, satisfactory decisions agreed to by people with different interests and knowledge can ordinarily be made.

To a very great degree, we have designed our governmental institutions to create such processes throughout our political system. The system of representation is designed to give citizens more or less equal, as well as ready, access to political power. The Administrative Procedure Act created highly structured proceedings to prevent agency administrators from ignoring major interests in wielding their substantial discretionary authority.[25] And we continue to tinker with our process of governmental decisionmaking through such things as the Freedom of Information Act, Government in the Sunshine Act, legislation designed to control ex parte communications between regulatory agencies and affected parties, and so on. Not only do we have a commonly shared ideal of an attractive decisionmaking process, then, we have also created laws and institutions which require officials to approach this ideal.

The problem, of course, is that despite our ideals, institutions, and laws, the actual process of decisionmaking rarely comes close to the ideal. The representation of interested parties in a decision is usually far from complete or fair. Similarly, simple busyness, as well as limitations on human cognitive capabilities, routinely frustrate intellectual ambitions for creative and thorough joint analyses of given issues.[26] Finally, and perhaps most important, it is always tempting to behave strategically in the process of discussion and negotiation rather than to enter the process in "good faith." The process can be deliberately biased by ignoring relevant interests or by granting formal rights of participation that are substantively meaningless. Similarly, in discussions, information about important consequences can be withheld or distorted, and preferences can be disguised so that a "fair division" of losses and benefits turns out to be much more favorable to one party's actual interests. Since such ploys are always possible and often occur, it is difficult for any party to enter the process of deliberation and negotiation in good faith. One's sense of competence and worldliness is at stake as well as the actual substantive and procedural stakes that will be affected in the process of choosing. In most actual circumstances, then, the problem for officials is how they should cope with a process that is likely to fall far short of an ideal process. What obligations do they have in confronting this common situation?

Three different standards for officials could be advocated. One standard is that officials should behave as though they were in fact operating within an ideal process. The justification for this standard is the categorical imperative: if officials are unwilling to discipline their own behavior to create a fair process they can hardly expect others to do so, and as a result, all hopes for a fair process will disappear. A second standard of conduct is that officials must manage their own actions in the process to compensate for the apparent weaknesses and injustices of the existing process governing their area of responsibility by deciding issues in ways that would be the result if the process were, in fact, fair and rational. The justification for this standard is that the officials' responsibility to do justice or serve the public interest takes precedence over their obligation to meet *apparent* process obligations where they depart from the basic requirements of an ideal process. A third standard is that officials must work to make the process "fairer." In the short run they must conform to the existing process, but because the current process is deficient, they must try to correct the process by drawing in additional interests, or shaping the process of deliberation in different ways.

In practice, each of these standards presents difficulties. The first standard — to behave as though one were involved in an ideal process regardless of its actual status — seems to me to run the risk of continuing both an unfair process and an unfair result. It is a noble position, but it seems to me to sacrifice too much of the officials' continuing responsibilities to create both fair processes and attractive results. The officials miss an opportunity to restructure the process, to represent unrepresented interests, and to insist on the value of their expertise.

The second standard — operating within the process to insure a result that officials think is just without regard to the rules that would govern their conduct in a fair process — runs the opposite risk. Justice may be done or the public interest served in a particular instance, but only at the price of further weakening the process. Moreover, there is always the chance that the officials' perception of the appropriate outcome is faulty because they do not have the ideal process to instruct them. Thus, they may weaken the process by championing nonexistent interests or by utilizing distorted information without doing any greater justice, or serving the public interest more effectively.

The third standard — making adjustments in the process to bring it closer to the ideal — seems the most attractive of the three. The only problem is that the officials' capacity to affect the process will usually be quite limited. Typically they face procedures built on law, well-defined institutional relationships, and custom. Many other officials and citizens will have important stakes in this process. Often no convenient forum to discuss a change in process will exist, nor will any authority to change the process be available. While this situation does not preclude officials from cumulatively making changes in the process, their term in office is often too short to produce much effect. To be sure, officials may, for some specific choices, be able to improve the typical process. And, of course, the force of this third standard is to oblige them to do so when they can. But still, there will be many situations in which they are more or less powerless to change the process in any significant way, and they will then face a choice between the first two standards.

In making up one's mind about what one owes to the process in a given situation, I would suggest the following principles. First, I think that public officials must accept the notion that the legitimacy of their actions depends crucially (I am tempted to say exclusively) on the extent to which the authorizing process for their actions approximated the ideal decision process. The closer the approximation, the greater the legitimacy. This means that officials have strong obligations to improve the decisionmaking process in their areas of responsibility, and to give great respect to the laws, institutional relationships, and customs that currently structure the process. It also implies that in ignoring or frustrating the process to achieve a specific aim, officials must accept a particularly heavy burden, since in this case the legitimation of their actions will be even weaker than it would have been if they had continued with the unfair but well-established process. Finally, this principle implies that most officials most of the time operate with surprisingly slender degrees of legitimacy. This does not necessarily mean that their actions are unjustified, but one of the conditions that could justify their action is often absent.

Second, as a corollary to the first principle, the officials' obligation to seek legitimacy through a process that approximates the ideal process increases as the action they contemplate becomes more important. An action may be important because it affects many people, produces effects in very sensitive areas, establishes new precedents, or involves some risk, however small, of very large adverse consequences. In effect, some actions require less elaborate procedures because the consent that is required covers a smaller, less important domain.

Third, I think it can be argued that the amount of legitimacy officials must secure through an elaborate process of consultation *diminishes* with the officials' own degree of accountability. If officials can be easily removed from office, they may be able to take greater risks with the legitimating process than they could if they were solidly entrenched. The reason is that removal from office is so thorough a repudiation of the official's actions that the process cannot only be repaired but strengthened. No permanent damage can be caused by someone who can easily be removed from office. So a civil servant with civil service protection should take fewer risks with the process than a political appointee who serves at the pleasure of an elected chief executive.

OBLIGATIONS TO FRIENDS AND COLLEAGUES

The ambiguities of an official's obligation to pursue the public interest and to conform to authorizing processes lead many conscientious officials to seek help and advice about where their duty lies. For such advice, officials are apt to turn to a relatively intimate circle of colleagues and friends. They turn to them partly because they trust their judgment and partly because they need their support. They need the good opinion of friends to comfort them when they are being criticized. And they particularly need the good opinions of colleagues to give them instrumental assistance and assure their future on the job. Moreover, when they turn to this circle of friends and colleagues, officials will find that not only do the intimates give advice, they also impose obligations of their own. The officials find that they owe them something that derives from personal loyalty and shared conceptions of ultimate purposes.[27] Thus, the advice and claims of colleagues and friends will figure quite prominently in the moral environment of a public official.

It is important to recognize that advice and claims from intimates are apt to be very powerful. The obligations are concrete and personal — not abstract. Moreover, they are familiar because they are similar to bonds that spring up in other realms of the official's life and are routinely honored, such as obligations to family and personal friends. Finally, the sanctions that these intimates can impose if they are disappointed, or, in their view, betrayed, are swift, vivid, and devastating to a person's conception of himself. Because duties to colleagues and friends are personal, familiar, and effectively guarded by social sanctions, these duties may often be given great prominence by officials.

These observations raise the question of exactly how much prominence should be given to these claims. We can see that they will be psychologically powerful. My view is that while one does owe friends and colleagues personal loyalty, these claims are much less important than the other claims we have discussed, and much less important than most officials make them. My guess is that more officials have been tempted into bad actions by responding to strongly felt obligations to friends and colleagues than by a badly distorted idea of what the public interest requires or a contemptuous attitude toward process.

Public officials owe colleagues and friends two things. First, they owe them notice that in their professional lives they serve their conception of what the public interest and authorizing processes require. They are obliged to do the *public's* business, not that of their friends or their own personal business. The interests and access of friends and colleagues with respect to public decisions must conform to these obligations. Of course, it will be difficult to maintain this distance. It requires an emotional attachment to conceptions of the public interest and authorizing processes that is as strong as an obligation felt to a friend. But I think this is the direction in which moral responsibility runs.

Second, officials owe friends and colleagues consistency in the independent stance they take toward the public interest and authorizing processes. I think this predictability and consistency is often what officials mean when they talk about another official's "integrity." They know where a person stands, understand the individual's reasons, and can trust that person not to change a position capriciously. It is capricious changes rather than disagreements that create a sense of betrayal. And the sense of betrayal is the sin that must be avoided in these intimate relationships. Given the "distance principle" cited above, friends or colleagues cannot reasonably feel betrayed if their interests are not accommodated or their advice not taken. They can feel betrayed only if they could not have guessed at the outset what stance their friend or colleague would take.

So officials owe their colleagues and friends clear signals of how they view obligations to the public interest and authorizing processes in particular circumstances.

OBLIGATIONS TO ONESELF

Notice that we have finally returned to the beginning of our inquiry. If obligations to the public interest and to authorizing processes are ambiguous in specific situations; and if friends and colleagues must be held at arm's length by a confidently held view of the duties of office; then, in the end, much depends on the individual official's conscience. Ultimately that individual must develop and remain loyal to a conception of the duties of a particular office, in a particular form of government, at a particular time, for the range of issues that occur. If much depends upon personal conceptions of duty, it is worth noting two troubling elements that insinuate themselves as one privately reflects on where duty and virtue lie. One element is personal ambition. The other is an astonishing capacity for rationalization. The two together are particularly poisonous.

Personal ambition is likely to be a major problem for public officials. After all, one must be more than a little arrogant to presume to govern others. With arrogance often comes ambition. Moreover, since continuing success seems to vindicate past actions, and since officials operating in their morally ambiguous environments often feel an acute need for vindication, officials may have a more than ordinary interest in continuing to be successful. Finally, we often think we see officials acting as though they were primarily interested in keeping their office or aggrandizing themselves rather than doing the right thing. It seems all too frequent that officials will explain inaction in an area where the public interest seems clearly to demand action but a suspect process of authorization prevents it by arguing that they are protecting their capacity to act effectively in other areas. Cynically we suspect the official is merely trying to survive in office. Similarly, active officials may claim that their unwillingness to rely on an elaborate process of consultation was necessary to achieve their purposes. Again, we cynically suspect the officials ignored the process to insure that they might claim credit for the action.

Clearly, selfish motives of public officials create moral difficulties when they guide actions.[28] That is particularly true in cases where simple stealing or deliberate deceptions of the public are involved. But I would argue that the desire to retain an office or to seek personal glory are hardly the worst sins of a public official. In fact, in our system of government, personal ambition is a key ingredient. We harness personal ambition to public purposes by forcing officials to be accountable. The best way for officials to stay in office and be praised is to meet their obligations to the public as they understand them. Note that because the system is designed in this way, the issue of whether public officials are acting out of self-serving or public-serving motives will always be obscure. When officials act on a policy, neither they nor we can be sure exactly what their motives are. If the action is well conceived and consistent with our aspirations, it will always be possible to see a self-serving as well as a public-serving motive. Perhaps the fact that we have designed the system in this way is part of the reason it is easy to become cynical about the motives of public officials: both self-serving and public-serving motives can always be inferred. Perhaps we err, then, and overestimate the importance of personal ambition as a threat to the moral stature of public officials.

Still, conscientious officials should determine how significant personal ambition is in guiding their actions. Fortunately, there are two rather simple tests they can apply. The first is to ask themselves whether they would be willing to be replaced in office by someone who shares the same values with respect to both outcomes and processes. Of course, it will always be easy to exaggerate the importance of modest differences in the stance of the proposed replacement in comparison with one's own stance. But if officials find themselves reluctant to leave office, or exaggerating small differences as they contemplate the imagined change, they should begin to be suspicious that personal ambitions and interests might be carrying too much weight in their actions.

The second test is particularly appropriate where officials seem to be sacrificing important values in one area because they believe they can make contributions in others. This situation often arises when officials feel particularly constrained by ties of personal loyalty to colleagues, and feel those with whom they serve are honorable despite their actions in given areas, but worry that their desire to stay in office is what is really influencing their willingness to continue in a job when important values are being sacrificed. The simple test here is simply to establish an arbitrary deadline in the future for reappraisal. If by that time the official has not been able to take actions that *advanced* important values, the apparent justification for "going along" can be readily seen as a rationalization and the official should leave office.[29]

In my view, the capacity for rationalization is a far greater enemy than personal ambition. It is a greater problem because the errors one can make if one allows this capacity full sway are much greater, and because it is much harder to see when it is operating on one's conception of duty. The only device that can protect one against rationalizations is a rather thoroughgoing, relentless skepticism about one's own conceptions, and enough time to become settled on a view that withstands this skepticism. Of course, one cannot take this time and effort with every action, but one should do it with *some*.

To the extent that the observations made in this essay will assist officials in rooting out rationalization and leaving only real justification for their actions, I will feel that I have accomplished a useful purpose. But I worry that I may only facilitate rationalization. And that is how skepticism works.

NOTES

1. See *The Federalist* (New York: Heritage Press, 1945), in particular, no 51. "If men were angels, no government would be necessary. If angels were to govern men, neither external nor internal controls would be necessary. In forming a government which is to be administered by men over men, the great difficulty lies in this: you must first enable the government to control the governed; and in the next place oblige it to control itself."

2. For an example of this kind of activity see Philip B. Heymann and others, *The Federal Trade Commission: A Failing Agency*, Kennedy School of Government Case *C14-76-119*, Harvard University.

3. The establishment of a separate cabinet level Department of Education is probably the most dramatic recent example of a shift in organizational structure that left the executive branch more vulnerable to influence by a narrowly interested professional group. For a general discussion of how structure affects the distribution of power see Harold Seidman, *Politics, Position and Power* (New York: Oxford University Press, 1970).

4. See the following cases: Mark H. Moore and others, *Methadone Maintenance (A) and (B)*, Kennedy School of Government Case *C94-77-065;* Philip B. Heymann and others, *The Bureau of Security and Consular Affairs*, Kennedy School of Government Case *C14-75-003;* and Joseph Bower and others, *William D. Ruckleshaus and the Environmental Protection Agency*, Kennedy School of Government Case *C16-74-028.*

5. A standard current complaint of public officials is that goals of legislation are left hopelessly vague, even contradictory, to allow passage in the legislature, and then turned over to officials to administer. The ambiguity and conflicts in the statutes then provide ample cause for interested parties to sue the government no matter what action an official takes, and the management of the program ends up in court. The court, in turn, tries to discern Congress' real intent by examining the legislative history. It also checks on the adequacy of the procedures an official used to reach a particular decision. It is a very clumsy process that puts officials in a difficult and ultimately hopeless position: they can work very hard in setting up a process and making a choice, but they have little reason to believe that their decision will be accepted as legitimate, final, and binding.

6. There are notorious cases of these in the literature on federal program implementation. See in particular Jeffrey Pressman and Aaron Wildavsky, *Implementation* (Berkeley: University of California Press, 1973).

7. Moore, *Methadone Maintenance (A) and (B)* (Case C94-77-065).

8. Nicholas Kotz, *Let Them Eat Promises: The Politics of Hunger in America* (Englewood, N.J.: Prentice-Hall, 1969).

9. Private correspondence with an official whose pseudonym is David Goldman.

10. Heymann, *The Federal Trade Commission* (Case C14-76-119).

11. For a discussion of the relationship between the extent of one's responsibilities and one's capacity to act see Charles Fried's concept of the "realm of efficacious action," in Charles Fried, *Right and Wrong* (Cambridge, Mass.: Harvard University Press, 1978), pp. 24-28.

12. This statement reveals a commitment to utilitarianism, since it suggests that a necessary if not sufficient condition for moral action is that one be aware of the consequences of one's action. A nonutilitarian, of course, could argue that the rightness of an action depended not at all on the consequences of the act, but only on the character of the action.

13. Again, throughout this discussion I am aware that I am revealing a strong utilitarian bias.

14. For a more complete argument on this point see Mark H. Moore, "Statesmanship in a World of Particular Substantive Choice," in Robert A. Goldwin, ed., *Bureaucrats, Policy Analysts, Statesmen: Who Leads?* (Washington, D.C.: American Enterprise Institute, 1980).

15. For an admirably clear discussion of the role of uncertainty in choices see Howard Raiffa, *Decision Analysis* (Reading, Mass.: Addison-Wesley, 1968). The fact of uncertainty in choices has important but as yet unstated implications for exactly how social science findings should be used in policy deliberations.

16. For a useful introductory discussion of these principles see Edith Stokey and Richard Zeckhauser, *A Primer for Policy Analysis* (New York: Norton, 1978), chap. 13.

17. Ibid., p. 279.

18. John Rawls, *A Theory of Justice* (Cambridge, Mass.: Harvard University Press, 1971).

19. Robert Nozick, *Anarchy, State and Utopia* (New York: Basic Books, 1974).

20. Rawls, *A Theory of Justice.*

21. On the concept of prima facie duties see R. M. Hare, *The Right and the Good* (Oxford, Eng.: Oxford University Press, 1973).

22. For an extended utilitarian justification for consultative processes see Charles E. Lindblom, *The Intelligence of Democracy* (New York: Free Press, 1965).

23. Ibid.

24. For a discussion of the important role that "due process" plays in facilitating implementation of choices see Roger B. Porter, *Presidential Decision Making: The Economic Policy Board*, chaps. 7, 8 (New York: Cambridge University Press, 1980).

25. For an excellent discussion of this important statute see Richard B. Stewart, "The Reformation of American Administrative Law," *Harvard Law Review*, vol. 88, no. 8 (June 1975).

26. For a stimulating discussion of the limits of individual cognitive capacities and the implications for policy deliberations see John D. Steinbruner, *The Cybernetic Theory of Decision* (Princeton: Princeton University Press, 1974).

27. For an illuminating discussion of this subject in a different context see Michael Walzer, *Obligations: Essays on Disobedience, War, and Citizenship* (Cambridge, Mass.: Harvard University Press, 1970), chap. 9.

28. For a discussion of this problem see Joel Fleishman's essay in this volume.

29. I am indebted to Jonathan Moore for this idea.

Douglas T. Yates, Jr.

2. Hard Choices: Justifying Bureaucratic Decisions

Questions of value and ethics hang over most public policy discussions like a cloud — or perhaps a thin vapor. We know the questions are critical and ubiquitous, but we typically have trouble setting our hands on them. In this essay, I wish to accomplish two things in considering value conflicts in public policy. The first is to bound the value problem so as to make the scope of discussion more manageable. The second is to suggest an analytical approach to value dilemmas that speaks to the value conflicts public officials face in their daily experience.

Before establishing my arbitrary boundaries and setting out my approach to value conflict, let me say a word or two more about the fundamental value problem as I see it. Unless we specify what kinds of officials, policies, and value problems we are interested in, we might include virtually every imaginable aspect of political life and behavior. The democratic process itself is a source of profound debate about values. So is any discussion of the role of representatives — be they Burkean or pluralist in their role definitions. So is any contemplation of individual interests or the public interest. So is any personalized account of morality — including canons of truth-telling, justifications of means (in relation to ends), and what is called, in old-fashioned terms, obligation and duty.

My strategy is to leave these tantalizing issues to others, in part because I have nothing fresh to say about them, in part, because other contributors to this volume seem to be grappling with these questions in a useful way. Rather, I want to pick out one corner of the map of officials, policies, and value conflicts that has been given much attention in an older literature but not recently. The area I have in mind concerns the role of appointive officials and bureaucrats as makers of public policy in a democratic society. I assume that they have some discretion both in designing the policy and in choosing the process by which the decision will be made. Moreover, I think significant values are at stake in both kinds of choices. I pick the value-choosing role of bureaucrats for three reasons: (1) it is commonly agreed that public policy is increasingly made by administrators, at the stages of both policy formulation and implementation; (2) emphasis on bureaucrats permits me to duck the debate about what constitutes proper representative behavior (when this depends on the choice of one or another broader democratic theory); and (3) in almost any democratic theory you choose, the choicemaking, "valuemaking" aspect of bureaucratic behavior is highly problematic. Whether policy and administration are separable or connected, it does seem odd in a democratic regime to give appointive officials a major role in value choices. It is not merely a matter of who guards the guardians — certainly a time-honored question — but more precisely, who regulates or controls the bureaucratic policymakers' values and how. I believe bureaucrats also play a further *critical* role in the realm of values to the extent that they set and administer the processes by which policy disputes are raised, argued out, heard, and disposed of in the decisionmaking process.

To avoid another long-standing empirical debate about the extent of bureaucratic independence and discretion (from statute or whatever), let me simply assert that bureaucrats are in the business of choosing and balancing values routinely — at least whenever they propose policy or interpret statutes. I can imagine someone replying that there are real constraints on the bureaucrat's ability to choose freely among different values. I cannot imagine anyone saying that the bureaucrat's role in value choice and balancing is a trivial feature of American government.

My first premise then, which is of particular interest and concern in a democracy, is that bureaucrats have a major role in making value choices and establishing processes by which competing values are dealt with in public decisions. Of course, if most public policy decisions turned out to contain only minor value trade-offs for the bureaucrat to worry about, my first premise might be correct but also quite uninteresting. In fact, in certain writings on bureaucracy and administration, the doctrine is advanced that decisions rest (or should rest) on criteria of efficiency and effectiveness (which criteria most reasonable people could agree upon and about which there is arguably only an interesting problem in terms of adequate measurement). Woodrow Wilson argued such a position and Robert McNamara may be understood, if slightly caricatured, to seek the same kind of value neutrality in dispassionate systems analysis, cost-benefit analysis, and the like. In this respect, it would be difficult to argue as a matter of principle that the government should receive less bang for the buck. As I will indicate below, I believe that there are some policy issues for which this kind of value neutrality, given the name of efficiency, probably obtains or is nearly approximated. But I believe that such policy issues are rare, a minority of public decisions.

Consider the current inventory of pressing public policy issues. These issues include affirmative action, busing, environmental protection, welfare reform, abortion, health insurance, energy policy, and energy "taxes," to name just a few. Now the heroic systems analyst might want to say that, analyzed carefully enough, these are really questions of benefit and cost and that different policies can be settled on efficiency or effectiveness grounds. However, on careful inspection, it turns out that this analytical heroism is at least incomplete and perhaps misguided. Taking any of the issues listed above, it seems plain that the public debate is, in the final analysis, concerned with the application of major public values, however understood, such as liberty, equality, justice, community. To take one example, busing can be construed as a strategy for increasing educational performance on average. But it is hard to avoid the conclusion that in a fundamental way, blacks are making equality claims and whites are making liberty claims (that is, freedom to maintain their neighborhoods); and the government may be seeking to alter existing notions of community.

So the first point is that the daily life of bureaucrats involves the identification and balancing of major public values. If these values were reasonably defined, it might be relatively easy for a bureaucrat to construct— implicitly or explicitly—a value impact analysis for a given policy and to specify relevant trade-offs.

Indeed, I think the first obligation of the appointive official or bureaucrat is to be *explicit* about the value premises and implications of public decisions. The reason for this goes back to the difference between legislators and bureaucrats mentioned above. We might exempt legislators from this value-accounting on the pluralist grounds that they are responding to constituent interests and that this response is considered a legitimate, indeed essential, way to justify value positions in a democratic society. Bureaucrats lack this justification of their policy decisions, and this is why their attention to providing a value analysis is of particular significance. If bureaucrats are going to make value choices, they should inform the rest of us value-laden voters and consumers of policies what the operative values behind public decisions are and how they conflict (when they do).

This value clarification is especially important where policy decision involves policy conflicts and trade-offs. It is there, most especially, that we citizens might want to know why the government is doing X rather than Y. (Obviously too, I believe that many interesting policy decisions will elicit and sustain a subtle analysis of value conflicts as they exist in different policy options.) Thus, if the first question of public policy is "What should government do?" any adequate answer should include a self-conscious assessment of the implications of policy for major public values such as liberty, equality, community, or the public interest.

This much may seem entirely unobjectionable. And we might suspect that given more time, bureaucrats could easily do value impact statements along with their myriad other analyses. In this halcyon world of philosopher-kings — Washington style — a new cover memo would emerge from officials which would comment on equality-efficiency trade-offs, liberty-equality trade-offs, and the like.

We might be happy to achieve this much if we believed the resulting discourse on values would offer clearer choices, illuminate policy dilemmas, and otherwise inform. Unhappily, we know all too well that the language of values is at present insufficiently precise to support impact statements that compare with those of economists, scientists, and other such experts.

I do not wish to delve into the substantive meaning of those timeless public values. I would offer instead a more modest approach to value clarification which will, I hope, add some additional criteria of assessment to debates about the ideas of liberty and equality themselves. I can make this point most clearly by using the example of equality arguments.

Most public officials would agree that equality has become a dominant idea in modern political discourse. Just think how many policy debates involve an equality claim on one side or the other. In a large number of policy disputes, we will find some equality claim in a strong if not ascendant position; and in a large number of policy disputes, we will find an equality claim in direct conflict with another equality claim. What are we to make of this? At first glance, it would seem that any hoped-for "value impact statement" has suffered a severe blow. For if it is hard enough to identify and trade off claims of liberty versus equality, for example, how in the world are we to assess conflicts between different equality claims as they arise in a particular policy dispute?

There is one other reason why equality is such an important but slippery principle. Many discussions about liberty, justice, rights of various sorts, and fairness revolve around the question of equality — that is, the "issue" can often be restated in terms of equal liberties, rights, and so forth. The idea of right seems to include an idea of equality.

However, the lamentable fact is that the concept of equality, in most of its formulations, is nearly empty. The simple equation $X = Y$ says very little without a great deal of further specification of what is being distributed in what amounts to whom and by what criteria. Perhaps the best way to write the basic equality statement is $? = ?$, so as to make the point that invoking the equal sign accomplishes precious little in the way of normative argument. We still have to figure out *who* is to receive equal shares and *what* is to be equalized.

It is possible to construct a basic grammar that highlights many of the persistent points of dispute in discussions of a principle like equality. On the *who* side, it is necessary to make clear in the first place whether we are talking about individuals or collectivities (such as a state or nation). If the former, is each individual to count discretely as one (unitary equality) or as part of some imagined class of people (for example, blacks, women, patients requiring kidney dialysis)? If the latter, how do we count or compare classes of people? Are we concerned about equality within groups (equal access to dialysis for all kidney patients) or equality between groups (that is, aggregate equality relationships between blacks and whites)?

So far this logic is indeed simple; and it would not be hard for a public official to make clear what accounting method he or she is using. However, there are also some interesting complexities here that are harder to disentangle. For example, how do you decide who to include in the relevant catchment area when adding up individual interest for the purpose of equalizing treatment? In the *Bakke* or *DeFunis* cases, concerning affirmative action policies, is the relevant catchment area the states of Washington or California or the nation as a whole? In thinking about equal claims to access to unspoiled wilderness in Alaska or the High Sierras, do you include the resident of New Jersey as well as citizens more immediately affected by Storm King or the Alaska Pipeline? The question is: Who has *standing* in the legal sense and how do we think about this question when residents of New York or New Jersey increasingly claim an interest in what happens to wildlife in Alaska or wilderness in California?

A second problem that the public official must increasingly think about is how to balance individual interests against corporate (in the broadest sense) and institutional interests. In this respect, what sense do we make of a claim of a group of urban residents who say they constitute a community or neighborhood and that the interests of that neighborhood should be treated equally (one-to-one) with other "neighborhoods." (This counting problem is, of course, familiar to all of us in the Virginia Compromise with the apportionment of votes to individuals in the House and to collectivities in the Senate.) My point is that increasingly we are faced with groups of individuals purporting to be indivisible, organic collectivities (more radical elements of the woman's movement and the Quebec "nationalists" come to mind), and unless we can figure out how to count interests (holding individuals equal or equalizing treatment of collectivities), any major problem of distribution is likely to be muddled. Put another way, until we can figure out this counting problem, we will have a hard time knowing whether we are making policy for individuals, say a truck driver; interest groups, say the Teamsters; or collectivities, say labor. Needless to say, the more public officials are asked to balance the interests of collectivities—business, labor, the frostbelt, neighborhoods, the young, the black community—the more difficult their task of calculation becomes. In the extreme case, the only logical result is corporatism, one vote or share for each entity. More frequently, the effort to equalize treatment of these groups leads to Theodore Lowi's interest group pluralism, where one group after another is accommodated by government. In the end, however, it is hard to know whether there is more or less equality as a result.

On the *what* side of equality arguments, there is a need to specify what the value is that is being distributed—money, opportunity, and so on. Then there is a need to make clear what further factors enter into the distribution—for example, need or merit of some sort. Finally, there is usually a need to specify the benchmark according to which equal distribution is measured. In the simplest case, if group X is way behind historically in its share of a value, does equality require an immediate equal result, a proportional increase, or merely an equal opportunity to catch up? This is essentially the problem of starting-line versus finish-line fairness related to the question of specifying the historical point at which the race began. My guess is that it is impossible to appraise the claims made by "disadvantaged" groups as well as "backlash" groups without specifying something about the historical benchmark to be used in making comparisons over time.

I have given this brief account of the simple grammar implicit in equality claims because I believe that although some of the terms may seem abstract, they are in fact pivotal issues in ordinary public decisions.[1] I do not expect public officials to torture themselves over all the nuances of normative argument. But they do have an obligation to attempt an explicit accounting of how they are applying the values and principles they seek to endorse.

A FIRST SUMMARY

So far I have attempted to make the following arguments about value discourse in public policymaking.

(1) Bureaucrats must choose between and implement values to a significant extent. They also play a major role in designing and implementing the processes by which value-laden decisions are made.

(2) In most but not all policy disputes, there are significant conflicts and trade-offs between values.

(3) As an example, we have seen that many policy disputes involve conflicting equality claims.

(4) Public officials cannot resolve value conflicts in any philosophical sense, but they can identify relevant values and the conflict they enter into.

(5) Moreover, public officials can and should make clear what language, what words, they are using in treating values.

(6) Further, as we saw in the case of equality, value discourse can be expressed in relatively simple terms that reveal not only what public officials are talking about, but also how they are doing their accounting—how they are counting heads and allocations.

From these points, I wish to draw one central conclusion that speaks to the problem of reconciling bureaucratic discretion and power with democratic norms. I believe the public official's fundamental moral obligation in a democracy is to pay increased attention to the definition and treatment of values the more these values are in conflict in a decision and the more difficulty there is in doing the accounting of who gets what. In the simple case where, for example, there is a clear and dominant equality principle at stake, and little problem in accounting, the public official may owe us as citizens no more than a terse statement of the justification for the public decision. But in more complex cases, where the value conflicts are great and the accounting problems are substantial, I believe public officials should provide a more thorough value analysis as one of the central justifications of public decision. Indeed, this is how I would define responsibility in bureaucratic decisionmaking. Without such an accounting, citizens can never know how and why their officials decided to act as they did. Without that knowledge, it is hard to see how the idea of democratic control of administration can be anything more than a dangerous fiction.

One public official who has made an attempt to perform explicit value analysis is former Secretary of Transportation William Coleman at the time of his decision on whether Concorde could land at Kennedy airport. In his written decision, Coleman performed a careful cost-benefit analysis that involved an explicit concern for legal, environmental, and political values. In short, Coleman sought to give the interested parties and the public a full accounting of his thought processes and of his own weighing of relevant values. As he wrote in his decision,

This decision involves environmental, technological, and international considerations that are as complex as they are controversial, and do not lend themselves to easy or graceful evaluation, let alone comparison. I shall nonetheless attempt in some detail to explain my evaluation of the most significant issues — those raised in the EIS, by the proponents and opponents of the Concorde at the January 5 public hearing, and in the submissions to the docket — and the reasons I have decided as I have. For I firmly believe that public servants have the duty to express in writing their reasons for taking major actions, so that the public can judge the fairness and objectivity of such action. Moreover, explaining our reasons in writing may help us avoid unreasonable actions. A decision that "cannot be explained" is very likely to be an arbitrary decision.[2]

The strength of Coleman's analysis is that his concern to spell out value considerations both enabled citizens to better understand the Concorde problem and, equally important, gave the citizen an opportunity to see what kind of person, with what kind of concerns and values, was making decisions in the office of the Secretary of Transportation.

Another fundamental reason the value-choosing role of bureaucrats is a critical aspect of policymaking in the American democratic system is that we increasingly lack any clear or coherent justification (or set of justifications) for government intervention in our society. There have, of course, been such doctrines in the past which at least appeared to be well understood if not always perfectly clear. In a much simpler world, those who advocated the view that the "government which governs least governs best" did at least have a decision rule that provided a guide to action. When in doubt, don't intervene. Keep government out. More recently, the New Deal faith in government as a potent instrument for solving critical social and economic problems also provided a kind of decision rule. The test was to identify "critical" problems and then explain why they deserved this definition. Of course, given an enthusiastic and adventurous government, the New Deal test for public intervention and action did not provide a clear or particularly stringent decision rule.

The most rigorous criteria for justifying public intervention are probably those of economic theory, but even here we have considerable difficulty sustaining any persuasive tests of appropriate government intervention. Modern economic theory contemplates a market mechanism that should be allowed to function unless certain market failures or other special conditions arise. Concepts of market failure, externalities, merit goods, and public goods are offered as exceptions to a general rule that the market should be allowed to operate "freely" — or at least within constraints imposed by antitrust policy, truthful advertising, and the like. Curiously, however, the exceptions to the market "ideal" have, in my view as a noneconomist, become the exceptions that very often disprove the rule. Put another way, in a complicated, intertwined economy, with a large public sector to begin with, it is easy for an alert economist to find market failures, externalities, and public goods in many different places.

If we cannot find justification for public action in a firmly rooted public philosophy, like "the government which governs least," or an economic theory, in earlier incarnations, what restraints or normative principles exist at all to suggest that government should *not* act on a particular policy problem? My answer is that in our present governmental climate, there are almost no such restraints or systematic principles. This means that a kind of "open season" exists for government, and indeed we have by now become used to a familiar pattern: if government finds a new problem like drug addiction or energy conservation or environmental protection, it will create a bureaucracy and throw a new program at it.

If this analysis is anywhere near correct, it strongly reinforces my central argument that bureaucratic policymakers are often deciding when, why, and how to act and are making substantial value choices for specific policy arenas, and in addition, are implicitly fashioning new rationales and precedents for government intervention. If this is true, it only reinforces my argument that bureaucratic policymakers owe citizens in a democracy a careful accounting of the reasons why they have decided to act, what public purposes they are pursuing, and what values they have emphasized as against reasonable alternatives. In addition, this accounting should both bolster the legitimacy of governmental action in given choice situations and strengthen the citizen's ability to comprehend the general role of government.

ADMINISTRATIVE PROCESS VALUES

Traditionally, the debate about bureaucratic power has not led to demands that administrative policymakers should justify their actions publicly and in substantive terms. We have tended to focus instead on "administrative process" values and, as such, to demand that bureaucracies be accessible, accountable, participative, responsive, and responsible. In the course of observing these process values, public officials may have to give reasons or substantive justifications, but that is not the central purpose of these administrative values. They involve at root certain tests of appropriate government procedure, and the measure of the tests is whether government is open to citizen claims and complaints and provides processes for participation, hearings, review, appeal, and remedy where an administrative error has been found to exist. These procedural values are at the heart of administrative law, and indeed, if we believed that these values and procedures were sufficiently powerful, we might pay far less heed to the substantive value dilemmas I have referred to above. More precisely, if we were confident that citizens possessed strong and well-established processes for discussing administrative issues and disputes, we might not be so interested in knowing *what* exactly citizens and bureaucrats are arguing about.

I am not satisfied that these administrative process values do the job and therefore provide substantial reassurance for those worried about democratic process in an increasingly bureaucratic state. My main worry is that there is considerable analytical confusion in our ordinary use of terms like accessibility, responsiveness, accountability, and participation. To take two examples: Does responsiveness mean being available to hear the complaints of a citizen or consumer, or does it mean recognizing those complaints and satisfying them? Does accountability mean simply that a government official can give a reason for an action or explanation of a policy, or does it mean giving reasons that are satisfactory to the citizen or consumer on the grounds that accountability entails substantive obligations on the part of the official and rights (if not authority) on the part of the citizen?

Or take participation. Does it mean that citizens are "heard," or heard and listened to, or heard, listened to, and, as a result, get their way? Put simply, does the test of successful participation lie in improved procedures for decisionmaking or improved decision results? Is it possible to have improved decision procedures without improved decision results? Further, who is to participate? How widespread must participation be? How many issues or decisions must be governed by participatory procedures for participation to be considered real? What of the nature of the participatory decisions? Is it enough that most minor decisions are participated in, or must citizen participation extend to some major issues, or to all major issues? Who decides what issues are minor or major?

We could, at the risk of considerable boredom, cut and slice into all of the administrative process values in the same way and show that, under careful examination, each apparently simple idea unpacks into a great many difficult questions and vaguely understood dimensions. Is responsiveness a procedural or a substantive notion? Is accountability? And so forth.

Aside from revealing considerable complexity, this exercise reveals two important general themes. First, for each administrative value, there is both a procedural and a substantive understanding. In the procedural sense, these administrative values entail greater communication and interaction between citizens and public officials. Thus, citizens would attend meetings and speak their minds: "participation." Government would establish new mechanisms so that the citizens could more easily approach officials: "accessibility." Government might establish new decentralized techniques that would bring officials closer to the problems that they must deal with: "responsiveness." Bureaucracies might make organizational changes designed to establish what bureaucrat is in charge of what program and who is to answer for breakdowns and failures: "accountability." The substantive construction of each value concerns the question of what kinds of decisions are made. The test of the value in this case is whether the recipients of the decision feel that the "right" decision was made. It is thus hard to avoid substance even when we are discussing process values.

Second, this analysis suggests that there is, in addition to the substantive and procedural distinction, a distinction between strong and weak constructions of the process values. The values are weak when they provide only mild forms of redress for citizens and strong when they go a long way toward changing the nature of proceedings or the resulting policy. Take, for example, the value of responsiveness. Let us look at how it may be defined in both substantive and procedural senses and in strong and weak senses in each case. In the procedural sense, responsiveness may be weakly defined to mean that bureaucrats will merely listen to an angry citizen who tries to press claims. In a stronger sense of procedural change, responsiveness may require that bureaucrats restructure their method of administration so that they can more quickly act on citizen complaints. In the substantive sense, responsiveness may mean, weakly again, that public officials will listen to what a citizen has to say and try to find answers that reflect the content of the citizen's concerns. In the stronger substantive sense, however, public officials might be required to do precisely what the citizen wishes — to respond directly, decisively, and quickly to the complaint that is being made.

So we see that our administrative process values have both strong and weak, substantive and procedural meaning and that the mere mention of the values which everyone is for — responsiveness, participation, accountability — tells us very little about what precisely is being asked for and therefore what government should provide.

This kind of confusion and conflict is only the beginning, for these administrative values are completely empty until one specifies what individuals, interest groups, or other government agencies want an official to be responsive or accountable. There is no simple or logical way to settle this issue. A black neighborhood that supports busing may ask city bureaucrats to be responsive to its claim and so may a white ethnic neighborhood that opposes busing. The Chamber of Commerce, the state government, and the federal government may ask administrators to be responsible, to uphold their "duty" to support local economic interests, state policies, or court orders. Being responsive or accountable per se provides no decisive way of settling value conflicts or making the usual hard choices between competing political interests.

In addition, the different bureaucratic values — responsiveness, accountability, and so forth — are often in direct conflict with one another. The greater the number of people participating in a decision, the less any individual can be held accountable for that decision.

There are many other practical conflicts among administrative process values. Providing for participation and accessibility and accountability takes time and administrative energy. Participatory mechanisms involving citizens and public officials are notoriously time-consuming because they are designed to nurture extensive discussion and debate. But if this is so, the value of participation conflicts directly with the value of responsiveness, which often requires or means that the government should act quickly without extreme deliberation. In addition, the point of participation, accessibility, and responsiveness is often to get particular exceptions or adjustments made for particular individuals or groups. But these exceptions will often conflict with the values of responsibility and accountability, which require that officials follow rules and laws and be able to give simple, clear, and therefore presumably general reasons for their decisions. Accounting for why X number of exceptions were made to a policy in the interests of responsiveness may not be impossible, but it is surely difficult to do if one is concerned to create an appearance of general, clear accountability.

So far I fear my analysis of "hard choices" has created more than its fair share of burdens and dilemmas for public officials. The first argument, that substantive value conflicts are both highly significant and pervasive, leads me to ask for a detailed account of a bureaucrat's value-accounting. The second part of my analysis, the examination of administrative process values, adds to the basic difficulty for bureaucratic officials by suggesting that these values are not a sufficient answer to the request for value-accounting and are themselves subject to very different interpretations and indeed may be in fundamental conflict with one another.

Having attempted to lay bare the critical role of the bureaucrat in value-choosing, I do not wish to wind up designing an impossible task for a public official or even one of Plato's guardians. Public officials cannot analyze the value dimensions and implications of every policy decision they face. Indeed, public officials not only face a variety of important new policy issues, but also administer hundreds of programs whose history may be traced back twenty, thirty, or forty years.

So which policies and problems should bureaucrats focus on if they accept the general moral obligation to exercise and illuminate significant value conflicts? One helpful answer to this question is provided by C. E. Lindblom in his development of the concept of incrementalism.[3] If Lindblom is right, there are many policy decisions that have evolved over a long period of time and are characterized by at least two important features of decisionmaking. First, in the course of a long evolution, such policies have been bargained over and adjusted so as to take into account a wide variety of different values and preferences. In institutions these are policies on which the president, Congress, the bureaucracies, and interest groups have been instructing and reviewing, appropriating and authorizing, administering and revising, to a greater or lesser degree. Under these conditions we can reasonably expect that the value issues contained in a policy have been wrestled over by many political actors and for a long period of time. Any attempt to seek fresh value clarification in such policy arenas would seem to me to discount the real virtues of incrementalism and the democratic processes it contains and reflects. The second feature of this kind of long-evolving policy is that ends and means, values and policies often become greatly intertwined and hard to separate.[4] Indeed, it may be a heroic feat to sort out the discrete value trade-offs from the substantive policy adjuncts, and it may well be wise not to try.

Another way to answer the initial question is to attempt to distinguish different kinds of policy problems — be they old or new — and then decide which kinds are most significant and suitable for value analysis.

At one end of the spectrum of public policy issues are those that involve highly technical or scientific issues. On matters concerning the Food and Drug Administration, the National Science Foundation, the National Institutes of Health, and to a lesser extent, the Atomic Energy Commission and weapons procurement in the Defense Department, the average person in a democracy is unlikely to be informed and enlightened in his or her value- and choicemaking role as a citizen by lengthy public argument about technical issues. Here the administrative process value of accountability may do the required work if in fact government officials explain (account for) their decisions to scientific peers and open the decisionmaking record to specialists interested in their highly sophisticated issues.

At the other end of the spectrum of public policy issues are those that involve fairly simple distributions to specified populations. Here one thinks of the great range of entitlements programs — allocations for food stamps, medicaid, welfare, veterans' programs, compensatory education programs, and programs for the elderly or the handicapped. In these cases, where X person with Y characteristic is said to have an entitlement to a government benefit, one or another administrative process value may well suffice to insure that a bureaucracy is meeting its statutory and normative obligations. I refer to the process values of accessibility and responsiveness; and we should notice in this regard that congressional staffers spend a great deal of their time seeking to insure in precisely this way that administrative officials are responsive to constituents whom they believe to be eligible for a particular program.

Of course, there is a great deal of space on the policy continuum between highly technical issues, where accountability may seem to be the appropriate government response, and highly distributive programs, often involving entitlements, where accessibility and responsiveness to individual claims may seem to fulfill the moral obligation of public officials to their clients. I cannot precisely define all the possible issues that occupy this middle ground and would not want to spend the time required to do so. Rather, I would argue that for issues that are not highly technical or distributive, the test of whether they deserve a careful value analysis depends on whether they (a) cut close to certain main public values and (b) have substantial policy implications. The test is of the depth of value conflict and the scope of policy impact. Applying this simple test, certain "new" policies clearly warrant careful attention: for example, busing, health insurance, abortion, affirmative action, environmental protection, open housing, and school financing. These are "potent" issues for value analysis, in my view, because one only needs to mention words like liberty, equality, community, and property rights to see immediately that these issues contain a great deal of value content.

In sum, without purporting to establish a precise formula for measuring policy significance, we might advance two criteria as useful guidelines: (1) a policy merits open public accounting when it either represents a nonroutine initiative by a bureaucracy or when it constitutes a marked departure from past practice, (2) a policy merits public accounting when it involves the application of a major social value such as equality, equal opportunity, personal liberty, or the public interest. This criterion is especially strong when a bureaucrat perceives a conflict to exist *within* a value (as in two competing definitions of equal treatment) or when two or more values are in conflict. Clearly, the two guidelines will often overlap and they are not fully dispositive of all interesting cases, but they do provide a starting point for a bureaucrat concerned to increase the level of open, public accounting.

VALUE CONFLICTS AND THE POLITICS OF INSTITUTIONS

Having said that bureaucrats are in the special and "suspect" position of having a crucial value-choosing role, I must also add that there is a perhaps ironic virtue in this privileged position. If bureaucrats do not illuminate, analyze, and educate citizens about value conflicts, what other institutions will? The simple point is that, with one exception, it is clearly not in the standard operating procedure of other major political institutions to perform this normative role. More precisely, we do not normally look to Congress for this kind of value clarification. As David Mayhew has persuasively argued, the role of members of Congress is not to weigh values; it is rather to attend to the distributive process and to capture benefits for their own constituents.[5] And it follows that if they are primarily concerned with the parceling out of policies and benefits to individuals, it would be counterintuitive to expect a systematic accounting of major value conflicts to emerge from Congress. If you start by asking and influencing who gets what, you simply do not reach the larger value issues and have no particular (or political) reason to do so.

Where else might we look in our institutions for value clarification of major policy issues? Perhaps to the presidency. But again, given what we know about the president's natural impulse to represent all the people as their collective national representative and executive, we should reasonably not have great expectations concerning the president's propensity to clarify value dilemmas. Rather, it is in the interest of the president, as agent of all Americans, to present programs and policies that merge, blend, and accommodate different values in a package that will have the chance, at least, of attracting broad-gauged national support. Put another way, a president who trafficked in sharply drawn value clarifications and trade-offs would be sawing off major constituencies at every turn of a trade-off, and I therefore see little incentive for a president to explicitly perform this difficult role of laying out and publicly evaluating different "hard choices."

If not the Congress or the president, then whom should we look to for help with our "hard choices"? In the last two decades, it has become something of a national habit to turn to the Supreme Court for the solution or at least the balancing of major public values. But there are numerous reasons to doubt the wisdom and efficacy of passing the buck of value clarification to the Supreme Court. In the first place, the Supreme Court is by design the least democratic institution in American national government. It would therefore be worrisome to a democrat if the nine justices were increasingly making and enforcing the society's most salient value decisions. In addition, the experience of the Warren Court suggests that the Court as an institution runs into difficulty when it is perceived as the central arbiter of values in our political system. Not only do the decisions of the Court become highly politicized when it is overloaded by major value conflicts, but its institutional legitimacy, which rests on its stance of being above the daily political battle, is likely to be strained as well.

Having seen the limitations of the Congress and the presidency as value classifiers and choosers, it would seem logical that we look back to the bureaucracy for an explicit, public treatment of value conflicts. For one thing, we have nowhere else to turn. But it is certainly ironic that we wind up back on the doorstep of the bureaucracy when I have argued above that public officials are a large part of the original problem — in that they both routinely make major value choices *and* typically do not illuminate in any persistent or satisfactory way the normative character of their "administrative" decisions. Nevertheless, at the risk of making the poachers into the game wardens, there are several good reasons why the major responsibility for examining "hard choices" and justifying public decisions in normative terms should be assigned to the bureaucracy.

In the first place, bureaucrats are not directly subject to the intense political pressures, especially the concern for reelection, that confront presidents and the members of Congress. For this reason, bureaucrats might reasonably be expected to possess (or develop) a degree of distance from political battles that would stand them well in performing the task of careful and thoughtful value clarification. In addition, one of the enduring values and justifications of bureaucracy, from Weber on, is that it will nurture an ethos of "neutral competence" — professional detachment, if you will — and the possibility of neutrality would seem to be an important precondition of useful value analysis. This is not to say that bureaucrats are usually or always neutral and detached in their policy assessments, for that would be a rash claim. It is to say that bureaucratic norms and traditions do provide some institutional support for neutrality and detachment. In the same way, as Hugh Heclo has shown,[6] the bureaucrat's greater longevity in office is apt to engender a longer time horizon than presidents or members of Congress typically possess, and an expanded time horizon might well increase an individual's ability to place value conflicts in a historical, evolutionary, "long-run" perspective.

A further qualification of bureaucracy for the task of value analysis is that administrative officials already possess substantial staffs and informational and analytical resources. To the extent that a value analysis requires a detailed knowledge of a particular policy or problem, the bureaucracy is perhaps best equipped to perform the role. Moreover, since bureaucrats stand at the intersection of policy formulation and policy implementation, they have the best vantage point for observing the evolving relationship between normative values and actual program impacts.

Most important, precisely because bureaucratic officials make important value decisions but usually do not discuss or justify them, the strategy of imposing the burden of performing value analysis and clarification on bureaucracy attacks the underlying problem for democratic decisionmaking at a major point of origin.

TWO POSSIBLE OBJECTIONS

Two other arguments advanced by Lindblom in his discussions of incremental decisionmaking pose potentially serious challenges to my definition of the value problem as well as to my strategy for dealing with it. I believe both arguments can be answered, but they do merit thoughtful consideration.

First, Lindblom writes that partisan argument is a virtue in democratic discourse.[7] I am inclined to agree with him that, given the difficulty of achieving full neutrality and objectivity about values, it is doubtless better to have open, explicit partisan debate. But if this is true, have I not contradicted this view by asking bureaucrats to perform a role of value clarification knowing that they can never achieve this full objectivity? The irony can be stated in even starker terms. Having worried about who guards the bureaucratic guardians in our state, is it not the effect of my argument to recreate the bureaucrats as a kind of aloof guardian of value analysis? Indeed, I think this contradiction or irony may appear to exist, but I would resolve it by saying that I would be perfectly happy for bureaucrats to argue for and against value positions provided that they perform the much-needed public service of arguing in an open and explicit matter. Indeed, I would expect that, given the likely diversity and range of bureaucratic views and interests, a public debate on values, even though a partisan one, would give us a far greater clarification of and exposure to value conflicts than we presently possess as citizens and supposed choosers of policies and electors of political leaders.

Understood in this way, explicit value analysis may be seen either as a compensation for possible defects in partisan bargaining or, from a different perspective, as a useful supplement to the process of bargaining and adjustment itself. To the extent that the bargaining process blurs or ignores basic value conflicts in the interest of facilitating accommodation, value analysis would have the effect of injecting an important missing element into policy — debate and decisionmaking. From a different vantage point, value analysis might be viewed as a supplement to normal bargaining processes in the sense that it would generate a broader range of issues at the political bargaining table.

The other argument Lindblom advances that bears directly on my analysis has been mentioned before. It is that values and policies are usually so intertwined in the evolution of policymaking that any attempt to dissect values (as if they could be isolated for inspection in a laboratory-style analysis) is apt to be fruitless if not impossible. As noted above, I have considerable sympathy with this argument, particularly as it relates to those policies that have been hammered out and negotiated over a long period of time in keeping with the canons of Lindblom's idea of incrementalism. At the same time, I believe that, as American government has increased its social programs and transfer payments, we are increasingly finding values like equality or equal opportunity playing a strong and independent role in the policy process. It is plain that major policies, like affirmative action and busing, to take only two examples, are being designed to explicitly advance notions of equality or equal opportunity; therefore to understand what such policies mean we *do* need to know what their guiding value (or values) mean or are understood to mean. Here is where the need for careful value clarification becomes so prominent. For if values such as equality or equal opportunity are not simple notions but rather unpack into a multitude of different conceptions and interpretations, then we need an open public discourse about value meanings and conflicts if we are not to fall into a kind of policymaking by slogan and highly subjective definition of public policy.

As we have seen in the case of Secretary of Transportation Coleman, explicit value analysis also forces public officials to show where they stand. It provides a reply to the problem of "faceless bureaucrats" and gives us an opportunity to appraise the value structure and the character lines of major public officials. This is a virtue in itself of some substantial magnitude.

TOWARD A NEW PUBLIC PHILOSOPHY

In sum, I believe that our government is increasingly a "bureaucratic democracy" — in which policy decisions are increasingly located within bureaucratic settings, and bureaucrats, at the stages of both policy formulation and implementation, play a highly significant role in decisionmaking and value-choosing. If this is so, we cannot have a viable discourse about our public philosophy if bureaucrats do not express and clarify major policy choices. One other Lindblom argument cuts deeply on this point. In a recent writing, he expresses the fear that there may be a troublesome circularity in our democratic process if public (and private) leaders are the major source of guidance to others who then feed back preferences to government based importantly on this guidance.[8] This is a perfectly fair claim, but it seems to me that citizens are in a worse position as democratic actors if bureaucratic officials do not articulate and clarify policy choices at all or hardly at all. Being subject to influence, guidance, or even indoctrination by public officials is one kind of danger for us. Being oblivious to the character and consequences of policy decision strikes me as potentially even more insidious. For while the possibility certainly exists with the first danger that our preferences will be engineered, there is also the possibility that we, as citizens, will retain some perspective or critical distance in appraising what government tells us we want. But where we do not even know what the debate is about because we cannot see into government and government is not "talking," the possibility of healthy skepticism or even independent judgment is greatly diminished.

Thus, I believe that the best hope for creating a more lively and cogent public philosophy is for bureaucratic policymakers to take the lead in opening up the debate. I do not know what substantive public philosophy is likely to emerge as a result, but I do believe an opening up of bureaucratic thinking and value-choosing is a procedural precondition of useful substantive argument—whatever its form or consequence.

NOTES

1. A dissection of different notions of equality has recently been attempted by a number of us working at Yale. See Douglas Rae and others, *Equalities* (Cambridge, Mass.: Harvard University Press, 1981).

2. Department of Transportation, The Secretary's Decision on Concorde Supersonic Transport, Washington, D.C., February 4, 1976, p. 7.

3. For a further elaboration and analysis see C. E. Lindblom, *The Intelligence of Democracy* (New York: The Free Press, 1965), and Lindblom, "The Science of Muddling Through," *Public Administration Review*, 19 (Spring 1959).

4. C. E. Lindblom, "Strategies for Decision Making," *University of Illinois Bulletin* (1971), p. 13.

5. David Mayhew, *Congress: The Electoral Connection* (New Haven: Yale University Press, 1974).

6. Hugh Heclo, *A Government of Strangers* (Washington, D.C.: Brookings, 1977), pp. 142ff.

7. Lindblom, "Strategies for Decision Making," p. 14.

8. C. E. Lindblom, *Politics and Markets* (New York: Basic Books, 1977), chap. 15.

Joel L. Fleishman

3. Self-Interest and Political Integrity

If I am not for myself, who will be for me?
If I am only for myself, what am I?

— Hillel, *Ethics of the Fathers*

For the administration of the government, like the office of a trustee, must be conducted for the benefit of those entrusted to one's care not of those to whom it is entrusted.

— Cicero, *de Officiis*

Watergate has bequeathed to American politics a new legacy of rules to constrain the behavior of politicians and their backers. The first major reform in the laws regulating political activity in a half-century has established a comprehensive set of restrictions that is not diminished in its significance simply because all of the goals of reform have not been attained. We have provided public monies to — and imposed enforceable ceilings on expenditures by — candidates for the presidency, limited the amount individuals and groups can legally give to all federal candidates, greatly extended the scope of public disclosure of contributions and expenditures, and created a federal agency to police the new regulations. We have tightened the laws regulating potential conflicts of interest in actions of government officeholders, and, by "sunshine" and "freedom-of-information" acts, have substantially enlarged the capacity of the public to scrutinize the behavior of its elected and appointed officials. As each new regulation has gone into effect, it has seemed to spawn its own evasions which, at least to the ears of some, cry out for even more regulation.

Many lawmakers, political activists, columnists, and members of the public are beginning to wonder if any end of regulation is really in sight. Unsure of exactly what the objectives of such political regulation are, and exasperated by our seeming inability to attain such of them as we can agree upon, one hears it said with increasing frequency that a better course of

52

action would be to junk the entire regulatory apparatus — laws, regulations, and regulatory agencies — and focus our energies instead upon identifying and electing to office public servants of character, men and women of integrity.

Even if that argument is a "cop-out," the subject of political integrity is surely worth examining irrespective of what should or should not be done about diminishing, retaining, or extending the specific regulations governing behavior of politicians or officeholders. If public officials lack integrity, no laws or regulations can infuse them with it, or indeed protect the public from the abuses of trust they feel free to commit, simply because they are without it. Surely, regulation can discourage the most egregious defaults, and does provide at least a modicum of protection to the public's interest, but no regulatory edifice, however far-ranging or minutely detailed, will ever be an adequate substitute for integrity in officials.

Such an assertion is likely to be unexceptionable, at least until we try to define what we mean by "integrity." What is conduct of good character in politics? How does society decide that it is so? What should an individual officeholder do when he is pulled in one direction by what he believes the public interest as a whole requires, and in the opposite direction by his desire to increase his program's budget or get himself a promotion? Wouldn't those who worry about politics be better off if there were some thoughtful discussion of these questions, and if we were able to attain some measure of agreement about what political integrity is, so that persons of pretty-good character, which is to say most people, would have touchstones when they come to hard turnings? In this essay I propose an interpretation of political integrity and attempt to define it in such a way as to make it useful to those who are engaged in politics, whether by voting, running for or serving in office, or otherwise thinking about it from time to time.

SELF-INTEREST AND POLITICAL INTEGRITY

Simply put, "integrity" means having a genuine, wholehearted disposition to do the right and just thing in all circumstances, and to shape one's actions accordingly.[1] There is no code of conduct declaring society's view of the right course of action in every situation, so each of us must puzzle out for ourself the moral solution to each dilemma we face. Some people seem to know instinctively what right conduct is, but they do not have a monopoly on integrity. Individuals may also be said to have integrity if their guiding intention is to do what is right, even if they require effort and time to unravel each knotty choice honestly in accordance with that criterion.

If public officials are to have integrity, they must therefore act ethically, insofar as they are able to know what is right, in each circumstance.[2] That is exceedingly hard to do because doing right in politics so often conflicts with doing well. The reason is that, at their root, many of the hardest cases in political ethics, just as in ethics in general, are conflicts between self-interest and the interests of others. For their ethical resolution, they require one to weigh the legitimate obligations one has to oneself, against what one owes to others who will be affected by what one proposes to do, and to adopt a calculus for choosing between them when the two sets of obligations clash. And how strenuously and frequently they do clash in political life! For example, every request to an officeholder by a political supporter is such a potential conflict. If the request is for appointment to a particular office, to grant it may or may not serve the public interest. To deny it will surely compromise the supporter's enthusiasm for the office-holder, and may even turn a supporter into an opponent. Similarly, every time a legislator's aid is sought by a prior or potential supporter or contributor, the same potential conflict is present.

The essence of politics is the exercise of power over others. Politicians exist because every organized society requires someone to wield that power for its survival and for the implementation of its wishes. Long before Lord Acton distilled his aphorism,[3] politicians and their critics knew the many different faces of power. Some are lured; others repelled. To some, it is the very reason for being in politics, to others only a necessary means of achieving the goals — personal or public or both — that attracted them to politics in the first place. Some, even if only a few, seek political office expressly to turn to their own uses that power over others. A larger group is sometimes tempted to do so. With power the essence of their existence, and with human nature so frail, it should be no source of wonder that many political actors succumb to that temptation.

But ethical dilemmas in public life are more complicated than the simple choice between serving oneself and serving others. Ethical dilemmas in public life nearly always arise in the context of a web of conflicting obligations created by the nature of the political system itself. Whenever one begins to act politically, one implicitly assumes, whether explicitly or not, a range of obligations to institutions, other individuals (who may or may not be politically active), other candidates, other officeholders, and a variety of interest groups, some yet to be born. While not terribly different in kind from the similar network of obligations that any person undertakes upon entering other varieties of continuing relationships — marriage, a particular profession, or an organization of any kind — the political network of obligations is more extensive because it embraces all of the others and then some. In fact, the actions of a political actor affect the lives and well-being of all other citizens who live, or who will live in the future, in the jurisdiction in which he chooses to act politically, and frequently beyond.

In addition, therefore, to the obligations that political actors may legitimately have to themselves, their conscience, their family, their relatives, and their friends, they also have obligations to a very large number of others. Consider, for example, elected American legislators. When they take the oath of office, they assume obligations to the Constitution, to the laws that may at any moment be on the books even if they seek to alter them, to the principles that animate their political efforts, to the majority view at any particular time on the issues coming before them, to individuals or groups who may be accorded special protection by the Constitution or by statutory law, to their own political supporters, to the members and the formal commitments of their political party, and to persons living in other political jurisdictions.

Obviously, so many obligations are bound to clash, and it is in such clashes that dilemmas are created for political actors. The obligations to which politicians give priority in such clashes tell much about the kind of people they are. For while such an intricate web of obligations indeed entails choices that are more complicated than choosing between oneself and others, it is surprising to note how most of them do boil down to that choice in the end. A "reputational survey"[4] of some sixty present and former members of Congress to identify the characteristics of those among their colleagues whom they regarded as ethical exemplars suggests the following conclusions.

Whether political actors have integrity is determined by how they resolve conflicts among competing obligations, and the key ingredient of political integrity is the extent to which persons give undue weight to their self-interest in reconciling them. To the extent that they are influenced by how particular reconciliations will affect their own career, wealth, or well-being — to the extent, in other words, that they are dominantly motivated by self-interest — the less political integrity they have. It follows, then, that any particular decision *determined* by the self-interest of a public official should be described as unethical. Whether the influence of self-interest on political action is the only determinant of political integrity is considered elsewhere. For our discussion here, suffice it to say that it is the central one.

Is this, then, to suggest that there is no legitimate space for self-interest in a politician of integrity? Obviously not, as we shall see. For the moment, however, this can be said. I do not refer here to self-interest in its ultimate or generic sense. For example, the pursuit of excellence in any field of endeavor — art, science, literature, or politics — is powered by a yearning for satisfaction in the pursuer; seeking that satisfaction is self-interested behavior at the most fundamental level, simply because it gratifies the self. To deny that self-interest would be to deny the basic spring of the most laudable of human action.

There is a less profound sense, too, in which self-interest may activate politicians of integrity. That is behavior that genuinely serves the interests of others, but is regarded by some philosophers as self-interested because it springs from the actor's preference for satisfaction through altruism rather than direct self-gratification. One might very well believe that an important goal for a civilized politics, as well as perhaps civilization itself, would be to increase the number of citizens and politicians who are self-interested in this sense.

But there is also a mundane sense of self-interest which may be tolerable in politicians of integrity. That is, to borrow from the law, what we might call for now an ordinary, reasonable, prudent degree of self-interest. We might define that as the amount of self-interest the public would find tolerable, perhaps even praiseworthy, and, in fact, the absence of which the public would find incredible in a human being, whether in politics or not. The task of distinguishing between this ethical form of self-interest and that which we would condemn as being unsuitable conduct for a public official of integrity would require more space than is available here. It seems enough, for now, simply to justify the self-interest criterion as useful, even if more work is needed in order to define it exactly.

DEMOCRATIC POLITICS AS GROUP STRUGGLE

The trouble is that our concern about self-interest flies in the face of much current thinking about politics. Ever since Harold Lasswell described politics as "who gets what, when, and how,"[5] scholars have come increasingly to view the political process as group struggle, a continuing contest of interests competing to maximize their self-interest. While that conception is not inaccurate as description, such models simply do not present the whole picture. They leave out, for example, the mass public as a whole, as well the large number of individual officeholders and groups seeking to maximize, not their self-interest, but what they regard as the public interest.

Even worse than their incompleteness, however, is the extent to which these models appear to have crossed the boundary from partial description to implied, even if unintended, *pre*scription. They tend to imply that, because some interests expressly use politics to maximize their respective interests, *all* groups and individuals should do likewise. Indeed, to the extent that they don't do so, their behavior is irrational and cannot be comprehended by the model.

As such models of political behavior have been taught to the last several generations of college students and have gradually worked their way into public consciousness, they have tended to foster increasing cynicism about the public-serving intentions of political actors. Indeed, one model—that of Anthony Downs—postulates that politicians

act solely in order to attain the income, prestige, and power which come from being in office. Thus politicians in our model never seek office as a means of carrying out particular policies; their only goal is to reap the rewards of holding office *per se*. They treat policies purely as means to the attainment of their private ends, which they can reach only by being elected.[6]

According to Downs, the pursuit of private interest by politicians is entirely consistent with the public interest. By a process analogous to Adam Smith's Invisible Hand, the function of a legislature—that is, generating socially beneficial laws—is conceived as an incidental consequence of the competitive struggle for power and office, "in the same sense that economic production is incidental to the making of profits."[7]

This model of politics, therefore, justifies the uninhibited pursuit of self-interest as long as the means chosen are technically legal. Outright bribery is forbidden, but, beyond that, anything goes.[8] Willful ambition and a host of other selfish motives are condoned because they are instrumentally useful.

This portrait of politics is not especially appetizing. It licenses a range of motives and practices that history and most of the present-day public would regard as debased, if not unethical. If deliberate sacrifice of self-interest for the good of the whole constitutes the most admirable and most ethical kind of politics, the greedy, blindly ambitious politician is the antithesis of our image of the statesman of integrity.[9]

The dominant pluralist view of politics, whether as mere description or as a normative theory, may then be one of the major causes of unethical behavior by political actors, including voters.[10] By glorifying, and therefore legitimating, the motive of self-interest, it encourages self-interested behavior at all levels of government, from the citizen in the voting booth to the president running for election. And self-interest does not exactly require encouragement for it to express itself.

A representative government depends for its survival over time on the support of the governed. What they believe about the motives and actions of those whom they elect to govern them greatly influences both popular support for the government and popular willingness to abide by its actions. Nothing—not errors of judgment, not waste, not inefficiency, not high taxes, not overregulation, not even the loss of a war—so shakes representative government at its root as does a belief by the public that the officials who govern act chiefly out of a concern for their private self-interest rather than for the public interest of those who elected them. When such a belief becomes pervasive among the electorate and persists over a long enough period, the public tends to lose faith not only in the officials who govern but also in the institution of government itself. Absent that faith, the public *will not* cooperate in carrying out the hard decisions, those involving self-sacrifice, which may be required in times of crisis or shortage. If public faith in the trusteeship nature of public office is the keystone of democracy's arch, self-serving behavior is the cardinal vice of public officials.[11]

In earlier times, when the public assumed, on the basis of all too much evidence, that most government officials were venal, a self-serving officialdom could be blinked away. After all, it was thought, that's the way public officials always are. Now that democracy in this country has begun to strive for that limited measure of purity that sometimes accompanies maturity, and we have decided, apparently, to try to conform our practice with our principles, public trust has become extremely vulnerable. The last decade, especially, has provided evidence that public confidence in government is eroding. The percentage of Americans voting for president has declined in every election since 1960. State, local, and congressional elections do not manifest so clear a pattern, but the overall trend has also been down. Even if causation is scientifically uncertain,[12] a good deal of opinion research data suggest a parallel decline in public confidence in government.

"Any objective analysis," Louis Harris reported in 1973 to the Senate Subcommittee on Intergovernmental Relations, "can only conclude that a crisis of the most serious magnitude now exists in the response and assessment of the people to their government." His conclusion was based, in part, on a finding that a majority of those questioned in his study believed that many public officials, both elected and appointed, "are in politics for their own enrichment in power or money, not for the welfare of the people they represent."[13] In a 1976 poll done for the Committee for the Study of the American Electorate (CSAE), nearly two-thirds of those polled believed that "quite a few of the people running the government in Washington are a little crooked." Nearly 90 percent believed that "what this country needs most, more than laws and political programs, is a few courageous, tireless, devoted leaders in whom the country can put its faith."

It is possible, of course, for a government to be effective in discharging some of its responsibilities even if its officials are believed to be using public office for private gain. Some have argued, indeed, that the concern about honesty and integrity is misplaced. What we need, they say, is a large number of competent decisionmakers in government, even if they are a bit shady personally. It may even be that the current public disaffection with government is more attributable to our visible lack of success at achieving collective aims than to public disillusionment with the integrity of officeholders. Or, put another way, government ineffectiveness is the cause, not the consequence, of public doubt. That widespread public mistrust of public officials tends to surface mainly in rocky times lends support to this view. But we are in rocky times, and are likely to remain so for the foreseeable future. We have more problems as a nation than we can solve with our own resources. Our enemies abroad perpetrate as much mischief as they can for us, and our allies are no more able to help us in dealing with our most severe problems than themselves. In such circumstances, public doubt about our government's integrity is a luxury we can no longer afford.

Direct pecuniary gain by public officials is not the central problem. For much of this century, most levels of government have had laws prohibiting personal pecuniary gain arising from the exercise of public responsibilities, and have enforced them for some time with considerable effectiveness. While violations of those laws have occurred recently, have been well publicized, and undoubtedly leap to the public mind when pollsters probe it, the problem is more subtle. On the 1976 CSAE poll cited above, a higher percentage than those believing that federal officials are crooked thought that the problem was that "candidates say one thing and then do another." In other words, many citizens believe that politicians lie or equivocate to get elected, and continue to do so in order to stay elected. Politicians are viewed as not standing for anything; they say what they think the public wants to hear. The main goal appears to be getting and keeping the office — the power, the fame, and the money — and not the representation of the public who elected them. And that is precisely the behavior assumed by Downs's model.

This public concern about self-interest not only applies to public officials as individuals, but also extends to the behavior of the bureaus, offices, and agencies in which public officials work. It has been given much credibility by the growing roster of scholarly treatments of government actions as dictated more by an organization's self-interest than by the interest of the public as a whole.[14] With the motives of both officials and agencies thereby tainted, what hope is left for the public? When the personal self-interest of officials combines with the interests of the organizations which they constitute, the public can see virtually no means of forcing bureaucracy to rise to the public interest. Redundancy of administration, proliferation of regulation, and interagency territorial battles appear to freeze policymaking and prevent solutions to pressing problems.

A similar phenomenon affects the workings of the legislative branches. To the public and the press, the legislatures appear also to be paralyzed by battles among contending interests, with too many legislators acting as advocates of one or another interest, and too few genuinely and chiefly devoted to the public interest no matter how the private interest chips may fall. The large recent increase in highly visible, well-organized, well-financed single-interest constituencies has undoubtedly contributed both to the reality and to the appearance of that paralysis.

Whatever else it has done, this growing sense of government as dominantly self-interested has intensified the normal adversariness with which the public usually, and certainly healthily, views it. A "we/they" syndrome is a result. Government has become more clearly "they"; the motive for its increasing intrusiveness must be to serve "their" ends, for it surely appears not to serve ours. As in Joseph Losey's film *The Servant*, the servant has become the master and the master, the victim. While there is some exaggeration in that stereotype, it substantially reflects present public attitudes.

This is obviously easier to describe than it is to treat. The truth is that the public's standards for public officials are ambiguous and contradictory. We want public officials to serve the general public interest, not "narrow, private" interests. We want public officials to act on the basis of *our* public interest, not of *their* self-interest, yet *their* self-interest is all too often determined by the extent to which they are able to please us, perhaps flatter us by reflecting our opinions. We want public officials who will do what we want when we tell them, but we also want public officials who will do what *they* think right. And when what they think is right happens to differ from what we think is right, we are extremely unhappy.

Moreover, to a large extent the nature of our politics forces a politician to be self-seeking. Individuals are, after all, required to push themselves forward as candidates for office, in other words to *seek* the office for themselves. After all, politics has always been recognized as an honorable means whereby ambitious, hard-working men and women might get ahead, make a living, perhaps even gain fame, money, and power to themselves. Yet somehow we feel it improper if used too blatantly to that end.

Can we make any sense of these paradoxes? Is all self-interested action unethical? If not all, what part and how do we distinguish permissible self-interest from that which tarnishes integrity? I suggest that the proper test for officials is one of dominant motive, or proximate cause. In assessing particular actions, we ask whether the official's conduct was caused by something other than career advancement. In weighing an official's cumulative career as a whole, we look to see whether its chief or only consistency over time is provided by career advancement. In voters, it is the extent to which the self-interested claim can be justified by testing it against generally accepted notions of merit, equity, fairness, and justice. In this essay, I concentrate on public officials only.

SELFLESSNESS AS THE PRINCIPAL CRITERION OF INTEGRITY IN PUBLIC OFFICIALS

Where else, in a non-totalitarian country, but in the political profession is the individual expected to sacrifice all — including his own career — for the national good? In private life, as in industry, we expect the individual to advance his own enlightened self-interest — within the limitations of the law — in order to achieve over-all progress. But in public life we expect individuals to sacrifice their private interests to permit the national good to progress.

—John F. Kennedy[15]

We declaim against "self-seeking politicians," but how do we define what a self-seeking politician is? Perhaps the best way to do so is to look for a moment at its polar opposite. Let us call such a person a politician of integrity, a statesman.

Most reasonable people with common sense would instinctively define such politicians as ones who, at the very least, are not self-seeking. They are the leaders whom we hold up as examples to the young; we measure the stature of other politicians against them; we like to think that we would emulate them under similar circumstances. Indeed, perhaps the most persuasive evidence of the importance we all place on the criterion of political selflessness in officeholders lies in that flood of admiration which wells up in us when a politician acts against short-term self-interest in reelection.

Every one of John F. Kennedy's heroes in *Profiles in Courage* manifested just that selflessness, some of them only for that one time in their lives. They all flew in the face of heated public opinion. They chose what they saw as the long-term national or public interest. They refused to bend with the wind by serving their short-term self-interest, by obediently deferring to popular sentiment. If the sacrifice of self-interest is not important to politics, why is it that such behavior arouses our admiration? Does the degree of our admiration depend on whether such heroic conduct was proven substantially wise by history? Not at all, if the choice was in fact determined by selfless devotion to what each then genuinely thought to be in the public interest. Did only those contemporaries who favored the policy advocated by the hero admire him? To the contrary, the record abounds in expression of respect, even by opponents. Is it only in exceptional times or with respect to the most serious issues that we admire such selflessness? That all of President Kennedy's cameos were of such events should not so mislead one.

I cite Kennedy's heroes not because I think they themselves constitute figures worthy of emulation. On the contrary, many were scoundrels, even by the standards of their own time. Perhaps some of them were seeking merely to apply a little gilt to lives of unrelieved dross. Perhaps some *were* making a bid for history, after lifetimes of slavishness to "the bubble popularity." But, the fact is that they all chose, on at least one occasion when the chips were down, to risk political suicide on the altar of principle, in other words to sacrifice themselves for something greater than themselves.

Nor do I suggest that any of them is a politician of integrity. Integrity is the way of a lifetime, not of an instant. While one admirable, ethical action deserves praise, it does not convert a lifetime of political self-service into a career of integrity. Whether they had integrity depends on their motivation over the long run, on the presence of wholeness, of consistency. What impresses me, however, is how powerfully appealing indeed their self-sacrifice must be if in our minds it can redeem — in other words, outweigh — an entire life of political skulduggery. How we thirst for it in politics, perhaps all the more because it appears there so rarely. I can think of no other trait in public officials that compels such widespread admiration. If that is true, then we are right in making selflessness the principal indispensable criterion of integrity.

The importance of selflessness in politicians is underscored by the fact that self-interested behavior is the principal target of laws designed to govern politics. While rules requiring public disclosure and regulating financial relationships in part constitute an attempt to insure fair competition among candidates for office or among interest groups and citizens supporting candidates for office, they are premised much more on the notion that neither the official nor his friends should be enriched at the expense of the public. To violate them is not only illegal; it is also unethical. To the extent that obedience to such regulations is a necessary component of political integrity, it is so because of their moral content and not because they constitute enforceable law. Indeed, as we shall see, there are occasions when officials can violate the law, if properly justified, without compromising their integrity.

It goes without saying that mere abstinence from rule-breaking is not particularly praiseworthy. While, as a general rule, we do not admire officials who break the law, neither do we admire them solely because they do not break the law. We expect them not to. Obedience to law is a threshold qualification, not a measure of attainment. In fact, the principal determinants of political integrity in candidates and officeholders are not, and cannot be, the subject of legal regulations. Integrity in politicians, like ethics in general, depends at root on the way *uncoerced* choices are made.

SELF-INTEREST AGAINST THE PUBLIC INTEREST

Many of the dilemmas confronting a public official occur when two interests collide. One is the official's personal self-interest, with self-serving behavior defined as actions taken principally to win an election, to increase popularity, to curry favor with powerful groups. The other is the public interest, defined as what the official sincerely believes to be to the long-run benefit of the public as a whole. Let us define the latter, in shorthand, as the greatest good for the greatest deserving number, over the longest possible range of time, while fully recognizing all the questions such a definition begs.[16]

They do not always conflict, but, as integrity may depend on how conflicts are resolved, it is important to discern whether there is a conflict, as well as how important the self-interest element is. It may very well be that, even where they do not conflict, a public official's actions can be unethical to the extent that self-interest dominantly motivates them.

The first question, therefore, that politicians who are concerned with integrity ought to ask themselves about a proposed action is "Where does my own direct private interest lie?" If the proposed course of action benefits their own interest, they should immediately be on guard. In other words, there is a presumption against it. If the action does not benefit their own interest, or is contrary to that interest, they are free, for purposes of this analysis, to proceed with it.

If the officials discover that the action would indeed serve their own private interest, they should then move on to a second question: "Where does the public interest lie?" If the officials' sincere perception of the public interest coincides with what their own direct private interest happens to be, the presumption raised by the answer to the first question is overcome. If, however, the public interest proscribes the proposed conduct, therefore heightening the presumption against it, it would be unethical for them to proceed.

Obviously, the determination of whether there is conflict between the officials' private self-interest and the public interest depends on the officials' honesty with themselves. Scrutiny of the most objective sort is required if they are to be able to discern the nature and direction of their self-interest, as well as to ascertain the nature and direction of the public interest. While an examination of motives is necessarily private, and while no one else can know for certain what the motive for a particular action may be, a consistent pattern of self-interested conduct by a public official would warrant an inference by the public and the press that the particular public official lacks integrity.

Because our test for the integrity of an officeholder rests on the officeholder's sincere perception of where the public interest lies with respect to a particular matter, we need not spend a great deal of time elaborating our earlier definition of what the public interest is. On the contrary, a moment's reflection will reveal that those persons whom we most admire — those whom we raise up as our examples of political integrity — disagree among themselves about what constitutes the public interest with respect to any particular matter. What distinguishes them from other public officials is that we do not suspect their motives. We do not worry that they are defining the public interest on the basis of what their own self-interest happens to be in the matter. We respect them because we know that it is *our* interest that they have at heart, even as we rely on their disagreement to sharpen one another's understanding, as well as our own, of what is genuinely in the public interest.

Indeed, for our purposes, such disagreement is inevitable, because each public official must define "the public interest" individually by testing the choices against underlying values that are often not explicit.[17] When officials describe an action as being in the public interest, what they mean is that they give greater weight to one or more values served by the proposed course of action than they do to a different set of values that would be served by an alternative course of action. For example, where is the public interest with respect to the provision of health services to the American public? When Senator Edward Kennedy urges a comprehensive health insurance program costing a great deal of money, he genuinely believes himself to be serving the public interest, defined as benefiting those in need of health care they cannot afford. When President Jimmy Carter proposed in the alternative a different, more modest series of steps toward health coverage, greater than the available but less than that to be provided under the Kennedy plan, he, too, believed himself to be serving the public interest defined as benefiting health needs while slowing inflation, and perhaps reducing it by avoiding the inflationary pressure of a larger budget deficit created by even greater health expenditures. What the public interest is, then, is determined by which values one wishes to maximize at how much cost to whom and when. Both Kennedy and Carter are concerned about the welfare of those less well off. Kennedy would provide for their health needs, even if as a consequence of so doing, they were required to pay more for everything else they buy. Carter would provide less amply for their health needs, in the hope that, as a consequence of a more modest extension of access to health services, they will end up less pinched by inflation.[18]

Similarly, it is entirely possible for public officials on different sides of an issue to be committed to the same underlying values. Most Americans, I believe, are committed to the principle that those who are better off in our society should carry their fair share of the burden of helping those who are worse off. What divides those supporting a particular piece of legislation with obvious redistributional consequences from those opposing it may be, not the underlying values that determine what is in the public interest, but different calculations as to whether the particular value will be served by the particular legislation, and whether there are other ways of serving it more effectively. A genuine conservative may, for example, favor redistributional values, and therefore the public interest as he sees it, while opposing particular redistributional tax changes. During a depression, such a conservative might very well favor tax incentives to industry designed to increase business investments or exports, and therefore to create more jobs, while opposing tax cuts for those less well off. The only accurate measure of that judgment is time. While it is not clear that such a judgment is usually right in any circumstance, it is also not clear that it is inevitably wrong.

A central problem with such an analysis is that what is in the public interest at any given time inevitably benefits one or more private interests to some degree or other. Unless one believes that it is always in the public interest for the less well off to win out over the better off in the short run, regardless of what the long-run consequences may be, some choices inevitably have to be made.

This problem is especially acute where the long-run public interest requires a course of action that appears to be to the short-run benefit of powerful, and therefore suspect, interests. Indeed, many current domestic and foreign issues—energy policy, for example—offer only alternatives having this characteristic.[19] The electorate, properly suspicious when the choice goes with the powerful private interest, may feel it has good reason to believe that it was the power of the private interest that caused the officials' decision rather than their perception of what the public interest required. Facing dilemmas of this sort, only public officials of unquestioned integrity, trusted by the public, have a chance to persuade the public that what appears to be in the short-run interest, for example, of the oil companies, is in fact—and more important—in the long-range public interest.

THE DILEMMA OF REPRESENTATIVELY ELECTED OFFICIALS

Necessity compels me to speak true rather than pleasing things . . . I should like to please you; but I prefer to save you, whatever be your attitude toward me.

—Daniel Webster[20]

Elected officials in a representative government face an additional dilemma of major consequence. That dilemma—the mandate/independence conflict[21]—arises out of the nature of the relationship between the voters and the officeholders they elect. Are public officials charged by representative government with an obligation to advocate their constituents' interest or preference or are they permitted to act more like judges, who decide in each situation on the merits of their electors' claims? If elected officials are to be regarded as having political integrity, is it necessary for them always to be either advocate or judge of their constituents' interests, or might they be advocate in some situations and judge in others? And how do they determine when to be which?

My preferred way out of this dilemma is for representatives to guide their choice by what they perceive to be in the long-run public interest, rather than the short-run interest or preference, of those they represent.[22] If they do so, the representatives are obliged to make explicit to those they represent how they calculate what is in the constituents' long-run public interest and how they distinguish it from what is called for by the constituents' short-run preferences.

If legislators take the opposite course—the pure "mandate" view of their role—no self-interest issue is present. If they assume that their role requires them in all cases to defer to the wisdom of those who elected them, and that their own independent judgment must not come into play, officials will invariably decide according to the short-run preference of their constituents, as best they can determine it. They are the agent, not the trustee. For them, that short-run preference is, on principle, a better guide to the long-run interest of constituents than their own speculation.

The problem for us is obvious. Since they always act according to the short-run public preference, they never need to know—indeed never can know — whether they do so because they believe that such a course is right in principle or because their self-interest in reelection is served thereby. For them, self-interest is never in question, and therefore any threat to their integrity from such quarter never arises. Integrity rests on making wise, selfless choices. It is for them to ascertain what their constituents want, not to choose.

None of the legislators I interviewed so described themselves, because, I suspect, the pure mandate view virtually eliminates choice, provides no role for leadership, and coincidentally diminishes the significance of their function.[23] Most cast their lot with Burke, playing the role of trustee when they feel strongly about an issue and that of agent when either they do not or their constituents do. Most would probably agree with George Canning, the early nineteenth-century British statesman, who formulated for his constituents the best reconciliation of the mandate/independence conflict I have seen:

It may happen that your own judgment may occasionally come in conflict with my own . . . In all such cases. I promise you not indeed wholly to submit my judgment to yours; . . . but I promise you that any difference of opinion between us will always lead me to distrust my own views, carefully to examine, and, if erroneous, frankly to correct them.[24]

Canning was a good enough politician not to spell out what would happen if after reexamination he remained firm in his view, but the implication is obvious. And, of course where a substantial preponderance of the public feels strongly about an issue, even Burke felt obliged to defer to them.[25]

For those legislators who assert their independence, the choice between public interest and popular preference is extremely vulnerable to considerations of the self-interest in reelection. The issue of integrity, therefore, frequently arises. When officials see a clash between their conscience, or their calculation of what is in the long-run public interest, and short-run public preference, and then let their self-interest be the proximate cause of their decision in the matter, the decision can well be regarded as unethical, and their integrity called into question.

IS A PUBLIC CAREER INHERENTLY INCONSISTENT WITH SELFLESSNESS?

No one gets into elective politics who doesn't have some ego to be fed and that includes me.
— Senator Philip Hart[26]

In an ideal world, the ethical person enters a public career with one clear presumption and one specific motive. The presumption is that he or she has some skills or talent that could be of use to the public weal. The motive is to put those skills or that talent to use doing the most possible good. Any rewards that come from doing a good job are benefits from the course of action chosen, and not causes of it, whether those benefits are power, influence, popular acclaim, or wealth. In the ideal world of public service, then, the only legitimate motivation is to serve.

Even in such a world, there is nothing inherently self-serving in seeking the highest position one can attain, so long as one's desire for office grows principally out of the greater good one can do by means of exercising its powers. If, however, the primary motivation for career advancement is personal power, the esteem of friends, or public acclaim, the pursuit of higher office would be unethical.

In the real world, however, motives are almost never self-evident, even, perhaps especially, to the one motivated by them.[27] In the first place, acting selflessly and touting one's selflessness are different things. Anyone with integrity will usually be uncertain whether his actions are entirely selfless, and would hardly claim that they are. The public surely has ample precedent for mistrusting someone who claims to be totally selfless. In the second place, persons enter public life as much for other motivations as out of a pure wish to serve the public. We enlist in the political campaigns of friends to whom we are loyal, or of candidates who stand for the principles—that is to say the definition of the public interest at that particular time—that we share. We seek or accept appointments to nonelective office in part because of the intrinsic satisfaction—maybe even fun—they would offer us, and then, having accepted, try to do the best job we can in serving the public interest as we define it.

Such motivations are not necessarily self-serving. Whether they are or not depends principally on the choices we make once we have entered into office. Are we independent actors contributing to public ends through official service, or do we use the office to flatter our ego? What value do we add to the public by occupying the office?

Officials with the highest degree of integrity are motivated by the desire to do as much good for others as possible, however they define it, irrespective of the consequences upon their election chances. A second group of public officials, much larger than the first, is motivated by the desire to do as much good as is consonant with reelection or promotion. Officials in both of these groups may be regarded as having integrity, so far as the test of overall career motivation is concerned, because the proximate cause of their decision to enter and remain in public life is to confer benefits on the public, even if those in the latter category do take account of their self-interest as a constraint. As a constraint, it is not pernicious.

A third group of elected public officials, however, is motivated principally by the desire to get elected and to remain in office. They will take no risks where self-interest in reelection is involved. For them, self-interest is the main objective, not a constraint. While not to be condemned as lacking integrity to the same extent as a fourth group—those who are totally unconcerned about doing good—the members of the third group give the public little to admire.

The essential difference between groups one and two, on the one hand, and groups three and four, on the other, is that the former are dominantly motivated by the public interest and the latter by their own self-interest. I suggest that the latter groups are what the public means by "self-seeking politicians."

But what about those who argue that there is no moral difference between serving others and serving oneself, explaining that it is all a question of which kind of satisfaction pleases one more? It may very well be that all values are relative; certainly no one has yet been able to prove some superior to others. In one sense, it cannot be denied that all human action is fundamentally self-interested, even totally benevolent action directed exclusively toward the good of others. Some men and women simply crave the satisfaction of giving to others more than they crave the rewards of getting for themselves. And who, we may well ask, is to judge which kind of self-satisfaction is superior?

Even if it is impossible to prove some human satisfactions generally superior to others—a task I leave for another time[28]—representative government is a special case which imposes on those who participate in it a set of obligations that establish value priorities for them. Some kinds of satisfactions are inherently contrary to the fundamental premises underlying representative institutions. Representative government is, after all, government of, by, *and for* the people.

I think, therefore, that the frequent public complaint about self-serving officials does have meaning. It is not enough to say that, because a dedicated servant of the public gets his satisfaction out of self-denying altruism, he is principally serving his own interest merely by serving in office. That kind of reductionism robs the words "self-interest" of any meaning at all, as well as that usually ascribed to them, and indeed invests them with a meaning that is directly contrary to what they are commonly taken as suggesting. If one accepts such a definition of self-interest, there becomes no way in which an individual can serve the public, in or out of office.

The institution of representative government imposes a hierarchy on the values that should motivate those seeking public office. Some satisfactions, therefore, are to be preferred over other satisfactions in those seeking a public career. If one accepts the interpretation of "the public interest" offered above, a love of the praise of history, for example, is a worthier satisfaction than a love of the applause of the present day. Some satisfactions, conversely, are harmful to representative public service. In that category fall a love of exercising dominion over others, a thirst for power for its own sake, and an incessant questing after higher office.

What about ambition itself? Most of the politicians described as highly ethical by those I interviewed do not appear overly ambitious. They are viewed by others as not using their present office or position as a stepping-stone to higher office. They view their present position as an end in itself, a position on which they will focus all of their energies without any attention to what their service will bring them in the future. My conclusion is, therefore, that people who always have an eye out for the next step up are in bondage to their own ambition. They cannot freely serve the long-run public interest because they are too busy courting the public's short-run opinions.

Now personal ambition seems to be a particular example of self-interest, one about which most of us feel somewhat ambivalent. We say we admire in young people ambition to get ahead, but what I think we really mean is that we admire the hard work, the wholehearted dedication to a job or to an organization or to a cause, the persistence, and the loyalty, which usually find their fullest expression in the service of personal ambition, but which surely exist in ample instances separate from it. The essential distinction is between overwhelming personal ambition, on the one hand, and intrinsic satisfaction in a position well held, on the other. There is a desperate futility (from the point of view of any personal satisfaction *other than* ego gratification) and a good deal of immorality in consciously using one office to attain a higher one, always seeking the satisfaction that lies beyond the present. Some politicians and a good part of the public understand the importance of having public officials dedicated to performing the job they hold with the passion, conviction, and dedication required to do justice to the possibilities of that position.

To what extent, therefore, does ambition vitiate integrity? If the dominant motive is to "get oneself ahead," the conduct is not laudable. If, on the other hand, the motive is to do a better job for the public — to make government more efficient, to use one's higher offices to make government better serve the interests of the governed — then ambition is unexceptionable, indeed laudable. That is personal ambition for the public's interest, not for one's own ego.

Is it then unethical somehow to want to be honored by the public, to seek the esteem of one's peers? Clearly not. But again the relevant distinction is between doing right, helping people who need help, preserving democratic government, achieving some measure of excellence, on the one hand, and being honored for its own sake, on the other. In the end, then, the desire for honor, which is inherently selfish, can be redeemed only by seeking to satisfy it through service to others. To the extent, therefore, that the late Senator Philip Hart, who was universally esteemed for humility, believed his own actions to be ego-based, what redeemed them, both in his eyes and those of all who knew him, were the "other-serving" ideals to which he was so obviously strongly and genuinely dedicated. There is, then, little substance to the charge that even altruistic public servants must necessarily be motivated by their own self-interest. Ambition in politicians of integrity is not self-serving; its objective is the service of others, of principles, of ideals, and of institutions.

TWO VARIETIES OF SELF-SERVING DECISIONS

The foregoing discussion suggests three standard situations:

MODEL I: The actor's direct self-interest is at stake in the decision, and in conflict either with the law or with what most reasonable people judging objectively would agree to be the public interest.
Prescription for Action: A presumption against the self-interested action. Strict scrutiny of the proposed action by the actor personally, as well as by the press, the public, or the courts.

MODEL II: The actor's direct self-interest is at stake, but *not* in conflict with what most reasonable people judging objectively would agree to be the public interest.
Prescription for Action: Ordinary soul searching as to the actor's motive, but no presumption against the action except among the saintly.

MODEL III: The actor's direct self-interest is *not* at stake, but the proposed action is contrary to law or accepted canons of morality.
Prescription for Action: A presumption against the act. It should be weighed again to be certain that self-interest of the actor is indeed absent, and weighed a third time to see if an impartial observer (or most reasonable people if they had the facts) would agree that, despite the presumption against the act, the benefits of doing it outweigh the costs.

MODEL IA: CONFLICT BETWEEN WISE POLICY AND SELF-INTEREST

Self-serving motivations are present in a variety of decision contexts. The most interesting ones involve a choice between a policy that is highly popular and a contrary one that officials believe to be required by the long-range public interest — that is, they believe it will be of greater benefit to this generation over the long run. A decision in accord with the popular view is therefore a decision motivated by the self-interest of the elected officials. A decision for the long-range public interest requires action against self-interest because, if taken, it may well result in their losing office.

All of John F. Kennedy's subjects in *Profiles in Courage* are examples of this dilemma. In each case, Kennedy directs our unbounded admiration to his hero by showing a desire to serve the long-run public interest, even if doing so entailed the sacrifice of his own career. In each of these examples, we could well have "understood" and forgiven a position contrary to that taken, on the ground that politicians, after all, are only human and no one should be required to commit professional suicide. But it is the courageous act, often the self-sacrificing act, by leaders such as these that sustains representative government. Without leadership, we are told, the people perish. One who cannot see some distance down the road, or, having seen refuses to reveal what is there, has no business putting himself at the head of his people.

MODEL IB: CONFLICT BETWEEN THE REQUIREMENTS OF LAW OR MORALITY AND SELF-INTEREST

A second category of Model I is that involving a self-serving justification for a violation of the law or common morality. This occurs, for instance, when public officials lie to protect themselves rather than the public. If President Nixon lied about his knowledge of Watergate in order to protect himself from impeachment, or even if he did not lie, but had refused to obey a court order compelling the release of the tapes, not in order to defend the principle of executive privilege but to protect himself from impeachment, his conduct would have been unethical.

MODEL II: NO CONFLICT BETWEEN SELF-INTEREST AND WISE POLICY

The typical example of Model II is the ordinary policy choice by a public official, which appears to be popular, and therefore in the official's self-interest, and which does not conflict with what most reasonable people judging objectively would agree to be the public interest. A recent example of Model II involves a member of the North Carolina House of Representatives who, as chairman of the Banking Committee, steered through the General Assembly a law permitting the establishment of stockholder-owned savings and loan banks. As soon as the bill had been enacted, he was the first person in North Carolina to start one of the new banks. While his direct self-interest was at stake, and was not in conflict with most people's view of the public interest, the extent to which his actions in getting the bill passed were ethical or unethical depends entirely on his motivation for pushing the legislation. Was he motivated principally by his own financial interests, or was his main concern to extend a new form of business opportunity to the larger community of the state, with benefits for both businessmen and borrowers? Persons with more concern for their own reputation and for the impact of their actions on the public's trust in government would not have taken the course pursued by the legislator in question.

Obviously, which way Model II cuts depends entirely on the actor's motive. If public officials choose their course of action because it seems to them, on principle, to be right, then whatever benefits accrue to them are incidental rewards for having done the right thing. If, however, they choose their course of action because they desire the benefits they anticipate will flow from the choice — in our example, personal pecuniary gain, or, in others, public approval, reelection, appointment to higher office — the decision they make — though it has good consequences — is an ethically tainted decision, tarnished by their pursuit of personal gain by means of their public trust.

If the well-intentioned choice turns out to be wrong, they have a very solid defense. They simply guessed wrong, or made a miscalculation as to unforeseen, possibly unforeseeable, consequences. And the public may well not hold it against them. If, however, the choice was self-interested in fact, and also goes sour, the officials have no honest defense. Take the Camp David Summit, for example. If President Carter had convened it principally in order to boost his personal popularity, and it had failed, he would have been roundly and justifiably condemned. If, on the other hand, his principal motivation for convening the Middle East leaders was a genuine belief that it was the only way to avoid continuing deterioration leading to war, and it had failed, he would have been praised nonetheless for a valiant effort, even if ultimately futile.

MODEL III: THE VIOLATION OF LAW OR MORALITY
WHERE SELF-INTEREST IS NOT AT ISSUE

Model III involves the attempted justification of violations of law or morality on the grounds of public interest, where the actor's direct self-interest is not at stake.

Cases involving lying by public officials show that the self-interest factor is really the principal distinction between justifiable and unjustifiable lying. The historical and philosophical literature justifies lying by public officials, as well as by others, on the basis of several criteria, principally the avoidance of great harm to others, or the conferral of great benefits on others. Those who have justified lying under these circumstances—best exemplified in the work of Sidgwick, Bentham, and Bok[29]—utilize some sort of utilitarian calculus to weigh the harm avoided/benefit conferred against the harm caused by the prospect of lying. That calculus requires deceivers to make judgments, however, about the effect of their intended lies on the public's interest, both with respect to costs and with respect to benefits. Even at the simplest personal level, with the innocent white lie, most thinkers reject the justification if the lie is told, not in the interest of the party being deceived, but in the interest of the deceiver. That is also the case in doctor/patient, lawyer/client, and other professional relationships.

It follows that the public would not object to such lies, but instead would demand that their public officials lie to them if they knew *for certain* that they were being deceived in the short run in order to advance their long-run interests. Precisely that is the justification accepted by historians for most of the international relations lies.

There are two problems. One is that the public's trust of public officials is so low at the present time that it hesitates to accept that it is being lied to in its own interests. And it must be acknowledged that recent events certainly justify most of that skepticism. The second problem is that even the public officials themselves frequently don't know whether they are lying to save their own skins or their country. It seems easier to be charitable to Richard Helms for allegedly misleading a U.S. Senate committee about CIA involvement in Chile than to Lyndon Johnson, who, in the 1964 election, as recounted by Sissela Bok,[30] did all he could to portray himself as "the candidate of peace," while he was at the very same time issuing orders for massive escalation of the war, and cautioning everyone in the administration to keep quiet about them until after the election. Not all public officials are so fortunate as Sir Stafford Cripps, whose well-known lie about his government's intention to abandon the gold standard appears to have been completely untainted by self-interest motivation.[31]

Most of us believe that honorable men can lie in some circumstances and still remain honorable so long as they intend their lies, insofar as their own reason can meticulously weigh them, to benefit the public interest rather than to benefit themselves by winning an election, concealing their illegal acts, or masking their policy failures. Similarly, while many of us may not agree with the premises of those who led the nation in the Vietnam War and kept it there, the self-interest test can help us considerably in separating ethical officials who supported the war from unethical ones. The former continuously acted on a set of premises and principles they believed to be true throughout, and did not appear to be motivated by self-interest, however wrong-headed we now regard their policies. The unethical officials, however, whatever their initial motivation, acted with a principal motive of either protecting their reputation by covering up their earlier mistakes or misleading the voters factually so as to gain reelection for themselves.

The task of sorting out one's motives is often arduous and time-consuming. Consider Elliot Richardson's role in the Saturday Night Massacre. Throughout his brief tenure as attorney general, Richardson attempted to promote the "national interest" with an unusual degree of self-consciousness. The discussion in the attorney general's office in the weeks leading up to the resignation of Vice-President Spiro Agnew and the Saturday Night Massacre were marked by self-conscious concern for the national interest and the judgment of history. In *A Heartbreak Away*, Jules Witcover and Richard Cohen describe Richardson's attitude on the Agnew resignation as constantly assuming "the role of the temperate Olympian—the one man with the public interest, national-interest overview."[32] During the months of crisis, Richardson frequently delivered soliloquies to his staff on the nature of political morality and responsibility, quoting often from classical authors. Clearly he felt the eye of history on him. Very few of his actions were spontaneous. Whenever an instinctive impulse to act in a certain way surged within him, he deliberately stepped back to analyze it at a cool distance. For example, once Agnew started to deny that he had accepted bribes or evaded taxes Richardson was morally outraged. He told his aides, "I can feel the old prosecutorial instincts coming out in myself as we get deeper and deeper into it. My first instincts were to worry about the ability to govern, to function. But now I am getting the feeling—'get the bastard.' " Upon reflection, however, Richardson overmastered his desire to "get Agnew," and decided that the national interest would be better served by Agnew's swift resignation than by "getting him" at a criminal trial. Elliot Richardson's behavior while attorney general had the mannered, stylized quality of a performance in a Noh play. He did not trust anything that occurred to him naturally. He acted only after having put himself at a distance from his own instincts. From this distance, he tried very deliberately to do what he thought was best for the national interest.

The role Richardson adopted strongly resembles that of the "impartial spectator" in Adam Smith's "Theory of Moral Sentiments" and the person in the "original position" described by John Rawls.[33] Like both of these imaginary philosophical spectators, Richardson tried to ignore his immediate attachments to particular individuals or causes, as well as to his own interests. He consciously pushed such considerations into the background and focused instead on the national interest. His attempt to get beyond partiality was again manifest in his self-assumed role as "counsel for the situation" during the crisis culminating in the Saturday Night Massacre. Richardson attempted to transcend the adversary role he normally would have taken as attorney general. His justification was that with the Justice Department in the process of investigating the White House, his normal role as attorney general had become self-contradictory. He could no longer be loyal to the White House at the same time he was responsible for prosecuting it. His solution of this dilemma was to transcend *both* roles. He abandoned the role of political adversary for the White House at the same time that he rejected the role of prosecutor. In this self-created role as "counsel for the situation," Richardson attempted to disengage himself from the particular interests to which an adversary role commits one. The national interest became his client. His role, as he envisioned it, was to be impartial, nonadversary, and disinterested.

Richardson's self-interest, however, was very much tied up in the decisions he made. His political future and his reputation in history were at stake. Furthermore, he had personal ties to many of the participants in the situation: his feelings for these people ranged from contempt to fear to respect. The existence of these emotional relationships undermined the idea of disinterestedness. Any course of action would please some and offend others. It was not in his immediate self-interest to offend those he liked or to please those he considered scoundrels.

Richardson was thus far from a perfect "impartial spectator." Yet his attempt to act as impartial "counsel for the situation," as the self-appointed advocate for the national interest, was not fraudulent. Human beings can apprehend experience from a variety of angles. They can artificially alter the terms through which they perceive and evaluate reality. Through an act of will, Richardson altered the power of the claims tugging at him. He scrutinized his instincts and the promptings of self-interest, and put himself at a distance from them. He shed the prejudices and inclinations which clothe us all. Once "outside" or "beyond" or "above" natural human partiality, he could see his responsibilities changed.

Richardson's perceptual shift toward "disinterestedness" coincided with his redefinition of role. At the same time that he chose to sever his affective ties to a particular interest, he redefined his role so as to avoid alignments with particular factions in the political and legal conflicts that swirled around him. Changing roles, he inevitably changed his audience. He shifted from conforming to the particular expectations of the White

House, or Archibald Cox, or his own self-interest, to a larger, more abstract audience — the national interest and history. When Richardson transcended his self-interest, he began to identify with the expectations of the national interest — the interests of everyone in America considered over the long run. He looked at himself as he imagined others would see him and acted in a way calculated to win their praise.

Take another example — the "dirty hands" dilemma so skillfully and artfully explored by Michael Walzer.[34] Applying the self-interest litmus test forces one to the second stage of examining just what is the justification for the violation of conscience one feels compelled by the dilemma to contemplate. If the justification for an act is the preservation of some clear public good — tricking or torturing a terrorist who is threatening the lives of innocent citizens — then the act is surely to be done, and the official is exonerated by the public interest justification, assuming the official *is* a good man or woman, has good judgment, and will use the minimal amount of force to achieve the objective. If, however, the justification is the self-interest of the official — winning election, preventing personal ill repute — then the contemplated act must not be done. Using Walzer's first example, to promise to award a contract in return for electoral support would be unethical and the solicitation to do so should be exposed.

The ethically questionable behavior described in cases of lying by public officials seems to me, therefore, to be more easily analyzed as either excusable or inexcusable almost entirely on the basis of a self-interest analysis. We might even have been able to forgive Nixon his cover-up if it were not so painfully clear that it was his skin he was protecting rather than either the national security or the power of the presidency.

Where the dilemma between lawbreaking and the public interest involves a conflict between one person's perception of the public interest and that of another, there is room for reasonable people to disagree as to the propriety of the proposed action. If we are convinced that self-interest is playing no role in an official's decision, then we are willing to allow that official much wider scope in reconciling the conflicting obligations that arise out of those differing perceptions of where the public interest lies. Where we are not so convinced, or where it appears that it is the official's self-interest that is in conflict with the public interest, there is little room for disagreement in the first place.

A PRACTICAL SELFLESSNESS:
THE REPRESENTATIVE AS TEACHER

Members of Congress who consistently play the role of judge of the interests asserted by their district, rather than advocate of them, or who consistently make decisions on the basis of what is good for the country as a whole, or even the international order, rather than on the basis of what is good for their district, run extremely grave political risks.[35] But the choice is not between politics and no politics. It is between long-range political considerations and short-range political considerations. Indeed, the principal challenge of representative politics is maintaining a balance between reflecting voter opinion and educating it. To the extent that officials can convince their constituents that their decisions are dictated by what they believe to be in the constituents' best interest, and do not rest at all on considerations about what is in the officials' own interest, they can diminish the political risks of such a course.[36]

There is also an intellectual difficulty. Without question, representation must embrace some forms of advocacy. As John F. Kennedy asked, "Who will plead for Massachusetts if our own Senators do not?"[37] Answering his own question, he elaborated:

Her rights and even her identity become submerged. Her equal representation in Congress is lost. Her aspirations, however much they may from time to time be in the minority, are denied that equal opportunity to be heard to which all minority views are entitled . . . Any Senator need not look very long to realize that his colleagues are representing their local interests. And if such interests are ever to be abandoned in favor of the national good, let the constituents—not the Senator—decide when and to what extent. He is their agent in Washington, the protector of their rights, recognized by the Vice President in the Senate Chamber as, "The Senator from Massachusetts" or "The Senator from Texas."

Indeed, if officeholders do not represent their constituents' narrow interests, whose interests do they represent? Those of the state, the region, the nation, those of the world at the present time, or indeed those of the world of the future? Inevitably, elected officials who counterpose the interests of others against those of their district are, in fact, substituting their judgment for the express preference of those who elected them and whom they are obliged to represent. In his well-known "Speech to the Electors," Burke put this view strongly:

Parliament is not a congress of ambassadors from different and hostile interests, which interests each must maintain, as an agent and advocate, against other agents and advocates; but Parliament is a deliberative assembly of one nation, with one interest, that of the whole—where not local prejudices ought to guide, but the general good, resulting from the general reason of the whole. You choose a member, indeed; but when you have chosen him he is not a member of Bristol, but he is a member of Parliament.[38]

However much one attempts to explain the inconsistency, such a substitution of judgment implies a sense of superiority over one's constituents, in effect saying that the representative knows better what is good for them than they do themselves. The popular conception of Burke's view goes only part of the way in providing a reconciliation.[39] It is simply not enough to explain to constituents that all one owes them is one's judgment. Representatives owe those who elected them at least that, and a good deal more.

The claims of constituents for the substantial reflection of their interests and preferences have a great deal of validity. On those occasions, rare or numerous as the case may be, when the representative's perception of the long-term public good conflicts with the short-term desires of those who elected him, he owes them at least an explanation of why he has decided as he has. But the obligation does not stop there. Explanations are a form of excuse, and far more than an excuse is owed. What is owed, in fact, is a strenuous effort to convince them that his view of what is in their interest is more accurate than theirs. Perhaps even greater than the obligation to reflect their views is the obligation to attempt to persuade the electorate that he is right and they are wrong about what is good for them. That dynamic, interactive process, with the elected representative leading as well as following the constituents' wishes, is what has always distinguished representative government at its best. If the reflection of citizen preference is the mother of representative government, surely the loving education of citizens' preference is the father. Without one or the other, there is no representative government. A politician who refuses to differ with his constituents when he thinks they are wrong, therefore, short-circuits representative government. Representative institutions that merely reflect the sentiments of the electors must necessarily blunder through one short-run decision after the other, leading ultimately to their own ruin.

Obviously, there are some limits to the extent to which a constituency will permit differences of opinion between itself and its elected representatives. In such situations, the theory of representative government requires that they elect a representative more congruent with their basic positions.[40] Such circumstances most often arise in connection with issues having tangible economic consequences in a particular district, although, of late, they also have tended to arise in connection with issues that are without tangible effects but are viewed as matters of morality, such as abortion or equal rights, or national pride, such as the Panama Canal Treaty.

If the issue is economic in nature — more jobs, for example, or the location of a vital installation such as a power-generating dam — which have a tangible impact within the local constituency, opposition to the district's interests by its elected representative in fact diminishes local well-being, whatever his reasons for opposing it. What kind of reason can conceivably justify such opposition? There are arguments of equity—other districts have greater need for the jobs or the dam. There are arguments of priority of claims—there are other national needs, perhaps with local consequences, for the same limited amount of funds. There are arguments of efficiency—the costs of such expenditure will increase the national debt, drive up inflation, and impose more burdens on the district in the long run than the benefits it will acquire in the short run. And of course there are other values that have to be served even in one's own district—environmental considerations, for example, which always come into play with respect to dams, and frequently with respect to industrial development.

When a representative makes a judgment in opposition to the express interests of his constituents, he is saying one of two things: what my constituents want is, in fact, bad for them and, in *their* interest I won't help, and indeed I will oppose; or, in the alternative, what my constituents want can be had only at a cost to others that I believe to be inequitable or unwise to impose.

These are the most difficult decisions for elected representatives, the decisions on which a vote against what the representative perceives to be the public interest will generally be understood and forgiven by political observers and his own peers. The conventional wisdom is that these are jugular issues, on which a self-interested position can be permitted without compromise to the basic integrity of the representative. But when a politician sticks to his principles, his own perception of what is in the long-range interest of those who elected him, even in the face of conflict with overpowering reality, he elevates himself into a class of superheroes. Some of the senators who figure in *Profiles in Courage* and others, such as North Carolina's late Senator Frank Porter Graham or Michigan's late Senator Philip Hart, appear to belong in this category.[41]

The more frequent response when faced with an issue of this kind is for an elected representative to take the unethical course on jugular issues, unethical because it serves his self-interest, and attempt to maintain his ethical stature with respect to all the others. In effect, he splits the difference, saying that such is the compromise required of all politicians. "I'll be ethical on some issues—those on which I feel I can 'safely' be motivated by my perception of the public interest—and unethical on others—those on which I feel I must, for whatever reason, be self-interested." In other words, what they are saying is that "it is, after all, a government we are running, not the Kingdom of Heaven." The trouble with such a course is obvious. The very decision about whether to act ethically or unethically in a given situation is itself highly prone to a self-interest decision criterion. Unless one is meticulous in deciding what is and is not a jugular issue, it is far too easy, because of the obvious self-interest that follows from the choice, to classify issues as jugular when they are in fact not so.

There is also some risk on the other side, a risk that if we set the standards of political integrity so high, most politicians will regard them as unrealistic and simply not bother with trying to live up to them. That is, of course, precisely why politics requires some superheroes in every generation, to prove that real-life politicians can maintain their integrity even while immersed in the often seamy world of politics. In this cruel and always-to-be imperfect world, we can never expect that all our politicians will be significantly superior morally to the electorate that chooses them.

In most generations, however, we are fortunate enough to have a few politicians who *are* morally superior, who will not under any circumstances tell a lie or decide an issue on the basis of how it will affect their career. When a Frank Graham sacrifices his own self-interest in winning an election on the altar of honesty with the electorate about a matter of great principle to him, and import to them, it gives other politicians the additional push they need to be somewhat better morally than they might otherwise be. It is the superheroes who move us closer, perhaps only by an inch at first, to the place we would prefer to stand and where representative government at its finest requires us to stand.

In serving that role, the political superheroes not only function as exemplars, but also serve as guardians for all the rest of us, in somewhat the fashion prescribed in Seneca's Eleventh Letter to Lucilius:

"Cherish some man of high character, and keep him ever before your eyes, living as if he were watching you, and ordering all your actions as if he beheld them." . . . We can get rid of most sins, if we have a witness who stands near us when we are likely to go wrong. The soul should have someone whom it can respect, — one by whose authority it may make ever its inner shrine more hallowed. Happy is the man who can make others better, not merely when he is in their company, but even when he is in their thoughts! And happy also is he who can so revere a man as to calm and regulate himself by calling him to mind! One who can so revere another, will soon be himself worthy of reverence . . . for we must indeed have someone according to whom we may regulate our characters; you can never straighten that which is crooked unless you use a ruler.[42]

THE PUBLIC SERVANT AS THE PUBLIC'S FRIEND

Over the last two decades, the balance has tipped very precipitously toward the short-run, self-interest candidates and officeholders.[43] The new tools for selling political candidates are nothing but means of acquiring instantly what politicians of integrity earn gradually. They help one cling to the superficial honor of office, while they demean the public trust. For those candidates who place their reliance on them, reelection is not the most important thing—it is the only thing. And the matter of motive, with which we have been so much concerned in this essay, is of little importance when, as Richard Fenno points out, the strategy is intentionally designed to mislead the voters.[44] An equally pernicious threat to politicians of integrity has been the growth of well-organized, single-interest constituencies on a broad national scale.

More than ever, the public seems to be famished for courageous and bold leadership, leaders who are willing to take risks, to imagine new ways of solving old problems. Only those whose motives are not suspect on self-interest grounds are sufficiently free from worry over the possible consequences of such initiatives to themselves to manage the boldness required. Correspondingly, it is only to the extent that the electorate senses that officials are primarily motivated by the public good that it is willing to trust them in unusual solutions or tolerate positions that are out of joint with the public's own views.

The conventional explanation of our public policy stalemates is that our problems are harder to solve today because they are more complex and because their solution requires the cooperation of more diverse and powerful interests with large antagonistic stakes. So far as it goes, that is an accurate statement. But an equally important cause is the shortage of public officials whom the public recognizes to be dominantly devoted to the public good, and so available to make decisions broader in scope than those that can be defined by the interests of contending parties.

Only the selfless official will get the benefit of the doubt, and benefit of the doubt is the crucial breathing room required for the birth of new solutions to old problems. Selfless public officials are to the body politic as selfless friends are to individuals. They help us see and choose what is in our long-term interest. They defend us from the strong temptation of short-run advantage, the sly or cunning words of those who would victimize us, or the seductions of those seeking to exploit us. Such friends reinforce what is best in both a nation and an individual, bucking up our desire, as well as our will, to do what is best for ourselves in the long run.

The key is selflessness. The reason we take the proffered advice—frequently painful or difficult in the short run—is that we believe the counselor to have *only* our long-run interest at heart, not his own, and not that of our adversaries or competitors. If the motives are suspect, so also is the advice. Without selfless public officials, the electorate has no recourses when confronted by the hard and painful choices that democracy must make from time to time — choices that require some to sacrifice and others to gain. Without selfless public officials, the public is bewildered by the task of discerning what is the public interest in situations where their several private interests are adversely affected. We know the public interest may require some private sacrifice, but how do we know that what claims to be the public interest really is? Not everything that demands sacrifice is in the public interest. Selfless officials can be trusted to exercise judgment without suspicion that they have been swayed by those who will be benefited by the sacrifices of the rest of us.

Our politics is impoverished, and the range of possible solutions to our problems diminished, by the tendency of many politicians to look to their own self-interest in reelection. That is not leading; it is following in the profoundest sense. And it is not the kind of behavior that strengthens representative government. Action against self-interest — standing up to the public on issues, educating the public — shores up our representative government. That is the risky ethical way of a politician with integrity, the way that makes our form of government the perfect form of government for imperfect men and women in an imperfect world.

It is just because the free creative world in which we live presents to us a continuous novelty of events that personal integrity is of such enormous importance. It is our only criterion of value. Our trust is given to certain leaders because their honor, their character, are the only things we can trust. We know they may have to change their minds, to break promises, to let us down, but if we trust them, if we can say of them they are honest men, we do not reproach them. We are sure that if they have broken a promise it was because they could not help it; if they did conceal some facts from us it was not for their own good but ours. That in the final resort they have given their lives to serve what they conceive to be a good end; that they are not in politics for their own advantage or glory.[45]

NOTES

Research on this chapter was made possible by the generous support of the Rockefeller Foundation and the Ford Foundation over several years. For their help in that regard, I am indebted to Joel Colton and Sanford Jaffe. I am greatly indebted, too, to my Duke colleagues James David Barber, Bruce Payne, and David Price, and to Steve Givens, my research assistant, for his assistance with much of the underlying research.

1. "Integrity" comes from the Latin *integer*, which denotes a whole,

intact quality. *The Oxford English Dictionary of English Etymology* (New York: Oxford University Press, 1966), p. 479. *The Compact Edition of Oxford English Dictionary* (Oxford: Oxford University Press, 1971) is, of course, more precise, defining integrity, in its general sense, as "the condition of having no part or element taken away or wanting; undivided or unbroken state . . . completeness; the condition of not being marred or violated; unimpaired or uncorrupted condition; original perfect state; unimpaired moral state, freedom from moral corruption; innocence, sinlessness; soundness of moral principle." For our purposes, the best definition of integrity given there is "the character of uncorrupted virtue especially in relation to truth and fair dealing; uprightness, honesty and sincerity" (p. 1455).

2. There is, of course, a contrary, cynical point of view, which holds that a successful politician cannot, by definition, be ethical and, therefore, cannot have integrity. It runs through much of the expert and popular literature about government. Some examples, all culled quickly from Burton Stevenson, ed., *The Home Book of Quotations* (New York: Dodd, Mead and Co., 1967), p. 1542, are the following: "Scrupulous people are not suited to great affairs," Turgot; "You can't adopt politics as a profession and remain honest," Louis McHenry Howe, *Address* to Columbia University School of Journalism, Jan. 17, 1933; "State-business is a cruel trade; good nature is a bungler in it," Lord Halifax, *Works*, p. 217; "No man, I fear, can effect great benefits for his country without some sacrifice of the minor virtues," Sydney Smith (Lady Holland, *Memoir*).

3. "Power tends to corrupt and absolute power tends to corrupt absolutely."

4. In the summer of 1977, I conducted a "reputational survey" of some sixty present and former members of Congress as well as political journalists to see if I could ascertain whom they regarded as ethical exemplars. The list of ethical exemplars was compiled by asking them to name those members they admired by virtue of their integrity and to whose judgment they deferred on "hard" questions. Only those whose names were mentioned by more than half of those in the larger sample were interviewed in depth. For the idea of approaching the issue in this fashion, I am in the debt of Fred Wertheimer, vice-president of Common Cause. Former Congressman L. Richardson Preyer, of Greensboro, N.C., who was on nearly everyone's list, made it possible for me to interview those of his colleagues whom I wished to see. My debt to him is enormous.

5. Harold D. Lasswell, *The Analysis of Political Behavior* (New York: Oxford University Press, 1948).

6. Anthony Downs, *An Economic Theory of Democracy* (New York: Harper and Row, 1957), p. 28.

7. Joseph A. Schumpeter, *Capitalism, Socialism and Democracy* (New York: Harper and Brothers, 1950), p. 282, as quoted ibid., p. 29. "Schumpeter's profound analysis of democracy forms the inspiration and foundation of our whole thesis." Ibid., n. 11.

8. Ibid., p. 30.

9. Downs's model acknowledges the existence of self-sacrificing altruism, and praises it, while preferring to build his general theory on self-interest. Ibid., pp. 27-28.

10. My concern is not dissimilar from that expressed by Christian Bay in his article, "Politics and Pseudopolitics: A Critical Evaluation of Some Behavioral Literature," *American Political Science Review*, 59 (March 1965), 39-51. Bay argues for a broader scope for the discipline of political science, so as to include "a more systematic articulation of the psychological and the normative perspectives of political behavior research." I am more interested in the assessment of the ethics of self-interest-motivated political actors. Although Bay and I would not appear to agree on the implication of our shared criticism, we do agree on one point—determinance of the economic model of political analysis. "I would define as *political* all activity aimed at improving or protecting conditions for the satisfaction of human needs and demands in a given society or community according to some universalistic scheme of priorities, implicit or explicit. *Pseudopolitics* in this paper refers to activity that resembles political activity but is exclusively concerned with either the alleviation of personal neuroses or with promoting private or private interest group advantage, deterred by no articulate or disinterested conception of what would be just or fair to other groups." Ibid., p. 40.

11. Thomas Jefferson ascribed to education the role of keystone. I am convinced that public trust is even more fundamental.

12. A variety of explanations have been offered for the decline in voting. Some argue that it is attributable to the growing disaffection of the less well off, while others contend that declining participation suggests satisfaction with things as they are. For an examination of alternative explanations, along with the most recent data, see American Bar Association, Special Committee on Election Reform, *The Disappearance of the American Voter* (Chicago: American Bar Association, 1978).

13. Cited in Robert Nisbet, *Twilight of Authority* (New York: Oxford University Press, 1975), pp. 14-15.

14. See, for example, Graham T. Allison, *Essence of Decision: Explaining the Cuban Missile Crisis* (Boston: Little, Brown, 1971), and Philip Selznick, *TVA and the Grass Roots* (Berkeley: University of California Press, 1949).

15. John F. Kennedy, *Profiles in Courage* (New York: Harper and Brothers, 1955), p. 7.

16. No single concept in all of political economy has suffered more analysis at the hands of philosophers, economists, and political scientists than "the public interest." While the overwhelming consensus of scholars is that there is no such thing as a definable general public interest, I remain unconvinced. Common sense, so greatly maligned by intellectuals, suggests that an "impartial spectator" can tell you, for any given problem, exactly what the public interest solution is. Ordinary men and women, in ordinary parlance, seem to know instinctively what it is. My shorthand definition embodies the results of my tentative groping toward clarity. It includes the

following elements: (1) the greatest good, defined as some balancing of aggregate wants (or preferences) and aggregate interests or benefits (irrespective of wants, that which is objectively beneficial); (2) the greatest deserving number (defined as some balancing of aggregate numbers of people and qualitative need or merit (a distributional criterion); (3) over the longest possible period of time. Obviously, this third element enters into the calculation of both what is objectively beneficial (in the first element) and what is distributionally desirable (in the second element), but it is so important to the maintenance of democratic governmental institutions over time that I list it as an additional element. This definition may not help anyone else, but it helps me. To begin one's own plowing of this acreage see, for example, Richard Flathman, *The Public Interest: An Essay Concerning the Normative Discourse of Politics* (New York: John Wiley and Sons, Inc., 1966); Glendon Schubert, *The Public Interest* (Glencoe, Ill.: The Free Press, 1960); *The Public Interest*, NOMOS V, ed. Carl J. Friedrich (New York: Atherton Press, 1962); Virginia Held, *The Public Interest and Individual Interests* (New York and London: Basic Books, Inc., 1970); and Theodore M. Benditt, "The Public Interest," *Philosophy and Public Affairs*, 2 (1963). The best summary in nontechnical language is contained in S. I. Benn, "Interests in Politics," *Proceedings of the Aristotelian Society* (Supp.), 38 (1964). See also the excellent discussion of "interest" in Hannah F. Pitkin, *The Concept of Representation* (Berkeley and Los Angeles: University of California Press, 1967), pp. 156-162.

17. My colleague David Price is undoubtedly correct in his belief that to the extent that we can increasingly make such underlying values explicit, we may be able to arrive at a sounder notion of the public good. See his essay in this volume.

18. Both Kennedy and Carter could argue in terms of John Rawls's criterion of benefiting the "least advantaged." "Distributive justice" arguments might incline one toward Kennedy, while "public interest" arguments might favor Carter. Examining such criteria of choice among policies is as much a component of ethical analysis as the more common form of attention to means used in attaining ends.

19. If it is in the public interest to discover and produce more oil domestically (with "public interest" defined as reducing the United States's trade imbalance and dependence on foreign political/economic influence, and increasing the fuel necessary for growth and job creation), if the revenue from higher prices for petroleum products can in fact be channeled into oil prospecting at less cost to the public than any other incentives or direct governmental actions to the same end, and if such a policy also included appropriate limits on oil company profits, could we not agree that higher fuel prices would be in the public interest and that so to describe them is an objective statement of where lies the public interest with respect to oil price decontrol?

20. Cited in Kennedy, *Profiles*, p. 74.

21. See Pitkin, *Concept of Representation*, pp. 144-167.

22. The issue of time frame is central in Edmund Burke's thought on

representation, and failure to take account of it has created much misunderstanding of his position on representation. As he said in his "Speech at the Conclusion," "I aim to look, indeed, to your opinions; but such opinions as you and I must have five years hence. I was not to look to the flash of a day." In his "Reflections on the Revolution in France" (1790), he elaborated: "mind must conspire with mind. Time is required to produce that union of minds which alone can produce all the good we aim at." Both quotations are cited in Pitkin, *Concept of Representation*, p. 181. See generally chap. 8 of Pitkin, "Representing Unattached Interests: Burke," pp. 168-189.

23. As Pitkin points out, there is not much empirical research on which role today's legislators envision for themselves. She cites a survey by Hadley Cantril, who asked the following questions: "Do you believe that a Congressman should vote on any question as the majority of his constituents desire or vote according to his own judgment?" "Should members of Congress vote according to their own judgment or according to the way the people in their districts feel?" "In cases when a Congressman's opinion is different from that of a majority of the people in his district, do you think he should usually vote according to his own best judgment, or according to the way the majority of his district feels?" The results "ranged from two-thirds in favor of constituency feelings, to more than half in favor of the representative's judgment." See Pitkin, *Concept of Representation*, p. 277, citing Hadley Cantril, *Public Opinion, 1935-46* (Princeton: Princeton University Press, 1951), p. 133.

24. Cited by Pitkin, *Concept of Representation*, p. 164, from Cecil S. Emden, *The People and the Constitution*, 2d ed. (Oxford: Clarendon Press, 1956), p. 27.

25. "Where 'the deliberate sense of the kingdom' on a great subject was known, Burke said that 'it must be prevalent' . . . when the people as a body . . . expressed their wishes 'strongly, decidedly, and upon long deliberation,' then their 'general sense' was to be taken for wisdom." Francis P. Canavan, *The Political Reason of Edmund Burke* (Durham, N.C.: Duke University Press, 1960), pp. 141-142, 146-147, as cited in Pitkin, *Concept of Representation*, p. 182.

26. Colman McCarthy, "The Trusted Man of Politics," *Boston Globe*, December 31, 1976, reprinted in *Memorial Addresses and Other Tributes in the Congress of the United States on the Life and Contributions of Philip A. Hart* (Washington, D.C.: Government Printing Office, 1977), pp. 6-7.

27. I realize that utilitarians would undoubtedly demand to know why motives should be valid objects of moral judgment in the first place. Jeremy Bentham, for example, argued that "a man's motives affect nobody until they give birth to action, and it is with the action and not with the motive that individuals and societies have any concern." Similarly, James Mill wrote: "all the value of acts consists in the consequences of acts; . . . if the acts are detached from their consequences, they are unmeaning contractions of muscles. As a buyer, it should not matter to me whether a mer-

chant sells to everybody at the same fixed price from a sense of duty to be honest or merely out of self-interested prudence. As long as the merchant is honest, for whatever reason, my interests are not affected." On the same principle, it should not matter whether my congressman is consumed by personal ambition, so long as his ambition has the incidental effect of producing policies I favor.

I believe that Bentham and Mill are wrong on two counts. The first grows out of my earlier stated view that representative government itself has inherent special values that place great weight on motive. The legitimation of self-interested political behavior, beyond all its effects on policy itself, which I explore next, has other consequences of a sort not usually taken into account by utilitarian calculation. Government is not the political equivalent of the economy. What may work to the satisfaction of most within the confines of a finite economic system designed to ration scarce resources, wreaks havoc when transferred to an infinitely more fragile political system of which the economic system is itself only a component part, an important one indeed, but still only one among many. We are told by both Thomas Hobbes and John Locke that governments were originally established, in theory, to serve our common *needs*, not our individual *wants*—our needs for security from the depredations of one another and from those external to our particular society.

Once the psychology of self-interest comes to pervade a political community, the delicate fabric of trust and respect, in which a government and its citizens are woven together, begins to fray. Without that trust, citizens have no reason to allow themselves to be persuaded by their elected leaders of the wisdom of particular policies, especially those requiring sacrifices by the public. Without that trust, the bonds of community are shattered. Without that trust, our politics becomes more a war of all against all. The utilitarians simply could not have imagined how dispiriting it would be to a nation or a state or a city when politicians are perceived "to act solely in order to attain the income, prestige and power which come from being in office." Downs, *An Economic Theory*, p. 28.

What then of the officeholder who believes as a matter of principle that the legislature will operate more efficiently—like a market—if all representatives vote their constituents' interests irrespective of their own judgment about what is best for the country as a whole as well as for their constituents in particular? There is an abundance of evidence going back at least as far as Aristotle that it is precisely such crowd-pleasing behavior—catering to the short-run whims of the mob—that brings about the decay of democracy into mobocracy. For who is more the demagogue than one who tells his constituents what they want to hear, even if he thinks they are wrong? If elected leaders do not seek to teach their constituents wherein they are wrong, who will?

A second way of answering Mill and Bentham is simply to co-opt their argument by relating motives to external, material consequences. The unabashed politics of self-interest does not make for "good" government even within the limited definition of "good" employed by the utilitarians. Uncompromising interest group competition leads both to political paralysis and to desperate short-term solutions designed merely to appease vocal, organized interest groups. Can there be any doubt that the psychology of self-interest which pervades the present debate over energy in this country is seriously impeding adoption of a wise, long-term energy policy, indeed of *any* coherent policy, wise or not?

This second answer to Bentham and Mill, however, is incomplete. It considers only the effects of self-interested motives on policy and the policy process. It is predicated upon the empirical observation that self-interest leads to bad policy outcomes. If it turned out that Downs's model of the political process were correct, and avarice and ambition in fact promoted socially desirable policies, we would be forced, under present assumptions, to praise avarice and ambition, motives we intuitively regard as being somehow dishonorable. Yet many of us, I think, are willing to exchange an increment of governmental efficiency and "good" policy for greater virtue, altruism, character, and good motives on the part of our political leaders. We do not value motives, therefore, only insofar as they lead to "good" policy.

28. While I cannot prove it either, and am not going to try, I confess that I do not subscribe to reductionist value relativism. I am convinced with Pascal that *la cour a ses raisons que la raison ne connais pas* (the heart has its reasons that reason knows not at all). Obviously one must temper one's confidence in employing this mode of knowledge with Jeremiah's warning that "the heart is deceitful above all things, and desperately wicked" (17:9), but Pascal's point still stands.

Most human beings, of no matter how great or little intelligence, instinctively admire, in themselves and in others, behavior that gives priority to the interests of others. The greatest satisfactions in life are regarded as those arising out of *giving* to others, with the implicit assumption, whether literally true or not, that what one is giving away one cannot keep for oneself. Memories of such generosity, in both the beholder and the giver, as well as in the receiver, mature and grow and remain full of vigor, while the memories of short-run self-serving pleasures have either faded entirely, or have been transformed into regrets.

The person who defers to strangers at doorways, or who stops his automobile at pedestrain crosswalks, *not* out of a desire to curry favor with either recipients or observers but from a wish to symbolize his deference to the interests of others, tastes a joy that those who, heedless of others, rush through doors or across pedestrian crossings blindly forego. The friendly, often surprised, wave of thumbs up or smile received in return is an acknowledgment that both receiver and giver know that an act of decency, of friendship, of human respect, has just occurred, a recognition that there is a bond of care between the two. Such thoughts remind me of the following lines from W. H. Auden:

Defenseless under the night
Our world in stupour lies

Yet dotted everywhere
Ironic points of light
Flash out wherever
The just exchange their messages.

(Quoted from "September 1, 1939," in *The English Auden: Poems, Essays and Dramatic Writings, 1927-1939*, by W. H. Auden, edited by Edward Mendelson, with the permission of the publishers, Faber and Faber Ltd., London, and Random House, Inc., New York.)

Are these altruistic acts really self-interested at their center, and if so, is the self-satisfaction derived by the actor similar to the usual category of self-interested motivations? While "yes" may be a reasonable answer to the first question, a "yes" answer to the second question would confound ethical analysis.

29. H. Sidgwick, "Classification of Duties — Veracity," in *The Methods of Ethics*, 7th ed. (London: Macmillan and Co., 1907), pp. 312-319; Jeremy Bentham, *The Principles of Morals and Legislation* (New York: Macmillan Co., Hafner Press, reissued 1948), p. 223; Sissela Bok, *Lying: Moral Choice in Public and Private Life* (New York: Pantheon, 1978), a superb work both substantively and methodologically, see esp. pp. 90-106.

30. Ibid., pp. 170-173.

31. Joyce Cary, "Political and Personal Morality," *The Saturday Review*, December 31, 1955, p. 6: "Cripps when Chancellor of the Exchequer in England was asked if the Government had any intention of leaving the Gold Standard. Cripps answered that there was none. But, in fact, the thing was already decided and Britain was off the Gold Standard within a week. Cripps was a man of the strictest truth, but if he had not evaded the question, misled the House, there would have been a major crisis; and the whole advantage of the operation would have been lost."

32. Richard M. Cohen and Jules Witcover, *A Heartbeat Away: The Investigation and Resignation of Vice President Spiro T. Agnew* (New York: Viking Press, 1974), p. 208.

33. Adam Smith, John Rawls, and other proponents of the "impartial spectator theory" claim that the most valid moral judgments are made by those who are not personally involved in a moral problem. If one's material or ideal interests are caught up in a particular decision, then one will be tempted to favor, consciously or not, one's own interests over those of others. John Rawls's requirement that the imaginary framers of his constitution be ignorant of their future social status under the political system they are erecting is designed to prevent class interests from compromising the impartiality of the constitution. Conflict-of-interest rules work on the same principle. The principle of impartiality is akin to the principle of generality, the concept that like cases should be treated similarly. An impartial spectator will have no motive for treating a particular individual or group differently from others because the decision has no bearing on his immediate self-interest. His life will be unaffected no matter what decision he makes, and therefore he can painlessly cast his vote for the general wel-

fare. For the "impartial spectator," the tension between self-interest and the public interest disappears because his self-interest is irrelevant to his decision.

34. Michael Walzer, "Political Action: The Problem of Dirty Hands," *Philosophy and Public Affairs*, 2 (Winter 1973), pp. 160-180.

35. Indeed, they violate every one of James McGregor Burns's prescriptions for success in politics: "If the Congressman were a modern Machiavelli, his advice to freshmen in Congress on 'How to Stay in Office' would be: 1) vote for the home folks first especially those who are well organized; 2) keep on good terms with the local party bosses; 3) stress the protection of your district's interests as a whole against the outside world; and 4) as far as possible, do not commit yourself on the important national issues that divide your constituents. But the Congressman is not Machiavellian and if he gave such advice he would speak in terms of the importance of following a safe and sane middle way, of the dangers of extremism and centralization, of the need for protecting local rights and 'interests.' " *Congress on Trial: The Legislative Process and the Administrative State* (New York: Harper and Brothers, 1949), p. 13.

36. There are obviously other kinds of things elected officials can do to build the kind of network of relationships between themselves and their constituents that will ease their difficulties, and help carry them through a period of acute difference with their constituents. The more they perform, for example, the wide variety of constituent services demanded today of representatives, the more constituents will trust them. The more often they are seen in their district, the more meetings they attend there, the more speeches they give there, the more responsive they are to inquiries for assistance as well as petitions for help, the more freedom of judgment they will acquire for themselves. As exhausting, tiring, fatiguing, as the satisfaction of these demands may be, and however unimportant they may appear when viewed from the long-range, national perspective, they are nonetheless vital to the effective functioning of representative government. When conscientiously performed, the varieties of constituent services combine with the educational functions discussed in the text in putting the lie to the implication of arrogance in a representative's decision to differ with his constituents.

37. Kennedy, *Profiles in Courage*, p. 16.

38. "Speech at the Conclusion," in Hoffman and Levack, *Burke's Politics*, p. 115.

39. That it is at root a misconception is clear from Pitkin's chapter on Burke. Burke did not understand that public sentiment ought to play a crucial role in his judgment. The question instead is one of balance. See Pitkin, *Concept of Representation*, pp. 168-189. Having said that, it is also clear that Burke did not carry his position to its logical conclusion.

40. And Burke so asserted. Ibid.

41. In his 1950 reelection campaign, Frank Porter Graham chose to take a strong public position in behalf of President Truman's fair employment practices legislation despite the overwhelming unpopularity of the

stand among North Carolinians. Philip Hart opposed the automobile industry and the drug industry, the two strongest economic interests in Michigan.

42. Seneca, *Ad Lucilium Epistulae Morales*, vol. I, "Epistle XI, On the Blush of Modesty," ed. Richard M. Gummere (London: William Heinemann, 1917), pp. 64-65.

43. See David R. Mayhew, *Congress: The Electoral Connection* (New Haven: Yale University Press, 1974), and David E. Price, "Ethics and Legislative Life: Thoughts on Representation and Responsibility" (Denver: LEGIS 50, 1978).

44. Richard F. Fenno, Jr., "U.S. House Members in Their Constituencies: An Exploration," *American Political Science Review*, 71 (September 1977), 916.

45. See Cary, "Political and Personal Morality," p. 6.

Donald P. Warwick

4. The Ethics of Administrative Discretion

A sound ethics of the public service should be constructed on two foot-ings: an accurate understanding of the behavior and environment of the public servant; and moral principles applicable to the dilemmas arising in public administration. An ethical framework built on an idealized concep-tion of what public officials do will tilt toward sanctimony or collapse into irrevelance; one erected on inadequate moral principles will incline toward cynicism or topple into description.

Our understanding of administrative behavior in the United States is now much more advanced than the ethical frameworks available for assess-ing that behavior. Recent empirical studies show that far from being cogs in an administrative machine, public officials exercise vast discretion in formulating and implementing public policies.[1] But if the central concern of organizational analysts has been with the politics of discretion, the pre-vailing focus among those writing about the ethics of administration has been on honesty, obedience, and personal integrity. The most commonly mentioned ethical dilemmas have to do with conflicts between conscience and obedience to superiors; the use of deception, bribery, and other mor-ally objectionable means; the uses and limits of administrative secrecy; conditions permitting or requiring "whistleblowing"; and the circum-stances calling for resignation from the public service. The emphasis of such writings has been on the dilemmas of professional integrity rather than the ethics of policy discretion.

In this essay I will review some common ethical dilemmas faced by pub-lic officials in the exercise of discretion, and suggest some ethical principles for resolving those dilemmas. The emphasis will not be on the familiar questions of conscience confronted by administrators—whether to lie for a seemingly good cause, to obey one's superiors when their directives seem

93

immoral, or to blow the whistle on corruption and other abuses of power. Nor will it be on the ethics of public policies themselves, such as the morality of using public funds for abortions or denying attendance at public schools to the children of undocumented aliens. Rather, the focus will be on the ethics of the administrative discretion used by officials in formulating and implementing public policies. The central ethical questions for this essay are those arising from the policy roles of the public official.

But what kinds of public officials will be considered, and why? The focal point will be career administrators and appointed officials who are expected to operate as civil servants rather than as politicians. They are the largest class of public servants and the principal implementers of many public policies. Moreover, because they can hide behind the screens of bureaucracy and don the robes of professionalism, they are often less subject to public accountability than elected officials. As Max Weber pointed out, a distinguishing characteristic of career officials is the possession of expertise appropriate to their niche in the organization. They present themselves, and are billed to the public, as experts in a certain sphere, functionaries whose decisions are guided by specialized knowledge not available to the ordinary citizen. Some of these individuals may be more astute politicians than the elected officials to whom they report (one thinks of J. Edgar Hoover of the FBI or Harry J. Anslinger of the Federal Bureau of Narcotics), and their specialized knowledge may sometimes be scant. But to the American public the raison d'etre of the civil servant is administrative expertise, and the key mechanism of accountability is hierarchy rather than politics. In the public mind, as in the lore of public administration, the civil servant is expected to execute policies devised by those with more direct electoral accountability. It is this gap between the image of the civil servant as executor and the reality of the civil servant as initiator that underscores the need for an ethics of discretion.

CASE STUDIES

The subsequent typology of policy roles will be more clear if it is set within the context of specific cases. Two principal examples will be used: the Methadone Maintenance Program developed by the Health Services Administration in New York City; and the international assistance program undertaken by the Office of Population of the U.S. Agency for International Development. A brief description of each will set the stage for more specific illustrations.

The Methadone Maintenance Program was developed by Gordon Chase,

Health Services Administrator under Mayor John Lindsay.[2] When Chase was appointed to this position in 1969 he had no direct responsibility for programs to combat heroin use. The unit then responsible for addicts was the Addiction Services Agency (ASA). Its approach was to encourage abstinence from heroin through supervised voluntary therapeutic communities operating under strict discipline. Another agency, the State Narcotics Addiction Control Commission, forcibly confined addicts in expensive treatment centers. There were also two private programs that tried to shift the addict's craving from heroin to an inexpensive synthetic drug called methadone. One was located at the Beth Israel Hospital, the other at the Addiction Research and Treatment Corporation (ARTC).

Shortly after taking office Gordon Chase decided that not enough was being done to treat the 100,000 or more heroin addicts on the streets of New York. Lacking formal authority to undertake new programs but believing that he personally should take action to fill the treatment gap, Chase resolved to establish a methadone maintenance treatment program. His first move was to send the Mayor's Narcotics Control Council a proposal to treat 15,600 addicts in less than a year. This number was inflated, but Chase thought that his memorandum would help to get key officials to think in terms of large programs and would create momentum. Then even before the mayor authorized him to do so and before funds were available, he began to recruit a dynamic and capable staff. The head of the new Bureau of Methadone Maintenance was Dr. Robert Newman, who was handpicked by Chase. Newman kept up the momentum by opening clinics in existing institutions, maintaining control and accountability through a tight monitoring and reporting system, pressing to meet deadlines, and working to overcome community opposition to clinics for "junkies." By June 1971, the city's methadone programs had treated 6,000 addicts, and by January of 1974 the figure had risen to over 20,000. Moreover, the apparent success of this effort had stimulated the Beth Israel Hospital to expand its intake of patients.

The Office of Population of the Agency for International Development (AID) provides a second example of bureaucratic entrepreneurship.[3] From the beginnings of the Point Four Program through the Eisenhower administration the prevailing attitude of the U.S. government was that birth control should not be part of foreign aid. At a press conference in 1959 President Eisenhower had declared: "This government will not, as long as I am here, have a positive political doctrine in its program that has to do with the problem of birth control. That's not our business."[4] But by the early

1960s the State Department was quietly conducting research on the "population problem" and even appointed a full-time population officer. Little happened within AID until 1967, when a concern with world famine led to congressional hearings on population and then authorization of expenditures for family planning. In that same year AID established a Population Branch and appointed Dr. Reimert T. Ravenholt as its head. Shortly afterward Philander P. Claxton, Jr., was installed as special assistant to the secretary of state for population matters.

Over the next eight years AID's population unit grew from a miniscule operation with a tiny budget to become one of the largest spenders in the foreign assistance field. This expansion was due in no small part to an effective alliance between Ravenholt in AID, Claxton in the State Department, congressmen concerned about the "population explosion," and interest groups stirring and supporting that concern. Also critical in forging links among the outside population lobby, AID, and the Congress was General William Draper. As a prominent public figure in his own right and as head of the Population Crisis Committee, Draper had the requisite visibility and connections to press the legislative case for AID. For his part, Ravenholt astutely used his swelling budget to build constituencies in the United States and abroad. A decade after taking office he was widely regarded as the czar of international population programs and a force to contend with in many spheres of action and research. What began as an obscure and controversial branch became the thriving Office of Population with a budget of over $150 million per year in earmarked funds (an exceptional practice in AID).

A TYPOLOGY OF POLICY ROLES

What are the most significant ways in which public officials exercise discretion in the performance of their duties? The principal spheres of discretion can be highlighted through a typology built around the concepts of policy formulation, implementation, and evaluation. The assumption is that public officials have scope for discretion in the initial development of policies or legislation, in the execution of the resulting programs, and in the evaluation of both policies and programs.

1. POLICY FORMULATION

The first realm of administration discretion is that provided by the formulation of public policy. Although it is hard to draw a sharp line between policy formulation and implementation, the distinction is clear at the extremes (for example, passing a law authorizing population assistance vs. delivering contraceptives to a client in India) and is helpful for present purposes. Public officials play both direct and indirect roles in formulating policies.

A. Direct role.

Despite the popular perception that civil servants merely execute policies set by their superiors, these officials can and do play a direct role in policy development. Their influence appears in several ways.

a. Seizing the initiative in a policy domain. Gordon Chase is a perfect illustration of the public official who plays a direct role in policy development by "grabbing the action" in a certain sphere, in this case the treatment of heroin addicts. By effective bureaucratic maneuvering Chase was able to establish his own dominance in this area, and to remove policy control from the Addiction Services Agency. The main ethical question posed by his maneuvering concerns the limits of administrative entrepreneurship. Should administrative responsibilities regularly be "up for grabs" by skilled operators, or do assigned responsibilities have some moral claim?

b. Drafting legislation. The public official, such as a career civil servant heading an agency, may propose legislation directly to a legislative committee, a legislator, or their staff. An example is seen in federal legislation and policy on drug abuse.

In the matter of drug legislation and policy formulation, the primary client group or constituency upon which Congress has relied over the years had been the criminal justice system. As is the case with other special interest groups, Congress has received from the criminal justice bureaucracy highly selected information consonant with its goals. As such, the development and administration of federal drug legislation enacted since the Harrison Licensing Act of 1914 bears the unmistakeable marks of its principal purveyors.[5]

The author adds that until recently the criminal justice/law enforcement bureaucracy "provided the major impetus for all drug control legislation and has assumed principal responsibility for defining the drug problem, categorizing the offenses, labeling the violators." These practices, which are common to many areas of public policy, raise the question of the proper role of public officials in proposing legislation. Specifically, what balance should be struck between narrow personal or bureaucratic interests and the broader public interest? And whose conception of the public interest should prevail?

c. Negotiating broad interpretations of policy. Laws are often passed or policies set at such a high level of generality that they must be defined operationally before any implementation can take place. A law to prevent drug abuse may simply authorize appropriate actions to control the spread of narcotics and to treat existing addicts. The officials of drug-related agencies may then lobby with the legislators to have the authorizing law interpreted to fit their interests or brands of competence. Criminal justice agencies may campaign for an operational emphasis on treatment, and the customs service for better inspection facilities at ports of entry. A critical ethical question is the point at which bureaucratic interests and the public interest begin to diverge.

B. Indirect role.

Public officials may also work to create conditions favorable or hostile to the emergence of certain policies. These indirect policy roles are well illustrated by the New York methadone program and by AID's Office of Population.

a. Creating the perception of a "problem." Public officials often use research findings, news releases, personal contacts, lobbying organizations, and other means to foster a sense of a "problem" requiring action by themselves or their agency. For over a decade the Office of Population has had calculated strategies for trying to convince the governments of the developing nations that they have a problem of excessive population growth. Countries have been rated according to the degree to which they are presently aware of their problem, and the consciousness-raising devices have been tailored accordingly. A 1975 paper by this office's policy unit (PPD) sets forth the following strategic principle.

PPD activity seeks changes in the policies of other sovereign governments, an extremely sensitive area for foreign assistance operations. The key instrument in this effort is not leverage — i.e., tying other assistance to the adoption of the desired policy measures — but a focussed, sequential program of persuasion. AID's role is to enlist and support indigenous forces who will themselves determine and implement whatever measures are needed to promote policy development.[6]

Stated more directly, AID's objective is to convince government officials and other leaders in the developing countries that they have a problem of excessive population growth, and that they should deal with it by setting up programs to control fertility. Among the steps which it takes to promote increased awareness of the "population problem" are conferences on population dynamics for selected opinion leaders; dissemination of literature designed to stimulate discussion of population issues; sponsorship of local research aimed at showing the deleterious consequences of rapid population growth; programs to show national planners how to calculate the impact of population variables on development plans; and overseas training in population dynamics for well-placed national officials.

AID's strategy raises a variety of ethical questions. Is it permissible to stretch the truth or to be highly selective in the presentation of data in order to dramatize an alleged problem? Is it the business of public agencies to whip up demand for their services? Should AID try to channel public attention toward the evils of population growth when there may be other problems, such as malaria control or sanitation, that are more serious for a given country? And whose values should govern the definition of seriousness? These issues arise in many kinds of public persuasion, but their ethical salience rises when the campaigns cross national boundaries and involve the cooptation of local elites through easy research money and other material benefits.

b. Mobilizing constituencies for action. Once there is a sufficient sense of a problem to legitimize action, public officials can take various steps to build up momentum. One of the most crucial is to convince outside authorities and supporters that they have a viable idea, know how to act on it, can spend money if it is given to them, and are likely to be "winners." In this respect Gordon Chase and Reimert Ravenholt acted in remarkably similar ways. Phyllis Piotrow writes of Ravenholt:

The first and most important element of Ravenholt's leadership was his own unshakeable conviction that he did indeed know what needed to be done and that he was personally well able to do it. His certainty and determination communicated itself to the rest of the Population Service. Working long hours under great pressure in an agency that still privately disapproved of the subject and resented its sudden affluence, Ravenholt drove the program forward partly by personal force.

Moreover, Ravenholt not only believed in his own judgement, he also believed that the population problem was susceptible of solution by the methods that he emphasized and with the means at AID's disposal . . .

Ravenholt's convictions were a source of strength within the program. They generated a strong loyalty and sense of direction among his own staff even when he was not completely correct.[7]

In the case of the methadone program, Gordon Chase faced the problem of gaining responsibility as well as money for a large-scale treatment effort. By submitting a seemingly outlandish proposal to the Narcotics Control Council, he hoped not only to get key officials to "think big" about heroin programs, but also to build momentum.

I believe that when you do things, that speed is terribly important in government. If for nothing else it builds momentum and allows you to get your program going . . . in managing the public sector speed is more important than just speed. Speed has to do with momentum. And in the public sector when you're trying to get something done in a place like New York City, everybody and everything seems lined up against you on the way to doing nothing.[8]

Beyond generating momentum through speed, Chase tried to create the impression that he would be ready to act effectively almost the instant that the city granted him authorization to do so. Toward this end he began to recruit a staff of doctors and managers who would show "character and drive" and be committed to the methadone program. They, in turn, fed him ammunition for use in his jurisdictional battle with the Addiction Services Agency and other critics. More important, they immediately set out to negotiate contracts with hospitals interested in operating methadone clinics should funds be forthcoming. Chase's mobilization effort bore fruit when Mayor Lindsay prepared a memorandum authorizing the HSA to establish a large methadone program.

Constituency mobilization may also be directed at interest groups outside the public service. During the 1960s and early 1970s it was an open secret in Washington that Reimert Ravenholt worked closely with the population control lobby led by General William Draper. The agency insider playing this role can feed the lobby information favorable to its interests, such as surveys purporting to show a massive popular demand for family planning, and can recommend tactics to enhance the agency's power position within the bureaucracy. Draper, for example, was able to persuade key legislators that funds for Ravenholt's population unit should be earmarked so that they could not be spent on other development activities. This decision, which was opposed by AID's administration, greatly fortified Ravenholt's autonomy and bargaining position with other bureaus.

Through adroit use of its funds, the public agency may further generate support for its preferred lines of activity by creating or nurturing clientele groups carrying out such activities. In the Philippines, AID provided financial assistance to a variety of nascent family planning organizations. As they grew and became more influential, they began to pressure the Philippine government to adopt an explicit antinatalist population policy and to support a national family planning program. When this step was finally taken, AID approached the government with an offer of substantial assistance, and soon became the principal source of foreign aid for Philippine population activities.

The administrative behaviors outlined here pose enormous challenges for an ethics of discretion because they flatly contradict traditional notions of hierarchical authorization. Nowhere is the gap between the normative theory and the behavioral practice of public administration so large as with constituency mobilization by agency officials. Far from being directed or authorized to act by their superiors, the officials in many cases seek to create the circumstances which will persuade or compel their superiors to grant them more jurisdiction, money, autonomy, or other benefits. The cardinal ethical questions raised by such practices are (1) the conditions under which officials are permitted or even obligated to step outside the formal chain of command to build support for their efforts; and (2) the ethical limitations which should govern the processes and contents of such transactions. Traditional normative theories of administration provide little help with either question.

2. POLICY IMPLEMENTATION

Public policies are rarely "formulated" once and for all and then implemented in machinelike fashion by compliant functionaries. Most policies are up for constant interpretation by the officials charged with execution, and by those with whom they must deal.[9] Not only are there lingering ambiguities stemming from the necessarily broad language of most legislation and policy directives, but also there are often dozens of choice points where conflicts, rivalries, overloaded schedules, and other practical constraints make ad hoc interpretation inescapable. Public officials play a positive role in the implementation process when they influence the speed, directions, priorities, methods, and other aspects of execution. They play a negative role when they work to stop, delay, or subvert implementation.

A. Positive roles.

Public officials can affect policy interpretation along the implementation chain in numerous ways.

a. Setting programmatic strategies. Very often public policies are deliberately drafted in broad language to permit flexibility of action by the executing agencies. The phrasing of Title X of the Foreign Assistance Act of 1967 (Programs Relating to Population Growth) was so general that its critics wondered what was excluded. It stated that the president could provide voluntary assistance for programs relating to population growth to governments, UN agencies, private nonprofit organizations, universities, hospitals, and "voluntary health or other qualified organizations." Partly because of its strong external constituency support and its firm backing in

Congress AID's Office of Population until recently enjoyed great freedom in setting its own programmatic strategies within the general framework of Title X. Ravenholt is well known for advocating direct provision of contraception, sterilization, and abortion services. While Congress did put restrictions on abortion, his preferences for an overall strategy largely became those of the Office of Population. Gordon Chase was similarly effective in channeling New York's amorphous narcotics control policies in the direction of methadone maintenance for heroin addicts. With Chase, however, it was more a matter of filling a policy vacuum than of negotiating a favorable interpretation of existing law. In either case a core ethical question concerns the moral principles, as distinct from the personal or bureaucratic interests, that should guide public officials as they translate broad policies into operational programs.

b. Determining priorities. Within an overall programmatic strategy there is usually ample scope for public officials to influence budgetary, geographic, and other priorities. The annual appropriation for AID's Office of Population provides considerable latitude for choice on spending. Under the rubric of population and family planning more or less emphasis can be given to door-to-door distribution of contraceptives in the developing countries. In the case of research the agency has discretion in allocating its funds between descriptive demography and operational research on family planning programs, as well as other categories. Further, within a given programmatic strategy and set of budgetary priorities, many areas of policy are open as to geographic focus. This is largely the case in the field of population assistance, where the Office of Population can, with a few exceptions, select the developing countries with which it wishes to work.

c. Establishing organizational arrangements. One of the broadest areas of discretion for implementing agencies lies in working out the precise organizational arrangements for carrying out a policy. Once he was granted authority to develop a methadone program, Gordon Chase had three institutional options: (1) to have the services provided directly through a city-operated agency; (2) to have the work done through contracts with private institutions; and (3) to create a "fiscal drop," a private organization "which would be legally responsible for the program but which would, in fact, be a front for the city agency that would actually manage the program."[10] Chase felt that working directly with the city would subject the methadone program to the gauntlet of clearances required by New York's "overhead agencies," such as the Bureau of the Budget. His initial preference was for the "fiscal drop," for that would permit maximal flexibility and less detailed accountability than the other options. However, criticisms of earlier corporations of this genre made a move in that direction politically inauspicious. Hence he chose the second option, contracting with private institutions, as the one that provided the best balance between freedom of action and control over program activities. It also allowed him to tap the vast resources of New York's medical establishment.

While the choice of organizational arrangements is an eminently practical matter, it is not without ethical implications. The foremost moral question raised by Chase's exercise of discretion centers on the proper place of accountability. Chase, like most skilled managers, wanted to be liberated from the "bureaucrats" who wield rules like whips and by nurture, if not nature, prefer caution to speed.

These overhead agencies could bring a large program to a standstill simply by losing a few of the thousands of pieces of paper that had to be processed to commit city resources . . . Theoretically, this mass of procedures made program managers "accountable" to the people of New York. However, from Chase's point of view, what the procedures really accomplished was to place major programs under the veto power of relatively obscure low-level bureaucrats who may or may not have been better able to judge the interests of the City than Chase.[11]

Anyone who has worked for the government can empathize with Chase's desire to bolt the bureaucracy, but the question of accountability remains. Should every enterprising executive enjoy the freedom sought by Chase? Are the "overhead agencies" nothing but a useless excrescence of bureaucratic torpor, or do they have some moral claim to supervise the operations of government?

    d. Staffing programs. Closely related to the choice of organizations are decisions about who will staff the program. Public officials often have the discretion to decide on the total staff size, their basic mission, their levels of compensation, and other job incentives. For the methadone program, Gordon Chase wanted managers who showed "character and drive" as well as excellent managerial skills. An ethical question arising in such talent searches is whether to raid other programs for their best people. Should a methadone program conduct an aggressive recruiting drive aimed at siphoning off the most astute managers from the city's health department or other agencies? If the lost talent can be easily replaced, there would seem to be no particular moral problem. But when the cost of recruiting for methadone is a decline in the quality of programs to control tuberculosis, lead poisoning, and other health hazards, agency entrepreneurship may clash with public welfare. Similarly, one wonders if it would be ethical, or even wise, for an organization such as AID to arrange for the salaries and fringe benefits of family planning workers to be significantly better than those offered to public health workers operating out of the same clinics. While this practice may have some justification as a means of compensating for a social stigma attached to work on birth control, it becomes morally dubious when its net effect is to lure scarce professionals away from essential services and to demoralize those who remain in their posts. The ethics of staffing would thus seem to hinge on the total context of a program rather than just on the needs of a single effort, such as methadone maintenance.

e. Selecting target groups. Within a given programmatic strategy, set of priorities, and institutional arrangement, implementing officials still have substantial scope for influencing the choice of target groups for a certain policy. An addiction treatment center may try to reach all the major categories of drug users, including alcoholics, or it may concentrate on just one. After it gained the necessary authority in this area, New York's Health Services Administration chose to deal only with heroin addicts and with a single treatment method: methadone maintenance. Critics have challenged both the politics and the ethics of this emphasis, mainly on the grounds that it "blames the victim" and shows a marked class bias.[12] Thomas Szasz, a perennial critic of social labeling, would go further to say that the very concepts of addiction and drug abuse are morally suspect. He opens his book *Ceremonial Chemistry* with this statement:

In its present popular and professional use, the term "addiction" refers not to a disease but to a despised kind of deviance. Hence the term "addict" refers not to a bona fide patient but to a stigmatized identity, usually stamped on a person against his or her will. Addiction (or drug abuse) thus resembles mental illness and witchcraft, and the addict (or drug abuser) resembles the mental patient and witch, inasmuch as all of these names identify categories of deviance and their occupants.[13]

The principal ethical questions raised by these criticisms are the degree to which public officials should consciously examine the assumptions and biases behind the identification of some groups as "problems," and the moral principles on which they should rely in choosing specific targets for public policy.

f. Pressuring for results. Policy implementation varies widely in the extent to which managers introduce incentives and adopt other means for producing results. Gordon Chase would fall on the activist end of the spectrum.

Chase did not rely entirely on the internal motivation of his program managers. As soon as the program began, he "started counting." A detailed plan for implementing the program was developed. Specific individuals were identified as being responsible for specific actions. Deadlines were established for each activity. A procedure for regular reporting was created.[14]

Chase also regularly informed his staff of the number of persons on their waiting lists who died from drug overdoses.

Pressure can be exerted as well on second parties dependent on the controlling organization for funds. According to reports from the Philippines, AID's Office of Population has leaned on the various population organizations receiving its funds for concrete evidence of performance effectiveness. This means, in practice, statistical documentation of the adoption of contraception and sterilization by a given organization's clients. The normal effects of AID's demands are augmented by the fact that, owing to AID's previous strategy of "buying into" a host of family planning organizations, there are now more agencies dependent on U.S. funds than AID can support. Since there are few alternative sources of funding, and the agencies want to stay in operation, they feel under considerable pressure to meet the de facto quotas set for them. As a consequence, employees in these units feel that they must sell not only family planning, but also the more effective methods of birth control.

These examples suggest two broad ethical questions. First, when there are risks to recipients of services, to what point should officials pressure for results from their subordinates? More specifically, what are the trade-offs between the quantity of service delivery and the quality of individual attention? Is it better to provide methadone maintenance to the maximum number of applicants, even if the cost is poor supervision of addicts and supplying methadone to some nonaddicts, or is a more cautious, controlled approach advisable? Second, what moral responsibility does an agency have for abuses wrought by its contractors in response to pressures for results? Does AID bear any responsibility if, in an attempt to meet expectations, a family planning clinic performs two dozen sterilizations without proper explanations of the risks of this procedure? These are very real questions in many social programs, but especially those involving hazardous drugs or medical interventions.

g. Maintaining safeguards. Closely related to the previous point is the degree to which implementing officials establish safeguards to protect the public and then insist on compliance with the procedures adopted. A critical issue in methadone maintenance is verifying the information presented by applicants to insure that they are, in fact, addicted to heroin. Providing free methadone to nonaddicts would obviously defeat the purpose of the program and create a new problem. The case material on the New York program suggests that Chase and his colleagues did not place strong emphasis on verification. This question also arises in research on human subjects. AID's Office of Population is one of the largest funders of research to develop new contraceptives, and as a federal agency, it is obligated to follow the procedures for subject protection established by the Department of Health, Education, and Welfare (HEW). There is a marked difference between AID and the Ford Foundation, however, in the stringency of the protection standards and the care with which they are monitored. From all indications, AID insists that its contractors follow the government procedures for consent and like matters, but it does not make a point of monitoring for compliance. The Ford Foundation, by contrast, has given considerable thought to the subtleties involved in protecting poor and illiterate research subjects in other countries and has taken a more activist stance in implementing its standards. In general, organizations whose trademark is "results" are wary of human subjects' protections and other safeguards which might slow down the attainment of quantitative targets. The crucial ethical question is again the proper balance between the protection of individual welfare and the attainment of performance goals thought to benefit the public.

B. Negative roles.

Public officials may also prevent, stop, delay, sabotage, obstruct, or subvert the implementation of public policy, often in ways that are perfectly legal and which they consider highly moral. The difference between positive and negative influence is that in the first case officials are basically working to move a policy forward toward implementation, albeit in ways congenial to their own predilections. With negative influence the essential orientation is toward rolling or holding a policy back from execution.

a. Failure to fund. Governments often have paper policies suggesting certain kinds of action, but this action is thwarted by a lack of funds. The stated aim of AID's Office of Population is to help individuals and couples achieve the desired number and spacing of their children. On its face this policy would imply attention to both sides of the fertility equation: excessive fertility and infertility or subfecundity. But given its latent mandate to check population growth, Ravenholt's office decided that all available resources should go to the provision of contraception, sterilization, and, to the extent feasible, abortion. If some of the agencies that it supported decided to provide services for infertility, AID did not object overtly, but its basic policy from 1966 to 1975 was to channel its monies toward fertility reduction. One ethical question is whether for reasons of either veracity or human welfare, administrators are obligated to implement with funding those policies they ascribe to their mission. How large a gap between rhetoric and reality is morally acceptable?

b. Inaction. The most formidable weapon in the arsenal of the public official is the power to do nothing. Case after case shows how assigned implementers can "sit on" a policy until sufficient heat is put on them to stimulate movement. Sometimes the reason for inertia is a moral objection to the policy, but more often it is disaffection, overload, or a blend of the two. A study of the Egyptian family planning program highlights the latter conditions. Implementing officials were assigned family planning duties over and above their normal responsibilities with no real incentive for performing the additional tasks. As a result, "for many personnel, family planning becomes one more thankless task that they have to take on, and even if their belief in and commitment to family planning is initially strong, such enthusiasm is apt to wane quickly in the face of overburdened responsibilities, program shortcomings, and lack of adequate compensation."[15] This example raises two ethical questions. First, what are the ethical obligations of officials to carry out assigned responsibilities when their working conditions are poor? And second, when there is more work to be done than time and resources to do it, what criteria should guide the choice of activities? If a nurse enjoys attending pregnant women but has a distaste for birth control, is this sufficient justification for deemphasizing family planning?

c. Obstruction. Public officials may further hinder implementation by setting up overt obstacles to policy execution. Many of these can be constructed from legal requirements, such as rules on hiring, firing, or tenders; interagency agreements; standard operating procedures; or precedents for clearance and concurrence. Officials typically have substantial impact on implementation through their decisions about whether to insist on a clearance, how quickly to process a request from the executing agency, whether to go "by the book" or to overlook slight deviations and infractions, and whether, in the end, to grant the required permission or approval. *Implementation*, the small classic by Pressman and Wildavsky, documents the overwhelming importance of just these kinds of decisions for the nonimplementation of a poverty program in Oakland, California.[16]

The ethically oriented analyst would distinguish between two kinds of obstruction: that motivated primarily by spite, bureaucratic expansionism, or other forms of self-interest; and that arising mainly from the official's desire to do a responsible job. Is there a difference, for example, between spite and conscience as a motive for obstruction? Do officials who believe that abortion is murder have the right, or even the obligation, to hold in as many stops as legally possible to slow down expenditures in this area? And is their exercise of discretion more or less permissible than comparable steps taken purely to settle scores with a bureaucratic rival?

d. Subversion. Another type of negative influence is seen when public officials deliberately take actions to undermine the motivation, commitment, political support, or other resources needed for implementation. A highly effective form of subversion lies in rumors about the harmful effects of a given program. Public health workers opposed to family planning could do considerable harm by either starting or not countering rumors that the contraceptive pill and the intrauterine device cause cancer, or that vasectomy leads to impotence. Stories of this sort have circulated in many of the developing countries, and have wrought palpable damage to government-sponsored population programs. One could ask if there are ever moral grounds justifying opposition by such devious methods.

3. EVALUATION

A third broad sphere of discretion lies in the evaluation of policies and programs. Evaluation constitutes a key link in the policy chain, for it is often the most direct connection between implementation and further policy formulation. The U.S. Congress typically funds social programs for one or two years, and then wants to know what progress has been made toward the original objectives. Sometimes program evaluation consists in tightly designed social experiments or other rigorous studies, while in other cases it is based on administrative statistics and personal impressions. In either case public officials may have ample scope for initiative.

Public officials may influence evaluations in at least four ways. The first is by helping to specify the methodologies used for a given assessment. With family planning programs it is much more difficult to demonstrate program impacts with tightly controlled, randomized experiments than with loose correlational studies. The astute program administrator may, therefore, steer clear of methods which could provide conclusive evidence of zero impact, and press for those allowing greater latitude for interpretation. Interestingly, a review of forty field studies on fertility control programs found only three that met the test of a true field experiment, and yet almost all offered conclusions about the putative effects of these programs.[17]

A second form of discretionary influence arises in the choice of the specific criteria for evaluating a program. With family planning programs there are several plausible indicators of programmatic success: changes in knowledge, attitudes, or interest related to birth control; evidence of behavior thought to be correlated with fertility control, such as seeking information about contraceptives; initial acceptance of some form of contraception; continuation with contraception over a certain time period, such as one year; a reduction in fertility for the region covered by the program; and a reduction in fertility causally attributable to the program intervention.[18] Experience with family planning programs suggests that it is much easier to obtain favorable results at the beginning than at the end of the list. People are more likely to show a change in attitude than a shift in behavior, and to accept contraceptives once than to continue using them for a long period. Reimert Ravenholt was apparently exercising this form of discretion when, in his annual reports to Congress from 1967 to 1975, he attached great significance to statistics on attitudes and "new acceptors," while paying relatively little attention to continuation rates and demonstrated impact on fertility.

The selection of evaluators offers a third area of influence. As every good administrator knows, the outcome of an evaluation depends in large part on who conducts it. In the evaluations done on its programs, AID's Office of Population has generally chosen specialists sympathetic to the family planning approach. The result has been reports that are rarely critical of the fundamental logic of AID's strategy. Finally, public officials can greatly affect the outcome of evaluations in their selection, interpretations, and reporting of the findings. Thus in several presentations to congressional committees, AID's Office of Population has cited statistics on fertility declines in certain countries as evidence of the effectiveness of family planning programs. Yet in some of these countries, such as Costa Rica, the decline had begun well before the programs were undertaken, and in others it was impossible to isolate the causal contribution of family planning services.[19]

The evaluation of methadone programs provides a perfect illustration of the points raised here. The case study of New York's methadone program, appropriately titled "The Entrepreneur's View," cites the following data on the program's outcome:

— although there was an increase in the total number of those who died from methadone overdoses from 1970 to 1973, the combined total of heroin and methadone deaths declined significantly.
— both the incidence and the prevalence of heroin use in New York City declined from 1972 to 1974.
— addict-related crimes decreased significantly in 1972.
— the retention rate for all patients in the methadone program is 76 percent after one year and 65 percent after two years.[20]

The authors conclude: "All in all, not a bad result."

Contrast this assessment with the views found in an article entitled: "Methadone: The Forlorn Hope."[21] Here the author challenges the notion that the use of licit methadone brought about a reduction in crime, and that it led to a decrease in overall drug abuse. The main reduction in crime, he contends, was in the realm of narcotics offenses rather than in street violence. Further,

The pattern found in most methadone programs was one of "poly-drug" abuse: when addicts were denied the euphoric reinforcement of heroin because methadone raised their tolerance to opiates, they quite commonly turned to amphetamines, cocaine, barbiturates, or other non-opiates.[22]

To make matters worse, the leakage of methadone from treatment programs created a new problem of drug abuse.

In 1974, the Drug Enforcement Administration reported that deaths from illicit methadone have surpassed deaths from illicit heroin, and that methadone now constitutes a substantial share of the illegal traffic in drugs. At best, 7.5 million doses of methadone distributed annually by government-licensed clinics seem to have had the effect of shifting drug-abuse from heroin to other equally damaging drugs.[23]

Epstein concludes that methadone programs are based on questionable assumptions and equivocal results, and were sold to the public as part of a broader "anticrime" program. In the end criminal behavior and addiction "proved to be more complex problems that did not lend themselves to simple chemical solutions."[24]

The most striking difference between these two appraisals is that they are based on noncomparable criteria of success. Where Moore and Ziering focus on a decline in heroin use, Epstein points to a rise in poly-drug abuse. Where the case study highlights the retention rate inside methadone programs, the critique underscores the emergence of a methadone problem caused by these programs. The authors seem to agree on the basic facts about methadone deaths and addict-related crimes, but interpret them in markedly dissimilar ways. It is hard to escape the conclusion that "the entrepreneur's view" on evaluation is, perhaps by design, slanted in favor of the New York program, while Epstein's view is somewhat biased against "the forlorn hope." The critical question, from an ethical standpoint, is the extent to which evaluation specialists and those who use their results are obligated to give a fair picture of a program's accomplishments and weaknesses. If there is, as I will argue, a basic obligation to be fair and truthful, whose standards of truth and fairness should prevail, and what procedural steps should be taken to protect them?

TOWARD AN ETHICS OF DISCRETION

The foregoing typology suggests a variety of ethical dilemmas arising from the use of administrative discretion. Should bureaucratic entrepreneurs seize the initiative in a policy domain when they see a compelling need, or should they follow established procedures? Should public officials mobilize outside constituency support to strengthen their bargaining position within the executive branch, or should they act only within their agency's hierarchy? How far should a program manager press for results when some individuals may be harmed as a consequence of strong pressures? Is it morally justifiable for officials to do nothing when they oppose a program, to obstruct or subvert it, or to carry out only those parts that fit their predilections and interests? Are officials obligated to design a completely fair evaluation of their programs and to present the findings in an accurate and evenhanded manner, or should they have some latitude for slanting the design and results? These are real questions for many administrators, and yet they have rarely been discussed in essays on ethics and the public service.

DIFFERENT TYPES OF GOOD

At root, most of these dilemmas arise from the pulls on the administrator created by different conceptions of the good to be promoted through public service. In many cases the tugging is not between perceived good and evil, but between two or more incompatible goods. Should I advance my own career interest or the mission of my agency? With the discretion that I have available, should I assist the constituencies on whose good will my agency's success depends, or pursue a larger notion of the public interest? At times, of course, an excess of one good can become an evil, as when the pursuit of careerism becomes blind ambition or service to clientele groups turns into supine deference. For present purposes it will be helpful to consider four kinds of good commonly sought by public officials, and the generic ethical dilemmas that they occasion.

The first two goods can be called external, for their prime beneficiaries lie outside the public agency. The broader of the two is the *public interest*, which is concerned with promoting and protecting the common good. As John Rawls observes, "The common good I think of as certain general conditions that are in an appropriate sense equally to everyone's advantage."[25] The public interest is not the same as what the public wants or the sum of the goods and services that the public requires. Rather, it is the set of conditions and outcomes providing advantage to the society as a whole. Although the specific content of the public interest can never be established in any precise fashion, its absence can be noted in undue concessions to special interests and in violations of procedural safeguards designed to protect the public at large. Of more narrow scope are *constituency interests*, or the goods sought by interest groups within the public. Most writers on democratic pluralism recognize both the legitimacy and the limits of serving these special interests. Without the impetus provided by political parties, clientele groups, and other constituency interests legislatures would often not be moved to act on pressing matters of the common good. Yet carried too far the tending of constituencies can lead to favoritism in dispensing benefits, partiality in the interpretation of regulations, and other abuses of the public interest.

Internal goods include the bureaucratic interest of the agency and the personal interest of the official. *Bureaucratic interest* commonly takes two forms: expansionism, such as seeking a larger staff, an augmented budget, broader jurisdiction, or other sources of organizational power; and protectionism, or the defense of the agency's domain against encroachment by other power contenders. These tendencies have been well documented for private as well as public agencies.[26] *Personal interest* is the individual pursuit of private advantage in the public service. The most common forms include attempts by officials to gain rapid promotions, to increase their political "clout" through internal and external connections, and to enhance their economic position by catering to special interests.

The core ethical dilemmas of administrative discretion arise from tensions among the four kinds of good. Some are conflicts between external and internal goods. Officials who push through a shoddy program to fortify a bureau's competitive advantage would be sacrificing the public to bureaucratic interest. Those who press for a program to strengthen their agency's hand at the expense of minority groups would be placing bureaucratic above constituency interests. Civil servants who sabotage an otherwise sound social program to gain a rapid promotion would be elevating their personal interest above the public interest. And a program manager who relaxes controls on the safety of contraceptive testing in the hope of winning a comfortable postretirement position with a drug company would be giving priority to personal over constituency interests. There are also potential conflicts between personal and bureaucratic interests and between constituency interests and the public interest. The former would be seen when a public official takes actions damaging his agency's image and standing with Congress in order to secure a better position in a rival bureau. The latter would occur when officials struggle with the balance to be struck between tax incentives for oil companies and the demands of the public interest for an equitable system of taxation.

The broad specifications for an ethics of discretion can now be set forth. Above all, the principles introduced should help the public official to resolve the dilemmas just outlined. This criterion rules out two approaches to the ethics of the public service. One is the search for institutional devices to promote ethical behavior and to prevent abuses of power. For example, in *Morality and Administration in Democratic Government* Paul Appleby singles out politics and hierarchy as institutional safeguards of the public interest. While valuable for governmental design, Appleby's model offers the public official little assistance on the ethical use of discretion within an existing system. Also of little value are the many treatises advocating universal moral virtues and strength of character as guarantors of ethical behavior. Prudence, justice, temperance, fortitude, loyalty, integrity, honor, and similar qualities are assuredly assets for the public official, but their implications for resolving dilemmas of discretion are often not obvious. The present quest is for moral principles that are neither properties of administrative systems nor diffuse qualities of individual character, but rather standards for adjudicating the competing moral claims arising in the exercise of administrative discretion.

ASSUMPTIONS ABOUT RESPONSIBILITY

Any ethics of discretion will rest on fundamental assumptions about the level of rationality and responsibility that we can expect of the individual official. The venerable debates in political theory over "realism" and "idealism" are as salient to organizations as to nation states. Shall we assume, following Machiavelli, Hobbes, and other "realists," that officials will invariably and selfishly pursue their own interests? If so, the search for an ethics of individual discretion would be largely superfluous, and our time would be better spent devising bureaucratic social contracts to regulate the contests for power. Or shall we accept the "idealist" view that reason does, or can be made to, prevail among public servants? In this case we should perfect the government's structure of hierarchy and rules, and instill these into public officials. Or shall we opt, with Reinhold Niebuhr, for a middle ground in which the interplay of interests is tempered by reason and responsibility?[27]

Given the state of organization theory these are not idle questions. One school of thought, which might be termed *administrative Darwinism*, holds that public officials are basically players in games of self-interest.[28] In this view officials are best viewed as bureaucratic politicians in search of power. Their modus operandi includes bargaining, strategic misrepresentation, intimidation, manipulation of information, and like tactics. The principal restraint, like the dominant motive, is self-interest, including a fear of detection, prosecution, reprimands, or other actions undercutting one's position in the arena of power. Personal ethics is largely irrelevant, for officials will never subordinate self-interest to altruism. The best means for insuring "ethical" behavior is to promote a healthy competition of interests with a few regulations to prevent flagrant abuses.

At the opposite end of the spectrum is a view that might be termed *Weberian idealism*. According to this school the public official should be guided above all by obedience to constituted authority, and specifically to superiors in the bureaucracy. The dutiful civil servant will be distinguished by informed compliance with all legitimate bureaucratic norms, including rules, regulations, manuals of approved procedures, clearances, and concurrences. The chief restraint on inappropriate means is obedient professionalism, a combination of conformity with directives from above and an internalized understanding of proper behavior for the career official. The place of ethics is to encourage and guide professional behavior, especially working within the chain of command. Constituency mobilization without the direction or consent of superiors, unofficial deals with allies in other agencies, end runs to circumvent the administrative hierarchy, and similar tactics are not the proper subject for an ethics of the public service, for they, like sin, should simply not occur. The norms for proper behavior are best expressed in Weber's ideal type of bureaucracy.[29]

Both views present enormous difficulties for an ethics of discretion. Administrative Darwinism effectively denies the need for such an ethics, arguing instead for the hidden hand of competing interests. Weberian idealism is more open to ethics, but would define it so narrowly that some of the largest areas for the exercise of discretion would be ruled out as illegitimate. The middle ground adopted for this essay might be called *dialectical acccountability*. Its key assumptions are that (1) the exercise of discretion is not only legitimate but unavoidable; (2) the pursuit of personal, bureaucratic, and constituency interests is morally acceptable provided that it does not work against the public interest or create other significant harms; and (3) public officials are neither fully rational in their administrative actions nor totally lacking in rationality. They rarely if ever seek all the possible alternatives for action, search for all the information relevant to each alternative, and weigh the advantages and disadvantages of each option for choice. But at the same time they are not blindly driven by organizational routines and by self-interest, so that reason can influence their decisions. Accountability is thus dialectical in the sense that moral choice involves the competing pulls of routine and reason, obedience and initiative, narrow interest and the public interest.

FIVE ETHICAL PRINCIPLES

Within the framework of dialectical accountability five ethical principles can provide guidance on the exercise of discretion. They are by no means exhaustive, nor are they always specific in their implications. No ethical standards, least of all those embracing a dialectical perspective, can provide a road map of moral behavior for the public official. The best that we can hope for is some signposts pointing toward the responsible and away from the irresponsible use of discretion. Here, as elsewhere in ethics, there will be more agreement on the paths to be avoided — the flagrant abuses of administrative power — than on the positive directions for discretion. Still it would be no small accomplishment if we could agree on the approximate boundaries of ethical behavior in the public service.

PUBLIC ORIENTATION

The first and most general principle is that the exercise of discretion should, on balance, serve the public interest. This does not mean that discretionary choices must be emptied of personal, bureaucratic, or constituency interests. Quite the contrary, there are many instances in which the public is best served by officials who appeal to private interests in mobilizing support for sound policies. Stephen Bailey states this point very well.

It is in appreciating the reality of self interest that public servants find some of the strongest forces for motivating behavior — public and private. Normally speaking, if a public interest is to be orbited, it must have as part of its propulsive fuel a number of special and particular interests. A large part of the art of public service is in the capacity to harness private and personal interests to public interest causes. Those who will not traffic in personal and private interests (if such interests are themselves within the law) to the point of engaging their support on behalf of causes in which both public and private interests are served are, in terms of moral temperament, unfit for public responsibility.[30]

Yet the public interest must be paramount for the responsible administrator, for it is the only one of the four goods that is fairly immune to selfish consideration. The pursuit of personal and professional interests is legitimate to a point, but it is easily susceptible to abuse. Loyalty to one's agency can and should be required of any public official, but it, too, can be abused when the quest for bureaucratic influence becomes an end in itself. And, as Bailey suggests, the astute administrator will and at times should tend the interests of relevant constituency groups. No apologies are needed for such service, nor for the return of favors to the agency, but the moral acceptability of these transactions ultimately depends on their consonance with the public interest. In the end, the common good must stand above the other three goods and act as the arbiter of ethical ambiguities in the use of discretion.[31]

The Methadone Maintenance Program suggests instances of possible conflict between personal and public interests. The initiator, Gordon Chase, was moved personally by the deaths and crime brought on by heroin use, and felt that other agencies were not doing enough to deal with the problem. At the same time, he also appears to have been motivated by a combination of personal and bureaucratic interests.

Chase was the first non-M.D. ever appointed to a high policymaking role in the health area. By nature, Chase was an aggressive manager. Given the importance of this job, and the close public scrutiny that would be given to his performance, Chase's natural aggressiveness was enhanced.[32]

While the information presented does not allow us to determine the balance between private and public interests, the case does raise some questions. If Chase's entry into the heroin field was prompted mainly by the desire to have new outlets for his "natural aggressiveness," one would want to know if such behavior was consistent with the public interest. Even more serious questions would arise if the cost of seizing the initiative for heroin was a deterioration in other health services under Chase's jurisdiction. Similar questions could be raised if, to enhance his own reputation as an effective manager of the methadone program, Robert Newman siphoned off the best talent from other parts of New York's health care system with a consequent reduction in services. The case material is inconclusive on all of these points, but it does highlight potential areas of concern.

REFLECTIVE CHOICE

A common barrier to the responsible use of discretion is the tendency for officials to follow, with little or no reflection, the organizational routines and conventional wisdom of their agencies. As March and Simon have pointed out, officials in most organizations operate under conditions of "bounded rationality."[33] Rather than approaching each new decision as a fresh exercise in conscious choice, they are inclined to follow the established procedures for generating decision-alternatives, evaluating those alternatives, and choosing. This is often not a matter of obedience to superiors who give orders, but of submission to operating procedures that may never have been ordered at all.

The second ethical principle, called reflective choice, enjoins the public official to push back some of the individual and organizational bounds on rationality so that deliberation may take place. Its purpose is essentially to make the official aware that discretion is, in fact, being used when otherwise these decisions might be passed off as "routine." The principle is dialectic in that it works at the junction of the deterministic forces of context and the liberating forces of consciousness.

Concretely, I posit that (1) the decisionmaking behavior of public officials will inevitably be influenced by environmental pressures and individual limitations of capacity and motivation; but that (2) within this context there is still ample scope for reflective choice. Official A may not be fully responsible for the fact that alternatives X and Y are not before her, but she can engage in sensible deliberation about the merits of those two possibilities. An ethics of discretion urging officials to soar above their bureaucratic context would be ethereal; one allowing them to dissolve into that context would be superfluous. Reflective choice lies on a plane between disembodied rationality and fatalistic realism.

A cardinal obligation of reflective choice is to be explicitly aware of the underpinnings of the problems addressed by public policy. Most policies are explicitly or implicitly aimed at resolving some "problem." Gordon Chase pushed through a methadone program to deal with the "heroin problem." Reimert Ravenholt and his allies urge attention to the "population problem." Policymakers are currently considering various measures for dealing with the "problem" of illegal immigration from Mexico. Astute politicians have long recognized that stirring concern about a deeply felt but vaguely articulated "problem" is a crucial prerequisite for effective action. After reviewing eight kinds of social interventions, Bermant and Warwick concluded:

If a modern Machiavelli were to compose a handbook called *The Intervenor*, she or he might begin with the axiom that the intervenor's most important task is defining the problem to be solved in a way that minimizes impediments to solution. In particular, the intervenor should define the problem so as to forestall the need to justify the intervention. If one does not have to explain why intervention is necessary, one can move quickly to consider how to accomplish it.[34]

The cases suggest that the most effective way to legitimate intervention is to portray it as promoting health or eliminating illness. These notions "evoke such reflexive responses of acquiescence that the targets are likely to consider it precarious, if not sacrilegious, to challenge diagnoses made in those terms."[35]

What, precisely, is a problem? Following Ralph Potter, we may say that this concept has three components:

— a *value:* a conception of some good to be promoted (health, welfare) or an evil to be avoided (poverty, illness, chaos);
— *facts:* empirical assertions about the area in question ("there are over 100 thousand heroin users on the streets of New York"); and
— *connection between facts and value:* statements indicating how the facts cited actually bear upon the value to be promoted or protected ("heroin users on the streets of New York are a major source of crime on the streets").[36]

Reflective choice implies, as a minimum, that public officials be clear about the values to be promoted or protected, rather than embrace them without examination; be reasonably sure that the information used is adequate and reliable; and be consciously persuaded that assertions linking facts to values are soundly based. Public orientation dictates that the values adopted should not unfairly reflect the biases or interests of a narrow segment of the society. Veracity, the next principle, enjoins against conscious distortion or falsification of information to foster a greater sense of urgency about the values at stake.

How well did Gordon Chase meet these criteria in establishing the New York methadone program? According to the case study by Moore and Ziering, Chase was consciously guided by a concern for two negative values: preventing death among heroin addicts, and reducing crime.[37] The key factual assertions were that (1) large numbers of addicts were dying of heroin overdoses; and (2) crime rates were skyrocketing. The connection between the factual assertion and the value of preventing illness seems straightforward: about 100 persons per month suffered death as a direct result of heroin consumption. In the case of heroin and crime, the connection is open to some question. Chase stated his belief succinctly:

The second thing was that all the crime rates were skyrocketing and particularly crimes that were considered to be addict-related like crimes against property: burglary, robbery, car theft . . . so that at that time drug addiction was starting to be considered the number 1 problem in the city.[38]

It seems doubtful that Chase critically examined the evidence linking drug addiction to crime in a direct, causal manner. Yet this connection was the prime basis for his judgment that drug addiction was the "number 1 problem" in New York. The case leaves the impression that Chase rather uncritically accepted a problem definition that was in the air and decided to get on with solving it.

Reflective choice also demands that public officials establish a plausible link between their proposed policy alternatives and the problem to be solved. One wonders if Gordon Chase, with the benefit of hindsight, would have been as optimistic as he was about the potential of methadone programs for reducing crime. Ethical responsibility does not demand that public officials become professional policy analysts, sifting pounds of murky concepts and tons of muddy data. But it does require that officials make a conscious and determined effort to ask explicitly about the connection between policies and outcomes, rather than take them for granted, and seek the best possible answer in the time available.

VERACITY

The third guiding principle is veracity, or truthfulness in the discharge of official responsibilities. Applied to the public service, veracity has three implications. The first is the obligation to avoid lying. While there has been much debate about whether official lies should be permitted for higher goods, such as national security, even the most ardent defenders of deception acknowledge that it should be exceptional. The general case against lying, and especially its cost for trust, has been admirably stated by Sissela Bok. As she observes, "*Whatever* matters to human beings, trust is the atmosphere in which it thrives."[39] In the specific context of the public service, lying or the suspicion of lying by officials has an added consequence—the proliferation of bureaucracy. When congressmen and other authorities distrust the information given to them by career officials or political appointees, they commonly establish their own mechanisms for cross-checking. These often take the form of staff assistants who pry into the innards of the bureaucracy and other bureaucratic controls, such as concurrence requirements, which retard governmental action.

The second implication of veracity is the obligation to be truthful in presenting information to superiors and to the public. There is a difference between an outright lie and a biased or distorted presentation of the truth. This distinction is aptly illustrated by Gordon Chase's memorandum to the Narcotics Control Council. In this document he proposed to establish "a citywide methadone maintenance treatment program to service 15,600 addicts over a twelve month period."[40] Yet in sending the memorandum to Robert Morganthau, the deputy mayor, he admitted:

The projection of 15,600 addicts in a 12-month period is plainly on the optimistic side—and may very well be downright unrealistic. However, this also doesn't strike me as particularly serious at this point (a) since it is probably well to set our sight high at the outset and (b) since—if we need it—we can always take more than 12 months to reach our 15,600 goal.[41]

The most reasonable interpretation is that Chase wanted to stir up interest in his proposal by making an exaggerated claim for the number of addicts likely to be reached, and yet did not wish to be caught in his own embroidery if the prediction did not materialize. Thus he sent the unqualified proposal to the Narcotics Control Council, but covered himself with his superiors in the mayor's office. He later justified this tactic on the grounds that the outlandish proposal was necessary to get people thinking about large programs, and to create "momentum." By the standards proposed here, these objectives, however laudable, would not justify the distortions of truth in the initial memorandum.

But there is another notion which may qualify the straightforward criterion of truthfulness in the public service. This is the concept of truth in the aggregate as distinct from truthfulness in any individual presentation. The prototype would be a policy arena in which five agencies of roughly equal strength are contending for influence on program design. Each is identified with a certain approach, and each is well armed with information designed to bolster that emphasis. In these circumstances it seems ethically justified for officials to present just one side of a case, provided that they do not introduce any false, distorted, or highly unreliable evidence. The reason is that the public, represented by the policymakers listening to the information, will have ample opportunity to sort out the truth of the matter by hearing five different perspectives on the same problem. Indeed, in many cases the possibilities for rational deliberation are enhanced by such advocacy. Hence where all contenders and the judges know that advocacy is the order of the day and that any single presentation is partial to a certain viewpoint, the test of truthfulness is met if officials make their case without significantly misrepresenting the truth. Where, on the other hand, a bureau or agency has virtually monopolistic control over the supply of information, truthfulness would require a more balanced presentation.

Veracity has, as a third implication, the obligation to respect the ability of others to gather and present true information relevant to public policy. This obligation has to do with the politics of data-gathering and reporting in the federal government. While AID's Office of Population need not go out of its way to support studies challenging its view of the "population problem," truthfulness would require that it not try to prevent or suppress such studies. Neither should a powerful bureau director, such as Raven-holt, use his or her discretion on funding to intimidate those who might come up with findings unpopular to the agency, or to pressure recipients for the "right" results. In the 1970s there was a running debate between the Office of Population and the U.S. Bureau of the Census about demo-graphic data on the impact of family planning programs. Census Bureau officials complained privately to the author about undue pressures for the "right" results, while Ravenholt argued that these officials were overly cautious and based their projections on obsolete data. Whatever the truth in that particular debate, it illustrates the twin dangers of administrative power and bureaucratic hesitation for veracity in the public service.

PROCEDURAL RESPECT

How should a responsible civil servant regard established procedures — the rules, regulations, clearances, manual orders, and precedents that are the stuff of bureaucracy? Every official knows that procedures can be es-tablished for the most flimsy reasons, including vanity and spite, and still acquire the same binding force as rules anchored in solid experience. Yet established procedures are perhaps the single most important source of accountability in the public bureaucracy. Stephen Bailey writes:

Rules, standards, procedures exist, by and large, to promote fairness, openness, depth of analysis, and accountability in the conduct of the pub-lic's business. Those who frequently by-pass or shortcut established means are thereby attacking one aspect of that most precious legacy of the past: the rule of law. Official whim is the enemy of a civilized order.[42]

What we can ask of the public servant is not reflexive compliance with every jot and tittle of the rulebook, but a fundamental respect for estab-lished procedure. The accountable official should neither be awed by nor scornful of an agency's rules. The essence of respect is not mindless deference but a willingness to show consideration for the established ways of handling the government's business. At times the procedures may have to be circumvented in the public interest and at other times they may have to be changed. But respect demands that such actions be the exception rather than the rule, and a last rather than a first resort. As Bailey notes, "The public servant who cannot recognize the paradoxes of procedures will be trapped by them. For in the case of procedures, he who deviates frequently is subversive; he who never deviates at all is lost; and he who tinkers with procedures without an understanding of substantive consequence is foolish."[43]

If procedures are neither sacrosanct nor senseless, what principles should guide decisions about exceptions? The most obvious and general principle is that established procedures should be observed unless there are compelling reasons for deviations. In seeking a principle to cover deviations, we might take as a model Kant's Categorical Imperative: "Act only on that maxim whereby thou canst at the same time will that it should become a universal law." Applied to the present question, Kant's norm might be restated as the Law of Procedural Reciprocity: "Seek exceptions to established procedures only when you would grant the same right to others in comparable circumstances." By introducing the notion of reciprocity in procedural deviations, this principle would rule out the great majority of potential exceptions to agency rules. Proponents of a deviation would have to demonstrate that their claims supersede those of others, and to accept that these others should, if they have equivalent claims, also be exempt.

By this standard, the officials in New York's Department of Real Estate (DRE) were fully justified in refusing to be hurried by representatives of Chase's methadone program. Their position seemed to be, "If we make exceptions for you people, we will have to make them for a lot of others whose requests are just as urgent as yours." DRE officials, moreover, may have felt uncomfortable with the idea of having to decide which of the city's programs deserved priority treatment. It is for this reason that such agencies often develop the operating rule of "first come, first served." While one could certainly not fault the methadone staff for seeking action as quickly as possible, it is hard to see that their efforts warranted special consideration. The critical question, as old-line officials would surely point out, is one of fairness. A bureaucracy simply cannot function with rules that are outnumbered by exceptions, and with procedural arrangements perceived as personalistic or otherwise inequitable.

RESTRAINT ON MEANS

Finally, the responsible public official will exercise restraint on the means chosen to accomplish organizational ends. Restraint begins as reflective choice, but becomes reflection guided by the public interest. This standard requires the official to hold back from using means that violate the law or the civil liberties of individuals, entail unfairness in the application of laws or administrative regulations, produce unjustifiable physical, mental, or social harm, or undermine citizen trust in government. The dialectic of accountability involves a tension between restraint carried to the point of inertia and a blind commitment to "results." The public is served neither by the risk-averse functionary nor by the proto-doer who delivers first and asks questions later.

The absence of restraint is well illustrated in the activities of the Central Intelligence Agency and the Nixon White House. Convinced that the end of national security justified almost any conceivable means, the CIA concentrated its efforts on the perfection of strategies and techniques. Thus if consciousness-altering drugs were a viable tool of national security, they could be tested on agency employees and others without informed consent and with no regard for harmful consequences. The suicide of Frank Olson, a scientist at the CIA, is testimony to the triumph of means over ethics. To judge from the spate of Watergate books, the Nixon White House was similarly motivated. The guiding question for many was not "how should we use discretion in the public interest?" but "how far can we go in pushing for the president's interest?" In *Blind Ambition* John Dean remarks:

For a thousand days I would serve as counsel to the President. I soon learned that to make my way upward, into a position of confidence and influence, I had to travel downward through factional power plays, corruption and finally outright crimes. Although I would be rewarded for diligence, true advancement would come from doing those things which built a common bond of trust — or guilt — between me and my superiors. In the Nixon White House, these upward and downward paths diverged, yet joined, like prongs of a tuning fork pitched to a note of expediency.[44]

Another example of the lack of restraint is AID's pressure on Philippine population programs to meet certain quotas for the delivery of contraception and sterilization. From all indications AID's urgings at the top were passed down the line of several programs, with the result that some clinic workers felt pressure to come up with acceptable numbers of clients. To the extent that AID's proddings simply encouraged clinic staff to work harder without violating their own professional and moral standards or abusing client trust, there would be no cause for ethical concern. But where the net effect was to encourage the medical staff to sell sterilizations to those who might prefer some other method, or to press for IUD insertions among women who sought a different contraceptive, the AID officials creating such pressures would be ethically accountable.

As a general rule, public officials are accountable for abuses that can reasonably be expected to flow from their pressures on others. Since abuses such as those described can never be entirely avoided, and the public interest is normally served by effective management practices, it is difficult to draw an exact line between acceptable and unacceptable pressures for results. The dialectical perspective, however, suggests a criterion which may resolve some of the doubt: the extent to which monitoring to prevent abuses is as strong as pressures to produce results. Where the penalties for neglecting safeguards are weaker than those for failing to meet quotas, the administrator could fairly be criticized on ethical grounds. Here, as elsewhere in the exercise of discretion, the test of ethical behavior is not the presence of abuses, which may be inescapable, but the overall balance of responsibility shown by the officials involved.

CONCLUSION

In this essay, I raise some basic questions about the kind of public servant who best serves the public, and suggest some answers. From an ethical standpoint is there room for ambition, even strong ambition, in the public service? Yes, provided that it is not blind and is directed toward the common good. Firmly secured to the public interest, the striving for success can be the flywheel of organizational action; unhitched from that axle it can sunder a government agency. And what is the place of courage? Do we want a bureaucracy populated with pusillanimous paper pushers, or should we seek the plucky, the spunky, and the nervy? Again it is a matter of balance. No public service could survive if its entire staff were modeled after Gordon Chase and Reimert Ravenholt, and few would attain distinction without leaders of their mettle. One reason that these individuals proved to be a rich source of examples was that they had the courage to break through the myriad obstacles to action in governmental service. "Perhaps the most essential courage in the public service," writes Stephen Bailey, "is the courage to decide. For if it is true that all policies have bittersweet consequences, decisions invariably produce hurt."[45] But fortitude and nerve must be geared to the public interest and be tempered by reflection, truthfulness, and restraint on means. This is an essential point of dialectical accountability.

The key question for an ethics of administrative discretion is responsibility in the generation and use of power. To develop a meaningful ethics of discretion we must lay to rest the notion that power is a fixed quantum entrusted to those at the top of a bureaucracy and dispensed in small parcels to those below. Power is created, destroyed, and applied at all levels of a public agency. And, *pace* Acton, it need not corrupt nor corrupt absolutely. The lack of power can be quite as corrupting to public officials, and quite as deleterious to the public interest, as a surfeit of discretion. In most circumstances the critical question is not whether officials should have discretion but when, how, and for what purposes it should be used. The criteria suggested here — public orientation, reflective choice, veracity, procedural respect, and restraint on means — may provide the embryo of an answer.

NOTES

This essay has profited greatly from the comments and suggestions of Stephen Bailey, Sissela Bok, James T. Burtchaell, and Reimert Ravenholt.

1. See G. T. Allison, *Essence of Decision* (Boston: Little, Brown, 1967); J. Pressman and A. Wildavsky, *Implementation: How Great Expectations in Washington Are Dashed in Oakland* (Berkeley: University of California Press, 1973); M. Halperin, *Bureaucratic Politics and Foreign Policy* (Washington, D.C.: The Brookings Institution, 1974); D. Warwick, in collaboration with M. Meade and T. Reed, *A Theory of Public Bureaucracy: Politics, Personality, and Organization in the State Department* (Cambridge, Mass.: Harvard University Press, 1975).

2. The principal source for this case is M. H. Moore and M. Ziering, "Methadone Maintenance (B); the Entrepreneur's View," case study prepared for use at the Kennedy School of Government, Harvard University, 1976.

3. The discussion of the Office of Population is based on two major sources: my own research on this agency between 1974 and 1979, and P. T. Piotrow, *World Population Crisis: The United States Response* (New York: Praeger, 1973).

4. Quoted in Piotrow, *World Population Crisis*, p. 45.

5. R. M. Susman, "Drug Abuse, Congress, and the Fact-Finding Process," *Annals of the American Academy of Political and Social Science* (1975), 417:16-26.

6. Office of Population, "Population Policy Development: Objectives, Strategic Concepts, Current Activities and a Draft Action Agenda for FY 76-78," unpublished paper, Agency for International Development, Washington, D.C., January 13, 1975.

7. Piotrow, *World Population Crisis*, p. 158.

8. Moore and Ziering, "Methadone Maintenance (B)," pp. 6-7.

9. See Pressman and Wildavsky, *Implementation*; E. Bardach, *The Implementation Game* (Cambridge, Mass.: MIT Press, 1978); B. Radin,

Implementation, Change, and the Federal Bureaucracy: School Desegregation Policy in H.E.W., 1964-1968 (New York: Teachers College Press, 1977); and A. F. Wichelman, "Administrative Agency Implementation of the National Environmental Policy Act of 1969: A Conceptual Framework for Explaining Differential Response," *Natural Resources Journal* (1976), 16:236-300.

10. Moore and Ziering, "Methadone Maintenance (B)," p. 14.

11. Ibid.

12. See A. S. Blumberg, "Drug Control: Agenda for Repression," in *Drug Abuse Control*, ed. Richard L. Rachin and Eugene Czajkoski (Lexington, Mass.: Lexington Books, 1975), pp. 1-34.

13. T. Szasz, *Ceremonial Chemistry: The Ritual Persecution of Drugs, Addicts, and Pushers* (Garden City, N.Y.: Anchor Press/Doubleday, 1974), p. xv.

14. Moore and Ziering, "Methadone Maintenance (B)," p. 14.

15. S. Gadalla, S. Mehanna, and C. Tennant, *Country Report: Egypt. Cultural Values and Population Policies* (Cairo: Social Research Center, American University of Cairo, 1977), pp. 96-97.

16. Pressman and Wildavsky, *Implementation*.

17. E. T. Hilton and A. A. Lumsdaine, "Field Trial Designs in Gauging the Impact of Fertility Planning Programs," in *Evaluation and Experiment*, ed. C. A. Bennett and A. A. Lumsdaine (New York: Academic Press, 1975), pp. 319-408.

18. Hilton and Lumsdaine, "Field Trial Designs"; J. Reynolds, "Evaluation of Family Planning Program Performance: A Critical Review," *Demography* (1972), 9:69-85.

19. For a general critique of the survey methods used for planning and evaluating population programs see A. Marino, "KAP Surveys and the Politics of Family Planning," *Concerned Demography* (1971), 3:36-75.

20. Moore and Ziering, "Methadone Maintenance (B)," p. 40.

21. E. J. Epstein, "Methadone: The Forlorn Hope," *Public Interest* (Summer 1974), pp. 3-24.

22. Ibid., p. 19.

23. Ibid.

24. Ibid., p. 22.

25. J. Rawls, *A Theory of Justice* (Cambridge, Mass.: Harvard University Press, 1971), p. 246.

26. See J. Thompson, *Organizations in Action* (New York: McGraw-Hill, 1967); W. H. Starbuck, "Organizational Growth and Development," in *Handbook of Organizations*, ed. J. G. March (Chicago: Rand McNally, 1965); and D. T. Dickson, "Narcotics and Marijuana Laws: Two Case Studies in Bureaucratic Growth and Survival," in *Drug Abuse Control*, ed. Richard L. Rachin and Eugene Czajkoski (Lexington, Mass.: Lexington Books, 1975), pp. 35-49.

27. The two works that best summarize Niebuhr's views on this question are: R. Niebuhr, *Moral Man and Immoral Society* (New York: Charles Scribner's Sons, 1932) and *Man's Nature and His Communities* (New York: Charles Scribner's Sons, 1965).

28. The view of organizations as arenas for games of power has been set forth most clearly in Allison, *Essence of Decision*. This approach is also seen in Halperin, *Bureaucratic Politics and Foreign Policy*, and especially in Bardach, *The Implementation Game*. As suggested by his title, Bardach seems to argue that implementation and organizations more generally are nothing but a set of games played by ill-defined rules. While the games analogy is not without merit as a lens for viewing public organizations, it carries strong overtones of cynicism and implies that in the perceptual world of the "players" there is little room for moral discretion. The anti-ethical bias is reinforced by the latent sense that the substance of what is being done is essentially amoral and even unimportant, while what truly counts is scoring points, or ultimately, winning. This seems to me a distortion and, in the extreme, a trivialization of what actually happens in the public service.

29. M. Weber, *The Theory of Social and Economic Organization*, trans. and ed. A. M. Henderson and T. Parsons (New York: Oxford University Press, 1947).

30. S. K. Bailey, "Ethics and the Public Service," in *Public Administration and Democracy*, ed. R. C. Martin (Syracuse: Syracuse University Press, 1965), pp. 283-298.

31. I am much indebted to James Burtchaell for helping me to clarify the position of the public interest vis-à-vis the other goods mentioned.

32. Moore and Ziering, "Methadone Maintenance (B)," p. 40.

33. J. G. March and H. Simon, *Organizations* (New York: John Wiley and Sons, 1958).

34. G. Bermant and D. P. Warwick, "The Ethics of Social Intervention: Power, Freedom, and Accountability," in *The Ethics of Social Intervention*, ed. G. Bermant, H. C. Kelman, and D. P. Warwick (Washington, D.C.: Hemisphere Publishing Company, 1978), p. 382.

35. Ibid.

36. The formulation summarized here is based on an oral presentation by Ralph Potter at a conference on international population held at the Hastings Center in 1973. For a related discussion see R. Potter, "The Simple Structure of the Population Debate: The Logic of the Ecology Movement," in *Population Policy and Ethics: The American Experience*, ed. R. Veatch (New York: Irvington Publishers, 1977), pp. 347-363.

37. Moore and Ziering, "Methadone Maintenance (B)," p. 3.

38. Ibid.

39. S. Bok, *Lying: Moral Choice in Public and Private Life* (New York: Pantheon Books, 1978).

40. Moore and Ziering, "Methadone Maintenance (B)," p. 5.

41. Ibid.

42. Bailey, "Ethics and the Public Service," pp. 291-292.

43. Ibid., p. 292.

44. J. Dean, *Blind Ambition: The White House Years* (New York: Simon and Schuster, 1976).

45. Bailey, "Ethics and the Public Service," p. 296.

II. Defining the Public Interest

Charles Wolf, Jr.

5. Ethics and Policy Analysis

I learn a good deal by merely observing you,
And letting you talk as long as you please,
And taking note of what you do not say.

— T.S. Eliot, *The Cocktail Party**

In discussions of ethics and policy analysis, two questions are important to distinguish but are often confused. The first concerns the fundamental ethical assumption that underlies policy analysis, is taken for granted by the institutions that sponsor the analyses, and is accepted (usually without examination) by the people who perform them. This fundamental assumption is that it is "better" — socially and individually, in general and in the long run — for society and its members to *analyze systematically* major issues of public policy: applying scientific methods to that analysis; subjecting the policy issues in question to an exacting process of compiling data, dissecting them, and trying to explain the relationships among the data; and attempting to predict (or "model") the consequences of possible policies, programs, or actions (or deliberate inactions) that may be chosen.

I refer to this as a fundamental ethical assumption for two obvious reasons: it is "ethical" because it relates to what is judged or presumed to be "better" for society and its members; and it is usually assumed rather than formally tested (although I would argue that there is a good deal of evidence to support it). It is worth noting that this assumption is not universally shared. It does not characterize other approaches to policy issues that are practiced and advocated.

What are some of these alternative approaches? They include reliance on intuition, or on revelation, scripture, the Koran, or *Das Kapital*, or on an oracular figure of some sort (wiseman, holyman, soothsayer, shaman,

*Harcourt Brace Jovanovich, 1964, reprinted with permission.

king, or dictator), or on discussion and bargaining among competing groups or interests to achieve consensus or, failing that, to arrive at compromises (again, without analysis as an important part of the process).

Most of these approaches share the view that systematic analysis, as I have described it, is irrelevant or inconsequential for arriving at "correct" decisions. Solutions instead are presumed to be known by someone, or to be embedded in some inclusive scripture. Hence, the proper recourse is to the qualified person in the former case, or to textual sifting and exegesis — a quite different sort of analysis — in the latter.

The discussion-and-bargaining approach differs from the others, but in a way that does not add very much to the role of policy analysis in policymaking. In this approach, a good policy choice is presumed to depend mainly on the process by which it is arrived at, rather than on its content or on the analysis that precedes it. Whether analysis is good or bad, complete or incomplete, accurate or not does not matter as long as the requisite discussion and bargaining proceed. Process is product, or at least dominates product.

The second ethical question concerns the choice of appropriate values, objectives, goals, and constraints to be adopted in specific policy studies. Expressed in more formal language, what should be the arguments in the utility function that is to be maximized? What should be the study's maximand? For example, should the appropriate goal or objective of a program or policy be to maximize total income (ignoring distributional consequences), or rather to maximize the income gains or the opportunities of a particular group (for example, the poor, the aged, minorities), or to maximize a particular type of benefit (say, housing, education, nutrition, clean air, family cohesion) for all, or for a particular group?

The observations I will make deal primarily with the second question. While this seems to me the more important and more constructive focus, this point of view can be challenged. Indeed, many people who regard themselves as professional ethicists and philosophers have the first question in mind when they address the subject of ethics in relation to policy analysis. To them, I have little to add to what seems to me a fairly sterile debate on whether or not it is "good" or "right" to analyze issues scientifically. I think the progress of civilization has been helped by extending the uses and reaches of systematic and scientific inquiry, rather than by restricting it. To be "cool and calculating" seems to me preferable to being "heated and emotional." It is indeed an essential part of what Walter Bagehot referred to as the "animated moderation" that characterizes a "polity of discussion" and contributes to progress and learning.[1]

SHORTCOMINGS AND IMPROVEMENTS

It is probably fair to criticize most policy analysis for defining too narrowly the objectives and constraints that are employed. Often the "values" (objectives, goals), in terms of which the predicted outcomes of alternative policies or programs are judged, have been chosen because they are convenient for the analysis and the analysts. These are not necessarily the objectives that are most appropriate or realistic, in the sense that they would be chosen or accepted by the public or by the constituencies on whom the policies or programs will impinge.

For example, the objective may be to maximize an income objective, or an educational or health objective (with the latter typically expressed in terms of some convenient intermediate or proxy measure, rather than in terms of educational or health outcome), for given dollar costs; or, alternatively, to minimize the dollar costs of achieving a satisfactory level of performance with respect to specific objectives so defined. Considerations of "justice" or "equity" — what particular groups benefit, and what groups pay, rather than how much are the total benefits and costs — are usually excluded, although not always.[2] It is even rarer, if indeed there are any precedents whatsoever, to find that the analysis includes consideration of such looser and still more elusive values as beauty, honor, and dignity among the objectives to be maximized, or the constraints to be adhered to in evaluating policy alternatives.

Even in those rare cases when distributional issues are considered, and attention is devoted to "justice" and "equity," inadequate attention is likely to be given to the wide range of standards that may be invoked for judging equity. Consider, for example, the differences, complexities, and ambiguities that result from interpreting equity according to various criteria: for example, equity in the sense of equality of opportunity; or equity in the sense of equality of outcome; or equity in the Rawlsian sense (that is, inequality can only be equitable if it is essential for providing advantage to the least favored);[3] or in the Kantian sense (the categorical imperative); or in the sense of "horizontal equity" (treating equally situated people equally) or "vertical equity" (treating unequally situated people in appropriately unequal ways); or in the Marxian sense ("from each according to ability, to each according to need"); or in the sense of the Old Testament; or in the sense of the New Testament.

Of course, observing that policy studies should give more attention to matters of equity, rather than focusing exclusively on efficiency, is only a part of the problem; and it is the easy part. The challenging and difficult part is *how* to do it: how to translate and transform the complexities pertaining to equity into practical terms, and into methods that can be employed effectively in policy analysis.

As previously noted, I think it is reasonable to criticize policy analysis and analysts for usually defining objectives, constraints, and costs too narrowly; once again, proceeding from analytic convenience rather than policy relevance. To put the point more formally, most policy analyses tend to define costs and benefits in terms of one or two dimensions, rather than the multiple dimensions that are really relevant for the policies being analyzed. For example, if alternative health insurance policies are being evaluated, the analysis clearly has to be concerned with their costs and with their expected effects on health status. But, in addition, a more complete analysis should address the probable impacts of the alternative policies on the health delivery system, on the behavior of physicians, and on the quality of care received by different social or income or ethic groups in society. In other words, a wider view of costs and consequences than one typically encounters in policy studies is desirable.

While granting and deploring these shortcomings of policy analysis as it is usually practiced, I believe that improvements are not likely to be found in exhortation about the importance of values and ethics, or high-sounding pleas to devote more attention to ethics. If discussion about the ethical dimensions of policy analysis is to progress from the fog of obscurantist rhetoric that has often surrounded it, that progress will be made by finding ways to bring broader values explicitly into the objective functions of policy studies, or to establish these values as constraints on the policy alternatives themselves.

How can equity considerations be introduced into policy studies, and what specific interpretation should be attached to equity among the alternative interpretations cited earlier? How different will the evaluation of alternatives be, depending on which meaning of equity or justice is used in the evaluation? And what methods can be employed to introduce still broader considerations relating to aesthetics, honor, dignity, human brotherhood, and so on?

I am not at all sure that this, or even most of it, can be done. Much of it may be genuinely beyond us. But if it is not beyond us, I am quite sure that we will need a lot of hard work, ingenuity, and inventiveness for these broader normative considerations to contribute to the improvement of policy analysis. Several examples suggest that encouraging, albeit modest, progress is currently being made along these lines.

One example is presented in a recent paper showing the diversity of equity criteria that can be formulated and applied for compensating those who are harmed by public policies and programs.[4] The various criteria correspond to some of the differing standards of equity referred to earlier: the Rawlsian standard of fairness, equality of opportunity, horizontal and vertical equity, and so on. In turn, the several criteria are used to derive compensation schemes to mitigate the losses imposed by regulation of fishing rights in a particular regional jurisdiction.

In a major policy study of alternative flood control projects in the North Sea estuary (the Oosterschelde) of the Netherlands, outcomes were evaluated according to a wide range of norms, including reduced risk of flood, environmental changes (and their effects on existing and new flora and fauna through the creation of a fresh water lake), losses and gains in recreational activities, and effects on oceangoing shipping.[5] Obviously, each of these norms reflects a different view of social values, of what is important to differing groups and interests in the Netherlands. The policy options (a massive and impermeable North Sea barrier, a storm-surge barrier with large flowthrough gates that would be closed during severe storms, and a system of large dikes around the estuary's perimeter to protect the land from floods) were evaluated according to these several norms, as well as the attendant costs and direct economic effects. The study's intention was to highlight the tradeoffs associated with each option, making the choice dependent on the relative weights assigned by Dutch policymakers to the conflicting norms.

A third example is provided by ongoing work comparing the effects of different health insurance systems, in terms of not only their economic costs but also their impact on the quality of health care. This is a most elusive concept. The innovation in analytic methods that I want to mention relates to the measurement of quality of care.

While one would like to measure quality in terms of medical outcome, this turns out to be extremely difficult for reasons having to do with the institutions of medical practice, with medical technology, and with the vagaries of medical recordkeeping and statistics. Pending progress on these intractable or at least difficult and resistant issues, quality is being evaluated according to two proxies: "best practice" (or acceptable practice) procedures; and patient "satisfaction." It is the latter proxy that directly relates to the normative and ethical matters of concern here. What is involved in this work is an attempt, by controlled experimentation and interviewing, to evaluate quality of care by trying to determine the *attitudes* and *perceptions* of patients concerning their health status, depending on the type and scope of health insurance in which they are enrolled.[6]

A variant of this approach has sought to determine the attitudes and feelings and satisfaction of patients depending on whether the ambulatory health care they received was directly provided by a physician or instead by physician's assistants or primary care nurse practitioners organized into teams with physician supervisors.[7] Attention to the feelings and attitudes of patients adds a new ethical dimension to the evaluation of quality of care. I might note in passing that this addition, while welcome and useful, is not without pitfalls and problems of its own. Using patient feelings and attitudes toward health care as a proxy for quality of care runs some obvious risks: for example, frill and deception might be substituted for substance, appearance might be emphasized at the expense of "the real thing," if the appearance or the frills make the patient more satisfied.

While other examples can be cited, the point is clear enough, even if it borders on the truistic: hard work, imagination, and ingenuity do result in progress toward bringing ethical and moral considerations more effectively into policy analysis. Even so, the progress we are likely to make in this way will be slow and only partial, under the best of circumstances. Whatever we are able to accomplish along these lines by hard work, ingenuity, and inventiveness, I think we must still look for wisdom, sensitivity, and good judgment to supplement the analysis. Clearly, these are attributes one would like to hope that policy analysts, and the university faculties who train them, possess or can acquire in some measure. Yet I would not want to rely as a matter of social policy on their acquisition and possession of these attributes in adequate measure. Nor do I think we know the best means for imparting these attributes, or nurturing the often modest natural endowments of them that one finds among students of policy analysis.

One approach to the cultivation of wisdom and moral sensitivity, currently much in vogue, is through using so-called "decision-forcing" cases in policy analysis curricula. These cases typically confront the student with a moral dilemma: for example, to withhold the truth or risk jeopardizing an important social program; to inflate a program's budget so as to provide a cushion against a budget cut or to estimate costs accurately; to "blow-the-whistle" on the practices of an agency or a senior official or to play it safe and try to remedy the practices from within. Wrestling with the dilemma may heighten moral sensitivity and develop ethical awareness. Or it may not do so. In passing, it is interesting to note that the curricula of many public policy programs are placing increased emphasis on the use of such decision-forcing cases at a time when law and business schools are having second thoughts about the possibly excessive emphasis they have accorded to such case materials.

Another approach is to expose students to the "great books," the moral philosophers, or the great thinkers and practitioners of policy analysis. Exposure to their writings and thought may incite and enhance the judgment and wisdom of the students by grounding them in a tradition which manifests these qualities. Herbert Goldhamer's *The Adviser* is perhaps the most notable exemplar of this approach.[8]

Still another approach is to sharpen the ethical sensibilities of students by giving them practice in applying differing criteria and differing objective functions in the formal evaluation of program alternatives. If the choice among policy options can be shown to be sensitive to the choice among criteria and objectives, perhaps the analyst's judgment and sensitivity and wisdom will be enhanced by the learning experience.

As I have said, we do not really know the best means of inculcating these crucial attributes. Consequently, using and testing all of them seems warranted. Doing so should be a high priority objective of the public management components of our curricula.

COMPATIBILITY OF ETHICS AND ANALYSIS: THE MORALITY OF ECONOMICS AND THE ECONOMICS OF MORALITY

We cannot be confident of our ability to acquire or to impart "wisdom," therefore we must devote more attention to what I alluded to earlier as a way of relating ethics to policy analysis: namely, a systematic and inventive effort to widen the scope of costs and benefits that are included in the objectives and constraints of actual policy studies. The aim of this widened range is to include in a tangible and accountable way the sorts of moral and ethical considerations whose absence in policy studies is frequently deplored by ethicists and philosophers.[9]

This way of formulating the issue is entirely compatible with the formal framework of policy analysis, including cost-benefit analysis, economic analysis, and other similar components of the larger field. It is not only compatible but, in my judgment, perhaps the only effective way of enhancing the moral content of policy analysis that is so strongly advocated elsewhere in this volume.

In asserting the fundamental compatibility between cost-benefit analysis on the one hand and ethical and moral considerations on the other, I disagree with Derek Bok, Daniel Callahan, and others who have repeatedly stressed their incompatibility.[10]

I was recently exposed to a somewhat exaggerated version of the incompatibility argument in the form of an invitation from one of the public policy schools to give a talk on "The Immorality of Economic Analysis." Although the title was perhaps intentionally hyperbolic—to stimulate audience interests rather than understanding, thereby posing a nice ethical issue in itself—it suggests a frame of reference very similar to the position I have associated with Bok: that is, economic analysis—attempting to calculate coolly (would heated calculations be preferable?) the precise costs and benefits associated with public policies and programs—is "immoral" because it ignores "higher" human values.

My own judgment leads in a different direction. In principle, *any* value, whether pecuniary or nonpecuniary, can be included in the maximand, or as a constraint on what is to be maximized. This can be done within the framework of economic analysis and cost-benefit analysis, *provided* we have the ingenuity and inventiveness to specify the relative importance of any particular value in comparison with other values, or, if not to do so ourselves as analysts, then to help the decisionmaker focus attention on this judgment.

Indeed, I would suggest that it makes far better sense to talk about the "economics of morality" than about the "immorality of economics,"[11] because the paradigm of economics is entirely consistent with, indeed is designed for, considering relationships among values. It is worth recalling that the standard title of economic treatises by the classical economists of the nineteenth century was "the theory of value." Of course, "value" was intended to mean "price": the theory of value dealt with the theory of price determination.

In more modern terminology, "price theory" is the core of microeconomic theory and economic analysis, including within it cost-benefit analysis. Microeconomic theory is fundamentally concerned with the determination and attribution of prices (that is, "values") to goods and services: equilibrium prices, shadow prices, monopoly prices, and so on. Essentially, the analysis of price determination is concerned with analyzing the forces and factors that determine the "value" of any good or service in terms of another good or service. The use of one "good," that is, money, as the numeraire in price theory readily permits a comparison to be made between any particular good or service and any other good or service simply in terms of their relative money prices.

This does not mean that money is the *only* value, or the only thing that matters. Nor does it preclude making the argument—whether persuasively or not—that some particularly cherished value defies monetary expression or that it transcends (that is, lexicographically dominates) all others. Using money as the numeraire simply means that money frequently turns out to be an extremely fruitful and convenient way of arriving at *relative* valuations among competing aims or goods.

Now I think it is fair to say that the position taken by Derek Bok and Daniel Callahan, as well as other professional philosophers concerned with ethics, tends to flout the relevance of price theory to ethics — hence the disparaging caption "the immorality of economics" referred to earlier. In contrast, I want to argue that there is a fundamental sense in which the notions, concepts, and framework embodied in price theory are likely to be central if we are to deal with ethical and moral issues in a usable and practical way in policy analysis.

I take as an initial premise that ethics is concerned with morality and moral values: individualism, freedom, truth, justice, love, beauty, generosity, humaneness, and tolerance. At a different level of aggregation, ethics is concerned with the values represented by the family, the neighborhood, future generations, and the environment. The issues for policy analysis are how to give recognition and attention to these values in formulating and evaluating alternative policies and programs in such fields as energy, health, education, defense, and social welfare, as well as how to provide recognition of these values in the implementation and management of public programs.

A second premise I would advance is that sometimes these "values" (or "goods") *conflict* with one another. If more of one value is to be sought and attained, it will likely be at some cost in terms of another value. Greater scope for freedom and individualism may result in outcomes that are inequitable or unjust. Generosity and humaneness may sometimes require a withholding of complete truth. Protecting and benefiting the family today may be at the expense of future generations. Preserving the environment for future generations may inflict costs and deprivations on living conditions for today's generation.

In the language of economics, or cost-benefit analysis, or policy analysis, there are "trade-offs" among social values and social goods just as there are trade-offs among private goods and values. These trade-offs can alternatively be expressed as "opportunity costs": the cost of one social or ethical value is the foregone opportunity to realize more of a conflicting ethical or moral value. The opportunity cost of achieving more of one ethical "value" is the "price" of that increment. More equal distribution of income and wealth may be achieved at a cost of less rapid growth. Legalized abortion enhances the freedom of women to make crucial personal decisions, but also rules out the potential freedom of aborted children to make *their* personal decisions. Insistence on cleaner air standards may be at the expense of greater vulnerability to an oil embargo, and so on.

Hence, I suggest that the tools and concepts of economic price theory (for example, demand functions, supply and production functions, possibility frontiers, substitution possibilities, and elasticities), are potentially useful and applicable to the analysis of ethical issues in connection with public policy. Opportunity costs are no less a characteristic of social and ethical values, or of morals, than they are of food, clothing, shelter, education, recreation, medical care, and other "economic" values.

An important conclusion follows from these two premises and the comments I have made about them: if ethical and moral values are to be better understood, and be more useful and more influential in public policy analysis and public management, then the opportunity costs associated with any single ethical value or group of values should be identified and evaluated in formulating and choosing among alternative courses of action. This is simply another way of expressing the point I made earlier: we should try to be more inventive and ingenious in seeking to introduce moral and ethical norms in the maximands, or alternatively as constraints, in policy studies. And, as I suggested earlier, notable, if modest, progress is being made along these lines.

Conflicts among values, and trade-offs between them, are frequent and typical, and they should occupy center stage when we address the subject of ethics and policy analysis. Nevertheless, it is also worth noting that there sometimes are instances where we can realize "trade-*ons*" among values: more of both economic and social well-being; more GNP *and* more equitable distribution; a healthier diet and also one that tastes better (at constant cost); a cleaner environment and also increased productivity; aesthetically pleasing housing at lower cost. Such instances of "trade-ons" or complementarities among values are usually less common than trade-offs and conflicts. But they should be sought, nonetheless. Programs and policies exhibiting such dominance are rare, hence especially to be esteemed when discovered or devised.

NOTES

1. See Bagehot's essay on the relationship between science and policy in his *Physics and Politics* (1867).

2. For two significant counterexamples see Charles Phelps and others, "Efficient Water Use in California: Executive Summary," The Rand Corporation, R-2385-CSA/RF (November 1978), and Adele Palmer and

others, "Chloroflurocarbon Emissions from Nonaerosol Applications," The Rand Corporation, R-2575-EPA (February 1980).

3. "All social primary goods—liberty and opportunity, income and wealth, and the bases of self-respect—are to be distributed equally unless an unequal distribution . . . is to the advantage of the least favored." See John Rawls, *A Theory of Justice* (Cambridge, Mass.: Harvard University Press, 1971), p. 303.

4. Joseph Cordes, Robert Goldfarb, and James Barth, " 'Equity' Criteria for Compensating Those Harmed by Public Actions," George Washington University, September 1980.

5. Bruce F. Goeller and others, "Protecting an Estuary from Floods—A Policy Analysis of the Oosterschelde," vol. I, "Summary Report," The Rand Corporation, R-2121/1-NETH (December 1977).

6. John E. Ware, Jr., and others, "Conceptualization and Measurement of Health for Adults in the Health Insurance Study," vol. I, "Model of Health and Methodology," The Rand Corporation, R-1987/1-HEW (May 1980), vol. V, "General Health Perceptions," R-1987/5-HEW (September 1978), and vol. VIII, "Overview," R-1978/8 (October 1979).

7. David Maxwell Jolly, "Patients' Acceptance of Physician's Assistants in Air Force Primary Medicine Clinics," The Rand Corporation, R-2620-AF (September 1980).

8. Herbert Goldhamer, *The Adviser* (New York: Elsevier-North Holland, Inc., 1978).

9. Although I have some quarrels with the particulars, I strongly endorse Duncan Macrae's efforts to integrate into policy analysis such normative stances as those relating to "the cost of stigma," vertical equity, the valuation of present versus future life, and so on. His work along these lines seems to me a move in the right direction. See Duncan Macrae, "Valuative Problems of Public Policy Analysis," paper presented at Association for Public Policy Analysis and Management, October 1979.

10. See Derek Bok, "Can Ethics Be Taught?" *Change* (October 1976), vol. 8, no. 9, pp. 26-30, and Daniel Callahan, "Ethics and Policy Analysis," paper presented at Research Conference on Public Policy and Management, Chicago, October 19-20, 1979.

11. Barbara Tuchman provides a revealing glimpse of the economics of fourteenth-century morality in her description of the "all-absorbing" controversy surrounding the Beatific Vision: whether the souls of the blessed saw the face of God immediately upon entering Heaven, or whether they had to wait until the Day of Judgment. "The question was of real concern because the intercession of the saints on behalf of man was effective only if they had been admitted into the presence of God. Shrines possessing saints' relics relied for revenue on popular confidence that a particular saint was in a position to make a personal appeal to the Almighty." In effect, the economic impact of the issue determined its moral (religious) importance. Barbara Tuchman, *A Distant Mirror* (New York: Knopf, 1978), pp. 45-46.

David E. Price

6. Assessing Policy: Conceptual Points of Departure

The development of "policy analysis" as an activity of governments and a focus of professional academic programs has been accompanied by an increasing concern with the normative assessment of public policy and of the process by which policy is made. Some analysts, to be sure, regard ethical reflection as "at most irrelevant to, at worst a positive interference with, the sort of work that is likely to prove productive."[1] But the political circumstances at the time many public policy programs were launched — the Vietnam war dragging on, and Watergate not far behind — led many to seek an antidote to the unreflective "utilitarian habit of mind"[2] that had informed many of the early applications of analytical techniques. Moreover, philosophers, theologians, and political scientists were increasingly and independently turning their attention to matters of public policy, often drawing on, or challenging, those economic theories upon which the policy analysts were also dependent; the debate surrounding John Rawls's *A Theory of Justice* and the launching of the new journal *Philosophy and Public Affairs* were symptomatic. Thus has "ethics and public policy" begun to develop as a subfield of philosophy and political theory. About half of the country's graduate public policy programs have incorporated an ethics course into their core curriculum, and similarly denominated courses have begun to appear among the offerings of other departments.[3]

Ethics, however, still compares unfavorably with economic and political analysis in the emphasis it receives in public policy and public administration programs. And what is taught or examined under the rubric of "ethics and public policy" is subject to a good deal of variation. The most familiar approach is to consider the dilemmas of individual policymakers as they face conflicting loyalties and pressures and reconcile their personal moral standards with the demands of practice. Does service as a public official

142

permit, or even require, one to violate constraints against deceit, coercion, and "corruption" that one would ordinarily regard as binding? If so, what sorts of constraints and standards *are* appropriate to the public role? Such questions, of course, have their *locus classicus* in Machiavelli, and a growing literature is devoted to exploring them in their modern setting.[4] Some of the essays in this volume conceive of the subject matter of "ethics and public policy" in this way. It is important to give such dilemmas searching consideration, for what is at stake is not simply the moral standing of individual practitioners, but also the integrity of democratic processes and the extent to which cruelty and deceit characterize our public life. Surely the Watergate experience has shown us that it is impossible to isolate personal ethics from public morality without impoverishing both.

In this essay, however, I want to suggest that a focus on the quandaries of the individual actor, while critically important, represents only one aspect of the attempt to bring ethics to bear on public policy. In fact, we would do well to recognize the extent to which such an emphasis plays to certain characteristic American prejudices about both ethics and politics. Too often we are prone to personalize the political order, to assume — Reinhold Niebuhr and Max Weber to the contrary notwithstanding — that upright individuals and "clean" processes will make for good policies. Too often we assume that the "ends" of our politics and policymaking will be readily agreed upon by all persons of good will, and that the critical ethical questions concern the employment of questionable "means." The fact is, however, that the ends toward which we ought to aim and the priorities we ought to adopt are anything but self-evident; these substantive questions, moreover, demand more straightforward attention than we would be likely to give them were we to take our cues solely from the everyday situations that individual actors experience as problematic. Hence the importance of a second approach to ethics and public policy: normative policy analysis. Here the focus is less on the ethical "binds" in which politicians or analysts find themselves, more on the terms in which they evaluate policy alternatives and their consequences.

Such an approach, while less common than the first, in some ways fits more naturally into the public policy curricula that are being developed across the country. Students are taught to analyze policy alternatives from a number of perspectives — through the use of cost-benefit analysis and other quantitative tools, with an eye to administrative costs and feasibility, in light of relevant political considerations, and so forth. It seems entirely appropriate — and quite important — that normative assessment take its place as a complement and a corrective to economic, managerial, and political analysis. The temptation is strong to regard ethical judgment as "soft" and "subjective," likely to prove irrelevant when the explicit trade-offs are calculated and the real choices are made. But such a stereotype is surely mistaken, for the ethical element in policy choice is irreducible, and ethical arguments can be as precise, as pointed, and often more powerful than those produced by other forms of analysis. The trick is to do the job well, with a full measure of discrimination and discernment. My intention in the present essay is to suggest one way in which such normative policy analysis might proceed.

A first step is to explicate some of the basic criteria we use in interpreting our general commitment to human well-being and the public good and in evaluating particular institutions and policies. I will examine four such concepts—liberty, justice, the public interest, and community—which offer different and sometimes conflicting points of departure for policy analysis. Through an examination of the debate surrounding affirmative action, I will then illustrate how one's conceptualization of an issue influences the arguments one regards as admissible and the conclusions to which one is drawn. Finally, I will suggest that while the American political culture has predisposed us to "individualistic" arguments predicated on liberty and distributive justice, it is important to give due weight to arguments that take fuller account of the needs and interdependencies persons experience in specific social settings. I will therefore conclude with a consideration of the idea of community—its origins in theories critical of liberalism, its scope, and the terms it suggests for policy evaluation.

CONCEPTS AND EVALUATION

One cannot think very long about the criteria of good public policy without raising broader questions of the social good—questions, that is, which are the staple of social and political theory. Indeed, one ventures into this field at peril without a substantial grounding in the classics of political thought. But those attempting to develop criteria for policy choice have understandably felt the need for a "linking" literature that would help one discover the policy implications of general social theories and ideals.[5] A good deal of the modern social philosophy that has been organized around the classic concepts of the public good has begun to develop such linkages. The danger that such attempts at translation and application will do violence to the profundity and subtlety of the traditions being drawn upon is very real—as Allan Bloom demonstrates in a telling, though overwrought and not entirely fair, critique of Rawls's use of Aristotle and Kant.[6] But I would regard the explication of such concepts, examining their foundations and their implications for political practice, as an essential and promising strategy for normative policy analysis.

This approach is very different, it should be noted, from expecting that cogent argument will arise naturally from the close examination of specific cases and problems. A Hastings Center report notes that persons working in ethics and public policy reject with near unanimity the idea of doing merely "abstract" theory. But the greater danger may well come from the opposite direction.[7] It is not immediately obvious, after all, what constitutes an adequate idea of distributive justice or the public interest, to what extent the two notions are compatible, and so forth. The terms, therefore, in which one might respond to a concrete problem are often quite unclear, and the probability that exchanging intuitive reactions to a given situation will lead to more sophisticated or systematic ways of thinking is frequently quite low. We have, in other words, some conceptual work to do. This work, moreover, might well have a reciprocal effect, informing and expanding the idea of the problematic with which we begin. Edmund Pincoffs has argued that "quandary ethics"—conceiving of the business of ethics as dealing with "situations in which it is difficult to know what one should do"—not only reduces morality to personal "conscientiousness," but also obscures the fact that the initial perception of a dilemma is itself morally significant.[8] A similar argument can be made about the relation of social ethics to policy problems. The articulation and refinement of our notions of the good society are important not only in providing us with the tools for dealing with policy questions that already give us difficulty or produce conflict, but also in showing us what sort of questions we *should* be asking.

An initial problem for anyone attempting to explicate the normative concepts pertinent to policy analysis is the indiscriminate way in which these terms are often bandied about. We commonly refer to "democracy," "liberty," and "justice" quite loosely, allowing them to become mere "hurrah" words, virtually synonymous with the "good" or "what I approve of" in politics and society. Joseph Schumpeter decried this tendency as he attempted to ask whether "democracy" as a political method was in fact likely to tap the "will of the people," much less to realize a "common good." For many, he lamented, the term had simply become "a flag, a symbol of all a man holds dear, of everything that he loves about his nation whether rationally contingent on it or not."[9] Isaiah Berlin has pointed up similar tendencies in his classic essay on "Two Concepts of Liberty." Noting that historians of ideas have recorded some two hundred senses in which "freedom" has been used, Berlin characterizes the term as "so porous that there is little interpretation that it seems able to resist." Yet he thinks it vitally important to mount such a resistance, for if such terms refer to social states and arrangements that are of value, and if they are to be of any help to us in identifying and safeguarding such conditions, certain conceptual boundaries must be drawn. "Negative" liberty, Berlin acknowledges, the freedom of a person or a people "to choose to live as they desire, must be weighed against the claims of many other values, of which equality, or justice, or happiness, or security, or public order are perhaps the most obvious examples." But when we engage in such "weighing" or, as the policy analyst's jargon has it, "trading-off," we should be aware of what we are doing. We are sacrificing something that we generally regard to be of value. It is best, Berlin insists, to be quite clear about this, rather than to convince ourselves that we are in fact pursuing some higher form of the value in question, as though all social ideals were necessarily unitary or compatible. Otherwise, the weighing process is likely to become distorted, and clear thinking about the normative implications of our policy decisions made much more difficult.[10]

Obviously, Berlin advocates such a bounded notion of negative liberty in the conviction that we will and should be less inclined to sacrifice this particular value lightly. Critics have argued that Berlin's notion of liberty as the absence of deliberately imposed constraints conceives of the relevant impediments too narrowly, and that he fails to discern how arguments or claims for "freedom from" a constraint necessarily contain or imply a "positive" notion of "freedom for" an action or state of being.[11] But the case Berlin makes for maintaining conceptual distinctions in theory and in application is, in general, a persuasive one. My purpose is to outline a series of concepts, each of which suggests distinctive perspectives on the public good and standards for policy assessment. My primary aim is not conceptual clarification, nor do I wish to "complexify"—lengthening the list of concepts which might give one slightly different angles of vision on a policy question—indefinitely. My focus will rather be on the general evaluative thrust that four criteria suggest, and on the kind of analysis of specific problems to which they might lead.

The treatment that Berlin and others have given the idea of liberty is a natural starting point, particularly for one working in the American setting. As Louis Hartz and others have argued, the ideology of economic and political individualism associated with the politically emergent bourgeoisie in eighteenth-century England and France came to be almost universally held in the new world. "We are a nation with no feudal Catholic corporate past, and no serious revolutionary party: a country lacking those two very different forms of a more collective understanding. We are John Locke writ large, seeing the individual standing separated from and prior to society."[12]

Lockean liberalism focuses on the "free" individual as the basic unit of the political order and the safeguarding of his life, liberty, and property as the fundamental purpose of the state. There has been less agreement as to the means by which this is to be accomplished, but the liberal bias is toward a minimal state. A natural harmony or equilibrium has frequently been assumed among free individuals and groups; safeguarding the life, liberty, and property of each has been regarded as a sufficient protection of the common good; and an extensive role for government in this connection has been regarded as at once unnecessary and dangerous.

A number of difficult questions await one who would translate this general commitment to liberty into public policy. The liberal tradition itself displays contending views as to who are the relevant agents of liberty in society, what are its proper objects, on what value-premises it is grounded, what means are appropriate to its realization, and how conflicts among liberties are to be resolved. Most Americans have regarded the objects of liberty simultaneously as the enjoyment of universal "rights" in which all persons have an equal stake, and the pursuit of particular "interests" which reflect individuals' different and manifestly unequal positions in society. The first notion of liberty relies on ethical postulates of individual autonomy and inviolability, while the second seeks to enhance what Jefferson — and later the utilitarians, with a somewhat altered meaning — termed the "pursuit of happiness." Those concerned with the first notion of liberty are generally wary of state power and of paternalistic interventions against the subject's will for his "own good," although modern discussions of "equal rights" have increasingly come to encompass not only the traditional constitutional immunities, but also an entitlement to the basic needs of life as a component of, or prerequisite for, effective freedom. The second notion of liberty, defended by Madison in *Federalist* 10 as "essential to political life" despite its promotion of inequality and domination ("Liberty is to faction what air is to fire"), has underwritten political arrangements ranging from laissez-faire to the "interest-group liberalism" of the New Deal but is compatible, in principle, with a wider range of functions for the state.[13] Clearly, any attempt to relate our general valuation of individual freedom to policy choice will have some groundwork to lay by way of analyzing and interpreting the many faces of liberty and right, and the claims each makes on or against the state.

Such an attempt also must recognize, with Berlin, that the maximization of liberty, however conceived, will be likely to impinge upon other social values. One can no longer rely on the glib assumptions of classical liberalism as to the viability of a system that minimizes constraints on the individual exercise of right and pursuit of interest. One must rather analyze and evaluate the social effects directly. The most familiar of the tools employed in this evaluative process, the notion of distributive justice, leads us to ask who is benefited and who deprived by a society's given pattern of liberties and entitlements. Such critiques imply that the institutions and usages of liberalism do not automatically serve human well-being, and that governmental intervention in economic and social processes, according to some criterion of what would constitute a fair distribution of society's basic goods, is necessary.

LIBERALISM AND JUSTICE

It is useful, in this connection, to reflect briefly on John Rawls's *A Theory of Justice*, both because of the book's central place in current debate and because of Rawls's attempt to develop an integrated theory that places liberty in its proper relation to our more general notions of justice. Rawls's efforts are reminiscent of the exhortations of David Braybrooke and C. E. Lindblom in their pathbreaking work, *A Strategy of Decision:* policy analysts must go beyond a mere listing of principles to specify how the criteria are related to one another and how conflicts among them are to be resolved in particular instances. While denigrating the "naive criteria" and "naive priorities" approaches to evaluation, however, Braybrooke and Lindblom are content, in the end, largely to rely on the vagaries of the political marketplace to weigh and balance their values for them.[14] Rawls is not.

Justice as fairness is not at the mercy, so to speak, of existing wants and interests . . . We are able to derive a conception of a just basic structure, and an ideal of the person compatible with it, that can serve as a standard for appraising institutions and for guiding the overall direction of social change. In order to find an Archimedean point it is not necessary to appeal to a priori or perfectionist principles. By assuming certain general desires, such as the desire for primary social goods, and by taking as a basis the agreements that would be made in a suitably defined initial situation, we can achieve the requisite independence from existing circumstances.[15]

Rawls begins with disclaimers reminiscent of Berlin's: "A complete conception defining principles for all the virtues of the basic structure [of society], together with their respective weights when they conflict, is more than a conception of justice; it is a social ideal. The principles of justice are but a part, although perhaps the most important part, of such a conception."[16] Yet Rawls's theory clearly represents an attempt to incorporate multiple criteria of evaluation and to specify their relations to one another. In particular, he sets out in his "first principle" of justice to secure the individual's "equal right to the most extensive total system of equal basic liberties compatible with a similar system of liberty for all." Liberty is to be exempted, in other words, from the distributive principles governing wealth, power, and the other "primary goods" of society. This would presumably have important policy consequences: schemes that would redistribute or increase the overall store of primary goods at the expense of "basic liberty" would be ruled out, as would, by virtue of Rawls's "second principle," policies that increased aggregate or average utility at the expense of the least-advantaged segments of the population.[17]

Brian Barry's book-length critique of Rawls is particularly interesting from our point of view, for Barry uses counterintuitive policy implications to cast doubt on Rawls's basic formulations. If, for example, in a developing society it were possible "to get a great increase in production with little more work by making, say, a small sacrifice of equal liberty," Barry asks, why would it be irrational or unjust to accept such a trade? Or might not one prefer certain "universal social services" to policies that responded more directly to the least-advantaged stratum's deficiency in primary goods? If such questions suggest that Rawls has gone too far in his attempts to specify hard-and-fast relationships among his criteria of evaluation, Barry suggests that in other respects Rawls has not been comprehensive or inclusive enough. For built into Rawls's method is the traditional liberal assumption that the sum total of individual goods (chosen, in Rawls's case, by persons in a hypothetical "original position" which guarantees their ignorance of their particular advantages and interests) will equal the collective good. On the contrary, Barry points out, the individual's wish to secure an ample supply of primary goods may, when universalized (as it must be), make for an absolutely intolerable, or at least suboptimal, end result.

It is quite rational to say that if you could specify your position you'd like to be a rich man in a fairly poor society, but if you're not allowed to make exceptions for yourself you'd sooner be poor in a poor society than rich in a rich one. An affluent society is a particular kind of society with its own advantages and disadvantages; whether one believes the advantages outweigh the disadvantages is a matter of judgment. It is certainly not settled, or even materially advanced, by the observation that people would rather have more money than less. The question of the optimal level of national income turns on the balance struck between the satisfaction that the consumer derives from goods and the costs imposed by their production (in pollution and resource-depletion) and often by their consumption too (noise, rubbish, etc.).[18]

Barry's critique thus points up the extent to which Rawls, despite his conviction that the basic principles of justice should not be subject to the determinations of the marketplace, nonetheless retains certain characteristic biases of the liberal-pluralist approach to politics. "Meliorative concerns," as they are expressed in our society, deal with "distributive properties . . . properties of groups or institutions that derive . . . from properties of individual persons," write Braybrooke and Lindblom, without any apparent sense of the social goods that such "distributive themes" might underemphasize or leave out of account.[19] The same can be said of Rawls's theory of justice. Despite his attempts at conceptual integration, Rawls largely omits those approaches to policy evaluation that would take the collective good as their point of departure.

This gap can at least partially be filled with the notion of the "public interest." Here the image suggested is not discrete individuals articulating their basic rights and interests and then concluding a compact for their mutual protection, but people gathered together, in society, to articulate the interests they hold in common and to devise means for their community-wide or society-wide implementation. Public interest calculations may derive from individual goods just as surely as do the quests for liberty and justice, but they allow one to assume *common* constraints, and compel one to think of *aggregate* impacts, in ways that can lead to quite different policy conclusions. News reports from Mexico, for example, periodically note the demands of peasants for economic justice in the form of land redistribution, while officials stress the likely adverse effect of such policies on the nation's food prices and levels of agricultural production. In the United States many would argue that the pursuit of distributive justice in the area of national health insurance could have disastrous consequences for the public interest in terms of rates of inflation and resources diverted from other national needs. It is far from uncommon for policy dilemmas to assume this form, and it is not clear that Rawls's or other theories of distributive justice can handle them adequately. The concepts that we bring to the evaluation of a political system and of the policy it produces remain multiple— sometimes complementary, sometimes conflicting—and some balancing among them seems inevitable. I want now to suggest, by reference to another current policy debate, that such analysis in terms of multiple concepts, while representing a kind of "complexification," can also help to classify, simplify, and move us toward the resolution of policy dilemmas.

AFFIRMATIVE ACTION: WHAT KIND OF ISSUE IS IT?

Much of the debate over affirmative action that has taken place in recent years has used the language of distributive justice. Proponents speak of compensating individuals or groups for past discrimination or deprivation and of giving them their fair share of jobs or educational opportunities, while opponents speak of the unfairness of denying a member of the majority group what that individual would have had coming were it not for the compensatory effort. Concentrating on that area of affirmative action policy recently highlighted by the *Bakke* case—the admission of minority candidates to professional schools—one finds proponents on both sides frequently conceiving of the process as a "contest . . . like a sporting event in which many compete for a few prizes."[20] The question then becomes how to make the admissions contest a fair and just one. The brief Alexander Bickel and Philip Kurland submitted for the Anti-Defamation League (ADL) in *DeFunis* v. *Odegaard*, for example, portrayed persons as "competing" on the basis of their "individual merit" for a limited number of places in an entering law school class. The school had, they argued, through its quota system, denied DeFunis the right to compete for a number of places solely because of his race; they left unclear whether it might have been permissible, having put all applicants in a single pool, to use a weighting system that disadvantaged DeFunis and other white applicants.[21] The U.S. Department of Justice argued the opposing position in the *Bakke* case a few years later, but still in terms of the contest model. Voicing a concern "to ensure that the effects of past discrimination are not allowed to mask an individual's merit," the Justice Department differed from the ADL only in arguing that it was legitimate to use race to identify those candidates who were likely to have been deprived and whose merit and potential might therefore be underestimated by the conventional measures.[22] Race, the government argued, should be taken into account, but the goal was still to make the contest among competing individuals a fair one. And what "fairness" meant was still reward according to individual merit.

While there is some plausibility in the Justice Department's argument that race is likely to be correlated with underestimated or unrealized merit, basing affirmative action programs on these arguments poses serious problems. The fact that there is an imperfect fit between race and deprivation has led George Sher and others to argue that reverse discrimination is "justified in favor of only those group members whose abilities have actually been reduced . . . by past discrimination."[23] Yet to establish and enforce criteria of eligibility for affirmative action programs that depend on one's

having suffered a demonstrable degree of deprivation would be quite difficult. Moreover, it seems likely, since these programs generally admit only
those deemed qualified to do advanced work, that those within the racial
or economic group picked will tend to be those whose background deprivation is *relatively* least severe. And what of those individuals from the majority group who are displaced? If they meet the standards society has set up
for those who would gain such prizes as berths in medical school, it seems
unfair to discount their qualifications because their background does not
display a vague quantum of deprivation. And it certainly seems inequitable that society's burdens of compensation should fall on them. "Correlative to the fact that those [in the preferred group] who have suffered least
from prior discrimination benefit the most from reverse discrimination is
the fact that [some of] those white males who have least participated in,
and least benefit from, past discrimination pay the most compensation."[24]

Thus will one whose main concern is to achieve justice among those individuals engaged in the admissions contest probably see affirmative action
programs as a blunt instrument at best. This is not to say, it should be
noted, that such programs would therefore be written off as *unjust*. Admission to professional school hardly constitutes a fundamental right or basic
human need. Under *any* system individuals who have met the basic standards will be denied scarce slots; under affirmative action the mix of those
chosen from among the qualified is simply changed slightly. Nor is anyone
being denied a place — and this of course is the crucial constitutional point
— "because the race or religion or sect or region or other natural or artifi-
cial group to which he belongs is the object of prejudice or contempt."[25] In
Thomas Nagel's terms, compensatory discrimination need not be "seriously" unjust to individuals. At the same time, one whose main concern is
to reward persons competing for admission according to their merit or
desert will be unlikely to regard such a policy with much enthusiasm.[26]

The case for preferential admissions as a positive instrument of distributive justice becomes somewhat stronger if we shift our attention from the
contest among individuals to the implications of the process for groups in
the society. Professional school slots are of value to racial minorities (or
women or persons living in certain areas) as collectivities — by virtue of the
services that indigenous professionals would render the collectivity, or perhaps the psychological rewards their elevation would provide for other
members of the (low-status) group. Thus may the traditional admissions
system, which appears to do justice to individual applicants in terms of
conventional notions of merit, actually contribute to group disadvantage
and help perpetuate broader distributive patterns that almost all would

acknowledge to be unjust. Owen Fiss has persuasively argued for the application of the equal protection clause not just to cases of discrimination among individuals but also to state action that results in group disadvantage; affirmative action, he argues, might be an area where these antidiscrimination and group-disadvantaging principles would conflict, with the second properly overriding the first.[27] For what is at stake is not simply specialized training opportunities for individuals, but also the more fundamental needs of large segments of the population. Nor, on the other side, can it plausibly be argued that affirmative action is *un*just to whites as a group; the rejection of scattered individuals implies no stigmatization of the group as a whole, and the broader shift of group advantage works, as Rawls would have it, in favor of those groups currently least advantaged.

The approach to ethics and public policy I have outlined, whereby a concept like "distributive justice" would be explicated and its terms clarified, would virtually force one to get beyond the simplistic arguments and assumptions of the ADL and the Justice Department in the matter of preferential admissions. But the value of the approach lies not just in "complexifying" our notions of what justice requires, but in suggesting that the problem might not be merely or even mainly a question of justice in the first place. In fact, the affirmative action debate will probably remain inconclusive and confused as long as the protagonists conceive of their problems in these terms; like Nagel and Dworkin, I find the aggregative perspective suggested by such conceptual points of departure as "the public interest" or "social utility" to be critically important in cutting through the conventional arguments.

A moment's reflection will show that even the "contest" model is not solely predicated on a desire to reward individual merit. In practice, of course, schools have always modified such admissions criteria in light of other institutional values and needs. But even if we assume that a purely meritocratic system could be devised and established, it is clear that such a system could scarcely be defended as rewarding competing individuals according to their relative "deservingness." Such a system would sometimes reward those who had worked hardest or overcome most, but often these candidates would be bypassed in favor of others whose intellectual and temperamental endowments seemed to equip them more adequately for successful practice. This seems appropriate, providing we do not interpret successful practice or the qualities that underlie it too narrowly, for the purpose of professional school admissions is less to reward deserving or admirable individuals than it is to identify those who will best perform the service that the profession offers the wider community. What counts as merit in such instances is tied to the social functions that earn doctors and lawyers autonomy and privilege as professionals in the first place. If the performance of these services requires a high measure of industry and competence, it may also dictate special efforts to train professionals who will, for example, practice family medicine or serve in minority or other underserviced communities.

There is no combination of abilities and skills and traits that constitutes "merit" in the abstract; if quick hands count as "merit" in the case of a prospective surgeon, this is because quick hands will enable him to serve the public better and for no other reason. If a black skin will, as a matter of regrettable fact, enable another doctor to do a different medical job better, then that black skin is by the same token "merit" as well. That argument may strike some as dangerous; but only because they confuse its conclusion — that black skin may be a socially useful trait in particular circumstances — with the very different and despicable idea that one race may be inherently more worthy than another.[28]

Those affirmative action proponents who have argued in terms of social consequences have tended to concentrate on two collectivities: the outside community being served and the medical school student body itself. The fact that so much of the debate of this issue has taken place in the courts has resulted in such arguments being either downplayed or translated into the language of "rights." Justice Powell's "leading opinion" in the *Bakke* case, for example, granted the legitimacy of a school's desire to promote the "robust exchange of ideas" through a diverse student body; he described the pursuit of such a goal as a component of academic *freedom*, which "long has been viewed as a special concern of the First Amendment."[29] The notion of a "compelling state interest" is available, of course, to justify those public interest goals that pertain to the wider community; the Washington Supreme Court, in fact, employed such a test in ruling against DeFunis. But the courts generally have placed a heavy burden of proof on one who would employ racial classifications to achieve such broader purposes — to show, as the lower court argued in the *Bakke* case, "that there are no reasonable ways to achieve the state's goals by means which impose a lesser limitation on the rights of the group disadvantaged by the classification," or, as Powell argued, to demonstrate that preferential admissions will in fact have a "significant effect" on the delivery of health services to underserved communities.[30]

Our earlier discussion of whether preferential admissions programs were demonstrably unjust suggests that placing such a burden of proof on benign racial classifications, as though they were equivalent to classifications that promised further disadvantage to those already suffering from societal prejudice, is unwarranted.[31] This is not to say measures undertaken in the public interest should not be scrutinized for their impact on individual liberty, procedural fairness, and distributive justice; indeed, our method would make such scrutiny an inescapable component of normative policy analysis. But it also forces one to develop arguments from social utility and the public interest and to take them seriously as values in themselves—a process that, on questions such as preferential admissions, can point up the limitations of the conventional terms of debate and aid us in transcending them.

LIBERALISM AND COMMUNITY

While "liberty," "justice," and "the public interest" thus provide benchmarks for the assessment of social policies and arrangements, no one of the concepts reduces readily to any of the others. Nor would policies designed to realize one of the ideals seem likely to coincide with, or even easily harmonize with, policies designed in light of the others. Surely one cannot profitably multiply such concepts indefinitely. But the history and usage of the notion of "community" suggest that it might be worthy of particular attention. Does it, in fact, offer a point of departure for policy analysis distinct from those suggested by the concepts of distributive justice and the public interest?

Our consideration of this question will be facilitated by considering some distinctions Robert Paul Wolff draws among the "values" (in the sense of "objects of interest") that persons seek:

(1a) A *simple private value* is a possible object of interest whose definition makes essential reference to the occurrence of a state of consciousness in exactly one person.

(1b) A *compound private value* is a possible object of interest whose definition is a truth functional construct of definitions of simple private values.

(2a) An *interpersonal value* is a possible object of interest whose definition makes essential reference to a thought about an actual state of consciousness in another person.

(2b) Among interpersonal values, a *social value* is any experience or state of affairs whose definition makes essential reference to reciprocal states of awareness among two or more persons.

Wolff indentifies "community" as a subset of (2b)—"the feelings, experiences, states of affairs, or sets of relationships . . . that conservatives and radicals alike miss in liberal society." As examples he points to three modes of community: *affective* ("the reciprocal consciousness of a shared culture"), *productive* ("cooperation in collective productive activity"), and *rational* ("discoursing together publicly for the specific purpose of social decision and action").[32]

I want to suggest below that Wolff's notion of community is itself unnecessarily restrictive. But his distinctions show how the community idea goes beyond the policy evaluations we normally undertake in terms of justice and the public interest. Wolff, it is true, assumes rather casually that "community" and the "public interest" designate "roughly the same idea" in our discourse. And Rawls is at some pains to argue that his conception of justice, while "individualistic . . . in its theoretical basis," nonetheless would serve persons who "need one another as partners in ways of life that are engaged in for their own sake . . . the successes and enjoyments of others [being] necessary for and complimentary to our own good."[33] But people, as Rawls conceives them, are bound initially to reason only in terms of "simple private values," however circumscribed their calculations may be (Rawls's version of the social contract denies to the parties any advance knowledge of their particular advantages or interests) and however persuaded Rawls may be that persons who are "secure in the enjoyment of the exercise of their own powers" will be "disposed to appreciate the perfections of others."[34] Nor do we generally use "the public interest" in a way that goes beyond Wolff's notion of a "compound private value." A "public" interest normally requires a collective articulation and implementation, and the good pursued is often not divisible into shares. But human interdependence enters at the point of *pursuing* the good, not as we conceive of the good or, for that matter, enjoy it. Public interest theories, in other words, challenge the sufficiency of liberal notions of the social contract and distributive justice, but they generally do so in terms of social ends that they share with liberalism. Indeed, much of the force of a theory like that of Mancur Olson[35] derives from his willingness to challenge the liberals on their own ground: it is precisely those goods that individuals independently desire, and for which in fact they might well vote, that would fail of realization without authoritative, often coercive, means of implementation. But that the good is still conceived in private terms is demonstrated by the strong temptation the individual experiences to play the free rider, to let others bear the cost of the common benefit.

The "communitarian" critique has confronted the ends of liberalism, and the notions of the individual and society on which they are premised, much more directly than have most theories of distributive justice or the public interest. What thinkers ranging from Burke and Tocqueville to Hegel and Marx articulated was a conviction that liberalism had radically underestimated the individual's dependence on the social environments that nurtured and conditioned him for his very definition of self; that what Wolff would term a "private" value, whether "simple" or "compound," was an abstraction which at best gave a partial and distorted representation of the goods people sought in society; and that a major task confronting modern social theory was to illumine the dialectic of dependence-independence that the self experiences in relation to its social/cultural environment. The liberal idea of an autonomous individual, fully formed outside of society and voluntarily entering into, or tacitly honoring, a compact in order to secure private values, was regarded as an empirical and ethical absurdity. Their constructive social ideals varied widely, but all assumed that what Wolff terms "interpersonal" and "social" values needed somehow to be expressed within and nurtured by the political order.

Carey McWilliams has identified a continuing, if often frustrated and faltering, quest for "fraternity" in the United States, rooted in Massachusetts Bay and later existing alongside (sometimes in conflict with, but just as often compensating for) the thoughtways and folkways of liberal individualism.[36] Communitarian thought in America never was embodied, as it was in Europe, in theories or political movements that represented "grand alternatives." But it did attain considerable force and coherence, particularly in the late nineteenth and early twentieth centuries—at first among scattered transcendentalists and utopians, and later among exponents of pragmatism such as Peirce, Royce, and Dewey; Cooley, Baldwin, Mead, and others seeking to shape the nascent disciplines of sociology and psychology; revisionist economists like Ely and Patten; and such proponents of Progressive reform as Croly, Lippmann, and DuBois. I have elsewhere sought to distinguish between such critiques and those of reformers who, less troubled by the privatistic, materialistic ends of liberalism, chose to focus on questions of distribution, regulation, and control.[37] It is social criticism in this latter mode, no doubt, that has remained ascendant in the United States. But communitarian strands have reappeared more often than is generally acknowledged, even as a component of policy evaluation.

Ideals close to what Wolff calls "social values" are at the heart of much American communitarian thought. Dewey and Cooley are particularly explicit in the paradigmatic role they assign to the primary group. "In its deepest and richest sense a community must always remain a matter of face-to-face intercourse."[38] But both men, and most of the communitarian thinkers of their era, were concerned not merely to preserve or to restore the reciprocal awareness and interaction of the primary community, but also to extend the essential values of community to arenas and spheres of life where this sort of intimacy was impossible. This brought them closer to European idealistic traditions than are, say, modern critics such as Wolff and McWilliams, who, in their insistence that community is rooted in mutual personal awareness and/or affection (and "like all such bonds, is limited in the number of persons and in the social space to which it can be extended"), reveal the extent to which they remain wedded to the idea of individual "moral autonomy" and to voluntaristic notions of how people articulate and implement common goals.[39]

I see no good reason to be bound by such limitations. We use the notion of community to encompass what Wolff would term "interpersonal" as well as strictly "social" values, and to refer to identification with collectivities and their purposes as well. Max Weber's definition bears this broader construction: "A social relationship will be called 'communal' if and so far as the orientation of social action . . . is based on a subjective feeling of the parties, whether affectual or traditional, that they belong together."[40] Such "feeling," to be sure, ties one to the values and purposes of other individuals; this imposes certain limits on the scope and generality of an effective community of identification and sentiment. It was for this reason, among others, that Progressive-era American communitarians were often reluctant to rely on the nation as the prime receptacle of communitarian attachment and focused instead on "provinces" and other associations intermediate between the family and the village, on the one hand, and the state on the other. The essential idea is that individuals recognize their interdependence, both as fact and as ideal, enhancing their sense of mutual sympathy and shared purpose, and assuming responsibility for one another's and the collectivity's well-being. The idea has its natural home in the face-to-face group, but there is no reason to confine it there.

The Progressive-era communitarians frequently thought it important to trace out the policy implications of their social criticism. Thus did Royce argue for the preservation of subnational "provincial" units as repositories of citizen loyalty, DuBois for the building of cooperative economic institutions among blacks, Cooley for the fostering of corporate awareness and *esprit* among occupational and professional groups. Often their concern was to preserve local and associational ties against the forces making for their dissolution, but they also sensed that if communal attachments and responsibilities were to find a place in twentieth-century society, they must be found—or perhaps deliberately fostered—in new locations. The early New Deal "community programs," for example, drew directly on Progressive-era communitarian thought; the key formulators and first administrators of these programs, M. L. Wilson and Rexford Tugwell, saw themselves as building directly on the ideas of Ely, Patten, and Dewey.[41] Subsequent invocations of the community idea have been less specific and more subject to interpretations in terms of concomitant objectives such as the redistribution of power and the attainment of self-determination for deprived groups. But the nurturing of community structures and sentiments has periodically recurred, particularly since the early 1960s, as a policy goal articulated across the ideological spectrum.

The most prominent current attempt to evaluate policy alternatives from a communitarian perspective is the "mediating structures" project which Peter Berger and Richard Neuhaus are directing for the American Enterprise Institute. Their idea is an important one: that public policy should protect, foster, and utilize those institutions—neighborhoods, churches, families, voluntary associations—that stand "between the individual in his private life and the large institutions of public life."[42] But the rationale they have developed is seriously flawed: it uncritically reduces the community idea to deference to group and local "particularism," adopts an indiscriminate status quo bias in considering which forms of associational life public policy should nurture, and falls back on an unsatisfactory balancing notion with respect to the values a communitarian strategy might ignore.

I have elsewhere developed a critique of the mediating structures project, suggesting several criteria which might make public policy more discriminating in its deference to and nurturing of group and community life.[43] My emphasis here will rather be on the possibility of *extending* the community idea. To what extent might communitarian values and perspectives, cultivated in the interstices of mass society, prove relevant to the assessment of larger-scale policies and institutions? And what relation might the community idea, thus extended, bear to those alternative conceptualizations of the public good discussed earlier?

COMMUNITY IN SOCIETY: SOCIAL ALTRUISM

Richard Titmuss, in his widely discussed book *The Gift Relationship*, has argued that "the extent to which specific instruments of public policy encourage or discourage, foster or destroy the individual expression of altruism and regard for the needs of others" may have important consequences, both for the viability of specific policies and for the moral tone of a society. His case in point is blood transfusion policy, which he compares in England, where the supply of blood comes mainly from volunteer donors, and the United States, where only 9 percent of those giving "approximated to the concept of the voluntary community donor who sees his donation as a free gift to strangers in society." The English system, Titmuss argues, taps values and attitudes associated with the "sense of community," while the American market in blood presupposes the "calculating 'economizing' behavior" by individuals that we associate with the shift from *gemeinschaft* to *gesellschaft*.[44] His findings thus may be read, in terms of our previous discussion, as indicating what might prove distinctive about policy formulated from communitarian premises. His answer, however, has little to do with the "social values" or "mediating structures" on which others have focused.

In comparing the effects of the two blood donor systems, Titmuss announces that he is willing, in part, to think "like an economist." He offers persuasive evidence, for example, that a commercialized system brings heightened risks to both donors and recipients, for it tends to attract penurious donors and to give them incentives to lie about how frequently they have given and about aspects of their medical history, exposure to disease, drinking and drug habits, and so on, that would render their blood infectious or otherwise disqualify them as donors. But Titmuss does not regard such economic arguments as conclusive. He speaks of social policies that foster and provide outlets for altruism as an "indicator" of "the quality of relationships and of human values prevailing in a society." But he also clearly regards them as an independent variable—a *determinant* of what sorts of values and relationships prevail in society: "The ways in which society organizes and structures its social institutions—and particularly its health and welfare systems—can encourage or discourage the altruistic in man; such systems can foster integration or alienation; they can allow the 'theme of the gift' . . . to spread among and between social groups and generations."[45] Titmuss' evidence does, in fact, suggest that voluntary giving has tended to increase most where payment for blood is not an option. But regardless of whether economic incentives in fact drive out altruistic motivations, the larger question at stake for Titmuss is what kind of society we wish to have. The fact that one lives in the kind of community where people act out of a sense of altruism and responsibility for the commonweal is valued as an end in itself.

Titmuss' "gift relationship" is not, in Wolff's terms, a "social value." In fact, he seems to regard the donor's altruism to be enhanced ethically by virtue of the fact that it cannot be reciprocated or even acknowledged. Similarly, the sense of community is seemingly valued all the more as the traditional boundaries of *gemeinshaft* are extended and such affirmations of solidarity and interdependence as occur take place among strangers. "The self is realized with the help of anonymous others."[46] This self is clearly not the autonomous, utility-maximizing individual of liberal theory. But neither is it the self of the organic primary community. Titmuss' self rather seems to be pursuing what Wolff would term an "interpersonal value," albeit with reference less to his fellows' specific "states of consciousness" than to their well-being more broadly conceived. Titmuss' citizen is motivated by a sense of solidarity and responsibility that encompasses the entire society, reinforced by the sense that his acts sustain unidentified fellow citizens who are in need.

Titmuss does not, however, portray his donor's motives as an abstract "complete, disinterested, spontaneous altruism." There must be "some feeling of 'inclusion' in society; some awareness of need and the purposes of the gift." A good number of British donors reported that a heightened sense of the need for blood had followed their own or their family's receipt of blood, experiences with war and accident victims, and so forth, and many also vaguely expected that they or those close to them would benefit from the altruism of others in the future.[47] Particularism thus exerts a discernible (though unacknowledged) tug on Titmuss' universalism, as indeed it must, one might surmise, whenever communitarian theory takes on an empirical referent. Giving does not thereby become a good directly attached to the expectation of reciprocation, much less a "social value" entailing mutual "states of awareness." But it does become understandable only in terms of experiences within and identification with a distinct human community, a unit with specifiable characteristics and boundaries, necessarily exclusive as well as inclusive.

Titmuss nonetheless does not mask his admiration for an indiscriminate and inclusive altruism that does not anticipate reciprocation. In light of this, his failure to extend his analysis to broader areas of social welfare policy is puzzling. He is content, by way of generalizing his argument, to note several examples—medical experimentation, organ transplants, foster care for children—of the "large and expanding social policy territory of stranger relationships and transactions of a non-economic character."[48] What these policy areas have in common is their dependence on extraordinary acts of giving by individuals; the donors, moreover, often have relatively rare and therefore valued characteristics or capacities, while the recipients are often persons with likewise atypical needs. But what of the policy problems that are more easily generalized to broad segments of the population, where both the needs addressed and the gifts required are less extraordinary, less tied to the particular circumstances of specifiable individuals? Titmuss has moved beyond the intimacy and reciprocity of the primary community in portraying the scope of social responsibility, but he still identifies what ethical initiatives might flow from the sense of community more in terms of the motivations of individuals and the sacrifices they make than in terms of policies and programs with a demonstrable link to the community's actual well-being.

This retention of what we might call a "personalistic" bias is, it seems to me, hard to justify. If we are to move, with Titmuss, beyond the notion of community as a simple "social value" — and I think the empirical circumstances and ethical imperatives under which we labor leave us little choice — then it seems unsatisfactory to retain a model of social responsibility or even altruism that is so closely tied to the notion of personal sacrifice. Personal giving for the relief of specified or unspecified others may have both intrinsic and instrumental worth for society, but so also may other forms of devotion and service to the commonweal. It is at this point that the Titmuss argument might lead us where he himself did not choose to go, into the broader question of how the supposed virtues of community might relate to, or modify, those quests for justice and the public interest in terms of which societies tend to justify their domestic policies. For surely the altruism and sense of community that lead one to give blood would not be irrelevant to questions of poverty, health care delivery, and so forth.

Titmuss' retort might well be that the presence of altruism among individuals is clearly requisite to the execution of the policies he has discussed, as opposed to the broader range of social welfare measures. But here we come upon the assertions made by various social critics in various ways, that communitarian values influence both the intensity and the direction of a society's quest for (among other values) distributive justice. Reinhold Niebuhr, for example, has discussed the relationship of "mutual love and brotherhood" to the "struggle for justice."

Systems and principles of justice are the servants and instruments of the spirit of brotherhood insofar as they extend the sense of obligation toward the other, (a) from an immediately felt obligation, prompted by obvious need, to a continued obligation expressed in fixed principles of mutual support; (b) from a simple relationship between the self and one "other" to the complex relations of the self and the "others"; and (c) finally from the obligations, discerned by the individual self, to the wider obligations which the community defines from its more impartial perspective.

But if the institutions of justice extend and broaden (and, to an extent, enforce) the communitarian ethic, brotherhood also exists in tension with justice, finding itself imperfectly fulfilled even in people's most ambitious attempts to institutionalize mutual responsibility. Such attempts require a calculation of rights and interests and a balancing of powers which is bound to be tainted by partial perspectives and inordinate self-seeking in practice. Thus does love continue to exert a positive pull on the quest for justice:

Insofar as justice admits the claim of the self it is something less than love. Yet it cannot exist without love and remain justice. For without the "grace" of love justice always degenerates into something less than justice.[49]

COMMUNITY EXTENDED

The Titmuss book and our reflections on it thus raise the possibility of extending the notion of community in two respects. First, as our human sympathies and sense of mutual responsibility encompass segments of society (and, indeed, the national and world communities) far transcending the proximate community, the possibility is raised that communitarian values will lead us to policies of widened scope. But as we move into such areas it also becomes doubtful that we can retain the voluntarism that Titmuss no less than Wolff finds at the heart of the communitarian ethic. Such voluntarism, it should be noted, was hardly conceivable in the traditional *gemeinschaft*. But the possibility we have raised is not a return to an ethic of status and ascription, but rather the implementation of communitarian values by means that do not depend upon individual initiative and altruism and that, indeed, may employ a measure of coercion and control.

The table lines out some of the distinctions we are working with and indicates a range of policies that (imperfectly) fit into the categorizations thus generated. We adopt the perspective of a citizen asked or constrained to contribute to a range of policy outcomes, all of which may be expected to benefit that individual and/or at least a few fellow citizens. According to the classical liberal view, most legitimate policies fall within category 1: individuals view them, at least initially, as securing their own life, liberty, and property; rationally and freely, they make whatever contributions and honor whatever constraints are necessary to the society-wide protection of such rights and interests. But as Mancur Olson and other theorists dealing with collective goods and the public interest have discerned, this voluntaristic assumption may frequently not hold, even when the self's desire for the good is relatively intense and the benefit enjoyed is quite tangible. The temptation is strong to play the free-rider, benefiting from others' contributions while withholding one's own, or to resist whatever contributions or

Policies categorized according to scope and the character of the citizen contributio required

		Primary recipient/beneficiary			
		Self	Self and proximate others	Unidenti- fied others	Collectivity
Character of contribution	Voluntary	1 Liberal conception of partic- ipation	3 Subsistence homesteads, community action programs	5 Blood donation (Titmuss)	7 Voluntary wa and conserva tion efforts
	Collective/ coerced	2 Union mem- bership, social security (Olson)	4 Cooperative farming (Tugwell)	6 National welfare minimum	8 Military draft, domes tic citizen corps (Barber)

constraints are necessary to extend the benefit in question beyond one's own immediate circle. Hence the likely need for coercion and constraint, even as we remain within the liberal world of the simple or compound "private value" (see category 2).

In categories 3 through 8 we enter the realm of communitarian policies, where one's identification with and sense of responsibility for other individuals or for the collectivity as a whole become decisive, both as a motivation for one's participation and as a frame of reference for judging the adequacy of specific policies. Category 3 encompasses Wolff's "social values": an area where liberal moral autonomy is retained but where liberty finds its object in relationships of cooperation and interdependence; the compound private values of the reformed liberal order are supplemented or supplanted by values that depend for their realization upon their being shared by a community in their formulation and their enjoyment. Here I am drawing on work I have done elsewhere (see note 41) on the community programs of the New Deal and the community action component of the 1964 Economic Opportunity Act—programs that set out to create or nurture enclaves within the larger society where mutual support and joint efforts could flourish.

The combination suggested in category 4 — communal interaction, but with the contributions of at least some members being rendered under constraint — is of course familiar to the student of the traditional community. But liberal critics have tended to portray communities and policies that fit these categories in ahistorical and myopic terms: as an oppressive, or alternatively, paternalistic and condescending, set of feudal relationships which antedated the dawn of "negative liberty," or as the collectivist end toward which any attempt to transcend private values in politics will inevitably tend. At the same time, the utopian left has tended to play down the fact that discipline and self-denial (recall Paul's description in Romans 12 of what is required of Christians as "members one of another") as well as moral autonomy and openness are likely to be integral to community building. In light of such tendencies, Rexford Tugwell's assessment of the planning and control that would be required to implement the community programs which came under his care during the early years of the New Deal takes on added interest.[50] Without such realism, one will be likely to sentimentalize the process of community formation and to underestimate its difficulty; moreover, under the guise of leaving moral autonomy intact, one might in fact leave the community open to ordering by its strongest and most resourceful elements. Several decentralized agricultural programs, cherished by M. L. Wilson and others as models of grass-roots democracy and cooperation, have proved vulnerable to just this sort of distortion. No more in the realm of social values than elsewhere can one assume the absence of power and constraint, or safely avoid attending to their responsible and equitable employment.

Titmuss' book is suggestive in its extension of communitarian values from category 3 to category 5; one's sense of social responsibility is universalized and the beneficiaries of one's gifts become not proximate others but strangers across the society. But in this broader realm, even more than in the face-to-face community, one can conceive of many policies to which communitarian values might point but which could never be implemented through voluntary individual gifts. Further applications of the community idea are suggested by categories 7 and 8, policies conceived in terms of their benefits not to specifiable individuals but to the society as a whole. Here too, it seems likely that to remain within the realm of voluntary action would be to limit the range and applicability of communitarian values unacceptably. Pertinent here is Benjamin Barber's proposal of "a moral equivalent of military conscription: a universal citizen corps in which every young American might serve for two years." Barber regards such service as differing from the armed forces precisely in its "generous and democratic" quality: "fellowship and equality rather than hierarchy, common discovery and cooperation rather than obedience, a rewarding altruism rather than the self-interest of survival." At the same time Barber seems to feel that participation in such a regimen of self-development and public service should (or would have to) rely on a system of conscription, whereby all would be compelled to serve.[51]

Analysts of Titmuss' persuasion would probably have very few problems with the proposed category 7. But they might see many of the policies falling in categories 4, 6, and 8 as not merely foreign but antithetical to the communitarian ethic as they have conceived it. Could they welcome a military system (or a universal citizen corps) that compelled young people to serve, or even a welfare system that provided for society's less-advantaged segments through an involuntary redistribution of income? They might reluctantly agree to the necessity of such measures, but hardly as the mark of a society that, by "encouraging the altruistic" in persons, fosters the community ideal. But I would argue that the idea of community functions not only as a stimulus to individual action, but also as an ideal in terms of which social policies might be evaluated. What is it, for example, that offends us about the idea that the sons of the rich might be able to buy their way out of military service, paying substitutes to go in their place?[52] Surely considerations of distributive justice, in part. But also, I think, the violence such a system would do to the notions of solidarity and interdependence held by the citizens of a nation faced by external threats. Such considerations might well lead to the institution of a military draft which, while unable to rely completely on the altruistic in individuals, might nonetheless lead them toward actions commensurate with the nature and the need of the community.

We thus, in closing, return to the questions with which we began: What does the community idea add to the policy generation and evaluation we undertake in terms of liberty, justice, and the public interest? The answer is clearest for policies in categories 3, 5, and 7, where personal adherence to the communal ethic is essential to the formulation and carrying out of measures that we might also want to evaluate and defend in terms of these other criteria. In categories 2, 4, 6, and 8 we are dealing with policies regularly defended by reference to norms of justice and/or the public interest, and typically implemented by public authority rather than through the spontaneous efforts of individuals. It would be a mistake, however, to assume that such policy questions lie outside the realm of the community idea. The policies we implement in the name of justice, and the deliberations we undertake as to what the common good or the public interest requires, should be (and for most people, I believe, are) underwritten by a sense of social interdependence, of mutual sympathy and shared purpose, and of responsibility for one another's and the collectivity's well-being. It is important not to sentimentalize this process: our moral imagination as often as not is distorted and limited, and public authority is necessary to extend and enforce whatever good intentions we are able to muster as a society. But it is equally important to recognize that any adequate and sustained effort to realize the social good will require means and motives that go beyond the terms of liberal individualism.[53]

Such attempts to extend communitarian thinking, however, also bring us, as they brought Dewey in the concluding pages of *The Public and Its Problems*, back to the idea's natural home in the proximate community. For it is only here that community as a "social value" is fully realized and that the mutual sympathies and cooperative efforts integral to the community idea are reliably nurtured. Attempts to replicate communitarian identification and loyalty in broader social settings, experience has taught us, are vulnerable both to faltering and failure and to dangerous distortions; their nurture in society's mediating structures is important, at once as an alternative, constraint, and guide to such broader expressions. The nurture of proximate communities is no substitute for the more inclusive quest for justice and the public interest, nor must it be allowed to degenerate into a mere defense of particularistic power and interest. But it represents a crucial and distinctive realm of policy initiative, worthy of sustained empirical examination and ethical defense.

NOTES

1. Peter Steinfels, "The Place of Ethics in Schools of Public Policy," A Report from the Hastings Center to the Ford Foundation, Hastings-on-Hudson, N.Y., 1977, pp. 10-11.

2. See Stuart Hampshire, "Morality and Pessimism," in Hampshire, ed., *Public and Private Morality* (Cambridge: Cambridge University Press, 1978), p. 4.

3. David E. Price, "Public Policy and Ethics," *The Hastings Center Report*, 7 (December 1977), supplement, pp. 4-6.

4. See, for example, Michael Walzer, "Political Action: The Problem of Dirty Hands," *Philosophy and Public Affairs*, 2 (Winter 1973), 160-180; David Little, "Duties of Station vs. Duties of Conscience: Are There Two Moralities?" in Donald Jones, ed., *Private and Public Ethics* (New York: Edwin Mellen Press, 1978), pp. 125-157; Bernard Williams, "Politics and Moral Character," in Hampshire, ed., *Public and Private Morality*, chap. 3; and Thomas Nagel, "Ruthlessness in Public Life," ibid., chap. 4.

5. Cf. Brian Barry and Douglas Rae: "There must be simplifying de-

vices standing between what we have called the general ground of evaluation ["the advancement of human well-being"] and evaluations of particular actions, policies, institutions, etc. Among these simplifying devices, the most important are political principles, criteria of evaluation derived from different interpretations of the general ground of evaluation, and emphasis on different aspects of it, plus factual beliefs about human behavior and society." "Political Evaluation," in Fred I. Greenstein and Nelson W. Polsby, eds., *Handbook of Political Science* (Reading, Mass.: Addison-Wesley Publishing Co., 1975), I, 377. Barry's and Rae's list of political principles includes the public interest, justice, equality, freedom, and democracy. See also Charles W. Anderson, "The Place of Principles in Policy Analysis," *American Political Science Review*, 73 (September 1979), 711-723.

6. Allan Bloom, "Justice: John Rawls *vs.* The Tradition of Political Philosophy," *American Political Science Review*, 69 (June 1975), 648-662.

7. See Steinfels, "Place of Ethics," pp. 12-13; and Price, "Public Policy and Ethics," p. 5.

8. Edmund Pincoffs, "Quandary Ethics," *Mind*, 80 (October 1971), pp. 565-567. The alternative, Pincoffs argues, is a return to the broader concern for "the best kind of individual life, and the qualities of character exhibited by the man who leads it."

9. Joseph Schumpeter, *Capitalism, Socialism, and Democracy* (New York: Harper and Row, 1950), chap. 11.

10. Isaiah Berlin, "Two Concepts of Liberty," in *Four Essays on Liberty* (New York: Oxford University Press, 1969), pp. 121, 167, 170.

11. See C. B. MacPherson, *Democratic Theory: Essays in Retrieval* (Oxford: Clarendon Press, 1973), chap. 5; and Gerald C. MacCallum, Jr., "Negative and Positive Freedom," *Philosophical Review*, 76 (July 1967), 312-334. MacCallum develops a model of freedom as a triadic relation— "agent x is (is not) free from y to do (not do, become, not become) z"— which is particularly helpful in analyzing policy disputes that involve claims about liberty.

12. William Lee Miller, *Of Thee, Nevertheless, I Sing* (New York: Harcourt Brace Jovanovich, 1975), pp. 221-222. See, generally, Louis Hartz, *The Liberal Tradition in America* (New York: Harcourt, Brace and World, 1955).

13. For an argument that John Stuart Mill's utilitarian defense of liberty does not require the constraints on state action that he wishes to maintain see Robert Paul Wolff, *The Poverty of Liberalism* (Boston: Beacon Press, 1968), chap. 1. For an examination of "rights" and "freedom" as "separate concepts that are intertwined in complex ways in our practice" see Richard Flathman, *The Practice of Rights* (Cambridge: Cambridge University Press, 1976), chaps. 7-8. The characterization of the New Deal is taken from Theodore Lowi, *The End of Liberalism* (New York: W. W. Norton, 1979), chap. 3.

14. David Braybrooke and Charles E. Lindblom, *A Strategy of Decision* (New York: Free Press, 1963), pp. 6-8. The extent to which these particu-

lar analysts are bound to the political marketplace is unclear. Lindblom's later book, *The Intelligence of Democracy* (New York: Free Press, 1965), reveals considerable sanguinity as to the overall rationality and equity of the give and take of pluralistic politics. *A Strategy of Decision*, at least in the chapters drafted by Braybrooke, reveals a livelier interest in the sorts of techniques and criteria a central policymaker might adopt. But the "incrementalist" strategy by which such an actor might rationally compensate for the absence of comprehensive analysis and might balance the values and demands of competing partisans is imperfectly reconciled with the "incrementalism" that the system as a whole unwittingly produces by virtue of the fact that every decisionmaker is reduced to the role of partisan, subject to checks and correctives from other "socially fragmented" decision centers. And while Braybrooke is reluctant to portray the policymaker as a cipher of the pressures and preferences of the political market, his arguments that the "normal" system will uphold the universalistic rules of the game, will respond to inarticulate and deprived groups, and will address "objective" needs are often unpersuasive. See particularly pp. 104-106, 185-186, 191-192, 218-221, 242-243. One leaves such a defense of the normal system — an able defense, relatively speaking — with a fresh appreciation for what Rawls is trying to accomplish.

15. John Rawls, *A Theory of Justice* (Cambridge, Mass.: Harvard University Press, 1971), pp. 261, 263.

16. Ibid., p. 9.

17. Ibid., sections 11-15, 26-28, 46. The precise wording of the second principle is as follows: "Social and economic inequalities are to be arranged so that they are both: (a) to the greatest benefit of the least advantaged, consistent with the just savings principle, and (b) attached to offices and positions open to all under conditions of fair equality of opportunity" (p. 302).

18. Brian Barry, *The Liberal Theory of Justice* (Oxford: Clarendon Press, 1973), pp. 75, 114-115, 119.

19. Braybrooke and Lindblom, *Strategy of Decision*, p. 170.

20. Winton Manning borrows the term from Ralph Turner, who contrasted "contest admission" and "sponsored admission" as ideal types. Manning, "The Pursuit of Fairness in Admissions to Higher Education," in Carnegie Council on Policy Studies in Higher Education, *Selective Admissions in Higher Education* (Washington: Jossey-Bass, 1977), p. 28.

21. Anti-Defamation League of the B'nai B'rith, Brief *Amicus Curiae*, *DeFunis* v. *Odegaard*, Supreme Court of the United States, October term, 1973, pp. 16-18.

22. U.S. Department of Justice, Brief *Amicus Curiae*, *University of California* v. *Allan Bakke*, Supreme Court of the United States, October term, 1977, p. 55.

23. Sher, "Justifying Reverse Discrimination in Employment," in Marshall Cohen and others, eds., *Equality and Preferential Treatment* (Princeton: Princeton University Press, 1977), p. 59.

24. Alan H. Goldman, "Affirmative Action," ibid., pp. 205-206.

25. Ronald Dworkin, "Why Bakke Has No Case," *New York Review of Books*, November 10, 1977, p. 14.

26. See Nagel, "Equal Treatment and Compensating Discrimination," in Cohen and others, eds., *Equality and Preferential Treatment*, pp. 13-15.

27. Fiss, "Groups and the Equal Protection Clause," ibid., pp. 148-149.

28. Dworkin, "Why Bakke Has No Case," p. 14.

29. *Bakke* v. *Regents of the University of California*, 438 U.S. 265 (1978) at 312.

30. *Bakke* v. *Regents*, 132 *Cal. Reporter* 680 at 690; 438 U.S. 265 at 310-311.

31. For an argument that Powell is mistaken and inconsistent in applying the same "strict scrutiny" test to both forms of racial classification see Ronald Dworkin, "The Bakke Decision: Did It Decide Anything?" *New York Review of Books*, August 17, 1978, pp. 23-25.

32. See Wolff, *Poverty of Liberalism*, chap. 5. The sections that follow are adapted in part from David E. Price, "The 'Quest for Community' and Public Policy," The Poynter Center, Bloomington, 1977.

33. Wolff, *Poverty of Liberalism*, p. 163; Rawls, *Theory of Justice*, pp. 264, 522-523. Cf. Rawls, p. 129: "Justice is the virtue of practices where there are competing interests and where persons feel entitled to press their rights on each other."

34. Rawls, *Theory of Justice*, p. 523. Also relevant is Rawls's argument that the standards of justice are compatible with, and indeed suggested by, the "morality of association," that second stage of moral development which grows out of the various roles and communities in which one is enmeshed. Note, however, that the sense of justice becomes more secure and less contingent as it becomes attached to one's third stage of development, the universalistic "morality of principles." See sections 71-72.

35. See Mancur Olson, Jr., *The Logic of Collective Action* (New York: Schocken, 1965). To argue that theories of distributive justice and of the public interest remain individualistic in certain key assumptions is not to assert that they are, in Barry's terms, purely "want-regarding." Rawls's idea of an "original position" is designed to bring egoistic calculations into line with our "considered moral judgments," to free justice as fairness from dependence on "existing wants and interests." *Theory of Justice*, pp. 21, 141, 148, 261. In *Political Argument* (London: Routledge and Kegan Paul, 1965) Barry treats "interest" as normally referring to a good instrumental to want-satisfaction (pp. 176, 184, 216); but for an argument that Barry unduly narrows our notion of the public interest, both by overlooking the need that is generally felt for its normative justification and by insisting on a strict criterion of common impact on "indeterminate" persons, see Virginia Held, *The Public Interest and Individual Interests* (New York: Basic Books, 1970), pp. 21-34, 115-124.

36. Wilson Carey McWilliams, *The Idea of Fraternity in America* (Berkeley: University of California Press, 1973).

37. David E. Price, "Community and Control: Critical Democratic

Theory in the Progressive Period," *American Political Science Review*, 68 (December 1974), pp. 1663-1678.

38. John Dewey, *The Public and Its Problems* (New York: Henry Holt, 1927), p. 211; cf. Charles Horton Cooley, *Social Organization: A Study of the Larger Mind* (New York: Scribner's, 1909), chap. 3.

39. See McWilliams, *Idea of Fraternity*, p. 7. The extent of Wolff's voluntarism is revealed in *In Defense of Anarchism* (New York: Harper and Row, 1970), but it can also be discerned in his earlier *Poverty of Liberalism*, especially chap. 2.

40. *The Theory of Social and Economic Organization* (New York: Free Press, 1964), p. 136.

41. See Price, "Quest for Community," pp. 3-8.

42. Peter Berger and Richard John Neuhaus, *To Empower People: The Role of Mediating Structures in Public Policy* (Washington: American Enterprise Institute for Public Policy Research, 1977), p. 2.

43. David E. Price, "Community, 'Mediating Structures,' and Public Policy," *Soundings*, 62 (Winter 1979), 369-394.

44. Richard Titmuss, *The Gift Relationship: From Human Blood to Social Policy* (New York: Vintage Books, 1972), pp. 12-13, 95, 211, 245.

45. Ibid., pp. 13, 225; cf. Peter Singer, "Altruism and Commerce: A Defense of Titmuss against Arrow," *Philosophy and Public Affairs*, 2 (Spring 1973), 312-320.

46. Titmuss, *Gift Relationship*, pp. 212.

47. Ibid., pp. 228-231, 238.

48. Ibid., pp. 213-216.

49. Niebuhr is working with an additional distinction, between *sacrificial* love (*agape*, love that "seeketh not its own") and *mutual* love or "brotherhood"; he portrays the former as standing in "judgment," not only of historical attempts to realize justice, but also of the mutuality of the community and all other "forms of human goodness in which self-assertion and love are compounded." See *The Nature and Destiny of Man* (New York: Charles Scribner's Sons, 1949). II, 72, 74, 82, 89, 248, 252, 258; "Justice and Love," *Christianity and Society*, 15 (Fall 1950), p. 7. *Agape* is generally thought of as the more distinctively Christian notion, a personal ethical ideal that it is impossible (or inappropriate) to institutionalize in human collectivities; it is interesting, however, to note that Titmuss' communitarian ethic owes at least as much to sacrificial as to mutual love.

50. Price, "Quest for Community," pp. 6-7.

51. Benjamin R. Barber, "Political Participation and the Creation of Res Publica" (Bloomington: The Poynter Center, 1977), p. 19.

52. I am indebted to Ronald Rogowski for the suggestion of this example.

53. On what grounds, Robert Nozick asks, is John Rawls justified in expecting that the better-endowed members of society would take any interest in his scheme of justice or willingly cooperate in implementing it? *Anarchy, State, and Utopia* (New York: Basic Books, 1974), pp. 189-197. It is a good question. Nozick's response is to retain a radically individualistic

social ethic ("There are only individual people . . . with separate lives and so no one may be sacrificed for others" [p. 33]) and to trim back the idea of justice accordingly. I am suggesting, by contrast, that the development and defense of an adequate notion of justice requires that we tap another stratum of social value and moral obligation.

III. Roles and Institutions

Bruce L. Payne

7. Devices and Desires: Corruption and Ethical Seriousness

For the Elizabethan generation "policy" meant actions which, although required by reason of state, were wicked as well as expedient.[1] In modern usage the term has shed its connection with cunning and dissimulation, and has come to mean more neutrally the government's course of action. The change reflects alterations in our philosophy of government and in our ideas about sin and virtue. Utilitarianism, the dominant moral framework of this age, has undermined the distinction between good acts and expedient ones, for both our private and our public lives.

The same period of time has brought with it much less development in our notion of political corruption. Now, as in the early seventeenth century, this phrase means illegal or irregular acts by public officials, motivated by their own pecuniary or political self-interest, and at odds with prevailing conceptions of the public interest.[2] A suggestion of individual moral decay has remained a more-or-less constant correlative over the whole period.

These different histories are compatible with observed reality. The nature and size of government, the shape and extent of policy, have been drastically enlarged. Desire for gain and a willingness to do wrong, on the other hand, are constant. Though corruption sometimes becomes more widespread, or of greater significance in relation to the survival of a regime, it remains formally and motivationally unchanged.

Among modern students of government there has been some interest (though not, perhaps, enough) in finding ways to reduce the incidence of corruption and to limit the damages it can cause.[3] Most of the resulting literature is concerned with changes in government structure or practice; considerably less has to do with honesty, or with character more generally. It is part of my purpose here to redress this imbalance; I mean to argue that while legal and organizational strategies are of great significance in fighting against corruption, attention to the problems of character is likewise necessary.

In the best recent work on corruption, the importance of personal honesty is recognized almost solely as a kind of residuum.[4] Individual virtue is understood to be helpful, even sometimes crucial, in maintaining responsive and legitimate government — but the discussions of organizational reforms and individual incentives are aimed at altering behavior, rather than motivation. This owes both to a realistic recognition that motivation is difficult to change, and to the liberal belief that governmental arrangements can be fashioned so as to produce decent government in spite of, or even by means of, narrowly self-interested individual acts and desires.

While no frontal assault on these assumptions is mounted, this essay argues that a direct concern with character is helpful in understanding political corruption and in reducing its incidence. Without undue optimism about human nature, it nevertheless may be possible to find ways of encouraging the good and decent motives in officials and citizens, and of inhibiting those coexisting vices with which humans are also variously endowed.

The title of this essay derives from the *Book of Common Prayer*. Since Tudor days Anglican congregations have confessed that "We have followed too much the devices and desires of our own hearts. We have offended against thy holy laws." The prayerbook view was that the proper remedy for sin is repentance, combined (God willing) with forgiveness and atonement; and the church threatened on the authority of St. Paul "no less pain than everlasting damnation to all disobedient persons" who followed "man's devices and instinct" rather than "God's wisdom, God's order, power and authority."[5]

These notions were largely rejected by the eighteenth-century thinkers, like Hume and Madison, of whom we are the heirs. They believed that men's predispositions might indeed be evil, but that human devices of law and agreement could use desire to control desire. Ambition was to be set against ambition, faction against faction, interest against interest, and earthly punishments and rewards arranged so as to keep self-interest from threatening the order.

These thinkers thought that private interest, the "pursuit of happiness," was ultimately much safer than those more apparently elevated ideals of righteousness and honor, ideals they thought had been productive of so many murderous wars. They hoped that men who looked to private needs and wants might be induced to moderate their striving for power and glory, that the promise of profit or the expectation of risk or loss would tend on the whole to favor peace and social harmony. Society was to be refounded on self-interest.[6]

The American constitutionmakers, in particular, saw in legislative and judicial self-interest the tools whereby executive corruption might be limited. And they planned more broadly that the potential for corruption throughout the governmental system could be limited by a pattern of checks and balances, and by requirements that governmental powers be shared.[7]

It is, then, hardly to be wondered at that American political scientists see the problem of political corruption as they do. But the very predominance in our society of the egoistic, mechanical, and legal approach of thinkers like Madison suggests we might look elsewhere for solutions to problems that remain unsolved. This is to say that the problem of corruption is not simply to be met by the development of more effective devices, that reform may require psychological insight and moral inquiry, and that it may be helped by the recovery of some older ways of thinking about wrongdoing.

CHARACTER AND CORRUPTION

It seems obvious that personal honesty plays a great role in opposing corruption and in maintaining the integrity of governmental processes.[8] Sanctions against corrupt behavior are notoriously weak, and penalties of any kind are low. Most corruption is probably undetected and unpunished; the great tides of reform have always revealed long-established patterns of corruption. Yet governmental officials in many jurisdictions and at many levels have reputations for personal integrity that seem for the most part well deserved.

There is no attempt here to assess the degree to which character is the determining factor in the incidence of political corruption. It strikes me as in principle impossible to isolate effects of character from those of law and governmental structure. Groups or governments that are serious about integrity will support it with organizational and personal incentives and with sanctions against misbehavior. The important thing to note is that many or most of those who have the opportunity for corrupt advantage do not seize it; only some who are tempted succumb. I think reflection and analysis can help us to see why some do and others don't, and can help us to identify ways in which the contribution of individual character to governmental honesty and reform may be strengthened.

More specifically, my purposes in examining the relation between character and corruption are these: (1) to promote more effective self-scrutiny by officials, and thus to encourage a deeper awareness and a higher degree of conscientiousness about problems of corruption, as well as about the whole range of moral dilemmas faced by officials; (2) to identify ways in which moral leadership in the face of corruption or temptation can be exercised by governmental superiors and subordinates alike; and (3) to consider what kinds of policy choices, whether about corruption or other problems, have beneficial or harmful effects on the characters of individual officials.

Before going on it may be important to enter a sort of disclaimer. I intend no special or technical meaning for the word character. As I understand ordinary speech, character refers to both psychological and moral characteristics—independence, greed, insecurity, confidence, virtue, aggressiveness, passivity, malice, untruthfulness, and the like. I suppose that using the word implies we can know someone—not fully perhaps (even Hobbes says of motivation that only God "searcheth hearts")—that we can say with some confidence of a person we know well what he or she is "really like."[9] Ordinary usage does not assume that knowledge of character requires knowing the causes of these traits, though judgments of character are likely to be modified and deepened by such etiological information.

Novels are often about character, and so is much biographical, psychoanalytic, and other psychological writing; Madison suggested in the tenth *Federalist* that government itself is a reflection on character. Pedagogically and theoretically my own preference in thinking about character is for stories before categories. Words are less elusive when they are tied to the particular acts and attitudes that exemplify them; stories have more staying power in our memories; and the real world, as it appears in history or in the transformations of good novelists, is always more surprising and instructive than the deductive structures of psychological theory or moral philosophy.

The story on which I want to comment is about Spiro Agnew accepting bribes for engineering contracts when he was governor of Maryland. It is in a way a case of old-fashioned garden-variety corruption, and it has the advantage of being the subject of a very good book by Richard M. Cohen and Jules Witcover, *A Heartbeat Away*.[10] Other tales might reveal something about other aspects of our subject, but the carefully considered insights and judgments of Cohen and Witcover provide a rich source for thinking about character.

The Agnew story has a certain helpful clarity. For reasons of personal profit, and in order to have the status and accoutrements of status he craved, Governor Agnew continued and refined a system whereby engineering firms were obliged to pay thousands of dollars to the governor and some of his associates, secretly and in cash, as kickbacks on the contracts they won for state work.

If this seems a simple and traditional case of crime and greed, one lesson may be that greed and illegality are rarely without complexity. Agnew's self-interested corruption was angrily upwardly mobile, and while he built a career on moralism, he seems to have been more than ordinarily obtuse about his own moral choices. Nor are Agnew's crimes unconnected with his conservative but strangely abbreviated ideology. In weighing the meaning of Agnew's crimes, one needs as well to consider the patterns of corruption endemic to Maryland politics. Agnew's claim that he did nothing unusual in taking illegal payments is a significant, if partial, truth.

These considerations merit some closer examination, as do certain further aspects of the Agnew case. The U.S. attorney who prosecuted him, along with Attorney General Elliot Richardson and others of Agnew's opponents, were in many ways typical anticorruptionists, and their attacks on Agnew prompt questions about the connections between our ideas of character and the realities of social class and political power. The sections that follow raise some of the topics we need to think about more fully in considering the relation between character and corruption.

GREED AND NEED

Spiro Agnew wanted more than money, but his pecuniary aspirations were not small. By corrupt means he managed to increase his income dramatically, though by how much remains unclear. He is known to have received $50,000 in cash while governor from one engineering firm, and an additional $10,000 from the same firm was delivered to him in his vice-presidential office. He received more than $50,000 in cash from another firm, $28,000 of that after he became vice-president.[11] Even if the well-documented bribes are larger than most of the others, it is clear the total was substantial. What was all this money for?

The answer seems to be that it offered an opportunity to live extremely well, to buy expensive clothes and meals, to maintain the social position to which Agnew somehow felt entitled. Scorning politicians for the most part, Agnew associated primarily with wealthy businessmen. He lived on their level, and imitated their ways. Cohen and Witcover see him as the authentic embodiment of "middle-class values, hopes and fears" of the "silent majority," a "creature of suburbia" who "seized upon politics as a vehicle to lift him out of mediocrity and obscurity."[12]

These unremarkable aspirations are, in the absence of countervailing ideals, motivation enough for Agnew's extraordinary greed, and his unusual success in getting what he wanted owed at least as much to chance as native talent. What is puzzling is the feeling of entitlement, Agnew's evident conviction that he deserved his illegal gains. My guess is that the only way to make any sense of this is to give amply recognition to the self-righteous anger that was evident in so much of Agnew's public life.

I am suggesting that Agnew's sense of his own unlimited right to rise, to reach a high position, was fueled by resentment, and not by the Horatio Alger hopes, hard work, and luck that can help in accounting for some successful careers. I say resentment because that is what I remember hearing in his voice, and because it makes sense in terms of the values by which he seems to have lived.

The point is that narrow and principally economic self-interest offers a less than satisfactory basis for making one's peace with the world. Assume that a person interprets social life mainly in terms of the restless striving of economic man, as mirrored in himself. Then ask what will happen when such a person meets patterns of distribution that leave him unhappily stuck near the bottom end of society while others, less restless and striving, attain far higher positions. Anger, settled and deep, is not an unlikely reaction. Something like this seems to have been Agnew's condition.

One can of course deal with the various and unequal ways in which property and income are distributed as John Winthrop did, explaining that God in his wisdom has ordained, in order to manifest the necessity of Christian love and social harmony, that at all times some must be rich and others poor.[13] Or one can believe (as I do) that many and diverse values and principles are important, and that in the face of injustice, different sorts of cures or compensations are available. There are also more systematic views: Marxists, for example, angrily decry the injustice of the whole scheme and urge its transformation. For one who is a capitalist, a materialist, and an individualist, the main available option would seem to be directing one's angry energy toward the task of moving up.

Agnew's ire at effete liberals and independent students may have other explanations, and surely the psychological roots of such attitudes are deep. My concern here is not to uncover the sources of personality, but merely to indicate an important connection. The anger, the ambition, and the feeling that taking bribes was somehow justifiable, all fit reasonably with a belief in the primacy and the rightness of economic motivation. The broad support that exists for this belief in our society is part of the culture in which bribery grows. So too, though perhaps less obviously, is the resentment of those whose economic striving seems to them inadequately rewarded. The angry self-righteousness of Agnew and many of those to whom he was a hero is a narrow and genuinely pathetic substitute for larger hopes or selves.

CONSCIENCE

Even at the end Agnew's self-righteousness was evident, but from the beginning it was coupled with a remarkable insensitivity about conflicts of interest or other ethical problems.[14] I think, as I have said, that it was associated in special ways with resentment, and with a narrowly economic view of life. I also believe it owed more than a little to deep feelings of insecurity, though I lack adequate material on which to ground any careful psychological analysis. Such inquiries, well supported biographically, can be instructive; but it is also important to ask about what was not there, and how it might have been. For this some less individualized analytic tools will serve.

What Agnew most obviously lacked was conscience. There is no evidence he felt guilty about what he did, no sign of inner turmoil, of any interior ethical code. A joiner who accepted the moral attitudes of those around him, Agnew never seems to have indulged much in moral questioning or conscientious scrutiny of his own motives. Socrates' constant theme, the Delphic injunction to know oneself, was hardly any part of Agnew's life.

Here again Agnew reflects an important aspect of our political culture. Action is regularly prized over introspection, and not alone by politicians. Academic analysts have often pointed to the dangers of self-doubt and the tormenting conscience, suggesting for example that Franklin Roosevelt's ability to put aside his scruples is preferable to the morally introspective approach of Woodrow Wilson. If effective action is indeed inhibited by an overcareful conscience, must we inquire after ways to a moderated conscientiousness? I do not think so. The notion of conscience need not suggest a kind of moralistic straitjacket that keeps us from the moral risks of political choice. It can mean instead a kind of internalized moral judgment that provides both strength and self-criticism for political action. Let me try to sketch a portrait of conscience seen this way.

The first word is an old one: sin. Whether we use it or not, the word denotes a common aspect of our experience. We do wrong, we have done wrong, knowingly, and willingly. Our own acts are judged by the moral feelings and standards we have developed. Sometimes we are only tempted, and avoid wrong or even manage to do right. But our sense of sin, our knowledge of willful wrongdoing, shapes our consciences.

Moral feelings are part of conscience. We feel the pull of others' needs, and must explain the reasons — to ourselves, at least — when we fail to respond. We see wrong and want it righted, we hear crying and believe it should be comforted. When we've hurt others, we have a desire for forgiveness and reconciliation, and in a more internal way our crimes demand expiation before they can be forgotten, or our rightness with the world restored.

These feelings come to us naturally and gradually, though not with similar power and effect to each. Likewise, we all grow up promising and being obliged to act by the commitments we undertake, for all that some feel the pull of obligation less keenly than do others. My own view is that being moral means, in part, owning these feelings, taking them seriously, and weighing our choices and our reasons in their light.

This view of morality shares something with Reinhold Niebuhr's "neo-orthodox" position (though it has no theological postulate), and while there are obvious differences of emphasis and approach, it is not necessarily opposed to forms of utilitarianism that value moral rules, or the attempt to choose consequences in terms of some desirable pattern of life. My purpose here is not to elaborate it into a competing philosophy, but rather to defend the notion of conscience as relevant to modern lives and helpful in coping with our problems.

PUBLIC DEBATE AND THE PUBLIC INTEREST

Agnew seems to have lacked a very developed sense of the public interest. He spoke about it, of course, but one always had the feeling the rhetoric was not quite serious. I think that feeling was justified, that much of Agnew's conservative, anti-big-government, pro-business, law-and-order ideology was adopted opportunistically, and that it functioned partly as a mask for his rather simpler belief in economic self-interest. This view may be unfairly skeptical; some of Agnew's commitments may have been held more deeply and sincerely than I am willing to believe.

His approach to debate is less subject to uncertainty. Agnew was sure of his own position and scornful of his enemies. More than most participants in the public controversies of our time, Agnew seemed not to feel the weight of the opposing arguments, the pull of the values represented by the views he was attacking. Part of this was surely tactical; many other politicians believe similarly that if they admit to some virtues in the opposition's argument they will weaken their own case. But Agnew's confidence in his own views was unusual enough to earn him an almost unequaled reputation for forthrightness, and among some groups, integrity. In a world of equivocations and howevers, Agnew spoke out clearly.

Those who like their controversy sharp tended to admire Agnew's candor even when they disagreed with his views; to others, Agnew's forthrightness seemed a fraud long before the admissions of corruption. His attacks on reporters showed no sense of the role and importance of a free press, and his law and order stance was hostile to the constitutional guarantees of fair judicial processes. Nor did he exhibit any care, in his attacks on the vices of big government, for the pressing human needs somewhat assuaged by machinery of the welfare state. These omissions were more than rhetorical. He wanted to score debating points, to win support, to further his strategic aims. If he cared about some values, they were few in number, and they were seen simply. About others, there is no evidence he cared at all.

Single-issue candidates and small-range ideologies have their uses in our political order. Sometimes the case must be made emphatically or even unreasonably if it is to become a matter of broad public concern. Nor can one hope to argue effectively or clearly if all the relevant values are always taken into account. But the dangers of partial political argument are real enough. Inured to oversimplifications, we often fail to demand from the parties in our debates any allegiance to the public interest.

By this last phrase I mean at minimum a willingness to have one's arguments and claims tested by some standard of the public good, a willingness to defend one's interests in terms of broader aims and aspirations present in society. I am not claiming there is agreement about what the public interest is, only that in a democracy those involved in politics must admit in principle that their interests are not unlimited, that they are properly adjudicated according to standards that refer to the good of the larger society. It should be evident that such a view ordinarily functions as a bulwark against corruption.

Agnew's narrow views of the meaning of good government are evident in his recurrent explanations of the bribes he accepted. It was important, he kept claiming, to realize that only qualified firms actually got engineering contracts from the government of the state of Maryland, and thus that there was nothing really wrong with the payments he accepted.[15] In such a claim other crucial values are utterly ignored: among them respect for the law, fairness and freedom from favoritism in governmental action, and the reputation for probity of government officials.

Corruption is presumably far more likely in an atmosphere where political ideology does not shape policy goals, and where commitment to the public interest is weak. We may not expect politicians to be moral philosophers, but we ought to demand of them some measure of commitment to principled objectives. And this duty of thoughtfulness, like other duties, should be greater as the position in government is higher. For more is always at stake — at the highest levels, even sometimes the legitimacy of the regime. It seems somehow particularly damning that Vice-President Agnew accepted bribe payments in the White House.

At his worst Agnew appealed to fear and anger, and skirted the edge of racist demagoguery. These are common tactics of narrowly self-interested opportunism; emotional appeals for the most part are too briefly effective to support a long-term program or an enduring party organization. Individuals intent on winning can regularly benefit from such a course, though only at the price of unacceptable risks to the stability and decency of the public order.

MORALITY AND MILIEU

Agnew's principal defense was predictable, and predictably unconvincing. He said the practices followed established custom, and proof is readily available that he was right.[16] Agnew added the novelty of an antimachine governor, with a reputation for integrity, accepting bribes; and it may be also that the level of his greed exceeded precedent. While few would agree that conformity to enduring practice excuses Agnew's acts, the pattern of corruption is worth the attention of anyone interested in reform.

One of the dimensions of the story, as Cohen and Witcover tell it, is a drama of lost faith, the confidence of Agnew's supporters in his uprightness and probity shattered by the revelations and the eventual resignation.[17] Their implicit message is the wise admonition of a long tradition in political journalism: pay attention to substance and not to style. Agnew's supporters were bamboozled, but they need not have been so surprised as they were. The defense of selfishness and the narrow moral horizons were evident in the public Agnew, for anyone who cared to look.

The bribers also have stories, as Cohen and Witcover make clear. They were mostly successful businessmen, respected in their communities, and there were quite a lot of them. Some appear to have been a bit victimized by the extortionate tactics of the politicians; others were evidently corrupters; and all benefited from bribery, at the expense of other businessmen and of the public at large. Lincoln Steffens long ago told the essential story of the interconnection between business power and political power, and in some ways the corruption of the business world made him angrier, because the businessmen then seemed the bigger hypocrites.[18] In the Maryland case the choice is more difficult, but it may be worth noting that there seem to be at least as many deeply corrupt businessmen as politicians in the story.

Reformers, on the other hand, are scarce in politics, and even rarer in business. The most worrisome thing about the Maryland political scene is the lack of any true reform movement. There were and are politicians never tainted with or even accused of corruption, but in the face of widespread knowledge about practices of bribery and other official illegality, it is noteworthy that no constituency for reform was ever built. The Agnew case emerged in a large-scale investigation of Maryland corruption, instituted not by state authorities, but by the office of the U.S. Attorney.

While Agnew's defense was transparent, it should perhaps be noted that the pervasiveness of corruption in a system can sometimes excuse, on rare occasions even justify, certain categories of corrupt acts. If laws are rarely or differentially enforced as a matter of course, for example, or if activities like gambling and prostitution are legally proscribed for symbolic reasons — enunciating values of a dominant group or stigmatizing activities without any real commitment to enforcement — then corruption of police agencies is to be expected. When changing these laws seems impossible, modest levels of bribery may even be tolerable, though a *policy* of official toleration for low-level corruption is likely to encourage worse crimes as well.

Illegal payments accepted, but not demanded, by police or other officials in return for routine and legal favors may be even less harmful. Christmas tips to the mailperson, for instance, may have such sanction in custom that they are not seen as criminal, even when accepting such gifts is formally prohibited. Most gratuities, however, are designed to secure more favorable treatment by officials — as when police are encouraged (bribed) to spend extra time looking out for the property of the giver. In such circumstances other citizens must be less favored, so that this kind of corruption will ordinarily be unfair, and indefensible.

Some defensible bribes can of course be found — a bribe to German or Austrian authorities for exit visas paid by a Jewish family in 1938, for example. Here the law is wrong, and no safe way to change or even to oppose it is available. But only *paying* the bribe is morally justified. An official's reasoning that accepting it serves a good end would not be persuasive: the end can be accomplished without requiring the payment. The distinction is more important than it may seem. Official illegality may always be discovered, and a principled defense of it can — in most regimes — encourage change, or foster other acts of resistance. Such a defense is less effective and less valuable when officials are shown to have acted for private gain. In a bad regime, however, an official might be justified in participating in *organized* corruption that would protect or aid the victims or potential victims of unjust acts. Here accepting bribes might be necessary, both to screen one's more decent motives, and to sustain the ability to offer aid. Such cases are obviously rare in a regime like ours.[19]

EXEMPLARS — CLASS AND CHARACTER

The Agnew story is unusual in that the heroes are almost as interesting as the villains. The officials who brought Agnew to justice are worth studying, both for the dilemmas they faced and for the examples they meant to set.

The five prosecutors were all hard-working lawyers, and for the most part they stayed within the established rules. Three were relatively low-level figures — assistant U.S. attorneys, one of whom, Barney Skolnik, had considerable experience in prosecuting cases involving the bribery of public officials. The two major figures were well-off and socially prominent politically appointed officials: the Brahmin U.S. Attorney General Elliot Richardson, and George Beall, U.S. attorney for Maryland, brother of a U.S. senator and son of a former senator.

The story of the prosecution is in some ways reassuring. Effective at fighting corruption and devoted to official honesty, these attorneys were nonetheless sensitive to competing claims of the public interest. A particular concern was the damage that might result from Agnew's accession to the presidency, and they devoted real care as well to the protection of his constitutional rights as a defendant.[20] (One aspect of prosecutory practice I found disturbing was the conferring of "use immunity" on unwilling witnesses at an early stage of the investigation.[21] Prosecutors have some responsibility to use the available tools if courts have found them constitutional — but they have sufficient discretion to refrain when they believe the courts have been unwise.)

Beall and his assistant Skolnik had suffered political interference during John Mitchell's tenure as attorney general;[22] in the Agnew case they and the others tried hard to reduce the potential for politically imposed limitations on their investigation. One may judge that in the end the culprit got off too lightly, but one can hardly doubt the sincerity of the prosecutors' judgment that Agnew's resignation was the most urgent priority. I remain critical of the prosecutors at this point — Richardson in particular could have been stronger in the plea bargaining — but Cohen and Witcover offer persuasive evidence that the major decisions were thoughtfully made and honorably motivated.[23]

The prosecutors were not without human and lawyerlike failings; they were occasionally affected by selfish considerations or pride, poor judgments were sometimes made, and lies were regularly told the press.[24] But on the whole the record is an admirable one. The deep and vigorous debates in the attorney general's office can serve as models for a careful weighing of the moral stakes of official choice. Richardson's willingness to take seriously the ideas and objections of subordinates was studied, but impressive — here was a public official genuinely concerned to meet the diverse obligations he faced.

There is, for all this, a disturbing thread running through the tale. Though the prosecutors came from moderately diverse backgrounds, three of the five most involved (Beall, Richardson, and Beall's assistant Baker) were members of prominent and wealthy families. Agnew, by contrast, was both arriviste and Greek, with educational attainments in the law and otherwise notably inferior to those of any of his foes.

The motives of reformers, and especially well-off ones, have often been attacked. Arguments have been advanced that the anticorruptionists, drawn from older elites anxious about questions of relative social decline, are simply trying to enforce the norms of their class against interlopers.[25] On this basis it may be thought that corruption is not chiefly a moral or legal problem, but rather principally a symptom of conflict between opposing social groups.

Now it may be true that it is easier to have high ethical standards when one is secure, and it is surely the case that many of the great American fortunes were built with the aid of massive illegality and corruption. Before such arguments can function as a justification for corruption or even an excuse for bribers, however, some further claims must be advanced. It needs to be shown, for example, that other avenues to the advancement of particular groups are indeed highly restricted, and further that the benefits of corrupt practices actually reach excluded groups. These benefits must, moreover, outweigh the interests of the public at large, and also of deprived groups, in more honest government.

In modern American politics such a case could be made only rarely and with difficulty. It is true that money can and does command political power, that WASP elites have retained much of their money and portions of their former social and economic clout, and that the slowness of actual social mobility contrasts sharply with prevailing social myths. No one has demonstrated, however, that the advancement by means of corrupt methods of some able persons, from relatively deprived groups, is anything like an optimum strategy for promoting the interests of those groups, or for increasing the opportunities open to their members. Noncorrupt strategies

—lawsuits, pressure group politics, social movements of various kinds—are all likely to have greater effects on larger numbers of people. Corruption is, in fact, more often directed against such efforts at equalizing opportunity than it is at accomplishing broad gains for the weak.

In this, as in so much else, Agnew's corruption was typical. Greek Americans won some symbolic gains from his success (and presumably suffered similar losses in his disgrace). But Agnew and the bribers—ethnically diverse, but all well off—got away with the money.[26]

The prosecutors were honest and serious public officials, angry and sometimes sickened by the illegality they discovered. While explanations of their attitudes in social class terms finally make little sense—plenty of people similarly placed in American society have behaved very differently—neither are wholly individual explanations adequate. While these lawyers do reflect values of their families and friends,[27] it seems more important that the Maryland attorneys were part of an office with a reformist tradition. Beall's predecessor, Stephen Sachs, had successfully prosecuted several important bribery cases, and Skolnik had been a part of Sachs's staff. There was, moreover, support and reinforcement from others in the Justice Department, and from Internal Revenue Service operatives with long professional experience in investigations of illegal profits.

The U.S. attorney and his staff were fortunate in having Elliot Richardson at the top of the Justice Department. Had the Watergate scandal not already cost John Mitchell his position, the Agnew investigation might have been abruptly canceled, and the prosecutors left with no recourse other than resignation in protest. It may be comforting to know that a deep commitment to honesty remained characteristic of many parts of the Justice Department even through Mitchell's term; but it is more than a bit scary to imagine what demoralization a few more years might have accomplished.

OTHER STORIES

Many of the great moral stories in literature have a satisfying completeness about them. Some characters, at least, know their sins, and by repenting of them embark upon a path of virtue (always to be distinguished from innocence). Occasionally virtue may even be attained: witness Hester Prynne at the end of *The Scarlet Letter*. The Agnew story, by comparison, leaves one with a sense of disquiet. Agnew has been vastly diminished but in no way transformed, and while some of the businessmen are disturbed by their complicity in crime, in only one or two cases is it suggested that any real changes have happened in their lives.

This failing could owe something to the fact that journalists and historians lack the omniscience of novelists: they do not know, and can not know, for sure. But I am prepared to assume the transformations really did not happen—not to Agnew, not to most of the others. Nor were they likely to. Among other things, these men lacked the social support, the expectations on the part of relevant others that their lives might be transformed.

This may suggest a role for renewed religious concern (can we believe that conversion has re-formed Charles Colson?), but it argues more directly for a revivification of language and a recovery of experience. What is needed is more, and more serious, conversation about the moral dilemmas of official life, thoughtful talk informed by criticism and interpretation, by ethical examinations of particular circumstances, by moral connoisseurship—the informed appreciation of ethical differences.

In literary portrayals of corruption, like *All the King's Men* (1946) or Henry Adams' *Democracy* (1880), attention is given to moral failings other than bribery, and especially to the moral blindness that can result from a self-righteous, or merely unthinking, confidence in the decency of one's own motives. Such stories do not serve to defend corruption, but they do argue that there are other forms of iniquity, some of them far worse, and that temptation is ubiquitous. Novels like these can also suggest more readily than can journalism or most academic writing the ways by which character is formed or altered.

Biography offers similar advantages, and one recent book is unusually edifying with regard to corruption: Robert Caro's *The Power Broker*,[28] a study of the public career in New York city and state of Robert Moses. Although Moses received no personal financial benefit from his dealings as parks commissioner (or any of the many jobs he often held simultaneously), the highway, public housing, park, and other projects he conceived are portrayed by Caro as a kind of fountain of corruption. All this was, of course, in the service of ends Moses believed to be decent and necessary, and he has been, if anything, less penitent than Agnew. A fair-minded observer, however, would probably conclude that Moses' "good-government" image served to shield many actions that never should have been tolerated, and that Moses often chose to work with corrupt individuals and groups in order to avoid procedural and democratic constraints.

There are, in fact, many true and many imaginary accounts that can illuminate the psychological and moral dimensions of the important problems of official illegality that we face. They can help us rediscover and make new old notions about character and wrongdoing, about self-interest, conscience, and moral seriousness. Without such renewal, these essential matters are likely to be studied formally and abstractly, an approach that risks pedagogic failure.

MAINTAINING INTEGRITY: LAWS AND IDEALS

We need to use what we learn about character in fashioning laws and governmental changes, and in shaping anticorruption efforts in the context of broader policy aims. Those who would speak only of personal qualities risk the charge of ineffectuality and even hypocrisy, and anyone who means to encourage individual virtue, at least in situations other than small groups, must admit that the support of law and governmental regularity are necessary. A few individuals behaving badly with impunity can weaken the commitment of many others to moral principles, or to conscience, or to habits of generosity. Nor are societies divided so easily into better and worse citizens or officials. We know laws are needed from the strength of our own desires, even if it happens that we ourselves have the means to control them.

There are counterproductive laws, as well. "Reforms" can easily be discovered that have had no real effect on reducing corruption, and which have at the same time increased official hypocrisy. While it will not be possible to inspect the whole arsenal of techniques that have been advocated or adopted in fighting corruption, it should be possible to ask about the likely effects on characters, and on official wrongdoing, of some of the major strategies.

There are many varieties of corruption,[29] and more-or-less effective strategies have been designed against each. The Australian ballot, secret voting, registration laws, and some of the legislation about campaign finance have, for example, vastly reduced the scope of electoral corruption. Nor should it be forgotten that America has for the most part succeeded in limiting corruption to venality; that scandals like Watergate, in which laws were violated to augment political power, are relatively rare, owes much to the strength of our institutional arrangements. Thus, the focus here is on venality. Which approaches have been effective against corruption and supportive of integrity in the lives of officeholders, and which have not?

ORDINARY DEVICES

When Agnew took office as Maryland's governor in 1967, the prospects for corrupt advantage were inviting. Decisions about engineering contracts involved relatively few people in state government, and the governor had broad discretion in awarding contracts, discretion not subsequently reviewed by any other authority. Interest in the possibilities of high-level corruption was faint in the press, and among most of Maryland's prosecutors and law enforcement establishment. Many of the usual controls, advocated for decades by reformers, did not exist. The result was a political order in which corruption was widespread, even, perhaps, expected. In such a situation three general types of anticorruption strategies seem called for: procedural reforms, investigations, and the reduction of unnecessary discretion. Each of these approaches has its distinct advantages, and each is likely to incur some costs.

The most important procedures in fighting corruption are those that ensure that an official's acts will be reviewed by others. Some reviews are appropriately conducted by supervisors. Opportunities for dishonesty are reduced when each decision must be explained and justified, when complaints can be heard, and decisions reversed, by higher authority. Reviews can also be carried out by auditing agencies, or by inspectors general, or by the courts. The expectation of regular review will tend to lower the likelihood of the discoverable forms of graft.

Other procedural matters are also important. Dishonesty is made more difficult when government documents are accessible to investigating agencies and to the public at large. Requirements of financial disclosure by officials increase the difficulties in making use of illegally gained funds. There are costs here, organizationally in the greater delays and enlarged disputes occasioned by openness, and personally in the reduced financial privacy of officials; but these costs seem, on the whole, acceptable. Secrecy must sometimes be maintained for reasons of national security; when the justification is merely administrative efficiency, however, the values of governmental integrity, to say nothing of democracy, must ordinarily be convincing on the side of openness.

Investigations perform a function similar to review, but they are more narrowly focused on the possibilities of criminal behavior, and they are usually conducted by outsiders, by law enforcement agencies — police, the FBI, district attorneys, or special prosecutors — or by legislative bodies, or by the press.[30] Techniques of investigation that encourage mistrust or risk unjust accusations may do more harm than good, but these cautionary considerations are no argument against well-run and even frequent investigations, occurring both regularly and randomly over time. A certain level of disgruntlement may exist in an organization that faces repeated investigations, especially when an in-house, undercover unit exists, but more substantial fears and greater demoralization will almost certainly occur in relation to rare investigations prompted by particular suspicions.

Corruption is likely to be further hindered when the reduction of official discretion accompanies increased review and investigation. Competitive bidding can be instituted for contracts, and merit systems can replace discretionary hiring and firing. Civil service, the great hope of the nineteenth-century reformers, has largely fulfilled its promise as an anticorruption device. The merit system may give too much job security to some whose merit is small, but it has protected the great body of government officials from arbitrary demands and from the application of political tests for employment. Relative financial security has weakened once strong economic incentives to peculation, and has removed the economic necessity of loyalty to party or political organizations.

More detailed laws of various kinds can reduce discretion still further, so that officials lose their powers to make exceptions, or to alter or adjust policy without recourse to the legislature, but there are obvious costs, in morale and governmental flexibility, of going further along this road. Laws about the zoning of property, for instance, can be much more specifically written, and the authority of zoning boards considerably narrowed. This may, however, reduce the ability of representatives to respond quickly to changing conditions or new possibilities, or to the expressed wishes of their constituents.

These reservations about reducing the scope of official discretion are of some force in relation to the procedures of review mentioned earlier. More laws and rules, more hierarchy, more bureaucratization, may indeed reduce corruption, but how much money and organizational effort is this goal worth? What are the costs in democratic values, in organizational morale, and in character, of pursuing these anticorruption strategies more vigorously?

The extent of corruption is vast, and the monetary costs of it are large. The Knapp Commission reported that in 1971, in New York City, "police corruption was . . . an extensive, Department-wide phenomenon, indulged in to some degree by a sizable majority of those on the force."[31] Levels of corruption rise and fall, of course—New York's reputation has improved decidedly in recent years—but similarly high levels have been characteristic of many cities in the recent past.[32] Recent scandals, like earlier ones, have revealed corruption in all levels of government—state and local and federal agencies—and in many fields—agriculture, foreign aid, the purchasing of office supplies, immigration, etc. It is evident that corruption is widespread; it seems fair to assume that it involves enormous sums of money. No one has estimated the costs for the corruption revealed in the recent GSA scandals at anything less than several billion dollars.

Thus it seems probable that any successful anticorruption efforts will survive the simpler tests of cost-effectiveness. The more difficult question is whether such strategies will affect morale and character and governmental effectiveness adversely. Clearly they will not, if they are only compared to the alternative of doing nothing; unchecked corruption is demoralizing, and it will probably eventuate in scandals that profoundly disrupt an agency's functioning. The problem is rather to determine which effective methods are least likely to have severely damaging collateral effects.

It has already been suggested that frequent investigations are to be preferred to infrequent and scandal-provoked inquiries. There are, however, other questions about how investigations ought to be designed and staffed. The ideal of a large, national, professional investigative agency, relatively independent of political control, is an attractive one, but it must be confessed that the FBI has on occasion misused its powers, intimidating officials and others.[33] It would appear, now that the days of J. Edgar Hoover and his immediate successors are past, that the FBI will remain open to press criticism and to legislative oversight, and that its procedures will be monitored by the courts with reasonable care. Potential for abuse remains, but the Bureau will probably be a major resource for any really broad examinations of large-scale official illegality.

The Agnew case shows what can be done by U.S. attorneys who are energetic in opposing bribery. While other important types of criminal investigations compete for the attention of their staffs, U.S. attorneys should probably be more involved than they are in probes of officials and agencies. The attorney general would be well advised to encourage or even to require greater efforts in this direction.[34] Nor should the potential of special prosecutors be ignored. From Charles Evans Hughes, whose investigations of New York's insurance companies were the springboard of a long and valuable public career, to Archibald Cox, special prosecutors have been among the more effective reformers.[35] That regular prosecutors resist such appointments as encroachment or reproach is not surprising, but special prosecutors can ordinarily, in fact, bring greater resources of money and staff to bear, with less cost for other anticrime work.

Investigations are essential for the serious work of reforming, or even for maintaining such governmental integrity as exists; but like punishment, their effects are primarily negative. Some processes of review, like audits are similarly designed to deter dishonesty. Others, however, can more directly encourage probity, and foster commitment to values associated with democracy and the public service.

The expectation that one's decisions will be reviewed by a superior, or by one's colleagues, does not necessarily provoke anxiety. Whether review means hostile snooping and implicit opposition to bureaucratic independence and creativity, or generally constructive criticism, depends very much on how it is conducted. As with investigations, review that is recurrent and expected will have a less damaging effect on morale than the occasional supervisory interventions occurring in response to outside attacks.

Review by peers or by higher authorities can serve to open a discussion of the moral stakes evident in particular decisions, and procedures of review — including those of formal complaints and hearings and appeals—can serve as forums for moral talk that might revive commitment to the animating ideals of an agency, or to the personal standards that guard against dishonesty. Too many bureaucrats try to think and act as if official misbehavior was inconceivable within their precincts, and then, in the face of scandal, are left with nothing more convincing than President Harding's lament, that he was unknowingly betrayed by his "God-damn friends."[36]

Agency chiefs and other high officials are in fact well placed to affect the culture of discussion in the government. It is not enough that they have integrity, however; they must also exemplify it and find ways of encouraging it. One means might be a kind of moral inquest or "grand rounds," an examination of the ethical aspects of some problematic case recently faced by the agency or by individual officials.[37] Even in ordinary reviews subordinates are taught the operative standards, learning whether or which rules and laws are to be respected, and how seriously conflicts among values are to be taken. A more formal process, for a few decisions that seem especially interesting, might have very great advantages in encouraging ethical seriousness.

One benefit of this kind of procedure is that moral commitments and attitudes will at least occasionally be expressed directly, and by those in authority. One of the consequences of the "toughminded" and "hardnosed" school of decisionmaking in the 1960s was the repression of moral discussion at high levels within the national administration. Although deep and largely unvoiced moral commitments were present, they were not available as tools of inquiry, nor helpful in questioning some of the assumptions of our policy in Vietnam.[38]

Many other promising approaches to reform are advocated. Some of these aim at reducing the price of bribery by organizational alterations, or at otherwise changing the structure of corrupt incentives.[39] Others would increase the penalties for corrupt acts, especially ones involving large sums of money, in order that large bribes might be as effectively deterred as small ones (and also, one supposes, so that the punishment might more nearly fit the crime).[40] As government grows more complicated, and as new ways of accomplishing its objects are developed, fresh opportunities for illegitimate gain arise. It seems only prudent to consider such remedies as modern analysts have devised.

Nevertheless, my own doubts about the efficacy of technical solutions remain strong; and they are indeed somewhat confirmed by the fact that the most recent and most advanced study of the political economy of corruption ends with a discussion of morality—albeit in terms that tend to reduce morality to one rather narrow version of democratic theory.[41] Democratic theory *is* relevant here; rule by the people is impossible when public choices are made corruptly. But other values must also have their place in any full consideration—among them justice, legitimacy, and equity.

IDEALS IN THE PUBLIC SERVICE

As a member of a U.S. Forest Service family, I grew up around people committed to the ideals of conservation and multiple use, the management of natural resources aimed at the greatest good for the greatest number in the long run. Those ideals, along with the thoroughgoing professionalism that supported them, were adumbrated by Chief Forester Gifford Pinchot in the administration of Teddy Roosevelt, and they have remained prime supports for the institutional integrity of the Forest Service, and for the enviable reputation of honesty and public-spiritedness that agency has maintained over the years. From my own observations I have no doubt that idealism, coupled with pride in expertise and public service, strengthened the habit of serious talk about the public interest, and supported the deep conscientiousness and honesty of the Forest Service officials I have known.[42]

Conservation was for Pinchot and his fellow Progressive reformers a part of the gospel of efficiency in the development of the use of natural resources.[43] As an ideal it has had its critics. Partisans of the free market have argued that the kind of efficiency it envisages is less than optimal, and preservationists have maintained an enduring skepticism about its bias toward use.[44] Conservation and the doctrine of multiple use have, however, retained their authority for Forest Service personnel, though not without the adoption of some preservationist goals.

That Forest Service idealism about conservation has been helpful in preventing corruption is instructive. The ideal is not so vague as to be shared by everyone, and it is not merely rhetorical; it is believed in and applied by a large number of officials across a broad range of problems. In public debate and in relation to concrete cases the ideal is given specific reference, and it serves as a guide in assessing those particulars relevant to a certain version of the public interest in the area of natural resources. It should be apparent that this is an ideal capable of contributing to the kind of ethical discourse that has been advocated throughout this essay. It supports a thoughtful weighing of the values at stake in a choice, and it fosters awareness of the public interest in the decisionmakers themselves.

I have said the language of conservation is not merely rhetorical, but that it is a piece of rhetoric need not be denied. Rhetoric is persuasive speech, or the art of influencing thought and action by words. Identifying it, as we do, with exhortation or with sophistry, we underestimate its usefulness and are suspicious of its relation to morality.

When we use rhetoric — which is most of the time, even in scientific writings — the ordinary obligations of truthfulness and logic apply. Persuasive language about morality need not claim certainty, or any greater confidence in the truth of ideas than one actually has. What it must do is to reach out to readers or listeners in a way that touches them, that enlists their imaginations, or their values, or their interests, or their fears.[45]

That ideals, and the rhetoric that supports them, can be extraordinarily dangerous is news to no one.[46] The greatest crimes of the century have come out of the passionate hopes of fascism and communism and nationalism. All ideals, even the worst, transcend narrow self-interest. What we need is not idealism per se, but decent ideals, visions of the public interest, that are not destructive of our most important and essential values.

Reform itself can be such an ideal at times when corruption seems of overwhelming importance. "The principle of my reform," said Lord Grey in 1830, "is to prevent the necessity for revolution." Had he not secured passage of the Great Reform Act, the manifest unfairness of the pre-1832 system of parliamentary representation would almost certainly have led to major political unheaval in England.[47] In the face of extraordinary municipal corruption in America, a Progressive movement was built in the early part of this century that played a crucial role in ending the power of corrupt machines in the cities.[48] The Progressive ideal of reform was accomplished, at least in part, by effective candidacies and by campaigns of exposure and political pressure. The structural reforms of Progressivism included some poorly chosen strategies seemingly aimed against politics of any sort; among these the initiative and referendum, the nonpartisan law, and the attacks on political parties seem the most conspicuous failures.[49]

Many other values — including ecology, equity, and (more strongly) justice, — function as ideals for those in the public service. Nor are those now planning careers in government bereft of decent aspirations for the common good. But it must be admitted that government is increasingly dominated by habits of thought and methods of analysis that seem to have little room for such hopes. Values of all kinds must be fitted into models and analyses in which the terms of comparison are fundamentally economic.

This represents something of a triumph of rationality, and it embodies the utilitarian faith that desires for pleasure and the avoidance of pain make all human goods commensurable. As a framework for analysis, and for the justification of policy choices, the idea of utility has obvious advantages. Benefits and costs can be analyzed across wide areas of policy, and outcomes in the marketplace or in politics can be seen as the result of consumer or citizen preferences, aggregated in ways that reflect the intensity of preferences. Ultimately policy resulting from a mixture of market forces, political pressures, and benefit-cost analysis can be seen as roughly reflective of the choices of an imaginary omniscient utilitarian decisionmaker — not an invisible hand, rather a kind of invisible digital computer.

In all this the pull of ideals seems almost irrelevant. While utilitarianism, like any good ethical theory, can surely accommodate them in some way, it does not call attention to them, or show us very clearly that they are needed, or even helpful.

With its focus on substantive ends, its individualism, and its compatibility with democratic principles, utilitarianism in some mode or fashion will no doubt continue to guide our public choices. It need not constrain our minds. Other ways of thinking — about conscience, or character, or civic virtue — may be better able to suggest the missing moral questions, or the goods or ends the analysts can include but are unlikely to discover.

For thinking more deeply and broadly about the problem of corruption, there are several places we can turn. One valuable recent study, for example, has traced the theory of corruption in some of the great political philosophers, arguing that unjust inequality is seen by thinkers as diverse as Thucydides, Plato and Aristotle, Machiavelli and Rousseau to be a fundamental cause of corruption.[50] The same study claims that the theory of corruption they share argues for educational efforts, broad political participation, and limits on the accumulation of great wealth as effective supplements to particular laws and structures.[51]

Traditional theorists were also concerned with character, and Plato was not alone in illustrating his thinking with specific persons. His portrait of Socrates remains near the center of any of our ideas about civic virtue. In the long run, the study of particular stories is preferable to any abstract analysis of character or virtue, though it may take much more time.

If we are serious about limiting corruption in the public service, we are going to need more than the devices of law and bureaucratic or economic incentives. We need to learn about the shape of honesty and integrity, as well as about the sources of vice. To study strength and weakness of character, or how civic virtue might be fostered, we could do much worse than starting with the Greeks. But we might do even better to look first at Americans, modern figures and old ones too. One good choice would be James Madison, whose whole labor of constitutional design was animated, and guided, by a deep and personal faith in the ideal of liberty.

NOTES

1. George L. Mosse, *The Holy Pretence* (Oxford: Basil Blackwell, 1957), p. 14. Hotspur contrasts "base and rotten policy" to the loyalty of "noble Mortimer." Shakespeare *I Henry IV* I, iii.

2. Joel Hurstfeld, "The Political Morality of Early Stuart Statesmen," *History*, 56 (June 1971), 235ff. Well before the seventeenth century "corrupt" had referred to acts, and persons, "perverted from uprightness and fidelity in the discharge of duty; influenced by bribery or the like; venal" (*OED*). Modern scholars writing about political corruption, however, rely more on law than on norms of "uprightness and fidelity"; hence my insistence that corrupt acts be both illegal *and* self-serving. Plunkitt's "honest graft," taking advantage of inside information about governmental decisions for personal gain, is corrupt according to this more strict view only when the law clearly prohibits such acts. See William L. Riordon, *Plunkitt of Tammany Hall* (New York: McClure, Phillips, 1905), pp. 3-4, and Arnold J. Heidenheimer, ed., *Political Corruption: Readings in Comparative Analysis* (New York: Holt, Rinehart and Winston, 1970), pp. 3-6. The inclusion of some reference to the public interest reflects ordinary habits of thought and speech, but the logical defensibility of this portion of the definition is disputed. Ibid., p. 6, and Carl J. Friedrich, *The Pathology of Politics* (New York: Harper and Row, 1972), pp. 161ff. My own view is that corruption should chiefly mean official, self-regarding, illegal acts or procedural violations; but some reference to the public interest must logically remain part of the concept. Corruption is a strong term, too strong for at least some minor self-interested violations of law or rules. Welfare officials might, for example, omit tedious but legally required paperwork. If this harms their clients or otherwise evidently injures the public interest, we may call such practices corrupt. Absent any harm to the public weal, the term could not apply.

3. The best of the recent studies is, in part, very practically oriented: Susan Rose-Ackerman, *Corruption: A Study in Political Economy* (New York: Academic Press, 1978). On an especially important part of the problem see Lawrence W. Sherman, *Scandal and Reform: Controlling Police Corruption* (Berkeley: University of California Press, 1978). A less hopeful view of the possibilities for reform is offered in W. Michael Reisman, *Folded Lies: Bribery, Crusades, and Reforms* (New York: Free Press,

1979). This last work does, however, offer some useful cautions about real and pretended reforms.

4. Rose-Ackerman, *Corruption*, pp. 2, 4, 12, 134.

5. *Sermons or Homilies Appointed to Be Read in Churches in the Time of Queen Elizabeth of Famous Memory* (London: C. J. Rivington, 1825), p. 118, "The Sermon on Obedience."

6. Compare the account of Albert O. Hirschman, *The Passions and the Interests: Political Arguments for Capitalism Before Its Triumph* (Princeton: Princeton University Press, 1977).

7. See Richard Bushman, "Corruption and Power in Provincial America," and Edmund S. Morgan, "Royal and Republican Corruption," in Richard B. Morris and others, *The Development of a Revolutionary Mentality* (Washington, D.C.: Library of Congress, 1972).

8. The Knapp Commission report on police corruption, in a section headed "Factors Influencing Corruption," says this: "The most important of these [factors] is, of course, the character of the officer in question, which will determine whether he bucks the system and refuses all corruption money; goes along with the system and accepts what comes his way; or outdoes the system, and aggressively seeks corruption-prone situations and exploits them to the extent that it seriously cuts into the time available for doing his job." *New York City Commission to Investigate Allegations of Police Corruption . . . Commission Report, December 26, 1972* (New York: George Braziller, 1973), p. 67.

9. Because his purposes were predictive, James David Barber, in his book *The Presidential Character: Predicting Performances in the White House* (Englewood Cliffs, N.J.: Prentice-Hall, 1972), defines the term more narrowly. His generalized psychological categories, "active-positive," and so on, are designed to assist voters and others in the task of choosing presidents, and for this they strike me as at least marginally helpful. In my view, however, the great strength of Barber's book is not its predictive apparatus, but its insights about the relation of character, in his sense and in the broader ordinary usage, to political performance. Telling the stories, pondering their meaning, comparing them to other stories, Barber's work can assist the sort of self-scrutiny I am urging. Hobbes's comment appears in the introduction to *Leviathan* (London, 1651).

10. Richard Cohen and Jules Witcover, *A Heartbeat Away: The Investigation and Resignation of Vice President Spiro T. Agnew* (New York: Bantam, 1974).

11. Ibid., pp. 97-99, 136.

12. Ibid., pp. 16, 17, 32.

13. John Winthrop, "*A Modell of Christian Charity*," written on board the Arabella, 1630, in Perry Miller and Thomas H. Johnson, eds., *The Puritans* (New York: Harper and Row, 1963), I, 195. This sermon owes much to the "Sermon on Obedience," cited in n. 5.

14. Cohen and Witcover, *Heartbeat*, pp. 23, 28-29.

15. Cohen and Witcover, *Heartbeat*, p. 22.

16. Ibid., p. 40.

17. Ibid., p. 33.

18. Lincoln Steffens, *The Shame of the Cities* (New York: McClure, Phillips, 1904).

19. But not impossible. Consider the morally wrenching difficulties faced by low-level immigration or public health officials who deal with undocumented aliens, illegally doing needed work in our country.

20. There were leaks damaging to the vice-president's public reputation during the investigation, but the prosecution team seems unlikely to have been responsible for many of these. Cohen and Witcover, *Heartbeat*, pp. 203-211. The White House emerges as the most likely source of the information that appeared in the press, though Agnew's staff of lawyers, or Justice Department lawyers, may also have been responsible. Cohen and Witcover carefully tell less than they undoubtedly know.

21. Ibid., p. 66.

22. Ibid., pp. 62-63.

23. See esp. ibid., pp. 313-316.

24. Ibid., p. 82. The defense for these lies, concerning whether the vice-president was under investigation, is that they served the important goal of helping to protect the early stages of the investigation from high-level political interference. This is only partially adequate. It may well be that the mutually advantageous relationship between press and prosecutors had in this case made the ordinarily ethically preferable "no comment" tantamount to admission. But surely some careful thinking in advance about the needs of reporters and prosecutors could have reshaped the pattern. That lying is a regular and rather casually accepted necessity for prosecutors is disturbing — there is great potential for abuse, and potential damage as well to the social strength of ordinary rules supporting truthfulness.

25. See, for example, William F. Whyte, "Social Organization in the Slums," *American Sociological Review*, 8 (February 1943), 34-39. "Politics and the rackets have furnished an important means of social mobility for individuals, who, because of ethnic background and low class position, are blocked from advancement in the 'respectable' channels." Quoted in Robert K. Merton, "Some Functions of the Political Machine," pp. 72-78, in *Social Theory and Social Structure* (New York: Free Press, 1957), reprinted in Jack D. Douglas and John M. Johnson, eds., *Official Deviance: Readings in Malfeasance, Misfeasance, and Other Forms of Corruption* (Philadelphia: J. B. Lippincott, 1977), p. 345.

26. One of the bribers, Lester Matz, is more interesting than Agnew on this score. He made handsome profits by purchasing favorable treatment from Agnew in Maryland. Yet he seems to have felt a need to transform some of his tainted gains into good works, giving generously to his temple and to other charities. Had Matz not agreed to the bribes, his business might not have prospered as rapidly as it did. But he was already doing quite well in nongovernment contracts. Matz's evident guilty conscience seems fully justified, but it, and the desire for atonement suggested by his willingness to testify, show a measure of decency in him almost wholly absent in any of his fellow criminals. See Cohen and Witcover, *Heartbeat*, esp. pp. 8-9, 94-99.

27. Compare, for example, Beall's rejection of Agnew's offer of a political appointment in 1968, in return for a switch to Nixon. Ibid., p. 31.

28. Robert Caro, *The Power Broker: Robert Moses and the Fall of New York* (New York: Alfred Knopf, 1974).

29. Among them bribery, extortion, conflict of interest, election fraud, direct theft of public funds or property, stigmatized by Plunkitt as "dishonest graft." Other types are suggested by the illegal acts of the Watergate drama directed against political opponents apart from the electoral process, and by related crimes committed to conceal earlier illegal acts.

30. Attempts to control police corruption are notoriously difficult, and internal investigatory controls have often proved inadequate. In his study of police corruption, Lawrence W. Sherman notes several instances in which investigations by the press were crucial in the discovery and the reform of corrupt practices; but Sherman also describes ways of making internal policing effective. Sherman, *Scandal and Reform*, pp. 244-256 et passim.

31. *Knapp Commission Report*, p. 61.

32. Sherman, *Scandal and Reform*, p. xxx. Sherman comments that "six years after the Knapp Commission hearings, corruption no longer appears to be widespread."

33. See, for example, Sanford Ungar, *FBI* (Boston: Little, Brown, 1976), pp. 355-357.

34. See Wayne Barrett's disturbing account of the weak anticorruption record of the office of the U.S. attorney for the southern district of New York. "Freedom to Steal: Why Politicians Never Go to Jail," *New York*, 13 (February 4, 1980), 26-32.

35. Robert F. Wesser, *Charles Evans Hughes: Politics and Reform in New York, 1905-1910* (Ithaca: Cornell University Press, 1967), pp. 40-48.

36. Francis Russell, *The Shadow of Blooming Grove: Warren G. Harding in His Times* (New York: McGraw-Hill, 1968), pp. 560, 571. Russell's book is another valuable story about character and corruption.

37. This plan was suggested by the "grand rounds" of the great teaching hospitals. There, cases are selected, often one each week, for full-scale discussion by leading members of the staff. Other members of the staff, and students, are an occasionally participating audience. Cases of all kinds are examined in this way, and in recent years they have focused occasionally on the ethical dimensions of the cases in question.

Another means of promoting ethical seriousness would be to encourage good writing about morally troubling decisions. Historians and scholars of the bureaucracy might well be encouraged to prepare short case studies available for reading within the agency and, eventually, by others.

38. On this point see David Halberstam, *The Best and the Brightest* (New York: Fawcett Crest, 1973), esp. pp. 87-88, 497, 595.

39. Rose-Ackerman, *Corruption*, pp. 221-228. Note especially her discussion of overlapping jurisdictions and competition, among low-level bureaucrats, to reduce bribe prices while maintaining some official discretions (pp. 137-166, 221).

40. Ibid., pp. 219-220.

41. Ibid., pp. 228-234.

42. My father, Burnett H. Payne, has retired after forty years in the Forest Service. His stepfather, J. Dennie Ahl, was a long-term employee of the Service, and so, too, is my brother, Brian R. Payne. Their enduring commitment to the public interest undergirds my best hopes for the decency and honor of government service.

43. Samuel P. Hays, *Conservation and the Gospel of Efficiency: The Progressive Conservation Movement, 1890-1920*, 2d ed. (New York: Atheneum, 1969), pp. 27-48.

44. Preservationists like John Muir believed in a different ideal; they wanted to maintain unspoiled the natural beauty of the wilderness. The conflict was at its most fierce during the Hetch-Hetchy dispute in California, which lasted until 1914 (see ibid., pp. 192-193), and there is still no full rapprochement. Disagreements in recent years between the Forest Service and the Sierra Club over the status and management of wilderness areas have continued the old opposition.

45. Bernard of Clairvaux said, "It is not enough to believe in general that God forgives sins; thou must also believe that He forgives thee." J. S. Whale, *The Protestant Tradition* (Cambridge, Eng.: Cambridge University Press, 1959), p. 46. These words, quoted to an anguished Luther by the Master of Novices at Erfurt in 1506, and never forgotten by him, suggest the essential point here. There is a personal, willing element in all knowledge. It is this element that marks the difference between teaching and telling.

46. Joan Didion notes one type of danger eloquently: "When we start deceiving ourselves into thinking not that we want something or need something, not that it is a pragmatic necessity for us to have it, but that it is a moral imperative that we have it, then is when we join the fashionable madmen, and then is when the thin whine of hysteria is heard in the land, then is when we are in bad trouble." *Slouching Towards Bethlehem* (New York: Dell, 1968), p. 163.

47. Michael Brock, *The Great Reform Act* (London: Hutchinson, 1963), p. 336.

48. It has been said that FDR and the New Deal destroyed machines and the corruption that went with them by federalizing relief and taking over many of the old functions of the machines. This seems unlikely. See Lyle Dorsett, *Franklin D. Roosevelt and the City Bosses* (Port Washington, N.Y.: Kennikat Press, 1977), pp. 3-5, 117n, who cites several studies that offer impressive arguments against this thesis. While the New Deal did centralize authority, many of its programs were locally administered, often by supporters of machines loyal to Roosevelt. Pressures against corruption could be effectively focused by the reformers on the more visible (and more responsive) national government, and the programs stayed relatively clean. Most of the machines have died, but for other causes—demographic changes, internal failures, and the repeated assaults of reform.

49. Grant McConnell, *Private Power and American Democracy* (New York: Vintage, 1970), pp. 38-50.

50. J. Patrick Dobel, "The Corruption of a State," *American Political Science Review*, 172 (September 1978), 958-973.

51. Ibid., p. 972.

Sissela Bok

8. Blowing the Whistle

"Whistleblowing" is a new label for a practice as old as government it-self. Whistleblowers sound an alarm from within the very organization within which they work, aiming to spotlight neglect or abuses that threaten the public interest. To sound such an alarm is to take great risks. The en-gineer who speaks out about a defective bridge, the chemical company employee who reveals undisclosed disposals of dangerous chemical wastes, the Defense Department official who alerts Congress to military graft and overspending: all know that they pose a threat to those whom they accuse, and that their own careers may be at stake.

A government employee who is wondering whether to speak out about abuses or serious neglect confronts a difficult choice. He has, at least in theory, the right and even the duty to speak out. The U.S. Code of Ethics for government servants asks them to "expose corruption wherever uncov-ered" and to "put loyalty to the highest moral principles and to country above loyalty to persons, party, or Government department."[1]

In practice, however, government employees know that whistleblowing often leads to personal loss: to dismissal, demotion, or reassignment; or to loss of collegial relationships and to sacrifice of reputation for "soundness."

A particularly damaging risk is that of being forced to undergo a psy-chiatric fitness-for-duty examination. Congressional hearings in 1978 uncovered a growing resort to such mandatory examinations, and found that they frequently result from conflicts between supervisors and em-ployees.[2] A person declared unfit for service can then be "separated" as well as discredited from the point of view of any allegations he may be making. The chairman concluded that: "There was general agreement . . . that involuntary psychiatric examinations were not helpful to the Govern-ment, unfair to employees and that the agencies placed psychiatrists in an impossible situation."

204

Outright firing, finally, is the most direct institutional response to whistleblowers. One civil servant, reflecting on her experience and on that of others, stated: "The reactions of those who have observed or exposed the truth about Federal Agencies have ranged from humiliation, frustration and helpless rage to complete despair about our democratic process."[3]

The plight of whistleblowers has come to be documented by the press and described in a number of books.[4] Evidence of the hardships imposed on those who choose to act in the public interest has combined with a heightened awareness of malfeasance and corruption in the government to produce a shift toward greater public support of whistleblowers. Public service law firms and consumer groups have taken up their cause: institutional reforms and legislation have been proposed to combat illegitimate reprisals.[5] Some would encourage ever more government employees to ferret out and publicize improprieties in the agencies where they work.

Given the indispensable services performed by so many whistleblowers—as during the Watergate period and after—strong public support is often merited. But the new climate of acceptance makes it easy to overlook the dangers of whistleblowing: of uses in error or in malice; of work and reputations unjustly lost for those falsely accused; of privacy invaded and trust undermined. There comes a level of internal prying and mutual suspicion at which no institution can function. And it is a fact that the disappointed, the incompetent, the malicious, and the paranoid all too often leap to accusations in public. Worst of all, ideological persecution throughout the world traditionally relies on insiders willing to inform on their colleagues or even on their family members, often through staged public denunciations or press campaigns.

No society can count itself immune from such dangers. But neither should it deny the right to speak out, or do without the safeguard whistleblowing provides in times of need. The effort, therefore, must be to consider both the costs of whistleblowing and its legitimacy: to see some instances of whistleblowing as justified, but not others. It is when it comes to singling out just which ones *are* justifiable, however, that opinions split. Charles Peters and Taylor Branch, in their book *Blowing the Whistle*, show how gaping the split can be.

The public reaction to two whistle-blowers, Otto F. Otepka and Daniel Ellsberg, clearly illustrates the disorienting spells cast upon fervent observers by the spectacle and drama of exposures from within—especially in cases that involve national security, as these two did. Otepka violated national security by slipping classified documents to veteran Red-hunter Julian T. Sourwine of the Senate Internal Security Subcommittee. He was fired for his transgressions in 1963, lost his position as chief of the State

Department's security-evaluation division, became a martyr of the right wing, and is considered by some to be the first whistle-blower in the modern period. Ellsberg violated national security by slipping classified documents, later to be called the "Pentagon Papers," to numerous senators and newspapers. He is being tried for his transgressions in 1971, has lost his security clearance at the RAND Corporation, became a martyr of the left wing, and is considered by many the capstone contemporary ideological whistle-blower.

Although these two men are ideological opposites, there are unmistakable similarities between their respective exploits . . . Ellsberg and Otepka operated by the same laws of motion in some ways, following their higher instincts regarding the public interest as they saw it, exposing treachery in places of power on questions of life and death. These similarities suggest that anyone who wants to fight institutional *rigor mortis* by encouraging people to speak out from within government is obliged to take his Otepkas with his Ellsbergs, and vice versa — to take a man like Otepka, who thought his bosses were ruining the country by being too sweet on Communists everywhere, with one like Ellsberg, who thought his former colleagues were ruining the country by killing people and lying about it.[6]

Are distinctions really so hard to make? Must we, as these authors suggest, take our Otepkas with our Ellsbergs? Are our judgments so politically biased that we must accept all who claim to blow the whistle if we are to avoid spurious distinctions between them? Or can we arrive at criteria for separating legitimate from illegitimate whistleblowing?

To be sure, a society that fails to protect the right to speak out even on the part of those whose warnings turn out to be misleading obviously opens the door to political repression. But from the moral point of view there are important differences between the aims, messages, and methods of dissenters from within the government. I hope to begin to explore these differences, and to set forth some general principles with respect to such practices.

In the first half of this essay, I consider the nature of whistleblowing and the reasons why it arouses such fierce disagreement on the part of participants and onlookers. In the last half, I discuss moral choice with respect to whistleblowing from two points of view: that of the agent worrying beforehand about whether or not to make a disclosure; and that of the policymakers who can influence both the practices that call forth whistleblowing and the responses to such acts.

THE NATURE OF WHISTLEBLOWING

The alarm of the whistleblower is meant to disrupt the status quo: to pierce the background noise, perhaps the false harmony or the imposed silence of "affairs as usual." For the act to be completed successfully, in the eyes of the person sounding the alarm, listeners must be aroused by the message and capable of response. A signal must be sent, a voice raised, to an audience that gains new insight and takes action. Three elements, each jarring, and triply jarring when conjoined, lend acts of whistleblowing special urgency and bitterness: dissent, breach of loyalty, and accusation.

Like all dissent, whistleblowing makes public a disagreement with an authority or a majority view. But whereas dissent can concern all forms of disagreement with, for instance, religious dogma or government policy or court decisions, whistleblowing has the narrower aim of providing information that sheds light on negligence or abuse: of alerting to a risk and of assigning responsibility for that risk.

It is important to see the difference between dissent on grounds of policy and the revelations of actual abuse or neglect which alone give cause for whistleblowing. In practice, however, the two often blur. Authoritarian regimes may regard dissent of any form as whistleblowing, and as evidence of an offense that in turn calls for public exposure and recantation. Someone may blow the whistle on an abuse in order to express policy dissent. Thus Daniel Ellsberg's revelations about government deceit and manipulation in the *Pentagon Papers* obviously aimed, not only to expose the misconduct, but also to influence the government's Vietnam policy.

Dissent from within is also seen as disloyal. The whistleblower, though he is neither referee nor coach, blows the whistle on his own team. In holding his position, and in working with those in his agency, he has assumed certain obligations to them. He may have subscribed to a loyalty oath or a promise of fidelity. Stepping out of channels to level accusations is regarded as a violation of these obligations. Loyalty to the agency and to colleagues comes to be pitted against loyalty to the public interest, to those who may be injured unless the revelation is made.

Because the whistleblower is an insider in the very organization he criticizes, his act differs from muckraking and other forms of exposure by outsiders, as when reporters expose corruption within a government agency. Pressure from within the institution adds to the internal conflict of loyalty. Fidelity to one's agency, to one's superiors, and to colleagues is stressed in countless ways. Yet in many political traditions there is also a strong sense of special obligation *to* the public on the part of government employees; the U.S. Code of Ethics, mentioned earlier, specifically asks that loyalty to the country be put above particular loyalties to "persons, party, or government department."

The conflict may be especially keen for those who take their role of "public servant" seriously, yet have strong bonds of collegiality and of duty to their agency as well. They know, too, the price of betrayal. They have seen what befalls the public servant who speaks out about matters such as defective machinery purchased at public expense. Organizations tend to protect and enlarge the regions of what is concealed, as failures multiply and vested interests encroach. "Power hides," as Carl Friedrich reminds us,[7] and secrecy, unless constantly checked, in turn strengthens the power *to* hide and the appetite for doing so.

Not only is loyalty violated in whistleblowing; hierarchy as well is often opposed, since the whistleblower is not only a colleague but a subordinate. Though aware of the risks inherent in disobedience, he often hopes to keep his job. At times, however, he plans his alarm to coincide with departure. If he is highly placed, resigning in protest may effectively direct public attention to the wrongdoing at issue.[8] Still another alternative, often chosen by those who wish to be safe from retaliation, is to leave quietly, to secure another post, and only then to blow the whistle. In this way, they can speak with the authority and knowledge of an insider without the vulnerability of that position.

Whistleblowing resembles civil disobedience in its openness: it differs from the anonymous warning as much as civil disobedience differs from covert breaches of law.[9] Unlike civil disobedience, however, whistleblowing is usually not a breach of explicit rules or laws; rather, it is protected by the right of free speech. Its purpose, moreover, is narrower than that of civil disobedience; it aims for change through revelation of accusations, rather than through more general political disobedience.[10]

It is the element of accusation, of calling a "foul," that arouses the strongest reactions on the part of the hierarchy. The accusation may be of neglect, of willfully concealed dangers, or of outright abuse on the part of colleagues or superiors. It singles out specific persons or groups as responsible for threats to the public interest. If no one could be held responsible — as in the case of an impending avalanche — the warning would not constitute whistleblowing.

The accusation of the whistleblower, moreover, concerns a present or an imminent threat. Past errors or misdeeds occasion such an alarm only if they still affect current practices. And risks far in the future lack the immediacy needed to make the alarm a compelling one, as well as the close connection to particular individuals that would justify actual accusations. Thus an alarm can be sounded about safety defects in a rapid transit system that threaten or will shortly threaten passengers; but the revelation of safety defects in a system no longer in use, while of historical interest, would not constitute whistleblowing. Nor would the revelation of potential problems in a system not yet fully designed and far from implemented.

Not only immediacy, but also specificity, is needed for there to be an alarm capable of pinpointing responsibility. A concrete risk must be at issue rather than a vague foreboding or a somber prediction. The act of whistleblowing differs, in this respect, from the lamentation or the dire prophecy.

An immediate and specific threat would normally be acted upon by those at risk. But the whistleblower assumes that his message will alert listeners to something they do not know, or whose significance they have not grasped. The reason that the danger is not known or understood is often that it has been kept secret by the organization or by certain members within it who are at fault.

The desire for openness inheres in the temptation to reveal any secret: sometimes also the urge to self-aggrandizement and publicity and the hope for revenge for past slights or injustices. There can be pleasure, too— righteous or malicious—in laying bare the secrets of coworkers and in setting the record straight at last. Colleagues of the whistleblower often suspect his motives: they may regard him as a crank, as publicity-hungry, wrong about the facts, eager for scandal and discord, and driven to indiscretion by his personal biases and shortcomings.

EFFECTIVE WHISTLEBLOWING

Given the internal and external pressures exerted by the elements of dissent, disobedience, and accusation in whistleblowing, it is little wonder that such acts are the exception rather than the rule; little wonder that, once undertaken, most are destined to fail.

For whistleblowing to be effective, it must arouse its audience. Inarticulate whistleblowers are likely to fail from the outset. When they are greeted by apathy, their message dissipates. When they are greeted by disbelief, they elicit no response at all. And when the audience is not free to receive or to act on the information—when censorship or fear of retribution stifles response—then the message rebounds to injure the whistleblowers themselves.

Whistleblowing requires *some* larger context where secrecy, corruption, and coercion are less solidly entrenched—some forum in which an appeal to justice can still be made. It also requires the possibility of concerted public response: the idea of whistleblowing in an anarchy is therefore merely quixotic.

Coercive regimes render whistleblowing an entirely different, often heroic, practice by their control over what is spoken, written, heard. If not only internal institutional protests are blocked, but even national warnings thwarted, international appeals may be the only remaining possibility. Depending on the severity of repression, only the most striking injustices may then filter through with sufficient strength to alert ordinarily indifferent foreigners. Alarms, like rings in the water, weaken as they move away from their point of origin; if forced to go below the surface to emerge later, they grow weaker still.

Such characteristics of whistleblowing, and strategic considerations for achieving an impact, are common to the noblest warnings, the most vicious personal attacks, and the delusions of the paranoid. How can one distinguish the many acts of sounding an alarm that are genuinely in the public interest from all the petty, biased, or lurid revelations that pervade our querulous and gossip-ridden society? Can we draw distinctions between different whistleblowers, different messages, different methods?

We clearly can, in a number of cases. Whistleblowing can be starkly inappropriate when in malice or error, or when it lays bare legitimately private matters having to do, for instance, with political belief or sexual life. It can, just as clearly, be the only way to shed light on an ongoing unjust practice such as drugging political prisoners or subjecting them to electroshock treatment; it can be the last resort for alerting the public to an impending disaster.

Taking such clear-cut cases as benchmarks, and reflecting on what it is about them that weighs so heavily for or against speaking out, we can then work our way toward the admittedly more complex cases in between these extremes. We can look at cases in which whistleblowing is not so clearly the right or wrong choice, or where different points of view exist regarding its legitimacy: cases where there are moral reasons both for concealment and for disclosure, and where judgments conflict.

INDIVIDUAL MORAL CHOICE

What questions might those who consider sounding an alarm in public ask themselves? How might they articulate the problem they see and weigh its injustice before deciding whether or not to reveal it? How can they best try to make sure their choice is the right one?

In thinking about these questions it helps to keep in mind the three elements mentioned earlier: dissent, breach of loyalty, and accusation. They impose certain requirements: of accuracy and judgment in dissent; of exploring alternative ways to cope with improprieties that minimize the breach of loyalty; and of fairness in accusation. For each, careful articulation and testing of arguments are needed to limit error and bias.

Dissent by whistleblowers, first of all, is expressly claimed to be intended to benefit the public. It carries with it, as a result, an obligation to consider the nature of this benefit and to consider also the possible harm that may come from speaking out: harm to persons or institutions, and ultimately to the public interest itself. Whistleblowers must therefore begin by making every effort to consider the effects of speaking out versus those of remaining silent. They must assure themselves of the accuracy of their reports, checking and rechecking the facts before speaking out; specify the degree to which there is genuine impropriety; and consider how imminent is the threat they see, how serious, and how closely linked to those accused of neglect or abuse.*

If the facts warrant whistleblowing, how can the second element— breach of loyalty—be minimized? The most important question here is whether the existing avenues for change within the organization have been explored. It is a waste of time for the public as well as harmful to the institution to sound the loudest alarm first. Whistleblowing has to remain a last alternative because of its destructive side effects: it must be chosen only when other alternatives have been considered and rejected. They may be rejected if they simply do not apply to the problem at hand, or when there is not time to go through routine channels, or when the institution is so corrupt or coercive that steps will be taken to silence the whistleblower should he try the regular channels first.

What weight should an oath or a promise of silence have in the conflict of loyalties? Those sworn to silence are doubtless under a stronger obligation because of the oath taken. They have bound themselves, assumed specific obligations beyond those assumed in merely taking a new position. But even such promises can be overridden when the public interest at issue is strong enough. They can be overridden if they were obtained under duress or through deceit. They can be overridden, too, if they promise something that is in itself wrong or unlawful. The fact that one has promised silence is no excuse for complicity in covering up a crime or a violation of the public's trust.

---

*In dissent concerning policy differences rather than specific improprieties, moreover, whistleblowing, with its accusatory element, is often an inappropriate form of warning. It threatens the public interest in that it so easily derails into ideological persecution. Many other forms of dissent exist when there is reason to voice policy disagreement or ideological differences.

The third element in whistleblowing — accusation — raises equally serious ethical concerns. They are concerns of fairness to the persons accused of impropriety. Is the message one to which the public is entitled in the first place? Or does it infringe on personal and private matters that one has no right to invade? Here, the very notion of what is in the public's best "interest" is at issue: accusations regarding an official's unusual sexual or religious experiences may well appeal to the public's interest without therefore being information relevant to "the public interest."

Great conflicts arise here. We have witnessed excessive claims to executive privilege and to secrecy by government officials during the Watergate scandal in order to cover up for abuses the public had every right to discover. Conversely, those hoping to profit from prying into private matters have become adept at invoking "the public's right to know." Some even regard such private matters as threats to the public: they voice their own religious and political prejudices in the language of accusation. Such a danger is never stronger than when the accusation is delivered surreptitiously: the anonymous accusations made during the McCarthy period regarding political beliefs and associations often injured persons who did not even know their accusers or the exact nature of the accusations.

In fairness to those criticized, openly accepted responsibility for blowing the whistle should therefore be preferred to the secret denunciation or the leaked rumor: the more so, the more derogatory and accusatory the information. What is openly stated can more easily be checked, its source's motives challenged, and the underlying information examined. Those under attack may otherwise be hard put to defend themselves against nameless adversaries. Often they do not even know that they are threatened until it is too late to respond. The anonymous denunciation, moreover, common to so many regimes, places the burden of investigation on government agencies that may thereby gain the power of a secret police.

From the point of view of the whistleblower, on the other hand, the choice is admittedly less easy. The anonymous message is safer for him in situations where retaliation is likely. But it is also often less likely to be taken seriously. Newspaper offices, for example, receive innumerable anonymous messages without acting upon them. Unless the message is accompanied by indications of how the evidence can be checked, its anonymity, however safe for the source, speaks against it.

In order to assure transmission for the message — through the press for instance — yet be safe from reprisals, whistleblowers often resort to a compromise: by making themselves known to the journalist, they make it possible to check the evidence; by asking that their identity not be given in the printed article, they protect themselves from the consequences.

From the public's point of view, accusations that are openly made by identifiable individuals are more likely to be taken seriously. Since the open accusation is felt to be fairer to the accused, and since it makes the motives of the whistleblower open to inspection, the audience is more confident that the message may have a factual basis. As a result, if whistleblowers still choose to resort to surreptitious messages, they have a strong obligation to let the accused know of the accusation leveled, and to produce independent evidence that can be checked.

During this process of weighing the legitimacy of speaking out, the method used, and the degree of fairness needed, whistleblowers must try to compensate for the strong possibility of bias on their part. They should be scrupulously aware of any motive that might skew their message: a desire for self-defense in a difficult bureaucratic situation, perhaps, or the urge to seek revenge, or inflated expectations regarding the effect their message will have on the situation.*

Likewise, the possibility of personal gain from sounding the alarm ought to give pause. Once again there is then greater risk of a biased message. Even if whistleblowers regard themselves as incorruptible, their profiting from revelations of neglect or abuse will lead others to question their motives and to put less credence in their charges. If the publicity matters greatly to them, or if speaking out brings them greater benefits at work or a substantially increased income, such risks are present. If, for example, a government employee stands to make large profits from a book exposing the iniquities in his agency, there is danger that he will, perhaps even unconsciously, slant his report in order to cause more of a sensation. If he supports his revelation by referring to the Code of Ethics for Government Service urging that loyalty to the highest moral principles and to country be put above loyalty to persons, party, or government department, he cannot ignore another clause in the same Code, specifying that he "ought never to use any information coming to him confidentially in the performance of government duties as a means for making private profits."

Sometimes a warning is so clearly justifiable and substantiated that it carries weight no matter how tainted the motives of the messenger. But scandal can pay; and the whistleblower's motives ought ideally to be above suspicion, for his own sake as well as for that of the respect he desires for his

---

*Needless to say, bias affects the silent as well as the outspoken. The motive for *holding back* important information about abuses and injustice ought to give similar cause for soul-searching. Civil servants who collaborate in the iniquities of so many regimes; business executives who support them through bribes and silent complicity; and physicians the world over who examine the victims of torture and return them to their tormentors: all have as much reason to examine *their* motives as those who may be speaking out without sufficient reason.

warning. Personal gain from speaking out raises a presumption against it, a greater need to check the biases of the speaker.

A special problem arises whenever there is a high risk that civil servants who speak out will have to go through costly litigation. Might they not justifiably try to make enough money on their public revelations—say through books or public speaking—to offset their losses? In so doing they will not strictly speaking have *profited* from their revelations: they merely avoid being financially crushed by their sequels. They will nevertheless still be suspected at the time of their revelation, and their message will therefore seem more questionable.

To weigh all these factors is not easy. The ideal case of whistleblowing—where the cause is a just one, where all the less dramatic alternatives have been exhausted, where responsibility is openly accepted, and where the whistleblower is above reproach—is rare. The motives may be partly self-serving, the method questionable, and still we may judge that the act was in the public interest. In cases where the motives for sounding the alarm are highly suspect, for example, but where clear proof of wrongdoing and avoidable risk is adduced, the public may be grateful that the alarm was sounded, no matter how low its opinion of the whistleblower.

Reducing bias and error in moral choice often requires consultation, even open debate:[11] such methods force articulation of the moral arguments at stake, and challenge privately held assumptions. But acts of whistleblowing present special problems when it comes to open consultation. On the one hand, once whistleblowers sound their alarm publicly, their arguments will be subjected to open scrutiny: they will have to articulate their reasons for speaking out and substantiate their charges. On the other hand, it will then be too late to retract the alarm or to combat its harmful effects, should their choice to speak out have been ill-advised (in both senses of the word).

For this reason, whistleblowers owe it to all involved to make sure of two things: that they have sought as much and as objective advice regarding their choice as they can *before* going public; and that they are aware of the arguments for and against the practice of whistleblowing in general, so that they can see their own choice against as richly detailed and coherently structured a background as possible.

Satisfying these two requirements once again has special problems because of the very nature of whistleblowing: the more corrupt the circumstances, the more dangerous it may be to seek consultation before speaking out. And yet, since the whistleblowers themselves may have a biased view of the state of affairs, they may choose not to consult others when in fact it would have been not only safe but advantageous to do so: they may see corruption and conspiracy where none exists. Given these difficulties, it would be especially important to seek more general means of considering the nature of whistleblowing and the arguments for and against different ways of combating abuse: to take them up in public debate and through teaching.[12]

INSTITUTIONAL POLICY

What institutional arrangements might best serve to protect the rights of dissenters, cut down on endless breaches of loyalty and false accusations, while protecting the right to speak out and assuring public access to needed information?

The most far-reaching set of changes, and the hardest to implement, involves the cutting down on legitimate causes for alarm. Reducing practices of corruption and cover-up, as well as opportunities for errors to go undetected, would reduce also the need to call attention to them. The necessary changes in review procedures, incentives, and obstacles go far beyond the scope of this essay; but so long as improprieties are serious and frequent, whistleblowing will remain a last resort for bringing them into the open.

The need to resort to whistleblowing can also be reduced by providing mechanisms for taking criticism seriously before it reaches the press or the courtroom. These mechanisms must work to counteract the blockages of information within an organization, and the perennial pressures to filter out negative information before it reaches those who make decisions.[13] The filtering process may be simple or intricate; well intentioned or malevolent; more or less consciously manipulated. Some abuses are covered up at the source; others sidelined en route to department heads; still others kept from reaching review boards or trustees.

Surveying the damage from such failures of communication, David Ewing has argued that managers have much to gain by not discouraging internal criticism.[14] In a recent survey, he found that over 60 percent of the business firms responding to a questionnaire claim that a senior executive's door is always open to anyone with a grievance.[15] A number of managements have other ways of welcoming the views of dissenters, and promise that no one will be unfairly dismissed or disciplined.

Such an "open-door" policy may suffice at times; but it is frequently inadequate unless further buttressed. In the first place, the promises of protection given by top management cannot always be fulfilled. Though an employee may keep his job, there are countless ways of making his position difficult, to the point where he may be brought to resign of his own volition, or stay, while bitterly regretting that he had spoken out. Second, it would be naive to think that abuses in industry or in government are always unknown to top management and perpetrated against their will by subordinates. If the abuse—the secret bombardment of Cambodia, for instance, or corporate bribing, or conspiracy to restrict trade—is planned by those in charge, then the "open-door" policy turns out to be a trap for the dissenter.

For these reasons, proposals have been made to protect dissenters in more formal ways. Independent review boards, ombudsmen, consumer or citizen representatives on boards of trustees, bills of rights for employees: these and other means have been suggested to protect dissenters while giving serious consideration to their messages.[16]

These methods of protection spring up and sometimes die away with great rapidity. They are often instituted without careful comparison between different possibilities. When they work, these methods have many advantages. They allow for criticism with much less need for heroism; for a way to deflect the crank or the witch-hunter *before* their messages gain publicity; for a process of checking the accuracy of the information provided; for a chance to distinguish between urgent alarms and long-range worries; and for an arena for debating the moral questions of motive and of possible bias, of loyalty and responsibility to the public interest.

Many of these methods work well; others fail. They fail when they are but window-dressing from the outset, meant to please or exhaust dissenters; or else they fail because, however independent at the outset, they turn into management tools. Such is the fate of many a patient representative in hospitals whose growing loyalty to coworkers and to the institution once again leaves the dissenter little choice between submission and open revolt. Still another reason for the failure of such intermediaries is their frequent lack of credibility. No matter how well-meaning, they will not be sought out if they cannot protect from retaliation those who turn to them for help. Even if they can give such protection, but cannot inspire confidence in those with grievances, their role will be largely a ceremonial one.

A comparative study of such intermediaries and means of protection would have to seek out the conditions of independence, flexibility, separateness from management, institutional good-will, fairness, and objectivity needed for success. Moreover, in looking at the protection given to dissenters, the entire system must be kept in perspective, so that changes in one area do not produce unexpected dislocations elsewhere. To what extent will increased due process make the entire institution more litigious? To what extent will protection in one place put increased pressure on another? Is it not possible, for example, that the increasing difficulties of firing incompetent federal employees have led to the growing resort to psychiatric fitness-for-duty examinations, and that these, in turn, have become a new weapon with which to combat critics?

A different method for reducing the tension and risk of whistleblowing is to state conditions expressly under which those who learn about an abuse *must* blow the whistle—when to do so, far from being disloyal, is not only right but obligatory. Laws or other regulations can require revelations, and thus take the burden of choice off the individual critic.

Such requirements to report exist in a number of places. The Toxic Substances Control Act, for instance, enacted in January 1977, requires companies producing chemicals to instruct their employees and officials to report chemicals that pose a substantial risk to health or to the environment. Once again, these requirements open up fields for study and for comparison. There is much to learn about how effective they are, how they may be combated within an industry, and how they compare to other ways of reducing neglect and abuse.

In order to be effective, requirements to report must be specific and enforceable. It is therefore not appropriate for them to be as open-ended and exhortative as the U.S. Code of Ethics in urging government employees to "expose corruption wherever uncovered." They must be limited to clear-cut improprieties, and used as a last resort only. Once again, here the lines must be firmly drawn against requiring reporting on religious or political belief or on purely personal matters. In many societies, citizens are asked to report "deviations," fellow workers to spy on one another, and students to expose the subversive views of their teachers or vice versa. No matter how great the need to eradicate corruption, these common precedents cannot be ignored.

If the requirements to report are properly limited and if they succeed in deflecting reprisals, they can effectively lessen the conflict of loyalty felt by the person obliged to report; they support, moreover, open revelations, and thus diminish the need to resort to anonymous accusations with all their disadvantages.

I have tried, in this essay, to look at the nature of whistleblowing, and at the problems—both individual and social—that it poses. I have found great differences in methods, in aims, in the messages conveyed, and in the degree of fairness to accused and accusers. I see no need, therefore, to "take our Otepkas with our Ellsbergs"—to treat all whistleblowers alike: no need to disparage all, nor on the other hand to offer unqualified support for all.

Rather, we must consider carefully the differences. I have tried to set forth steps that individuals might take in deciding whether or not to sound the alarm in a particular situation, and to consider institutional steps to allow for dissent and criticism in the public interest, while cutting down on unnecessary, erroneous, or harmful resorts to the panic button.

NOTES

I have drawn on this essay for a paper entitled "Whistleblowing and Professional Responsibilities," in *Ethics Teaching in Higher Education*, ed. Daniel Callahan and Sissela Bok (New York: Plenum, 1980), pp. 277-295.

1. Code of Ethics for Government Service passed by the U.S. House of Representatives in the 85th Congress and applying to all government employees and officeholders. Compare the requirement in the Code of Ethics of the Institute of Electrical and Electronics Engineers (Article IV), that members speak out against abuses threatening the safety, health, and welfare of the public.

2. "Forced Retirement/Psychiatric Fitness for Duty Exams," Subcommittee on Compensation and Employee Benefits, Committee on Post Office and Civil Service, House of Representatives, November 3, 1978, pp. 2-4. See also the Subcommittee Hearings, February 28, 1978.

Psychiatric referral for whistleblowers has become institutionalized in government service, but is not uncommon in private employment. Even persons who make accusations without being "employed" in the organization they accuse have been classified as unstable and thus as unreliable witnesses. See, for example, Jonas Robitscher, "Stigmatization and Stonewalling: The Ordeal of Martha Mitchell," *Journal of Psychohistory*, 6 (Winter 1979), 393-408.

3. Carol S. Kennedy, "Whistle-blowing: Contribution or Catastrophe?" address to the American Association for the Advancement of Science, February 15, 1978, p. 8.

4. For case histories and descriptions of what befalls whistleblowers see Rosemary Chalk and Frank von Hippel, "Due Process for Dissenting Whistle-blowers: Dealing with Technical Dissent in the Organization," *Technology Review*, 81 (June/July 1979), 48-55; "Dissent in Corporate America," *The Civil Liberties Review* (September/October 1978); Louis Clark, "The Sound of Professional Suicide," *Barrister* (Summer 1978), pp. 10-19; Helen Dudar, "The Price of Blowing the Whistle," *The New York Times Magazine*, October 30, 1977, pp. 41-54; David Ewing, *Freedom Inside the Organization* (New York: E. P. Dutton, 1977); Ralph Nader, Peter Petkas, and Kate Blackwell, *Whistle Blowing* (New York: Grossman Publishers, 1972); Charles Peters and Taylor Branch, eds. *Blowing the Whistle* (New York: Praeger, 1972); Alan S. Westin and Stephen Salisbury, eds., *Individual Rights in the Corporation* (New York: Pantheon Books, 1980).

5. For an account of strategies and proposals to support government whistleblowers see "A Whistleblower's Guide to the Federal Bureaucracy,"

Government Accountability Project (Washington, D.C.: Institute for Policy Studies, 1977).

6. From "The Odd Couple," by Taylor Branch, in Peters and Branch, eds., *Blowing the Whistle*, pp. 222-223.

7. Carl Friedrich, *Constitutional Government and Democracy*, 4th ed. (Waltham, Mass.: Blaisdell Publ. Co., 1968), p. 55.

8. See Edward Weisband and Thomas M. Franck, *Resignation in Protest* (New York: Grossman Publishers, 1975). See also Albert Hirschman, *Exit, Voice and Loyalty* (Cambridge, Mass.: Harvard University Press, 1970).

9. There are great variations in the degree of furtiveness or anonymity of any one message. Thus a leak through a newspaper may be made by a person known to the reporter, but unknown to the readers — disguised, perhaps, as a "highly placed official" or even wrongly characterized in order to mislead those seeking to identify the source of the leak.

10. I rely here on the definition of civil disobedience offered by John Rawls: "A public non-violent, conscientious yet political act contrary to law usually done with the aim of bringing about a change in the law or the policies of the government." See *A Theory of Justice* (Cambridge, Mass.: Harvard University Press, 1971), p. 364. See also Hugo Bedau, "On Civil Disobedience," *Journal of Philosophy*, 58 (1961), 653-661. A combination of whistleblowing and civil disobedience occurs when, for instance, former CIA agents publish books to alert the public about what they regard as unlawful and dangerous practices in the intelligence community, and in so doing openly violate and thereby test the oath of secrecy that they have sworn, but that they now regard as having been unjustly required of them.

11. I discuss these questions of consultation and publicity with respect to moral choice in chap. 7 of *Lying* (New York: Pantheon Books, 1978).

12. The debate must take into account, too, the larger issues of public and private morality recently discussed in a number of articles: must public servants sometimes act so as to go against their personal ethical standards? Are there differences between public and private morality? If so, by what moral criteria should one evaluate the choices confronted by public officials? See Alan H. Goldman, *The Moral Foundations of Professional Ethics* (Totowa, N.J.: Rowman and Littlefield, 1980); Stuart Hampshire, "Public and Private Morality," in Stuart Hampshire, ed., *Public and Private Morality* (Cambridge: Cambridge University Press, 1978), pp. 23-53; Thomas Nagel, "Ruthlessness in Public Life," in Hampshire, ed., *Public and Private Morality*, pp. 75-91; Michael Walzer, *Philosophy and Public Affairs*, 2 (Winter 1973), 160-180; Richard Wasserstrom, "Lawyers as Professionals: Some Moral Issues," *Human Rights*, 5 (1975), 1-24; Bernard Williams, "Politics and Moral Character," in Hampshire, ed., *Public and Private Morality*, pp. 1-24.

13. John C. Coffee in "Beyond the Shut-eyed Sentry: Toward a Theoretical View of Corporate Misconduct and an Effective Legal Response," *Virginia Law Review*, 63 (1977), 1099-1278, gives an informed and closely

reasoned account of such "information blockages," such "filtering out," and possible remedies.

14. David W. Ewing, "The Employee's Right to Speak Out: The Management Perspective," *The Civil Liberties Review* (September/October 1978), pp. 10-15.

15. David W. Ewing, "What Business Thinks About Employee Rights," *Harvard Business Review* (September/October 1977), pp. 81-94.

16. An example of an unusually thorough and articulate review of allegations by government whistleblowers is provided by the Final Report of the Review Panel on New Drug Regulation, 1977, Department of Health, Education, and Welfare, chaired by Norman Dorsen.

Dennis F. Thompson

9. The Private Lives of Public Officials

While citizens have won greater recognition of their privacy in recent years,[1] public officials have found their private lives subject to greater public scrutiny. Courts have made officials more vulnerable to criticism and comment by weakening the legal protections against libel and invasion of privacy of public figures.[2] Candidates and officials have been forced to disclose their financial affairs and medical condition, and the press has extensively publicized their drinking habits, sexual conduct, and family life.[3] I shall argue that we should respect the privacy of some public officials less than that of ordinary citizens, but to justify this difference we must examine the rationale and limits of the privacy of officials more closely than has usually been done.

When should what would otherwise count as the private life of a public official become a matter of public concern? Alternatively, when may a public official properly claim that certain activities are part of his or her private life and none of the public's business? By "private life," I mean to refer to those activities that may be known, observed, or intruded upon only with a person's consent. The dimensions of this sphere of privacy are not always clear, since they partly depend on conventions that are neither absolute nor always stable. But within this sphere, however defined, individuals are understood to have a right to control information about themselves.[4]

The question of the privacy of public officials arises for both politicians and bureaucrats when they decide what to disclose about themselves, and to whom to disclose it. The question also confronts the many officials who have occasion to decide what to reveal about other officials, and to whom to divulge it. Personnel officers, in particular, must often decide whether to probe into what might be regarded as the personal affairs of a prospective or current employee of the government. Members of the press, too, encounter the question in deciding what to print about an official, and so do members of the public in determining what to consider in assessing a candidate for office.[5] However, the secrecy or confidentiality that officials claim for some governmental business should not count as a question of privacy, or as a part of private life even by analogy. When officials legitimately keep governmental business secret from other officials or from the public, the reasons must relate exclusively to the special nature of the policy, institutional effectiveness, or the privacy of other citizens — not to the individual rights of privacy of the public officials themselves.[6]

Rarely can a public official's claim of privacy be resolved simply by consulting the law. Although the law gives some guidance, it does not settle the question. Privacy law remains relatively undeveloped, as it applies to public officials, and in any event legal rights and duties do not exhaust moral ones; individuals retain considerable discretion.[7] Moreover, defending your right of privacy in court can be self-defeating; even if you win, you often sacrifice your actual privacy in the publicity that attends the court proceedings.[8] But where the law is silent or inconclusive, political ethics cannot wholly fill the void. The pertinent ethical principles are often in conflict, and the variables affecting the conclusion are numerous. It is therefore not possible to stipulate a set of rules that would determine in advance what should count as the private life of a public official. It is possible, however, to establish a basis for the privacy of public officials, and then to outline the factors that should be considered in deciding to what extent a public official may claim a private life.

The idea that the privacy of officials should be respected for the same reasons as should the privacy of citizens makes sense only within a theory that assumes that everyone's private life has at least prima facie priority over the claims of public life. Theories that do not accept this assumption conceive the problem in very different terms. Plato's *Republic*, for example, abolishes the foundations of any private life for the guardians who rule the ideal state — eliminating the family and private property in order to create unity in the state. Adeimantus objects that the guardians will not be happy if they have to give up the pleasures of private life. Such happiness, Socrates replies, is "senseless and childish"; the guardians, after all, will enjoy a better and more honorable life than other citizens. Anyhow, the aim should be to make the whole society good, not to make one section of it happy.[9] One reason that Plato does not lament the eclipse of a private life is that he shared with many classical thinkers the view that private life is inferior; it connoted, as its etymological origins suggest, a deprivation.[10]

Even Aristotle, who thought that Plato had gone too far in his quest for social unity, still conceived of private life as deficient; the private realm of the family and household could satisfy bodily needs and the like, but not the distinctively human quality of reason, which could be actualized only in the public activity of the polis.[11] The primacy of the public remained prominent in some modern political thought: in Rousseau's vision of a society where "every citizen will feel himself to be constantly under the public eye,"[12] in Hegel's exaltation of the ethical superiority of the state where "public and private ends are identical,"[13] in Marx's critique of the class bias of bourgeois claims for private life.[14] From none of these perspectives can the privacy of public officials or rulers be readily justified as an extension of the privacy of citizens; if the privacy of the latter is suspect, so a fortiori is the privacy of the former. Furthermore, privacy in the form that liberals seek usually becomes an issue only in a large and diverse society. Such privacy is not possible in small, closely-knit communities, and it would not be so necessary in a more homogeneous or in a more tolerant and humane society.

Although early liberals did not explicitly discuss the modern notion of individual privacy, their theories supplied a framework that could comfortably accommodate it. Beginning with a concept of a relatively asocial individual or "small families," they demanded justification for each intervention by society or the state into the natural liberty or the private sphere of the individual.[15] As later liberal theorists and liberal societies, sometimes reluctantly and sometimes unwittingly, circumscribed this private sphere, it became important to stake out more precisely what if anything was left for the individual.[16] The hope was (and is) that at least the privacy of the individual (in the narrow sense defined above) could be salvaged. It is not my aim either to defend or attack these views of the privacy of citizens, but rather to see what implications follow for the privacy of public officials if we accept, as many theories and many societies do, a presumption in favor of the privacy of citizens. Since officials are citizens too, the presumption quite naturally implies that the private lives of officials and citizens should be equally respected; I shall call this the presumption of uniform privacy. But there are also good reasons for granting officials less privacy than citizens; these reasons give rise to what I shall call the principle of diminished privacy.

THE VALUE OF PRIVACY

The presumption of uniform privacy depends on showing that privacy has value for public officials for the same reasons, or for reasons just as strong, as does privacy for ordinary citizens. Privacy has two general kinds of value for the individual — instrumental and intrinsic. An instrumental justification holds that privacy contributes to liberty by ensuring that individuals can engage in certain activities free from observation, intrusion, or inhibiting threats.[17] A public official needs such protection, sometimes even more than citizens, because if his or her privacy is violated, the exposure is likely to be greater. Privacy also supports fairness and equal opportunity by guaranteeing that private activities that are irrelevant to public duties do not affect an individual's chances for gaining public employment.

It is important to distinguish the instrumental value of privacy from the separate values of liberty and fairness, both where they coincide and where they diverge. If an activity is private, an official may claim not only that the activity should not be disclosed (the privacy argument), but also that if for some reason the activity is disclosed, it should not be used against him (a liberty or fairness argument). Generally, if an activity is protected by privacy, it would also be protected by a principle of liberty or fairness, but some activities (for example, expression of political opinions) that are not private may still enjoy protection under a principle of liberty or of fairness.

The instrumental justification, though important, does not fully capture the distinctive value of privacy, and therefore some philosophers have sought a justification in certain human relations in which privacy seems to play an intrinsic role. These relations may involve a general respect for persons (for example, recognizing how one's observation can change the nature of someone else's private activities or self-conception),[18] or more specifically they may be relations of love, friendship, and trust, which presuppose a certain degree of privacy.[19] On these views, privacy is justified even if none of the usual harmful consequences (such as loss of job) are likely to ensue. Because many public officials live under the glare of publicity, the moments alone and with their family and friends are or should be precious, and especially stand in need of privacy. Moreover, if officials are to sustain a conception of their own personalities that is at all independent of their public reputation, they need to be able to escape the public eye from time to time. Without such escape, an official may suffer what Erving Goffman calls stigmatization: "The figure the individual cuts in daily life before those with whom he has routine dealings is likely to be dwarfed and spoiled by virtual demands (whether favorable or unfavorable) created by his public image."[20]

Most of the arguments for the value of privacy to the individual may also be reformulated as arguments for the value of privacy to society. If privacy protects the liberty and equal opportunities of individual officials, it also can increase the pool of available talent for public positions; unorthodox and sensitive persons are less likely to be discouraged from seeking and holding public office, and often such persons bring diversity and competence that government always needs. By respecting the privacy of public officials, we may encourage greater respect for the privacy of citizens: officials who are in the habit of honoring the privacy of other officials are perhaps more likely to respect that of ordinary citizens; officials demonstrate, by their own example, the importance of individual privacy in society. Finally, the titilating details of private lives tend to divert our attention from the larger issues of public life. The quality of deliberation in a democracy is debased when sensationalist exposés of private activities displace discussion of questions of public policy.

The presumption of uniform privacy underscores the value of the private lives of public officials, but the presumption cannot always be sustained. Public officials are not simply ordinary citizens: officials have power over us, and they represent us in other ways.[21] From these differences follows the principle of diminished privacy for public officials; that principle may in several ways override the presumption of uniform privacy. Because officials make decisions that affect our lives, we want to make sure that they are at least physically and mentally competent; that they do not abuse their power for private ends and are not vulnerable to the improper influence of others; that they pursue policies of which we approve; and (more speculatively) that they demonstrate moral sensitivity and anguish when they are forced to "dirty their hands" by choosing one of two courses of action, both of which are wrong.[22] Their public conduct may reveal much of what we need to know, but in many instances, if we are to hold officials accountable for the power they exercise or will exercise, we need to learn something about their private lives.

It is sometimes suggested that some officials (presidents, congressmen, ambassadors, and some lower-level officials) represent us not only in their public decisions but also in what would otherwise be their private conduct, which symbolically stands for our own conduct.[23] Usually such a view is accompanied by a demand that political leaders observe higher standards of personal morality than expressed in the "least common denominator of society's . . . standards."[24] Presumably on this view, we want leaders to represent our aspirations, not necessarily our own behavior.[25] Beyond the symbolism, officials by the example of their own private lives can also have an effect for good or ill on the way that citizens conduct their personal lives. Public figures who deal gracefully and courageously with personal difficulties — an errant offspring, marital problems, alcoholism, breast cancer, death of a loved one — not only excite admiration but invite imitation. To be sure, these benefits of diminished privacy might be achieved, and no doubt sometimes are, simply through hypocrisy; it is the appearances that are effective. But since for other reasons, such as those relating to accountability, citizens will properly inquire to some extent into an official's private life, the strategy of hypocrisy cannot be prudently recommended either to society or to officials.

Nevertheless, probity in one's personal life is certainly not a sufficient condition for making moral public decisions (many of the major Watergate conspirators evidently lead impeccable private lives), and it is probably not even a necessary condition. Indeed, admiration of the private virtue of officials may lead us to neglect (or even mistakenly excuse) the public vice they perpetrate through the decisions and policies they make in office. With respect to most officials most of the time, the chief reason for prying into private lives is to hold officials accountable for these decisions and policies. An official may choose, for prudential or for supererogatory reasons, to disclose his or her private affairs, but beyond what is directly relevant to holding an official accountable for the duties of public office (in ways I shall try to specify), the principle of diminished privacy does not cogently extend.

Although everyone's privacy deserves respect, public officials must sacrifice some of their privacy for the general good of democratic society, including the protection of the privacy of ordinary citizens. One form of this argument for the priority of the principle of diminished privacy is largely utilitarian in character — that the interests of the larger number of citizens take precedence over those of the smaller number — and hence does not fully respect individual rights or interests of officials. If we could assume that officials consent to the limitation of their privacy, we would have a more satisfactory basis for diminished privacy, and indeed many writers have maintained that the act of seeking or holding public office constitutes such consent.[26] Such an act does seem to involve more of a real choice than the status of being a citizen, which is sometimes (dubiously) counted as proof of consent. But while some degree of consent to less privacy does seem to follow from holding some kinds of public office, such consent is not sufficient to negate all claims of privacy for officials. In the first place, the vast majority of public officials (postal employees, clerks, schoolteachers) do not, and should not be expected to, consent to relinquishing rights that an ordinary citizen enjoys simply because they hold a state-supported job, which otherwise is like any other job in society. Since public employees now constitute such a large part of the working population, they surely cannot be generally required to sacrifice rights as a condition of such employment, and in fact the Supreme Court has rejected the "privilege" doctrine that once warranted the government's denying constitutional rights to public employees.[27] In the second place, even for those officials at higher levels who might be said to consent to some diminished privacy, the argument from consent does not by itself suggest what these officials should consent to. The appeal to consent does not eliminate the need for some criteria, or at least for a framework of considerations, to specify the scope of diminished privacy.

The rationale for diminished privacy provides reasons that any citizen, including a public official, should be able to accept insofar as he or she accepts general principles of democracy. But the rationale does not justify an unlimited or general exposure of the private lives of anyone; it implies that private lives become public only to the extent necessary for certain specific purposes, chiefly to ensure accountability. This implication yields two kinds of criteria that should govern any potential intrusion into the private life of an official: substantive criteria, which specify the kinds of positions and activities that should affect diminished privacy; and procedural criteria, which proscribe certain kinds of methods of inquiry and investigation. While the substantive criteria indicate (more or less determinate) boundaries of private life, the procedural criteria prohibit the use of certain methods to probe private life, whatever its boundaries may be.

THE SCOPE OF PRIVACY: SUBSTANTIVE CRITERIA

It is commonly said that the private life of a public official should not be disclosed unless it is relevant to his or her official position.[28] This view is, at best, a shorthand statement of the substantive criteria for diminished privacy. The ways in which private lives may be relevant are complex. How much privacy a public official should sacrifice depends not only on the nature of the position he or she holds, and the nature of the (presumed) private activities, but also on the relationship between them. For example, the more influential the position, the less are more intimate activities protected. Moreover, the nature of position and the nature of the activity are themselves complex terms, and each needs to be analyzed separately.

The most important feature of the nature of the position is usually thought to be the level of authority or influence that the official exercises. Consistent with the aim of accountability, we assume that we need to know more about officials who wield more authority over us. The authority need be neither formal nor direct. Typically, top White House aides, as much because of their close association with the president as because of their actual authority, invite more inspection than other officials of similar rank in other offices. It is doubtful someone less close to President Carter than Hamilton Jordan should have had to endure public scrutiny of his marital difficulties, his father's stroke and death, his conduct at Sarsfield's Bar, and his comments about the wife of an Egyptian ambassador at a private party.[29] Notice that if privacy depends partly on the level of the position, an interesting corollary follows: an official should not demand that subordinates disclose more of their private lives than the official would properly reveal of his or her own.

We must consider not only the level of the position but also the kind of issues with which an official deals. Griffin Bell's confirmation as attorney general ran into opposition when it was revealed that he belonged to several private clubs that excluded women and blacks. Although Bell should have disclosed this fact himself, he did resign his memberships, conceding that they were incompatible with the office of attorney general, a "symbol of equality before the law."[30] That no similar objections were raised against Secretary of State Cyrus Vance or Defense Secretary Harold Brown, who also belonged to discriminatory private clubs, suggests that most people regard the close connection between the issues with which the attorney general deals and his club memberships as a significantly distinct factor. It would be better of course if no Cabinet members belonged to discriminatory clubs (and still better if no such clubs existed), but the reasons for denying privacy to the attorney general's club memberships are even more compelling than the reasons for denying it to that of other officials at roughly the same level. When we consider positions where the connection between memberships and the issues dealt with on the job is more tenuous (and the positions are at lower levels of government), we encounter claims of "associational privacy" that would protect the privacy of the memberships. Courts have held, for example, that a policeman's membership in a nudist society is his "private life" and none of "his employer's concern."[31] In several cities, policemen have won the right to belong to the John Birch Society, secretly if they wish.[32]

Still another aspect of the nature of the position is the form of the appointment—whether, for example, the official is an elected representative, a political appointee, or a career civil servant. This aspect makes much less difference than is usually thought. Once we take into account the level of the position and the kinds of issues dealt with, most of the differences between the various forms of appointment disappear. We are entitled to know more about a congressman than an analyst in the Office of Management and Budget because the congressman usually has more influence and deals with a more general range of issues. How much we should know about the congressman depends on our theory of representation — whether we assess, for example, his character or only his public position on issues[33] — but whatever theory we adopt, his privacy will be determined by much the same criteria that we use for political appointees. The press and the public generally ignored the excessive drinking of Hugh S. Johnson, the head of Roosevelt's National Recovery Administration, just as they later overlooked the drinking habits of many senators and congressmen. We should want to object to the tacit protection from public comment that these men enjoyed since their drinking evidently had a significant effect on the performance of their public duties.[34] But we would not be inclined to distinguish the cases on the ground that one is a political appointee and the others elected representatives.

Similarly, the traditional distinction between political appointees and career civil servants, which in Max Weber's view justified granting more of a "private life" to the politically neutral administrators than to politically committed politicians,[35] has now lost most of its significance in the higher levels of the American federal bureaucracy. For most of the top nonelected executives in the federal government, the line between political appointment and career service no longer clearly divides politicians and generalists who make policy from administrators and specialists who implement it.[36] How much of the private life of top executives should be known therefore ought to depend more on their influence and the kinds of decisions they make than on the form of their appointments.

However, the form of appointment affects privacy in one important respect — not what is known but who should know it. Insofar as we assume that civil servants are at least initially responsible to their superiors and the norms of the professional service (an assumption not dependent on our completely accepting Weber's concept of bureaucracy), the circle of persons who know about the private lives of civil servants should be smaller and more specific than the wider public who should know about political appointees and representatives. It is essential for some officials to know perhaps even more about the private life of an intelligence agent, a code analyst, or a Strategic Air Command employee, because of the responsibilities they have, than about the private life of a congressman or an assistant secretary, but it is not necessary or appropriate for so many people to know.

How much an official's privacy should be diminished also depends on the nature of the activity in question — its character and its effects. Although the content of what should be private is largely conventional, a general feature of many private activities is intimacy. We usually expect privacy for our physical condition and our personal relations with family, friends, and certain associates (those with whom we have "privileged" relationships), and for activities carried on "in private" at home. The boundaries of what is intimate are neither precise nor absolute, and even the most intimate facts about a public official may not be protected if they are highly relevant to the performance of his or her duties. But we should be inclined to say that the more intimate the activity, the more compelling must be the connection with the official's position; and, conversely, the less intimate, the less compelling the connecton has to be. Consider the legal requirements for financial disclosure that now apply to legislators and high officials in the executive and judiciary.[37] The chief purpose of the requirements is to expose potential conflicts of interest — a purpose obviously related to holding officials accountable. But the relevance would not be strong enough to overcome privacy objections if private financial affairs were not at the edge of intimacy. Our attitude would be very different toward a requirement, for example, that officials list all their friends, the frequency of contact, and the nature of the relationships.

Even though the relevance of financial disclosure outweighs the claim of privacy, it should not be an excuse for publicizing all other personal information that may pertain in some way to the financial affairs. Senator Edward Brooke, who in divorce proceedings (according to a Massachusetts Supreme Judicial Court justice) deliberately overstated by a relatively small amount his financial liabilities, complained that the public had no right to intrude into "every bureau drawer, every clothes closet, every item in my checkbook, every personal agreement" with members of his family.[38] If Brooke misrepresented his financial worth in the divorce proceedings, he may have also done so in his financial statement to the Senate Ethics Committee, and in either case, the public is entitled to know about it. To the extent that the press went beyond reporting these facts and others necessary to make sense of them, however, Brooke's complaint has merit. Even some of the proponents of the requirement for financial disclosure concede that medical bills, church contributions, and many other items on personal tax returns should not have to be disclosed.[39] A California court struck down, on privacy grounds, a state law that required all public officials to disclose major financial investments; a less broadly drawn statute — limiting who must disclose, what must be reported and to whom — probably would have passed judicial scrutiny.[40]

If otherwise intimate activities are carried on in a way that violates public duty or risks public notice, they lose the protection of privacy. In the past, members of Congress usually connived at the sexual improprieties of their colleagues, and even when they did not (as when they forced House Speaker David Henderson to resign in 1903 because he was sexually involved with a daughter of a senator), the press did not report them.[41] But beginning in the summer of 1976, the public was treated to an orgy of sex exposés: no less than seven congressmen were reported to have engaged in illicit sex, or to have attempted to do so. Six of the episodes involved misuse of public funds (for example, Wayne Hays kept a mistress on the House payroll) or encounters with the law (for example, Allen Howe allegedly solicited two policewomen posing as prostitutes) and therefore could hardly be considered private matters.[42] But the seventh case, which was not always distinguished from the others, might be plausibly regarded as an invasion of privacy. In the middle of Representative Don Riegle's campaign for a Michigan Senate seat, the *Detroit News* reported that seven years earlier he had an affair with an unpaid woman member of his staff. The claim that the incident reflected badly on his judgment and maturity did not receive much credence (a church official remarked, "Remember, he's not running for bishop"), but the reports of the incident distracted the candidates from further discussion of the more substantial issues in the campaign, such as school busing and criminal law.[43] Apart from the effect on the privacy of the candidate, the quality of public debate generally suffers if such scandals become an issue, unless they involve abuse of office or violations of the law.

A public official can properly claim that much of his or her family life is private; at stake is not only the official's privacy but that of other people. An example of a practice that violates such privacy is the so-called "transfer technique," involving an investigation into an official's family circumstances to see if he could be persuaded to resign by reassigning him to a location his family would resist. This technique would be no more acceptable if the aim of the investigation were to reward the official with an assignment his family liked.[44] Some facts about family life (such as marriage and divorce) are of course a matter of public record.[45] It is surely proper that these facts be considered when assessing a public official if they are relevant to the office, according to the criteria we have noted elsewhere. But the official has no obligation to reveal the details of life behind the public facts, and often an obligation to other parties not to do so. New York Governor Nelson Rockefeller quite properly resisted pleas to explain the reasons for his divorce and remarriage in 1963.[46] Some family members of public officials become, formally or informally, officials themselves (such as the first lady, or the spouse of an ambassador) and should expect no more privacy than other officials with similar influence and similar functions. In other cases, facts about a family member of an official—a spouse's health, a son's delinquency, or marital problems—might bear on the capacity of the official to do his or her job. But even here, it would seem better to publicize the effects (if and when they occur), rather than the causes. We did not really need to know about Joan Kennedy's third miscarriage or her hospitalization for alcoholism—or about Nancy Kissinger's surgery for a stomach ulcer and her treatment for ear discomfort.[47]

However, when a candidate for public office makes his family life a campaign issue (for example, by portraying himself as a "good family man"), he opens to public inspection what might otherwise be private. The candidate can hardly complain if the press looks into his family life to verify his boast. But again there are limits. That Philadelphia Mayor Frank Rizzo campaigned on a law-and-order platform probably does not justify the extensive publicity given to the fact that his daughter was about to marry a person twice arrested for bookmaking.[48] Because Spiro Agnew was piously lecturing America on parenthood at the time, Jack Anderson and Brit Hume reported that Agnew's twenty-four-year-old son had left his wife and was living with a male hairdresser. Anderson and Hume now regret the story because it was "going after the son to expose the father."[49] But the real objection is not that Agnew's statements could not legitimately be said to invite scrutiny of his family (arguably, they could). Rather, the objection should be that the effect of the story depended on readers' assuming that a person's sexual preference is a matter of public morality.

Beyond how we characterize a private activity itself, how we assess its effects should also influence the scope of privacy of officials. We may distinguish two general ways in which an otherwise private activity may affect an official's public responsibilities: (1) the direct effects that bear upon the official's capacity to perform the specific duties of the job; and (2) the indirect effects that result from other people's attitudes toward the official's private life. In general, it would be better if neither kind of effect were publicized until it showed up in official performance; to probe possible causes before they have produced public consequences usually is to risk exposing affairs that are legitimately private. But we often cannot follow this principle, especially when we are evaluating a candidate for high office.

The direct effects constitute the stronger basis for diminished privacy, and, when the evidence for the effects is compelling, may override claims based even on intimacy if the official holds an influential position and deals with certain kinds of issues. Although a person's physical condition is conventionally regarded as particularly private in our society, some writers have argued that candidates for public office should have physical examinations, the results of which should be publicly announced.[50] Similar proposals for psychiatric examinations of candidates are less persuasive, chiefly because we have less confidence about the validity or objectivity of such examinations.[51] But a candidate or official who has experienced severe mental or physical problems in the past should not conceal this history. Senator Thomas Eagleton, it is generally agreed, should have told not only George McGovern in July of 1972 but also the public about his three hospitalizations for mental problems. No intimate details perhaps were necessary; a statement such as the one he was eventually forced to issue would have been sufficient, had he volunteered it earlier.[52] Since mental illness still carries a stigma in our society, the decision to disclose it can never be easy. Eagleton may have been correct that his past mental and physical problems would not affect his capacity to do the job, but a public official cannot be permitted to make that determination alone — at least not one who aspires to the highest offices.

Officials at lower levels of influence and with less serious mental and physical problems do not, of course, have the same obligation to divulge such information, certainly not to the general public. Dr. Peter Bourne, a close aide to President Carter until he was forced to resign, recognized this difference in his efforts to protect the privacy of Ellen Metsky, his administrative assistant, by using a fictitious name on her prescription for methaqualone, a powerful and controversial sedative. Defending himself, Bourne appealed to the Code of Ethics of the American Medical Association, which prevents a doctor from revealing confidences about a patient.[53] The Code does not countenance violating the law, however, and using fictitious names on prescriptions infringes federal regulations on the dispensing of controlled drugs (laws to which the president's chief adviser on drug abuse must be especially sensitive). That Bourne's conduct may have violated the law would not necessarily settle the issue, however, since many believe the law to be too rigid in this area (the practice of using fictitious names for patients apparently is not uncommon, and is seldom prosecuted). But the rationale for the law itself is cogent, and there are alternative means for protecting the privacy of officials without abandoning the general purpose served by the law. For example, pharmacists and others who divulge the identity of patients to unauthorized persons could be made subject to stiff penalties.

The indirect effects of private life on public duties raise further problems. The question of such effects typically arises when an official is alleged to have engaged in controversial activities (such as adultery or homosexuality) that are commonly classed as matters of private morality.[54] Since the evidence that such an activity directly affects an individual's ability to do a job is usually meager, the objection turns on the reaction of other people to the knowledge that an official engages in the activity. Public reaction, it is said, undermines confidence in the agency in which the official works, and could impair the ability of the agency to win support for its decisions and policies. (The argument from the possibility of blackmail is similar since it depends on public disapproval too.) Often the objection is a disingenuous way of expressing moral disapproval of the practice, and often the evidence for the indirect political effects is weak. However, even if the likelihood of the political effects is great, we should still consider other factors, such as the nature of the position, and the importance of the decisions and policies that are likely to be affected. When a Mr. Norton, a GS-14 budget analyst in NASA, was dismissed for allegedly making homosexual advances near Lafayette Square in Washington in 1963, the press did not publicize the incident, and the D.C. Court of Appeals ordered him reinstated.[55] But when Walter Jenkins, a close aide to President Johnson, was charged with homosexual activity in the men's room of a Washington YMCA in 1964, the incident received wide publicity and Jenkins promptly resigned.[56] Even if Jenkins had not suffered a nervous collapse at the same time, and even if the press had not learned of the homosexual incident, Johnson and his staff probably would have concluded that the risk of serious political effect justified their setting aside any claim by Jenkins that his sexual preferences were no one else's business.

The level of the position and the importance of the issues do not settle the matter, however, for we still should want to say that indirect effects resulting from misconceived moral principles and prejudices ought to be disregarded. Certainly strict liberals, following John Stuart Mill, would argue that activities like homosexuality are self-regarding and should be free from any kind of social intrusion.[57] Mill and other liberals would not apply the distinction between self- and other-regarding activities directly to public officials in the same way as to citizens. But they would insist that, if the only effects on an official's performance in office spring from the reaction of people who fail to respect this distinction, the effects should be disregarded. Critics have argued that Mill's distinction is impossible to maintain, and, further, that society should try to enforce standards of a public morality that does not in principle treat any activities as always self-regarding or private.[58] It might be possible to abandon Mill's distinction and still achieve his purpose — for example, by distinguishing moral principles from mere prejudices, and then showing that disapproval of homosexuality and similar practices is a prejudice, not a proper part of either a public or a private morality.[59] In any case, the question of whether we count indirect effects as sufficient to override claims of privacy cannot be settled without judging the justifiability of the views that create the indirect effects, and such a judgment must ultimately rest on a general theory of liberty and society. Public attitudes toward otherwise private conduct should alone warrant neither disclosure of the conduct, nor sanctions for the conduct if it is disclosed.[60]

THE SCOPE OF PRIVACY: PROCEDURAL CRITERIA

Some procedural criteria that prohibit intrusions into private lives also protect many other activities. These criteria follow from the prohibition against force and fraud, and often, but not always, involve the breaking of the law. The break-in at the office of Dr. Henry Fielding to collect psychiatric information to discredit Daniel Ellsberg, the planting of a spy on McGovern's campaign staff to look for "dirty stuff—who was sleeping with whom . . . who was smoking pot,"[61] a newspaper reporter's posing as a friend to extract confidences from a newly elected politician[62]—all of these may be challenged as improperly forceful or fraudulent, quite apart from whatever invasion of privacy may have occurred. Other criteria, however, derive more specifically from the value of privacy, and it is these on which I concentrate here.

It is often not possible to tell in advance what private activities may be relevant to our assessment of official performance, but this fact should not warrant unlimited inquiry into private lives in the hope that something relevant may turn up. This is not to say that an investigation, prompted by independent evidence and seeking further specific evidence relevant to official performance, should be proscribed merely because it might uncover some purely private information in the process. However, even if the boundaries of private life cannot be precisely delineated, we presume that *some* beliefs and activities are protected (as the rationale for uniform privacy stressed). We should therefore not use methods that intrude into potentially private areas in a way that by their nature cannot discriminate among activities that are legitimately a matter of public concern and those that are not. We should choose, for example, methods that give the official some control over what information about himself is disclosed; and we should always seek, among available alternatives, the method that is likely to intrude to the minimum degree necessary. A brief analysis of cases in three different areas will illustrate how these procedural criteria can be applied.

Surveillance of an official in his home generally transgresses the constraints imposed by the procedural criteria. Some surveillance of this sort may be illegal, such as the wiretaps placed on the phones of Morton Halperin and other aides to Henry Kissinger in 1969 to discover the source of leaks that were alleged to have damaged national security.[63] But whether legal or not, any such surveillance should provoke ethical qualms. When a reporter asked Kissinger in 1974 if he had any doubts about the "ethicality" of these wiretaps, he replied that if any of his subordinates had been found guilty of security leaks, it would have "reflected badly on [his] own judgment," evidently suggesting that because the taps involved risks to his own reputation, they were not morally objectionable.[64] Showing that a practice is not in your self-interest does not dispose of other, often more important, ethical objections, including those based on privacy.

Although officials who bring their personal activities and belongings into public space should expect less privacy, they should still not be subjected to unlimited observation. Surely an official should be able to have a family picnic at a park without worrying, for example, whether a photograph displaying his slovenly table manners or some other indecorum will appear in the morning paper.[65] Nor should it be impossible for an official to hold a family funeral in a church without his every reaction being photographed or commented upon. That Henry Kissinger's garbage may betray some information of public concern should not license members of the press or anyone else to rummage around in it, whether or not it is in a public place.[66] It is sometimes supposed, however, that once an official arrives at his office, all privacy protections disappear. The legal counsel for the Los Angeles County Office in Pomona defended the continuous monitoring of conversations in that office, maintaining that public officials "have no reasonable expectation of privacy" on the job.[67] To be sure, most of what goes on in a government office is public business, but even here a preserve of privacy might be staked out. The importance of such a preserve, as well as the difficulties of defining it, can be illustrated by the case of Otto Otepka.

Otepka was an official in the State Department's Office of Security until he was dismissed in 1963.[68] Otepka's critics charged that Otepka had improperly supplied the Senate Internal Security Subcommittee with classified information, and had in other ways demonstrated disloyalty to his superiors within the department. Otepka and his defenders maintained that he had been ousted merely because of his zealous security checks on prospective appointees (especially Democrats), and his denial of security clearances to some of them. Quite apart from the merits of these arguments, the methods that Otepka's superiors used to accumulate evidence against him raise some problems of privacy. Not only did his superiors conduct surveillance of his home and tap his telephone, but they also gathered the trash he discarded in his wastebasket and burn-bag, attempted to search his desk at night, drilled open his office safe where he kept private papers, and planted a secretary to report on his conversations. It could be argued that the surveillance at the office, because it took place on government premises and involved government property, did not violate Otepka's privacy. Moreover, the information the investigators were seeking was part of the political process and, though it might be protected by norms of confidentiality, could not be considered part of Otepka's private life. Yet it seems that an official should still be able to claim control over some information or activities even on the job. He should be able to determine to some extent when his private thoughts even if written become a part of the political process; perhaps even some unofficial conversations with his secretary or colleagues deserve similar protection. The line between the official and the private on the job is hard to draw, and probably need not be drawn at all if investigators have good reason to believe, for example, that a government employee is passing secrets to enemy agents. But a general warrant to engage in indiscriminate searches and surveillance on the job ought not to be conceded. Whatever methods are used, they should permit some significant area of private life to persist, however it might be defined.[69]

Employment tests and interviews are a second area where questionable methods are sometimes used. One objection to some of these tests and interviews is that the questions asked are not relevant to the job — questions, for example, that delve into driving habits, religious affiliation, birth control methods, dating relationships, or the marital and financial status of parents.[70] Such questions would usually be disallowed (except perhaps for sensitive intelligence positions) by the substantive criteria we have already discussed. But tests often seek information that is arguably relevant to the job and nevertheless violate the procedural criteria because they intrude indiscriminately into private lives. Personality tests probe characteristics — reliability, self-confidence, general psychological stability — that may significantly affect a person's capacity to do a job. (Whether such tests accurately identify these characteristics — which is doubtful — is a separate issue.) Congress directed the Peace Corps to select volunteers of sound "mental health," and the Corps implemented this directive by administering to volunteers the Minnesota Multiphasic Personality Inventory, which asked for "true" or "false" responses to statements such as "Once in a while I laugh at a dirty joke," "I loved my mother," and "During one period when I was a youngster I engaged in petty thievery." Other tests required federal employees to complete these sentences: "I feel ashamed when _____" and "I secretly _____" and "My childhood _____."[71] Such indiscriminate rummaging in the minds of individuals would in general run afoul of the procedural constraints on diminished privacy. Although surprisingly few employees objected to them (even in the Peace Corps), personality tests can hardly be regarded as fully voluntary. The individuals taking such tests nevertheless retain some control over the information they disclose, even if they must resort to wile to protect themselves. In this respect, the polygraph test is even more objectionable because the individuals at least theoretically relinquish even that degree of control over information about themselves. The test procedure often involves other objectionable practices as well: the reactions of the subject, who is encouraged to read pro-polygraph literature planted in the waiting room, are observed by a "receptionist" and reported to the examiner, who includes the observations as part of his evaluation.[72] The Civil Service Commission in 1965 sharply restricted the use of polygraph tests, but the government continued to administer a substantial number to employees each year.[73]

Interviews themselves may also raise privacy questions. The case of Ed Deagle illustrates how this can happen, as well as how the issue of privacy can become entangled with other ethical questions.[74] An army officer who had served in Vietnam, Deagle in 1971 sought a post as assistant administrator for program analysis in the Environmental Protection Agency in the Lindsay administration. The head of the agency was about to hire Deagle when members of the staff raised questions about Deagle's moral character, based on his previous support of the war, which he now repudiated. Deagle agreed to a series of further interviews with the staff, but objected to the last one, with Geoffrey Stokes and John Leo, as an "invasion of privacy." The interview, Deagle thought, took the form of "an inquisition," in which Stokes and Leo pried into his "views on some very fundamental things." Deagle could not very well complain that his participation in the conduct of the war was a private matter, though he could (and did) object to the ways in which the EPA staff took into account his war record. Among the objections were: (1) that the members of the agency were not competent and did not have the authority to decide whether or not he was a war criminal; (2) that to disqualify him because of his earlier views on the war would be to apply a political test for public office in a way that resembled the tactics of McCarthyism; and (3) that his earlier views on the war were not relevant to an administrator's position and would have no significant impact on staff harmony and morale unless members of the staff improperly ignored (1) and (2).

None of these objections is, strictly speaking, based on privacy: was Deagle merely confused in claiming an "invasion of privacy"? Although privacy is not the only important issue in this case and Deagle may not himself always have distinguished it from other issues, his privacy objection should be taken seriously. In principle, Deagle might have maintained that his conversion to an antiwar view was a private matter, but he of course felt that he had to disclose his current beliefs, in part to avoid misinterpretations of his military service.[75] Some staff members doubted that his conversion was genuine or complete; they wondered, for example, to what extent his opposition to the war was based on moral rather than merely pragmatic grounds. Stokes and Leo suspected that if they asked him only about the war, he was clever enough to give the "right" answers. They wanted him to "reveal what kind of person he was"; to test the sincerity and depth of his conversion, they attempted to conduct an interview that probed his personal views on a whole range of "basic values." The result was an interview that evidently proceeded indiscriminately, violating the procedural constraints we have been examining. That the interview also covered some topics relevant to his performance in the agency or may have raised some doubts about his general reliability does not remove the objection to undertaking such an interview in the first place. An interview that tests sincerity and searches for the "whole person" in this way is not likely to respect any boundaries of the private life of a candidate, however narrowly those boundaries may be drawn. Even if the sincerity of Deagle's views on environmental reform had been the primary issue, such an inquisitory interview would have been inappropriate. His past public record, and his responses to questions of obvious pertinence to the job, should have given agency officials sufficient information to decide whether to hire him.

To be sure, how wide-ranging an interview or an employment test may be depends partly on the nature of the position to be filled. A candidate for Congress, for example, who seeks to represent us on a wide range of issues, may be less entitled to object to probing interviews (though partly because a more diverse public assesses the propriety of the questions and the adequacy of his responses than could do so in Deagle's case). Yet current practice often seems to be the reverse of what would be called for by the nature of the position. It is lower-level, more specialized, public employees who have been more often subjected to personality and polygraph tests and probably also to improper interviews. In any event, whatever the nature of the position, the procedural criteria remain in force.

A third area to which procedural criteria apply concerns the personnel records of public employees. Here too methods should be selective and give officials some control over information about themselves. Even if we optimistically assume that the records contain only relevant or necessary information, we have not disposed of the privacy problem. First, like any employer, the government properly collects a great deal of personal information about all employees (for example, relating to medical insurance, life insurance beneficiaries, and home mortgages). Although personnel officers need access to this data, other officials, including the employees' superiors, and the press and the public, do not. The method of record-keeping, therefore, should distinguish between such personal information, which could be kept in completely separate files, and job-related information, which would be available to an employee's superior or in some circumstances to a wider public.[76] Second, individual officials should have some control over all of the records about themselves, specifically the right to see what is in their own files, to determine who else sees them, and what is included or excluded from them. The Privacy Act of 1974 gave federal employees the right to examine their personnel files, but legal provisions are not likely to solve the problem completely, since officials have been known to maintain "ghost files" containing confidential information unknown and unavailable to their subordinates. The State Department kept such a file on Murray C. Smith, III, a young foreign service officer who was "selected out" (involuntarily retired) in 1971, evidently partly on the basis of this file.[77] In this case, the information concerned his public antiwar activity, but the same procedure could well be used to collect private information, and even if the employee knew about it, he would be unlikely to challenge the abuse formally, for fear of publicizing the sensitive information more widely.

The private lives of public officials deserve protection because the privacy of all citizens has value. However, because officials must be held accountable in a democracy (in part to safeguard the privacy of others), they should not expect to enjoy the same protection as do ordinary citizens. What the scope of the private life of officials should be depends on a manifold set of criteria that do not by themselves yield precise boundaries. The criteria are best conceived as a framework of factors about which citizens and officials should deliberate when questions of privacy arise, and as a guide that suggests when such questions ought to arise. In democracies, especially the imperfect ones we know, it is important to seek justifiable boundaries between public and private life. The purpose is not only to secure the privacy of officials and citizens; it is also to ensure the publicity of affairs of public import. Spurious claims of privacy shield officials from needful scrutiny by a democratic public and subvert democratic processes of deliberation and accountability. The private lives of public officials are as important for what they exclude as for what they include.

NOTES

I am grateful to David Johnston for assisting with the research for this essay and providing comments on an earlier version of it.

1. Alan F. Westin, *Privacy and Freedom* (New York: Atheneum, 1970), pp. 349-364, 367; Kent S. Larsen, ed., "The Privacy Act of 1974," in *Privacy: A Public Concern* (Washington, D.C.: Government Printing Office, 1975), pp. 162-178; and David W. Ewing, *Freedom Inside the Organization* (New York: Dutton, 1977), pp. 133-138.

2. Alfred Hill, "Defamation and the First Amendment," *Columbia Law Review*, 76 (December 1976), esp. pp. 1211-1218; and Clifton O. Lawhorne, *Defamation and Public Officials* (Carbondale, Ill.: Southern Illinois University Press, 1971), pp. 213-228, 265-283.

3. Congressional Quarterly, *Congressional Ethics*, 2d ed. (Washington, D.C.: Congressional Quarterly, Inc., 1980), pp. 48-57, 75-88, 182-203; and Brit Hume, "Now It Can Be Told . . . Or Can It?" *More* (April 1975), pp. 6ff.

4. See Stanley I. Benn, "Privacy, Freedom, and Respect for Persons," in *Privacy, Nomos XIII*, ed. Roland Pennock and John W. Chapman (New York: Atherton Press, 1971), pp. 1-3; and Charles Fried, *An Anatomy of Values* (Cambridge, Mass.: Harvard University Press, 1970), p. 141. "Private" is often used in a broader way than "privacy," so that almost any activity can be private with respect to some wider group or with respect to the government (for example, a private club, a private company, the private sector). However, this broader notion of private raises the question of the legitimate scope of intervention by the government and other members of society in the whole range of economic, social, and political activities. The distinctive claims made in behalf of a private life, though related to this general question, are better conceived as based specifically on individual privacy. For an illuminating analysis of the concept of the private see W. L. Weinstein, "The Private and the Free: A Conceptual Inquiry," in *Privacy, Nomos XIII*, ed. Pennock and Chapman, pp. 27-55.

5. In some cases it is useful to distinguish between permissive, obligatory, and supererogatory disclosure by an official whose privacy is in question and by other persons who challenge his or her privacy. But in most cases, the crucial issue is usually whether the official has an obligation to reveal aspects of what would otherwise be his or her private life, and whether other people have an obligation not to disclose or to consider these aspects.

6. Westin, *Privacy and Freedom*, pp. 42-51, argues that organizations may claim confidentiality on the same grounds that individuals claim privacy. Although parallels exist (for example, privacy protects the liberty of both individuals and organizations), we would generally accept a claim of confidentiality by a government organization only if we accept the ends it is pursuing and regard confidentiality as a necessary means. A claim of individual privacy may be warranted whether or not we accept the ends the individual is pursuing.

7. For a survey of the application of existing legal doctrine to the privacy of public officials see Robert M. O'Neil, "The Private Lives of Public Employees," *Oregon Law Review*, 51 (Fall 1971), pp. 70-112. The most developed aspect of the law concerns the relation between libel of public figures and the First Amendment (see Hill, "Defamation," pp. 1206-1313), but since most cases have involved matters of public controversy, the question of how far the private life of a public official is protected has not been resolved. "Some aspects of the lives of even the most public men fall outside the area of matters of public or general concern" (*Rosenbloom v. Metromedia, Inc.*, 402 U.S. at 48 [1971]), but the court has not determined what those aspects are. Whatever they are, they would evidently be more protected than public aspects: see *Gertz v. Robert Welch, Inc.*, 418 U.S. at 347 (1974).

8. See Note, "Application of the Constitutional Privacy Right to Exclusions and Dismissals from Public Employment," *Duke Law Journal* (December 1973), pp. 1054-1055, 1062.

9. Plato, *The Republic*, trans. Paul Shorey (Cambridge, Mass.: Harvard University Press, 1963), I, 315, 475-483; II, 141 (419a, 464b-466d, 519e-520a).

10. See Hannah Arendt, *The Human Condition* (Chicago: University of Chicago Press, 1959), pp. 23-69.

11. Aristotle, *Politics*, trans. H. Rackham (Cambridge, Mass.: Harvard University Press, 1967), pp. 5-13, 85-89 (1252a-1253b, 1263a-1263b).

12. Rousseau, *Considerations on the Government of Poland*, in *Rousseau: Political Writings*, trans. Frederick Watkins (Edinburgh: Dent, 1953), p. 244; and *The Social Contract*, trans. Maurice Cranston (Baltimore: Penguin, 1968), bk. III, chap. 15, pp. 140-141. In other moods, Rousseau celebrates the charms of private life; see, for example, *Emile*, trans. Barbara Foxley (London: Dent, 1963), pp. 438-439; and *Les Rêveries du promeneur solitaire*, ed. Raymond Bernex (Paris: Bordas, 1966).

13. Hegel, *Philosophy of Right*, trans. T. M. Knox (Oxford: Oxford University Press, 1962), p. 281, Addition to paragraph 265; cf. pp. 155-158, paragraph 258. Hegel nevertheless appreciates the ethical value of private life, for example in the family (pp. 110-122, paragraphs 158-181).

14. See, for example, Marx, "On the Jewish Question," in *The Marx-Engels Reader*, ed. Robert Tucker, 2d ed. (New York: Norton, 1978), pp. 33-35.

15. For example, Hobbes, *Leviathan*, ed. C. B. Macpherson (Baltimore: Pelican, 1968), chaps. 13-14, 17, 21; and Locke, *Two Treatises of*

Government, ed. Peter Laslett (Cambridge, Eng.: Cambridge University Press, 1960), *Second Treatise*, chaps. 2, 7-9.

16. Kant's ideal state, traditionally liberal in many ways, nevertheless already removes from the private sphere the provision of welfare. *The Metaphysical Elements of Justice*, trans. John Ladd (Indianapolis: Bobbs-Merrill, 1965), p. 93. By the mid-nineteenth century, John Stuart Mill is striving to maintain a private sphere merely for self-regarding action: *On Liberty*, in *Collected Works*, XVIII, ed. J. M. Robson (Toronto: University of Toronto Press, 1977), pp. 276-291.

17. Here it is less important what those activities are than that some significant zone of privacy should be generally respected. Our broader interest in privacy, as Thomas Scanlon points out, is in "having a zone of privacy in which we can carry out our activities without . . . being continually alert for possible observers, listeners, etc." "Thomson on Privacy," *Philosophy and Public Affairs*, 4 (Summer 1975), 317-318.

18. Benn, "Privacy, Freedom, and Respect for Persons," pp. 3-13.

19. Fried, *Anatomy*, pp. 140-147; James Rachels, "Why Privacy Is Important," *Philosophy and Public Affairs*, 4 (Summer 1975), 323-332; and Jeffrey H. Reiman, "Privacy, Intimacy and Personhood," *Philosophy and Public Affairs*, 6 (Fall 1976), 26-44.

20. Erving Goffman, *Stigma* (Englewood Cliffs, N.J.: Prentice-Hall, 1963), p. 71.

21. Officials in nongovernmental positions also exercise power over us, and insofar as they do, the principle of diminished privacy applies to them too.

22. See Michael Walzer, "Political Action: The Problem of Dirty Hands," *Philosophy and Public Affairs*, 2 (Winter 1973), 160-180.

23. On the forms and difficulties of symbolic representation see Hanna Pitkin, *The Concept of Representation* (Berkeley and Los Angeles: University of California Press, 1967), pp. 92-111.

24. Edward N. Stirewalt, "Yardsticks for Rulers," *Washington Post*, August 1, 1976, p. C-1.

25. In some cultures the expectations about leaders may differ from ours (or at least from those we admit to): Sukarno's "massive preoccupation with sex" was said to be "a matter of admiration rather than disapproval in Indonesia—a demonstration, perhaps, of Sukarno's continuing virility and thus of his political potency as well." J. D. Legge, *Sukarno: A Political Biography* (New York: Praeger, 1972), p. 336.

26. Paul A. Freund, "Privacy: One Concept or Many," in *Privacy, Nomos XIII*, ed. Pennock and Chapman, p. 187; and Westin, *Privacy and Freedom*, p. 375. Cf. *Gertz v. Robert Welch, Inc.*, 418 U.S. at 344-345 (1974): "Public officials . . . have voluntarily exposed themselves to increased risk of injury from defamatory falsehoods concerning them."

27. William W. Van Alstyne, "The Demise of the Right-Privilege Distinction in Constitutional Law," *Harvard Law Review*, 81 (May 1968), 1439-1464.

28. For example, William L. Rivers and Wilbur Schramm, *Responsibil-*

ity in Mass Communications, rev. ed. (New York: Harper and Row, 1969), p. 164.

29. By issuing a thirty-three-page statement on the Sarsfield's incident, the White House may have generated more publicity than would have otherwise occurred. Press Secretary Jody Powell claims, however, that the report was an "in-house memo," given only to reporters on request (letter to author, May 12, 1978).

30. *Washington Post*, December 22, 1976, pp. A1, A5; December 23, 1976, pp. A1, A17; and December 24, 1976, pp. A2, A15. For a discussion of the relevance of Senator Robert Byrd's earlier association with the Ku Klux Klan and his possible nomination for the Supreme Court see John L. Hulteng, *The Messenger's Motives* (Englewood Cliffs, N.J.: Prentice-Hall, 1976), p. 68.

31. *Bruns v. Pomeyleau*, 319 F. Supp. 58 (D. Md. 1970). Nudism, the court solemnly observed, is not the only recreational activity for which policemen must remove their weapons.

32. Benjamin R. Epstein and Arnold Forster, *The Radical Right* (New York: Random House, 1967), pp. 180-181.

33. See Pitkin, *Concept*, pp. 144-167.

34. See Arthur M. Schlesinger, Jr., *The Coming of the New Deal* (Boston: Houghton Mifflin, 1959), pp. 105-110; and Hume, "Now It Can Be Told," p. 6.

35. Max Weber, "Bureaucracy," in *From Max Weber*, ed. H. H. Gerth and C. Wright Mills (New York: Oxford University Press, 1958), pp. 197, 199.

36. Hugh Heclo, *A Government of Strangers* (Washington, D.C.: Brookings Institute, 1977), pp. 34-83, 154-155.

37. Congressional Quarterly, pp. 75-88, 182-188.

38. *New York Times*, August 2, 1978, pp. A1, A14; and June 21, 1978, p. A18.

39. Congressional Quarterly, pp. 75-88.

40. David Arnold Anderson, "A Constitutional Right of Privacy Protects Personal Financial Affairs of Public Officials from Overbroad Disclosure Requirements," *Texas Law Review*, 49 (January 1971), pp. 346-356.

41. *Congressional Quarterly Weekly Report*, 32 (June 19, 1976), 1565.

42. *Congressional Quarterly Weekly Report*, 32 (June 19, 1976), 1564; and *Washington Post*, October 24, 1976, p. E1. All won their elections in the fall except Hays, who did not run, and Howe, who ran in a Mormon dominated district in Utah. Cf. Wilbur Mills's escapades with Fanne Foxe in the tidal basin in 1974. For cases involving lower level officials see O'Neil, "Private Lives," pp. 75-76.

43. *Washington Post*, October 26, 1976, p. A5.

44. U.S. House Committee on Post Office and Civil Service, Subcommittee on Manpower and Civil Service, *Final Report: Violations and Abuses of Merit Principles in Federal Employment* (Washington, D.C.: Government Printing Office, 1976), p. 163.

45. Marriages not on the public record may also be fair game. If Presi-

dent Kennedy had been previously married and the record suppressed, as was widely rumored, the press should have reported these facts. See Tom Wicker, *On Press* (New York: Viking Press, 1978), p. 111. Bigamous marriages are also properly a matter of public concern, not merely because they are illegal, but because they may demonstrate an official's attitude toward a major social question. See "Newspaper Wins Bigamist Case," *The News Media and the Law* (April 1978), p. 25.

46. *New York Times*, May 5, 1963, pp. 1, 28, 72.

47. *New York Times*, August 29, 1969, p. 15; Hume, "Now It Can Be Told," p. 8; *New York Times*, January 9, 1976, p. 29; February 12, 1976, p. 13; and February 12, 1975, p. 4.

48. *Trenton Times*, July 28, 1978, p. 1 (Associated Press story).

49. Hume, "Now It Can Be Told," p. 8. For somewhat similar cases see Rivers and Schramm, *Responsibility*, pp. 164, 169.

50. Alan L. Otten, "No More Tiptoeing," *Wall Street Journal*, September 4, 1975, p. 10. The Judicial Council of the American Medical Association has held that a "physician may not discuss the patient's health condition with the press or the public without the patient's consent." AMA, *Opinions and Reports of the Judicial Council* (Chicago, 1977), sec. 6.09. Presumably, proposals for announcing the results of physical exams assume that the candidate would give his consent.

51. For an example of such a proposal see Harold D. Lasswell, *Power and Personality* (New York: Norton, 1948), pp. 186-187.

52. Theodore H. White, *The Making of the President 1972* (New York: Atheneum, 1973), pp. 263-275; and *Congressional Quarterly Weekly Report*, 30 (July 29, 1972), pp. 1851-1852.

53. *New York Times*, July 21, 1978, pp. A1, A8.

54. That such practices are against the law does not necessarily remove them from the private sphere, since it can be argued that the law should be changed. The controversy over the alleged use of marijuana and other drugs by members of the White House staff illustrates the interplay between legal, moral, and political considerations in this area. See *New York Times*, July 22, 1978, pp. 1, 7; July 23, 1978, p. 20.

55. *Norton v. Macy*, U.S. Court of Appeals, D. C. Circuit, 417 F.2d 1161 (1969). That Norton did not "openly flaunt" his homosexuality seemed to be a factor in the court's decision. A later case upheld the dismissal of a homosexual public employee, evidently because he publicly pursued an "activist role in implementing his unconventional beliefs." *McConnell v. Anderson*, U.S. Court of Appeals, Eighth Circuit, 451 F.2d 193 (1971), *cert. denied*, 405 U.S. 1046 (1972). The courts generally have not sufficiently distinguished between the public practice of the homosexual activity itself, and the advocacy or public knowledge of the activity; the former may sometimes be relevant but the latter seldom should be.

56. Theodore White, *The Making of the President 1964* (New York: Atheneum, 1965), pp. 367-372. That the first newspaper editors who learned of the Jenkins incident did not print it, and that Senator Goldwater did not make it an issue in the presidential campaign, suggest that many

people believed that homosexual incidents of this sort should not be widely publicized (whether or not they should be grounds for dismissal).

57. John Stuart Mill, *On Liberty*, pp. 223-224, 280-283.

58. For a sample of the controversy since Mill see Richard Wasserstrom, ed., *Morality and the Law* (Belmont, Calif.: Wadsworth, 1971).

59. For example, Ronald Dworkin, "Lord Devlin and the Enforcement of Morals," in Wasserstrom, ed., *Morality and the Law*, pp. 55-72.

60. It is therefore too simple to say, as Tom Wicker does, that "a reporter should write and a newspaper should print what they know." On his view, even if a reporter believes for good reason that, say, an extramarital affair of a politician is not any business of the public, he should still report it; the reporter has no right to impose on his readers his moral judgment about what is relevant to public duty, Wicker maintains, and moreover other papers would print the story anyhow. *On Press*, pp. 111-112. But on many topics the press already exercise discretion about what is relevant, and in principle they could do so with respect to private lives too. Furthermore, the decision to publish information about private lives is no more morally neutral than the decision not to publish it.

61. J. Anthony Lukas, *Nightmare: The Underside of the Nixon Years* (New York: Viking, 1976), pp. 126-138, 218-219.

62. Rivers and Schramm, *Responsibility*, p. 166.

63. Lukas, *Nightmare*, pp. 66-84.

64. "Kissinger's Threat to Resign—June 11, 1974," in *Historic Documents of 1974* (Washington, D.C.: Congressional Quarterly, Inc., 1975), p. 495.

65. But see Rivers and Schramm, *Responsibility*, pp. 165-166.

66. *New York Times*, July 21, 1975, p. 27.

67. Ewing, *Freedom*, p. 130.

68. See Taylor Branch, "The Odd Couple," in *Blowing the Whistle*, ed. Charles Peters and Taylor Branch (New York: Praeger, 1972), pp. 222-245; and Committee on the Judiciary, Subcommittee to Investigate the Administration of the Internal Security Act and Other Internal Security Laws, *State Department Security, 1963-1965* (Washington, D.C.: Government Printing Office, 1967).

69. For some cases involving seizure of personal effects from employees' lockers and trunks see O'Neil, "Private Lives," p. 97.

70. Alan F. Westin, "Privacy and Personnel Records," *The Civil Liberties Review* (January/February, 1978), p. 30.

71. Westin, *Privacy and Freedom*, pp. 259-268.

72. U.S. Congress, Senate Committee on the Judiciary, Subcommittee on Constitutional Rights, *Privacy, Polygraphs, and Employment* (Washington, D.C.: Government Printing Office, 1974), p. 5.

73. "Use of Polygraph in Personal Investigation of Competitive Service Applicants and Appointees to Competitive Service Positions," in *Federal Personnel Manual* (Washington, January 1972), chap. 736, Appendix D; and *Privacy, Polygraphs and Employment*, p. 2.

74. See Diana Gordon and Jane Downing, "The Deagle Affair," Ken-

nedy School of Government, Harvard University, 1976; or P. G. Brown and P. Vernier, "Morley Affair," ICCH Public Policy and Management Program, Boston, 1980.

75. An analogous dilemma confronts a candidate for a federal administrative post when he is subject to a "political affiliation check." It may be to his advantage to have investigators go beyond his public party registration and scrutinize his general "political concepts and philosophies." But often this is done without the candidate's knowledge and for supposedly nonpolitical career positions. See House Subcommittee on Manpower and Civil Service, *Final Report: Violations and Abuses of Merit Principles*, pp. 190-192, 201, 204.

76. See Ewing, *Freedom*, pp. 136-138; and Westin, "Privacy and Personnel Records," pp. 28-34.

77. Robert G. Vaughn, *The Spoiled System* (New York: Charterhouse, 1975), pp. 308-309.

Lance Liebman

10. Legislating Morality in the Proposed CIA Charter

Two large themes have figured prominently in recent political discussion. One is the asserted need to raise the moral level at which political activity is conducted: to increase the ethical content of public life by constraining for the collective welfare the pursuit of self-interest by individual participants. The second theme is a new realism about the machinery of public regulation of social affairs: growing recognition that legislative enactment of collective goals is not self-implementing, that the results of official action are often less satisfactory than their proponents expected, and that the conventional arsenal of intervention weapons is poorly adapted to certain battles in which it is nonetheless employed.

The connection between these two themes seems obvious but is rarely noted. As a result, we hear of deregulation, of substituting incentives for command-and-control regulation, and of the unfortunate tendencies of large bureaucratic organizations at the same time (and sometimes in the same voice) that we hear of the desirability of the Federal Election Campaign Act, the Massachusetts Ethics Commission, the Permanent Special Prosecutor, the Whistleblower Protective Act (formally titled the Federal Disclosure and Accountability Act), and the Government in the Sunshine Act. Each of these is an effort to expand government so as to control government, and each is likely — if the general critiques of regulation have bite — to result in important unhappy consequences, whatever the good it may also achieve.

The contradiction, of course, is only typical of our present temper. We seek many goals for which government seems the only possible agent. We are dissatisfied with some of what government is doing, but are hardly confident that we would be more satisfied were the efforts not being made. Using government so much, we naturally attend to its processes. When those seem flawed, we turn to general schemes of legal reformation: to

248

codes, to charters, to reorganizations. As with so many other occasions of public intervention, we enact new rules, not with certainty they will succeed, but because taking no action seems unacceptable. Our imagination has not provided adequate alternatives to the restricted set of mechanisms we routinely use, and our intellectual tools do not permit refined analysis of the likely consequences of employing specific institutional arrangements in the pursuit of particular ends.

In this essay, I attempt to take a small step on the intellectual path hinted at above by examining — staring at, shaking gently — one recent attempt at legislated morality, the proposed National Intelligence Charter. This statutory proposal was the fruit of extensive and serious consideration by a special committee of the U.S. Senate of the asserted abuses of American intelligence activities. One purpose of this essay is to see what insights are possible about the proposed law and about the difficult set of problems the law addresses. A larger purpose is to treat this bill as an example of attempts at legislated public ethics, and to seek generalizations about the capacity of democratic processes to formulate and enforce collective judgments of official morality. It is perhaps unnecessary to say that the context discussed here — the attempt to achieve institutional reform of the nation's intelligence services by statute — is not the typical context but rather the hardest one, because of the inherent aspect of lawlessness that is characteristic of the spy business. Achieving a fine-tuned control of lawless spying (so much but no more) is either difficult or impossible. But the spy context is nonetheless provocative in terms of the general problem.

There really was a post-Pearl Harbor consensus. The United States, a reticent power, could not stay out of world affairs. We were too strong and too good. Since we could accomplish so much, we were obliged to try. In any event, we would inevitably be drawn in eventually, so we had better stay involved. Indeed, we could avoid large confrontations through prudent manipulation, and we could also remain ready — could obtain knowledge and practice — for the time when something big would occur. Iran (restoring the Shah, and overthrowing Mossadegh), Guatemala (overthrowing Arbenz), and Italy (subsidizing Christian Democracy) are examples of behavior — "operations" — justified by this consensus catechism. [1]

The OSS-to-CIA, Bedell Smith-to-Allen Dulles model is logically stable. The model includes:

(a) a permanent organization, as much a company as AT&T;

(b) honest reporting to the president, and sometimes to other executive officials;

(c) a long leash from the president — "do things generally in the service of interests we jointly understand (anticommunism, pro-U.S. companies), but don't tell me about everything";

(d) a similar relationship with a few trusted congressional leaders, who however will be inattentive, unstaffed, and uncritical of unpublicized excess;

(e) cooperation with a wide variety of establishment institutions and individuals within the United States;

(f) according virtually no respect to the laws or desires of any foreign states except (sometimes) Britain.

This, says organization theory, is a recipe for an institution that will:

(a) be fat and lazy, because no one is monitoring its activities;

(b) permit individual frolics, since goals are very general, decentralization is inevitable, and central authority can sidestep if called on the carpet;

(c) gather vast quantities of data, but hesitate to become committed to disprovable predictions (I have never seen a CIA document; I would bet my piece of the Fenway Park wall that they are a lot like the *Newsweek* "Periscope");

(d) always be engaged in one or two fantastic ventures, of the sort that could be the subject of a movie.

But observe the solution to the legitimacy problem. The country wants what it is getting. The president approves, sort of. A few senators approve, sort of. Congress more broadly *could* intervene and does not, therefore impliedly ratifying the supervision members assume is being given by the special committees and the president. The citizenry, fed a diet of lightly fictionalized exploits, is happy. Other countries cannot or do not complain, for various realpolitik reasons. And everyone assumes what Richard Helms firmly believes: you can have this sort of organization or not, but you can't have half of it, or have it under procedural bounds. Assuming (or, if they think about it, believing) that to be the choice, most members of Congress, accurately reflecting their constituents' values, cast an appropriately secret positive vote.

This stability has now been undermined. Several developments combined to bring about the breakdown. We did badly abroad: among other setbacks, we lost a war. The press changed: in a period of public skepticism, media owners and managers found profit and status through spectacular revelations about institutions once treated as sacrosanct; also, this more concentrated industry had capital to invest in well-educated reporters pursuing long-term quests for prize-earning scoops. Congressional leadership weakened. Communism looked a different sort of enemy. American leaders and institutions appeared less deserving of trust and support. The CIA itself was exposed for domestic behavior outside its apparent bounds, for bumbling overseas, for compliance to the requests of a discredited administration, and for projects (kill Castro with poison cigar smuggled by Mafia intermediaries) symptomatic of an international order that, if it was not the cause of President Kennedy's death, was certainly not compatible with our highest professions and aspirations.

When the Senate Select Committee on Intelligence was formed in 1976, and published a draft National Intelligence Reorganization and Reform Act in 1978, the postwar intellectual structure explaining intelligence activities must have looked permanently shattered. (Richard Helms: "I don't think we ever in the history of this country want to go through again what we did in 1975 over intelligence, and anything that would stop that, I would be in favor of.") Recent U.S. spies were publishing their memoirs, and even telephone directories of their former colleagues. Newspapers were printing whatever they could ferret out about failed adventures. Perhaps most threatening, a notion was in the air that Congress was responsible both for the monies spent on these dubious activities and for their moral validity. Yet, in an age suddenly marked by public disagreement over what it is right for us to do and by quick changes in standards (so that what seemed right recently might be indefensible when reelection is necessary), acceptance of such responsibility would be exceedingly uncomfortable.

The relevant question was therefore quite clear to the senators who considered the problem: Could America have some spying without the abuses that had occurred in the past? Was there a third way, between entering a nunnery on the one hand (that is, giving up virtually all of the operational work, and perhaps also quite a bit of the information-gathering* conducted by the CIA in the recent past) and, on the other, returning to the days of unchecked delegation to a permanent unelected agency of the power to spend our money and to risk compromising our other goals and our good name? To succeed, the committee would have to avoid a demand for U.S. renunciation of spy work (a call that would either be unheeded or, if followed, would give up foreign activities seemingly favored by voters and called for by the logic and structure of America's 1970s historical role

---

*It must be true that a large amount of all the useful information obtained by intelligence organizations comes from satellite observation, collection of legally available materials, interviews with cooperative observers, and then—most important and difficult—perceptive distillation of insights and conclusions. What is unclear is whether the additional contribution from cloak-and-dagger fact-gathering, while episodic, is nonetheless of great significance.

and position), yet somehow achieve a greater degree of legitimacy and support for those activities than the weakened postwar system could sustain.

In seeking a new set of rules and procedures, the committee found virtually no help in stated international agreements. Countries may approve or tolerate spying, but they do not say so, and they do not reach public agreements as to its norms and bounds. There is a common-law record of arrests, expulsions, retaliations, and suppressions, but attempting to build generalizations on national behavior in this area would be fruitless. Facts would be hard to compile and assess, and actions so often respond to immediate considerations that at best they reveal only a little of continuing views about appropriate conduct.

The committee also obtained scant help from the possibilities represented by changes in the individuals holding particular positions. Assume a world where Helms is director and he reports in full to President Johnson and to Senators Russell and Stennis. Now assume Turner as director reporting to President Carter and to Senators Bayh and Cranston. If Bayh is different from Russell, then this is a different arrangement. This much change, however, while it may produce a different result in some important particular matter, is hardly a fundamental alteration. Passage of time has produced different senior senators, with somewhat different ideas and constituencies. If anything, the switch from ad hoc reporting to the armed services/appropriations titans to a specific intelligence committee could by itself be counterproductive: deeper immersion may tend to produce even less perspective, even less fresh review. Compare the theories of regulatory capture.

The one plausible reed for those seeking to predict the new committee's conduct is its staff. In what my children call "olden times" (the sixties, for example), the senators reviewed without staff help. Now we are in a period of larger congressional staffs, and certainly much more independent and assertive ones. It is a contingent fact that the intelligence committee staff is capable, honed on anti-CIA experience, and out to establish its role before a fuzzy-liberal constituency. Might there be some long-lasting reason to expect such a staff to take up a position that is regularly adversarial to the operating agencies? Is this like a car-safety agency whose only measurable impact is recalls, so that one can predict that the agency will order recalls of more cars every year? Does not the cooptation outcome seem equally likely? Indeed, adversariness probably requires a historical period of fundamental division between the policies of those running national security affairs and a significant segment of educated opinion. End that schism and there will be no reason to expect skeptical and intensive review by the committee staff of agency activities and proposals.

Even if the existence of new committees and a new staff led to tougher review of budgets and activities, and some restraints on imaginative exploits,* it would hardly satisfactorily legitimate the ventures. A few elected representatives, and staff picked by them, would be part of this process, but the reviews would inevitably be late and fragmentary (indeed, if they were full and early, the effectiveness of the activities would be compromised significantly). Most important, while appraisal by a subgroup of the Congress can import a broader perspective than that of full-time spies, the process of consultation and decision remains a set of unconnected benefit-cost calculations with the currency—the relevant values—unstated. This certainly represents no progress toward public consideration of the sorts of activities America should conduct, or—especially—of the sorts we should forswear.

The intelligence context highlights the deceptive attraction of procedure as a mechanism for enforcing ethical norms. Our tolerance of intrusive, clumsy, and sometimes draconian official authority is mitigated by the wide range of institutional arrangements that decentralize coercive power, requiring disclosure, persuasion, compromise, and barter. Rules of process frequently enforce power-sharing. Information is essential to effective participation. Just as the securities laws enhance investor participation in economic markets by granting access to relevant facts, so rules of notice and hearing, of sunshine, and of stated reasons and explanations add to the capacity of persons and groups to make effective use of rights to participate —even as voters—that would otherwise be nugatory. The second purpose of these procedural requirements is a function of the fact that no matter how much participation is authorized, modern government must to a large degree be the exercise of authority by a few on behalf of others. In theory and in practice, this idea of trusteeship has always lived in rough tension with the notion of the political marketplace as a locus for self-serving (but public-benefiting) competition for the status and power of office. Rules requiring that conflicts of interest be avoided (or at least revealed), that campaign contributions be disclosed, and that explanations of official action be provided are imperfect efforts to discipline investitures of authority that are legitimate only as service to others.

The proposed CIA charter illustrates both of these explanations for pro-

---

*Effective congressional oversight might require protection for intelligence agency foot soldiers seeking to rat on their colleagues, yet freedom to complain to Congress seems inconsistent with the standards of discipline and secrecy usually associated with a bureaucracy of spies. The proposed Federal Disclosure and Accountability Act, popularly known as the Whistleblower Protective Act, specifically does not apply to the armed forces, but is ambiguous about whether its umbrella extends to the CIA.

ceduralism. The bill would have Congress informed, early and often, on matters they previously were not told about. Indeed, in this one instance, statutory change has already occurred. A 1974 amendment to the Foreign Assistance Act, adopted with little discussion or attention at the height of agitation over CIA misdeeds, and now codified as 22 U.S.C., section 2422, forbids expenditures "by or on behalf of the Central Intelligence Agency for operations in foreign countries, other than activities intended solely for obtaining necessary intelligence, unless and until the President finds that each such operation is important to the national security of the United States and reports, in a timely fashion, a description and scope of such operation to the appropriate committee of the Congress." This, the Hughes-Ryan amendment, presumably does not apply to U.S. intelligence organizations other than the CIA. To some degree, the legal change — the one enacted in 1974, and the somewhat modified version proposed in the charter — seeks increased power-sharing, not by requiring approval, but by making an opportunity for veto (through congressional control of funds and authority to enact substantively limiting laws) effective. Also, of course, the notifications increase the opportunity for informal congressional advice to the executive officials, a role that may not be legal authority by some definitions but is certainly sometimes of great significance. Second, there is here an attempt to emphasize that the president's authority to order activities, given indirect statutory approval by the 1974 amendments and by the proposed intelligence charter, is to be conducted in the service of certain (unstated and undefined) public goals, so that the duty to report is a mild injunction that he consider "the national security" and be clear about how it is served by his decision.

Requirements of notice and disclosure are probably the weakest type of power-shifting restraint. The restraint is least effective when publicity is merely an aid to citizens in general, assisting them in their function of legitimating officeholders with ballots. Citizens are inattentive. As voters, they must often choose among imperfect alternatives. No law achieves revelation of everything, and sometimes the revelation of more leads to the recognition and comprehension of less. Requirement of disclosure to organized, financed, prepared users is a far more significant method of enforcing power-sharing. In the context of foreign intelligence, it is hard to have a view on whether, over time, congressmen want the responsibility as well as the information, and whether other claims on their attention are compatible with a real role. One can only be confident that without information, congressional participation in the process of decision is impossible. The hearings on S. 2525 presented a fascinating contrast. Former CIA director Colby insisted on meaningful congressional oversight, and stated that without it, democratic approval is impossible. ("Exposure to specified Members of Congress . . . will give our American intelligence greater, rather than less, strength in the long run and avoid the . . . sensational hindsighting . . . of the last several years.") Former director Helms said that congressmen can't and won't perform the task responsibly, and therefore that some alternative form of legitimation — delegation to honorable executive branch officials, plus conversations ("not committed to impersonal treatment such as would be the inevitable result of exchanging written documents . . . papers in this town have a way of turning up in the strangest places") with a very small number of specially selected members of the House and Senate, is what he seemed to have in mind — must do.

Of course, disclosure rules, like all constraints on authority, are sometimes in conflict with effective government. There will be leaks. Compare William Colby, writing about the 1974 amendment in *Honorable Men* (p. 423): "I was going up there [to Capitol Hill] to report on every new step taken in the Angola, Kurdish, and other covert operations currently underway . . . Sadly, the experience demonstrated that secrets, if they are to remain secret, cannot be given to more than a few Congressmen — every new project subjected to this procedure during 1975 leaked," with the same Mr. Colby, testifying in 1978 before the Senate Select Committee: "The particular danger of exposure of intelligence secrets is not, in my mind, a bar to proper constitutional supervision. This committee, in its years of history, has given evidence that it can keep the secrets it has been given." Paperwork itself is burdensome. Mr. Helms: "S. 2525 would seem to demand . . . at least 67 separate conditions under which written reports would be made to the Congress. This blizzard of paper would be so heavy as to turn the examination of it over to the committee staffs, which in turn would be running the intelligence community, or, as former Director George Bush put it, 'micromanaging the intelligence business.' " Nonetheless, without information there can almost never be participation, and so the correct question about information is who should have what role in the process of decision. When Richard Helms, as a CIA functionary, authorized an agent to pose as a personal representative of Attorney General Robert Kennedy, and in that guise to recruit a Cuban assassin to kill Castro, but did not tell Kennedy, we are convinced Helms was wrong because we feel Kennedy should have been part of a decision to use his name in that way. When Helms did not tell the Warren Commission about attempts to assassinate Castro, saying they never specifically asked, we feel he was wrong if we believe that the question whether the public should know everything relevant to President Kennedy's death even at some compromise to CIA purposes properly rested at that point with Chief Justice Warren and his colleagues rather than with Helms.

The bill's other main type of restraint, the requirement that the president state a substantive view, raises somewhat different questions. The sponsors exhibit their upbringing in a world of written presidential justifications for selling arms to Turkey after it invades Cyprus, written statements that arms sales will not have "a significant adverse effect on the combat readiness of the Armed Forces of the United States," presidential findings that a "nonmarket economy country" does not deny emigration as a condition of commercial agreements, inflation-impact statements, and so forth. The procedural requirement that the president determine that intelligence activities serve U.S. security interests is not itself power-sharing (not, that is, like a requirement that search warrants be granted by a judge, that treaties win consent, that the FBI budget be authorized as well as appropriated, or that new debt be approved by referendum). Nor does it provide standards for the president's decision — what evil to do in order to obtain what information, what governments to destabilize, and what falsehoods to spread before foreign readers. This is a version of proceduralism that assumes standards cannot be formulated (or agreed to) and discretion must be left, in the end, to those who held it before, but that the exercise of that discretion can be affected through channeling and ordering of what and who is heard and who must accept responsibility for the outcome. Or, to put the question baldly, does it matter if a commissioner of highways must hold a public hearing on the environmental consequences of a new road, file an environmental impact statement, and then personally certify that transportation improvement outweighs environmental costs?*

The requirement of a presidential statement has two important aspects. First, it probably tends to push decisions to a higher level of consideration within the government. Yet I do not think discretionary U.S. intelligence decisions have often been made outside the consensus view of the highest levels of the national security operation, including presidents. Thus I do not see why channeling more decisions to a higher bureaucratic level will in this instance produce different decisions. The committee would seem to be proposing checks on a runaway, self-serving set of organizations. I doubt that is an accurate diagnosis. (Another interesting question is whether, if

*Put aside the possibility, brought to mind by the environmental analogy, that existence of the procedure will in fact transfer some part of final discretionary authority, because in fact — contra the statutory language — judges will be reviewing the validity of the final choice. Even in America, substantive judicial review of intelligence activities seems far-fetched.

the full-time workers and the political masters were in disagreement, requirements for approval would be effective. How important would be the workers' control of the evidence, the arguments, and the means of formulating issues so as to circumvent reporting and appraisal requirements?)

The second significance of the requirement of a presidential statement is that *the president* must sign. He cannot, therefore, later say "I didn't know." (What Eisenhower, by consensus account, was supposed to do over Francis Gary Powers would now be made unlawful as a matter of domestic statute.) The idea that personal responsibility for a presently secret action will lead to different actions (much less, better ones) is fascinating. Is it because a politician will always take credit for successes, but can be charged with failure only if a signature is in the files? Or is it because a leader obliged to sign will think longer, and therefore better, or will give the risks a heavier weight than is involved in a more casual approval, or will somehow make it *his* decision rather than his acceptance of something undertaken by the agency pursuant to discretion delegated to it? Some sort of institutional analysis is underway here, but I fear it is only convincing on a premise that until now the intelligence agencies have been acting in ways that are not the president's, and therefore policies that are more his than theirs would more satisfactorily reflect his—that is, a national electoral—constituency. If the premise is rejected (and I think that taking the last forty years as a whole the premise is exceedingly difficult to document), the analysis crumbles.

There is, in the context of intelligence activities, a different problem with the Senate committee's procedural rule, important even if obvious. Personal presidential responsibility is significant only if the decision or action is known or may become known. If secrecy survives, a signature in the bowels of history will not alter events. If the committee meant to open the books at some defined point in the future, and in effect to share the authority of those now part of the process with a larger group of citizens who would render society's verdict at a point soon enough in time to be incompletely discounted when decisions are made, that is what the committee should have said, rather than asking for a signature but saying nothing about when or by whom the approval would be known and evaluated. Again, procedure matters as an agency of shared authority. The appropriateness of procedures can be evaluated when the structure of distributed power is understood.

Finally, therefore, because the proposed CIA law does not seek the sharing of presidential authority—a sharing believed, probably correctly, to be ruled out by the nature of the decisions and by the locus of foreign policy authority in our governmental structure—its requirements of consideration and consultation can be of only limited effectiveness. The proposed law would matter to the extent that it effectively brought new participants into the process. If they are members of Congress (and, sometimes, staff), decisions could change to the extent that the new participants had different views or responsibilities, or to the extent that the larger number of persons with knowledge made wider dispersion of certain information inevitable (or compromised certain possible actions). Thus the important question is who should participate in what public decisions. Once that is answered, it is possible to draft laws that so distribute information as to make the distribution of participatory authority effective.

A different argument is possible. If the society had a norm or a rule or a statute or a policy, then perhaps the president (or the secretary of defense or the director of Central Intelligence or the agency's mission chief in Ouagadougou) is more likely to obey if he can be charged with personal responsibility (by whom? when?) than if he merely fails to prevent violations by subordinates. For this to be a motivating explanation for the personal responsibility requirements, however, there must be such rules.

The discussion above was compatible with an assumption that all intelligence activities are ruleless: that in both their information-gathering and their operational functions, intelligence agents are licensed by their employing nations to function outside those nations' conventional criminal and civil rules. This assumption emphasizes the need for particularized judgments—continual (and often, presumably, very difficult) calculations about risks vs. benefits, needs vs. desires, short-term vs. long-term, personal commitments vs. institutional necessities. This is the stuff of spy fiction and, I suspect, of the spying life. In very general ways, historical development influences the making of those decisions. Presumably spies today are able to distinguish between Eurocommunism and other kinds, realize guerrilla movements can survive the death of a single leader, and see that the interests of the United States are not identical to those of ITT. They may even weigh more heavily today than previously the "cost" involved in taking a life or perpetuating a falsehood or violating someone's privacy. (It is different to say that they may today rate as more substantial the domestic cost of revelation of such actions.) But can the society do more, in an organized way, than expect that its intelligence agents will gradually respond to such historical developments?* Can it, to be specific, agree within itself on

---

*There are institutional ways to assure or speed the adaptive process. Short tenures, early retirement, diverse recruitment, and in-service training come to mind.

answers to particular dilemmas, and then express and enforce them? Is it possible to achieve democratic expression on hypothetical matters of great seriousness and contingency? Is it possible, that is, to subject the grey world of spying to majority regulation on terms that include considerations of both policy and morality? The proposed bill contains attempts to do this, three of which I will mention.

(1) In section 132, after forbidding any "entity of the Intelligence Community" from hiring "any United States person following a full-time religious vocation," the bill similarly forswears hiring Americans "whose travel to a foreign country is . . . part of a U.S. government program designed to promote education or the arts, humanities, or cultural affairs" to "engage in any intelligence activity . . . while . . . participating in any such program." (The third virgin category established by section 132, though with more qualifications, is journalists.)

Why would such a provision be enacted? Notice that deception alone is not forsworn — it could not be if spying were to survive. Diplomats, business people, tourists, and foundation-supported scholars can all be hired by the CIA. Why not government cultural grantees? The reason must be that these individuals are obvious targets of suspicion (more so than their colleagues paid by someone other than the U.S. government? May the CIA "launder" its money through the Kaplan Foundation?), and ones whom the target nations do not need to welcome. If it were thought that cultural travelers never supplied much good intelligence anyway, it would be easy to make a medium-term calculation that more is gained for knowledge and amity than is lost to intelligence, taking into account the loss to cultural relations if no such rule were enacted. (Ought we to look at this more cynically, as if the world of arts and letters now has lobbying strength equal to that of journalism and religion? I doubt it.)

What would happen if this provision were enacted? Surely casual hiring of the listed category of travelers would stop or lessen. That much faith in bureaucratic effectuation of a major legislative intervention seems well placed. But is there reason to fear that the general purification will make occasional use of such persons irresistible, investing them with at least a marginally greater likelihood that others will credit their virginity? Are those who so employ them meant to be given the defense (seemingly available in the language of the present draft of the legislation) that their spying was not "while . . . participating" in their cultural work? On the whole, this provision seems quite conventional: not particularly an ethical limitation, rather one based on a legislative judgment of longer-term prudence and policy, which subordinate officers with short-term goals may be tempted to subvert, thus posing issues of management, discipline, and — conceivably — criminal enforcement.

(2) Hiring dons is surely a minor issue for spy agencies. Assassination is a major matter. Section 134 of the proposed law makes life imprisonment the possible punishment for conspiring "to kill any foreign official because of such official's office or . . . political views." There is an exception for war (or the quasi-war of the War Powers Resolution), but this provision does not have the exception (available for hiring priests and professors) for presidential determination of "a grave and immediate threat to the national security of the United States." Why not assassinate foreign leaders? Because that is a two-way street, as we may have learned with great trauma? Because we are attempting, in the mildest way, to civilize even that most unruly world espionage, and this — the extreme act — is the starting point in an effort at unilateral renunciation hoping for enemy response? Or because we really believe that much, including killing, is legitimate in foreign affairs, but not assassination, and that this means is so dirty we are prepared to renounce it? There is surely ethical content to section 134, but the foundations of the policy are not easy to state considering the various other dirty means we seem quite clearly to be declining to forswear.

In any case, are we ready to say we would not have killed Hitler in 1935 (or 1938 or November 1941) or Idi Amin in 1978? Will these cases be debated in Congress? Conspiracy is a broad notion; it is not inconceivable that Americans could have been criminally liable in the Allende death had section 134 been the law. Are the criminal laws always binding? Would we want a president to decline to discuss a Hitler assassination, on the grounds that the statute, perhaps enacted years earlier, is the final word? Are there absolutes in terms of means, which a democracy can proclaim and then enforce against it own highest agents?

(3) Finally, consider section 135, a catch-all, with the remarkable title "Prohibitions against particular forms of special activities." The United States would be proclaiming its unwillingness to perform any "special activity . . . likely to result in":

(1) the support of international terrorist activities;

(2) the mass destruction of property;

(3) the creation of food or water shortages or floods;

(4) the creation of epidemics or diseases;

(5) the use of chemical, biological, or other weapons in violation of treaties or other international agreements to which the United States is a party;

(6) the violent overthrow of the democratic government of any country;

(7) the torture of individuals;

(8) the support of any action, which violates human rights, conducted by the police, foreign intelligence, or internal security forces of any foreign country.

Only items (1), (2), (3), and (6) could be done during wartime or upon presidential determination of a "grave and immediate threat." Presumably (4) and (5) are barred by treaties or other statutes even as acts of war. It is possible to argue that Senate ratification of the International Covenant on Civil and Political Rights, giving legal content to the Universal Declaration of Human Rights, would have implications for the legality of some of these intelligence methods as a matter of domestic civil law. Also, inferences can be drawn from 22 U.S.C., section 2304, the 1976 Human Rights amendment to the Foreign Assistance Act, that the United States, committed by statute to using its influence and its foreign expenditures to improve the status of human rights abroad, should not be authorizing its own agents to violate those rights.

There is a great deal of ambiguity in section 135 — words that do not define themselves, such as "terrorist," "torture," and "human rights." There seems to be a rather casual answer to such valuable law school (not to mention undergraduate philosophy) class-provokers as whether to use torture to save the kidnapped child. But more interesting for present purposes is the ban on "violent overthrow of . . . democratic government." "Democratic" surely does not refer to the country's name for itself. But was Chile democratic in 1973? Is South Korea today? Iran? Turkey? Egypt? Is this meant to be an authorization to the president, the select congressional intelligence committees, and the so-called intelligence community to engage in both violent overthrow of regimes not meeting whatever is our test of democraticness and the use of nonviolent means to influence disputes over power in democratic countries?

I suppose the provisions' authors were thinking about Chile (Guatemala?), a case their language has certainly not covered with shining clarity. Meanwhile, they go a long distance toward granting domestic statutory authority for a vast range of interventions all over the globe. Does the U.S. public support such an authorization (restricted, of course: we can't use U.S. priests or assassinations), and are we willing to authorize the actions without even the hortatory statements of relevant considerations that the bill contains for certain other ventures? Do we not feel moral restraints applicable to the use of destabilizing economic policies, financial subsidies to foreign politicians, "plantings" in foreign media, infringements of the privacy of foreign nationals? Why is the assassination of a regime better than the killing of a leader? Why not help foreign police violate human rights if we retain the legal authority to do it ourselves? And so on. Here the attempt to codify public morality may not go as far as is politically possible.

But are detailed prohibitions of the sort listed in S. 2525 appropriate? Several of those who testified at the Senate hearings on the proposed charter said that such prohibitions are offensive. Most eloquent was Clark Clifford, former secretary of defense. A distinguished lawyer, Mr. Clifford was all for a charter—all for establishing legal authority for activities now grounded on only the vaguest statutory footings; all for personal presidential responsibility; and all for such procedural devices as meetings of the National Security Council and reports to congressional committees. But he was "unalterably opposed" to the enumeration of prohibited activities. His reasons are interesting. First, it is "demeaning" to say, for example, that the United States should not assassinate. Not that we would do it: "Of course, the United States will not engage in such activities," but it is unaesthetic to say so. Second, we may sometimes need to do the prohibited deeds: "The fact is [prohibitions] create problems, and in the last analysis, these decisions have got to be made by the President . . . It would be entirely possible under some circumstances that with all of this language an emergency might arise in which a President would say I have but one duty, the duty to my country to take a particular action, and it might be inconsistent with the language of this particular prohibition. I suppose he would have to take it." This is, of course, not really a contradiction. Clifford is saying that usually one does not do these things, that legislation can only express norms so commonplace that they would be followed anyway, and that no laws will constrain in the gravest emergencies. He is saying that it is not possible for democratic processes to adopt significant general rules applicable to this realm of governmental activity, and that intelligence activities, "by their very nature, must be conducted by a few chosen officials in secret." How, in present conditions, that is compatible with public trust, which Mr. Clifford acknowledges as, "once dissipated, . . . the most difficult of public attitudes to reestablish," he does not say.

Robert Bork, former solicitor general, took Clifford's aversion to statutory prohibitions even further, arguing that they might be unconstitutional as an infringement on presidential authority to conduct foreign relations and to command the military. Professor Bork had an answer to the question of what to use in place of statutory rules: "One way is the establishment of a strong tradition of the ways in which it is permissible or impermissible for an intelligence agency to behave." Bork applauded our "strong start in establishing just such a tradition through the investigation, discussion, and public airing of past behavior of the intelligence agencies," yet he opposed the reporting requirements of S. 2525 for seeming "to spread American intelligence information so broadly as to ensure leaks and diplomatic complications." Like Clifford, Bork sees the problems: laws can be rigid; publicity can be harmful; yet unpublicized, unregulated intelligence agencies will frequently behave inefficiently, and will sometimes do outrageous things, as recent experience demonstrates. Without a degree of publicity, there is not likely to be public confidence. And without informed consideration beyond the executive branch, how can there be a process of democratic decision about the hard cases, the ones not resolved by uttering proverbs or by assuming that the instincts of a gentleman are necessarily sound?

The point, of course, is that language has its limits: its ambiguities, its euphemisms, its contradictions. As Orwell understood, loose language is a sign of loose thought. But bad *legislative* language reflects an incomplete, an unsatisfactory, process of collective decision. A country whose citizens do not want to decide whether to authorize assassinations, or to decide which ones are right, cannot have a statutory CIA charter that does anything more than empower the president to make decisions.

Consider the language of S. 2525 purporting to guide presidential decisions. According to section 131(c), the president should not approve a "special activity" (a marvelous euphemism for shady operations interfering in the politics of other nations) unless, after "careful and systematic consideration," he makes a "written finding" that the activity:

(1) . . . is essential to the national defense or . . . the foreign policy of the United States;

(2) the . . . benefits . . . justify the . . . risks . . . [and]

(3) . . . less sensitive alternatives would not . . . achieve the . . . objectives.

If passed, these provisions would give the president an authority he exerts now with no legislative support. It would tell him that in exercising his authority he should pledge allegiance to the flag each morning and call his mother on her birthday. That is, the language does not express a majority view of any significance as to which "special activities" the agents of the United States should be told to attempt. Certainly, the draft law offers no guidance for the routine situation where the gain is potentially significant on certain (but not all defensible) analyses of the world situation, where there could be real embarrassment if the venture came unstuck in some not-entirely-farfetched way, and where there are less risky ways to do it that however seem less efficacious. But Congress does not want to confront that sort of factual context, nor does the citizenry. Yet without putting real cases, and struggling over them, and distinguishing them from each other, there cannot be conclusions that create a moral framework for the official actions, and certainly not a framework of democratic morality.

Reaching democratic agreement about the issues identified above would be exceedingly difficult. The experience since the Senate committee submitted its proposed charter provides empirical evidence of some of the difficulties. As of early 1981, no legislative action had been taken, and none was in prospect. Hearings had been held at which persons experienced in the intelligence community vied at finding the proposed norms unnecessary and unduly constricting; the apparent contradiction was not emphasized. By all appearances, the public noticed not at all. That public undoubtedly wants effective and successful intelligence operations serving the short-term and long-term national interest; probably is embarrassed when frivolous or evil activities are revealed; and may want America to lead an active search for higher standards of public international morality. But we would just as soon avoid making these general views specific, and we show no inclination at all to make choices when particular procedures, arrangements, or activities place the general goals in conflict. So far, the institutions of government have not forced the citizenry to sacrifice its inclination to avoid painful choice.

In this vital sense, therefore, the story of intelligence ethics is an example of the difficulty of American government in the last quarter of the century. Our machinery of government is imperfect. It cannot set prices, allocate scarce goods, deter undesired conduct, or abolish disease. But our central public problem is not the high cost and incomplete benefit of the goals we crudely pursue, but rather an obtuseness in refusing to see basic choices among incompatible ends, and our never-ending desire to blame government and government officials when decisions have not been taken, choices have not been made, resources have not been committed. Unwilling or unable to imagine, agree on, and establish either moral or prudential norms for this aspect of official life, we are then free to complain when operations miscarry or new views make past practices seem dubious.

The outlook for the world of intelligence remains standardless delegation: assignment to officials of vague mandates to pursue a wide range of serious national tasks, weighing their goals and limiting effective means as they see fit. To the extent that these officials—the president and his chief national security appointees for the highest matters, high-level officials of the intelligence agencies for mid-level activities, probably every operating employee for some matter—share coherent cultural attitudes, decisions will reflect that set of values. Without such, and with the institutions for considering (much less promulgating) such values having failed so signally, these delegees of national authority are indeed "out in the cold."

NOTE

1. Among the sources for the factual interpretations upon which this essay is built are Dean Acheson, *Present at the Creation* (New York: Norton, 1969); Philip Agee, *Inside the Company: CIA Diary* (New York: Stonehill, 1975); Ray Cline, *Secrets, Spies and Scholars* (Washington, D.C.: Acropolis, 1976); William Colby, *Honorable Men* (New York: Simon and Schuster, 1978); Victor Marchetti and John D. Marks, *The CIA and the Cult of Intelligence* (New York: Knopf, 1974). After the essay was completed I read Thomas Powers, *The Man Who Kept the Secrets: Richard Helms and the CIA* (New York: Knopf, 1979), a book of real distinction filled with specific material that I regard as consistent with the argument set out here.

Dennis F. Thompson

11. Moral Responsibility and the New York City Fiscal Crisis

Most discussions of the moral obligations of public officials concentrate on what officials ought to do — the justifications they may give for their decisions and policies. But there is a problem of moral assessment that is partly independent of the acceptability of justifications: it focuses on the excuses officials give for these decisions and policies. Even when officials admit that a particular decision is wrong, they may still disclaim responsibility for it. Because many political outcomes are obviously unjustifiable, an official often has a motive to look for an excuse; and because many outcomes are the product of the actions of many different people, an official usually has an opportunity to plead that other people are to blame. In politics, excuses are thus at least as common as justifications. Yet except in the literature on the morality of war, the question of the moral responsibility of public officials has not received much attention. I take up that question here by identifying and analyzing three major categories of claims that officials and their critics put forward during one episode in the 1974-75 New York City fiscal crisis.

One reason that the question of the moral responsibility of officials has been neglected is that it is often assumed to be determined by an official's legal or political responsibility.[1] This assumption is a mistake. Unlike morality, the law limits the scope of responsibility for reasons of policy and administrative efficiency. Under certain conditions, you are not legally, though you may be morally, responsible for failing to warn of a crime that someone else is about to commit, for giving bad advice to someone who commits a wrong, or for the harmful consequences of a decision made within the discretionary authority of public office.[2] Under other conditions, you may be legally but not morally liable for certain kinds of harms, such as offenses of strict liability.[3] Political responsibility, similarly, does

266

not imply that the person whom we hold accountable for an outcome actually brought it about, or even could have done anything to prevent it from happening. Simply occupying a political office that has jurisdiction over the outcome in question is normally sufficient to make an official politically responsible. Officials sometimes lose elections because of governmental actions over which they had little control, and though this strict liability in politics may be morally justifiable, it cannot be equivalent to moral responsibility.[4]

RESPONSIBILITY AND EXCUSES

The categories of excuses I present here derive from a concept of moral responsibility that is common to a wide range of conceptions of morality in both philosophical and ordinary moral discourse. Two kinds of excuses — based on what may be called causal and volitional responsibility — are familiar enough in everyday moral life. We excuse persons for a harm insofar as their actions did not cause the harm, or insofar as the actions were not the product of their own will. Sometimes in private life, but more frequently in public life, we encounter a third kind of excuse: an appeal to the requirements of the role or office an official holds. Indeed, the first two kinds of excuses are often indeterminate without some reference to role or office. But the excuse of role, I shall suggest, must be cautiously circumscribed if it is not to undermine the idea of moral responsibility altogether.

It is tempting to suppose that we can settle the question of causal responsibility in a value-neutral way, even if the definition of the harm in question obviously involves evaluation. But whether a person (especially a public official) is to be excused on the ground that he or she is not the cause of a harm can rarely be determined without referring to noncausal considerations, some of which include value judgments. Consider this incident which took place in Sydney, Australia.[5] A motorcycle policeman gave chase to a speeding motorcylist; both were traveling at about 70 mph when a passenger stepped off a bus into the path of the policeman's cycle and was killed. In the ensuing public controversy, some people agreed with the police, who charged the original speedster with causing the death. But many others took the view that the policeman was the cause since he should not have been traveling at such high speeds under these conditions. Thus an argument about who was the cause, even in a case where the law provides some guidance, seems to depend in part on an interpretation of the policeman's role (what one would reasonably expect a policeman to do in these circumstances).[6]

In general, there appears to be no satisfactory way of using strictly causal criteria to single out one person as "the cause" of some policy. In the past of any event for which we wish to assign responsibility, we can find an infinite number of other events, each of which is a necessary condition of the given event, and therefore each of which equally deserves to be designated "the cause" of the event.[7] Which event or events we take to be the cause will depend on what the purposes of our inquiry are (for example, explanation, social reform, or moral criticism). It is therefore better to adopt a weak criterion of causal responsibility, requiring only that one be *a* cause of an outcome in the sense that the outcome would not have happened but for one's act or omission.[8] Since this criterion is relatively easy to satisfy, causal excuses are rarely valid, though they appear in many different guises in political discourse.

While it is difficult to escape responsibility by appealing to causal excuses, it is also difficult to fix blame by invoking causal responsibility. That an official is causally responsible does not imply that the official is the agent we should blame for a harm — unless we adopt the theory of responsibility expressed in the nursery rhyme, "for want of a nail . . ."[9] Causal responsibility merely makes an official a candidate for the ascription of moral responsibility, usually along with many other people.[10]

Whereas a causal excuse would completely remove one from the chain of events leading to a harmful outcome, a volitional excuse would detach only one's will from this chain. Following Aristotle, we may consider two kinds of volitional excuses — those of ignorance, and those of compulsion.[11] Ignorance (not knowing that a certain description applies to one's action) does not always count as a valid excuse, or even as grounds for mitigation. Only if the ignorance is not negligent (only if, for instance, the official should not have been expected to know that his action would have certain harmful consequences) would we be prepared to accept the excuse. In the case of public officials, standards of negligence largely depend on how we understand the formal and informal requirements of roles or offices. The question is not so much "What did the official know and when did he know it?" but rather "What should he have known?"

Similarly, we cannot decide whether compulsion should excuse officials without deciding what their roles require of them. We may legitimately expect persons who hold public office to resist some extreme pressures more than if they did not hold office. But the compulsion that officials cite to excuse their conduct usually differs from the threats, torture, and the like that lawyers and philosophers typically discuss.[12] When public officials plead that they had no choice, they often may be interpreted as saying that they did not choose the *range* of alternatives within which they made their decision. Like Aristotle's sea captain, the official should be seen as confronting two disagreeable alternatives (to jettison the cargo or let the ship sink), and holding an office that requires a choice between them.[13] Officials who decide correctly under difficult circumstances of this sort expect to be praised; so in some sense they must be responsible for such decisions. Yet in another sense they cannot be fully responsible, because if they make the wrong decision, we do not blame them as much as we would if their choice had not been limited to a narrow range of alternatives (assuming of course that they had nothing to do with causing the range to be so limited). Excuses of compulsion therefore need to specify precisely how a range of alternatives constrains the person who invokes the excuse.

Both causal and volitional responsibility when applied to public officials thus depend on an interpretation of their role.[14] The idea of role identifies the special requirements (or the special permissions) that a person acquires by virtue of holding a particular office. What would usually be excused in private life (say, ignorance of macroeconomics) could become culpable in public life (as in the office of secretary of the treasury). The idea of role also delineates a moral division of labor which, within limits, may be justified on the ground that it promotes a more efficient pursuit of moral ends, just as a political division of labor ideally contributes to political efficiency. Not everyone need to try to right every wrong in an organization.

Nevertheless, the idea of role, as John Ladd has argued, can undermine moral responsibility.[15] Since officials, at least initially, do not determine the requirements of the roles they hold, they cannot be said to be fully responsible for the consequences of acting according to those requirements. Also, an official can use a role as a way to evade responsibility, pleading, "That's not *my* job."

However, even relatively fixed roles leave a great deal of space for personal responsibility.[16] First of all, an official chooses whether to accept the role, and whether to continue in it. Second, most roles permit some discretion, and we assess how well or how badly an official exercises this discretion partly according to general moral standards that are not defined solely by the role. We may, for example, criticize a social worker for being condescending or a policeman for being bigoted. Third, officials may be held responsible for conduct not only in a particular role, but also in their general role as public official, and for how they resolve conflicts between their particular and general roles. We may blame officials when, for example, they act merely as advocates for their own bureaus, rather than as agents of the government as a whole. Finally, even when the structure of roles is the chief source of a moral failure, and officials have given the best performance they can in their faulty roles, we may still impute a continuing responsibility to these officials, charging them with calling attention to the structural defects and initiating changes to correct them. Officials have this continuing responsibility because their knowledge of the defects and their ability to test whether the defects can be changed are usually greater than the knowledge and ability of ordinary citizens in these respects. The excuses of ignorance and compulsion are therefore less accessible to officials.

In all these ways, the moral responsibility of persons persists behind the impersonal structure of roles in public organizations. If there is a "constant threat to morality" from dividing responsibility according to offices or roles, as Ladd fears, there is equally a constant threat to morality from spreading responsibility throughout government and society ("all of us are responsible for justice and for the common good").[17] If we understand the idea of role in the variegated and dynamic way I have suggested, it can counteract both of these threats.

DISCLOSURE IN THE FISCAL CRISIS

Much more could be said about the theoretical problems posed by these categories of excuses, but since their meaning also depends on the political context in which they are used, I turn to an actual episode where officials sought to defend themselves against charges that they failed to fulfill their public duties. For this purpose I examine some of the excuses over which officials and their critics contended in the New York City fiscal crisis during the period from Abraham Beame's inauguration as mayor in January of 1974 to the collapse of the market for city securities in the spring of 1975. The principal sources for the accusations and excuses are a report by the staff of the Securities and Exchange Commission (SEC) and the city's official response to this report, plus interviews with eight participants in the events.[18] My aim is not to adjudicate this dispute, but rather to see what it can tell us about the possibilities and limits of ascribing moral responsibility to public officials.

A full analysis of the responsibility in this crisis would have to examine the whole range of policies adopted during this period and earlier, such as wage settlements, and changes in the welfare and educational systems.[19] It would also consider the role of other people besides city officials—for example, the bank officers who functioned in the crisis much as public officials, and others in the city's corporate elite, and would examine, as well, the social and economic structure of the city. But to make the analysis of the case manageable, I concentrate mainly on one official—the mayor—and on the issue that attracted the most attention of Beame's official critics —the accusation that city officials deceived the public by failing to disclose the true state of the city's finances.

What was at stake here was not simply a matter of "full and fair disclosure." Beame's accusers as well as his defenders saw the disclosure question as significantly affecting the welfare and the livelihoods of the millions of people who depend on the city's financial health. It would therefore be a mistake to view the issues in this case as involving mainly the obligations of officials to investors. The controversy about these obligations reflected deeper questions concerning the duties of officials to all citizens. Nor was disclosure mainly a matter of legal obligation. Although the SEC's report charged that city officials had violated certain laws, the legal case was never very persuasive, and was later completely dropped.[20] The force of the critics' accusations derives from the moral obligation of officials in a democracy to keep the public informed of such vital facts as the financial condition of the government.[21] The issue is also moral in a sense more directly pertinent to the analysis of excuses: the responsibility at issue is based, not on legal or political criteria, but on criteria of moral agency.

When Beame became mayor in 1974, he faced the most severe financial crisis the city had known at least since 1933. The crisis had its origins in long-term social and economic trends.[22] More and more people who depended heavily on the services of government—the poor, the ill-educated, the aged—had moved to the city in recent years. City employees, now organized into strong unions with political power that mayors could not ignore, had won expensive wage settlements. At the same time, industry had begun to move elsewhere, and the city's tax base consequently could not keep pace with the growing demands for services and wages. All of these trends were exacerbated by the recession of 1973-74, which swelled the ranks of the unemployed, added to the welfare rolls, and reduced tax revenues (which came more from sales taxes than from relatively stable property taxes).

Other cities suffered from many of these same problems, and New York officials might have been able to muddle through, as officials in other fiscally troubled cities were doing, if New York were not so dependent on the confidence of investors. New York has proportionately far more outstanding debt than do other comparable cities, and must enter the market continually to "roll over" large quantities of short-term notes.[23] Some of these notes were issued to finance long-term capital projects, but the city had rarely attempted to convert them into long-term debt. The city also needed short-term funds to ease the cash flow problem that arose because revenues such as taxes and federal aid came in later than the expenditures they were supposed to cover. Finally, the city had to issue new notes both to finance the current year's deficit and to refund outstanding debt from previous years. As a result of all of these borrowing needs, the city had to issue notes every month or so no matter what the market conditions might be, and by 1975, they were quite unfavorable for New York City securities. Given these circumstances, city officials naturally believed they had to put the best possible face on the city's financial condition.

Beame and other officials could not be held responsible for most of the circumstances that created the crisis, but they could be—and were—blamed for the decisions they made to cope with the circumstances. As the city continued to issue short-term notes through late 1974 and early 1975, top officials did their best to make them appear attractive to investors. In November 1974, the city expanded the public market to a broader class of citizen by reducing the minimum size of the notes from $25,000 to $10,000. Throughout this period, Beame and Comptroller Harrison Goldin attempted in frequent public statements to assure investors that city securities were completely safe.[24]

Beame and Goldin admitted that the city had serious fiscal problems but insisted that investors had nothing to worry about. The principle of "first lien" would protect them: the state constitution required the city to use revenues to pay off all outstanding debt before making any other expenditures, including payrolls. SEC arguments notwithstanding, city officials were probably correct in their legal interpretation of the principle of first lien; the Court of Appeals in November 1975 declared the moratorium on city notes unconstitutional.[25] Also, Beame and Goldin were no doubt sincere in their intention to respect the principle. "As far as I was concerned," Goldin said, "I was going to pay the bond and note holders first. It was as simple as that."[26] But the political facts may not have been so simple. It hardly seemed likely that the city could refuse to pay the wages of policemen, firemen, and other employees in order to meet their obligations to creditors, and in fact in November 1975 creditors were forced to wait while the moratorium was enforced.

Although critics claimed that Beame's statements underestimated the size of the city's budget deficit, they generally did not accuse him of trying to conceal the fact that the deficit was very large. The main charges centered on several allegedly deceptive accounting practices (or "gimmicks," as the critics called them). First, the city had increasingly used the capital budget to fund operating expenses.[27] This "capitalization of expenses" had been common at least since 1965. By 1975 the expenses funded by the capital budget totaled $722 million, compared to $195 million just five years earlier. This practice certainly helped balance the operating budget, but it dangerously undermined the city's long-term financial health. Yet no one had tried to keep the practice secret. As comptroller, Beame himself had publicly criticized it; during 1974 and 1975 other officials as well as the press continued to call attention to its dangers.

A second "gimmick" also had a long history: the budget for any fiscal year recorded as liabilities only money actually spent in that year, while it showed as receivables not only funds actually collected but also those estimated to be earned that year which were expected to be received in future years.[28] Examples of these "accrual basis receivables" are water and sewer charges and the yearly estimate of sales taxes (the "June accrual"). On the liability side, the city recorded its contributions to the pension funds two years later than the liabilities were actually incurred. Although these practices were sanctioned (and, arguably, encouraged) by state law, they effectively hid a portion of the city's cumulative deficit. The SEC staff asserted that the city's annual reports of 1973 and 1974 "failed to explicitly set forth that the City recognized revenues on an accrual basis and expenditures on a cash basis."[29] Although officials did not attempt to conceal this practice, neither did they go out of their way to publicize it.

The most controversial and complex "gimmick" involved the alleged overstatement of receivables. The SEC report claimed that officials did not reveal that "the City carried disputed receivables on its books, did not reserve against the possibility of non-collection, and borrowed against these receivables by issuing RAN's [Revenue Anticipation Notes]."[30] Apparently few if any bank officers and others outside the government realized that the budget included significant amounts of these uncollectible receivables.[31] (In the foreword to the comptroller's annual report of 1973-74, however, some of these receivables are designated "unaudited," thus, city officials maintained, serving to warn investors.)

The city overestimated the receivables in two general categories. First, the amount of federal and state aid officials claimed the city would receive proved to be greatly inflated. When the federal government announced a spending program for the city, city officials would typically record the funds as receivables and borrow against them. If (as often happened) the federal government later decided to reduce or eliminate the program, the city, while protesting the decision, would keep the funds on the books, without indicating that they were in dispute.

The other category of overestimates comprised real estate taxes; as much as 80 percent of all these taxes may have been overstated.[32] The city made no allowance for the fact that some of the taxes could never be collected. The law permitted officials to "roll over" tax anticipation notes for five years before writing them off as uncollectible. In earlier years the number of write-offs had not been very large, but in 1974, as more and more owners abandoned buildings during the recession, the amount of permanently uncollectible real estate taxes became significant. The recession may have also been a cause of the accounting practice that some regarded as the most serious instance of deception. The budget did not show that some $126 million of the city's uncollectible real estate taxes were on city-owned property. Some owners defaulted for so long on their real estate taxes that the city foreclosed on their property. But the city's books, often for several years, continued to show this city-owned property ("in rem") as a source of receivable real estate taxes.

Despite the prevalence of these accounting practices, Beame denied that he had misled the public in any way, and his response to his accusers can serve to illustrate some general features of the ascription of responsibility to public officials. I shall consider the ways in which Beame used or could have used each of the three kinds of excuses mentioned above.

EXCUSES OF CAUSE

In reply to the charge that officials generally did not disclose how precarious were city finances and the market for city bonds, Beame asserted that "anybody who didn't know what was going on was either asleep or had his head in the sand."[33] Beame's plea here illustrates two different forms of the causal excuse. First, Beame could be understood as appealing to a principle of *novus actus interveniens*: subsequent voluntary intervention by other people cancels his responsibility for any harmful consequences.[34] City officials publicized many of the most serious financial problems, and also some of the questionable accounting practices.[35] Officials regularly called attention to the large deficits, and certainly did not conceal the practice of capitalizing expenses, or the practice of recording revenues on an accrual basis while showing expenses on a cash basis. That "the public did not take heed" of this information, city officials argued, is not our fault.[36] This kind of excuse may be acceptable insofar as officials disclosed all the important problems and "gimmicks," but in fact they did not do so, and many citizens (including investors) did not know "what was going on."

City officials no doubt believed that these people should have known, and could have known, without officials taking positive steps to reveal any more than they did. If these people had taken the trouble to inform themselves, it might be argued, Beame's not publicizing the city's financial plight more actively would not have mattered. This plea, a second kind of causal excuse, is analogous to what in the law of torts is called "additional causation": if the actions of two (or more) persons are each independently sufficient to bring about a certain harm, both persons are liable for the harm, and if one of them is also the victim of the harm, he cannot recover damages.[37] This analogy breaks down, however, because the victims of nondisclosure were not merely or mainly the investors, but (so Beame's critics pointed out) everyone who depended on the viability of the city. The argument from additional cause at most shows that other persons could also be considered to be a cause of the harmful consequences; the argument does not absolve Beame since his actions would also count as a cause.

But neither can a causal argument establish that Beame is chiefly or especially responsible for the incorrect impression that many people had of the city finances. One such causal accusation resembles the legal doctrine of the last clear chance: the person who failed to take the last available opportunity to prevent a harm is the "proximate cause" and is solely responsible.[38] On this view, although Beame inherited the accounting practices that misled the public, these practices should be considered mere "background conditions." Beame and his colleagues had the last clear chance to do something about them, and are therefore responsible for whatever harm they caused.[39] The trouble with the argument is that we cannot determine what a last clear chance is simply by looking at causal chains. Beame insisted that he did not have a real opportunity to disclose more than he did; the risks to the city of doing so were too great.[40] Perhaps Beame was wrong, but to show that, his critics would have to say something about how much he should risk for the sake of disclosure and what we may legitimately expect of a mayor in these circumstances—in short, the kind of considerations raised by volitional and role responsibility.

EXCUSES OF VOLITION

When we turn to volitional excuses, we encounter a doctrine that would make the question of moral responsibility turn simply on whether Beame and city officials deliberately misled the public. This doctrine—stated most absolutely by Kant—holds that you are morally responsible only for what you *intend*.[41] "What you intend" is to be understood as "what you yourself do," as distinct from what happens as a result of what you do (even if you can foresee the result). In a notorious example, Kant insists that you must tell the truth even to a murderer who asks you where your friend, his intended victim, is hiding. You are responsible only for your own intentional act (truth-telling or lying), and if you tell the truth you cannot be blamed for what other people do as a result of your honesty.

Whatever one makes of this doctrine in private life, it is too simple to account for the problems that public officials face. Whether we describe Beame's intention as deception partly turns on how much he knew about the budget. But what he knew at any particular time depended partly on what he had said at a previous time, since his statements at each stage of the crisis may have encouraged or discouraged other officials to discover and report information to him at some later stage. Moreover, even if Beame deliberately failed to disclose significant facts about the city's financial condition, whether we characterize this decision as "deceiving the public" or "saving the city from bankruptcy" (or some combination of the two) depends on what he could have done differently in face of what other people were likely to do as a consequence of his decisions. Thus, we cannot adequately assess Beame's responsibility without considering what he should have foreseen of other people's actions, and how these foreseeable actions constrained his own decisions. We cannot assess his responsibility without considering, that is, excuses of ignorance and compulsion. Let us briefly examine an example of each.

Beame and Goldin claimed that they did not know, or at least did not appreciate the significance of, the fact that the city counted as expected income real estate taxes on property the city itself owned.[42] Their claim is plausible since a change in ownership of such property often did not show up on the books for a long time. Nor is there any compelling reason to suppose that in ordinary circumstances Beame should have known about this practice. Normally we would blame lower-level officials, who are in the best position to discover such problems. Nevertheless, the question of responsibility here — and in similar cases — cannot be settled by looking only at the formal duties of officials. It has been suggested that in the fiscal crisis lower-level officials believed that any effort to scrutinize the real estate taxes (about which they may have had suspicions) would not be viewed favorably by their superiors.[43] Insofar as Beame's public statements and other actions discouraged lower-level officials from questioning the estimates (whether or not he intended this effect), he would have to bear the responsibility for his own lack of knowledge of them. (We might of course blame lower-level officials to some degree as well.)

Beame and his defenders also invoked the excuse of compulsion; again like Aristotle's sea captain, Beame in effect pleaded, "I had no choice." He could not change, and perhaps could not even publicize, some of the misleading accounting practices. For example, if city officials had removed from the books the millions of dollars in disputed federal and state grants, they would, they believed, have weakened the city's case for collecting these funds from Washington and Albany.[44] More generally, if Beame in his public statements had not emphasized the positive aspects of the city's financial prospects, he would, he believed, have brought about the bankruptcy of the city—with the subsequent losses of jobs and city services, creating especially great hardships on the poor.[45] The course Beame followed, his defenders argued, gave the city time to work out a more satisfactory arrangement with federal and state support, cushioning the effects of the crisis on the city's residents. As the *New York Times* declared in a headline: " 'Deception' May Have Kept the City Solvent."[46]

Even if this line of argument is valid (the SEC report disputed it[47]), it should be understood as a justification rather than as an excuse. It would therefore not absolve Beame of the responsibility for the consequences of his decisions about disclosure. As I have suggested, the fact that other people and other forces may have determined the alternatives from among which an official has to choose does not relieve the official of the responsibility for the choice. However, the compulsion involved here does warrant a different description of what the official is responsible for. Perhaps the SEC staff did not have grounds to charge Beame and other officials with deception. But even if they did, they should have characterized Beame's action not simply as choosing deception but as choosing deception rather than, say, bankruptcy of the city. A more complex way of ascribing blame does not eliminate an official's responsibility, but may narrow its scope.

EXCUSES OF ROLE

An excuse of role often comes to the rescue when the other kinds of excuses alone fail to exonerate an official. We have already seen that the acceptability of Beame's plea of ignorance about some of the budget "gimmicks" assumes that overseeing detailed accounting procedures is simply not part of the mayor's job. Such a plea is sometimes well grounded, but only within certain limits. The validity of the excuse presupposes that either all are doing their jobs properly within the structure, or that any faulty performance in a role is not attributable to the person who invokes the excuse. But in the fiscal crisis neither of these presuppositions held.

The division of labor that defined the various roles had broken down, and in a manner that reversed the standard problem that role morality is supposed to create. Usually, one objects to role morality (or an appeal to excuses based on role) because it seems to license officials' taking a narrow view of a policy or decision, imposing the parochial perspective of their particular office on the whole government. But in this case, the source of the problem might be better understood as misplaced public-spiritedness: each official trying on his own to consider the welfare of the city from a general perspective, and consequently neglecting some of the duties specific to his own office. Officials in the Bureau of Accountancy, for example, may have been encouraged to think too much about the city-wide economic and political implications of what should have been routine accounting judgments. If some officials laid aside the normal conception of their roles — in effect they were playing mayor — Beame himself could no longer assume that doing his own job was sufficient. Under these circumstances, the excuse of role carries less weight, and an official may become responsible for failures that would otherwise have been imputed to other agents.

Another limit of the excuse of role can be brought out by scrutinizing Beame's claim that many of the questionable accounting practices had been instituted long before he became mayor in 1974. If we grant that the practices could not easily be changed in the midst of the crisis, it is reasonable to excuse Beame, as mayor, for the existence of the practices, on the ground that he inherited them from his predecessors. But among his predecessors were: Abe Beame, comptroller, 1970-73, 1962-65; Abe Beame, budget director, 1952-61; and Abe Beame, assistant budget director, 1946-51. That we excuse Beame the mayor does not entail, as an undiscriminating use of the excuse of role might suggest, that we excuse Beame the comptroller. The moral responsibility of officials attaches to persons not offices, and ascribing such responsibility cannot be entirely determined by any one role a person holds.

It is not only in the excuses officials use that roles may absorb persons but also in the accusations that officials make. Official reports by their nature often tend to examine individual responsibility only in the particular episode under investigation; they rarely consider an official's past record or his subsequent conduct.[48] This same tendency sometimes shows up in American political life more generally. Public officials may be blamed for immoral (or incompetent) performance in one role, but then appear to start with a clean slate once they leave the old job and take up a new one. No doubt this recycling of discredited public figures has structural sources

— a systematically limited circulation of elites, for example. No doubt it is also made possible by the fact that many people do not disapprove of these characters at all. But it is reinforced by any mode of imputing responsibility that completely identifies officials with the temporally discontinuous roles they hold.

To stress some of the limits of the excuse of role is not to deny that expectations of role do, and should, restrict an official's actions in various ways — sometimes very significant ways. Beame, for example, could hardly have ignored the pressures of the New York banking community. The role of a mayor in an American city, given the prevailing economic system, imposes certain constraints on his actions, and therefore circumscribes his responsibility for these actions, even when the overall results may be regarded as unjust. But even here moral responsibility need not be completely extinguished. If because of the constraints of a role, an official escapes blame for a particular decision or policy, the official does not necessarily escape responsibility for seeking to change those constraints or at least for criticizing them. Criticism of one's own past and current performance, however rarely public officials engage in it, may be the last refuge of moral responsibility.

To establish the general conditions under which the excuses public officials use are valid, we would have to look beyond the New York City fiscal crisis, and examine a wide range of cases where officials seek to escape blame for decisions and policies that are morally controversial. But the analysis here should suggest the outlines of a general view of responsibility that can be applied to the conduct of public officials.[49] Such a view, supplemented by justificatory principles of morality, should help preserve the idea of personal responsibility in public organizations, which by their nature offer many opportunities for officials to evade responsibility (for example, through excessive use of the excuse of role).

The task of establishing moral responsibility in particular cases and in general is likely to be complex in a democratic political system. It will not be possible at all unless most political processes are open to public scrutiny, so that citizens can trace in detail the paths of responsibility that lead to important decisions and policies. It will not be worthwhile unless political processes are responsive and accessible to citizens, so that they can give effect to their moral judgments about political leaders. But along with these practical political prerequisites remains the theoretical necessity of understanding the basis of the moral responsibility of public officials, and more specifically the excuses they use.

SELECTED PUBLIC STATEMENTS OF MAYOR BEAME
AND COMPTROLLER GOLDIN[50]

News release, Office of the Mayor, October 22, 1974:

The Mayor emphasized that the City's credit position was "solid and strong," even though the national economy is under the stresses of both inflation and recession, and even though these inflationary-recessionary trends are "creating some budget balancing problems for the City."

The Mayor said, "There is absolutely no question about the City's ability to repay all of its debts on time, and that this ability has improved over the last fifteen years."

Letter of mayor and comptroller, published in the New York Times, November 11, 1974:

Bankruptcy means that liabilities exceed assets or that credit obligations cannot be met—a situation in which the City of New York, even in the darkest days of the Great Depression, never has found itself, nor will it . . .

It should be clear, in connection with our municipal budget, that the Constitution of the State of New York makes our New York City bonds and notes a first lien on all revenues which include the real estate tax, all of the City taxes, fees and permits, all state aid and all Federal aid.

Over and above the constitutional, legal and moral guarantees afforded to investors in New York City notes and bonds is the fact that they are investing in the world's wealthiest and soundest city as far as these obligations are concerned . . .

This picture should be very reassuring to all city investors.

A recitation of these facts should by no means be construed as complacency in the face of the city's budget difficulties. While we have not always agreed on ways and means to place the budget in balance, we do agree that tough fiscal decisions and reforms, including substantial capital budget reductions, will have to be made in order to cope with runaway inflation, unemployment, business recession and the carryover effects of past fiscal practices . . .

We will do what needs to be done in the general interest of taxpayers, for the preservation and strengthening of the city's economy and to insure the continuing soundness of the city's obligations as an investment medium.

News release, Office of the Comptroller, December 1, 1974:

The budget deficit "should not impair confidence in the essential soundness and safety of the City's obligations."

Speech by the comptroller, December 20, 1974 (at the City Club of New York):

New York's budget problems should be of only marginal interest to investors, who are protected by the State Constitutional guarantee making New York City bonds and notes a first lien on all revenues.

Joint statement of mayor and comptroller, January 11, 1975:

This City is not bankrupt, near bankrupt nor will it ever be bankrupt. This City has always repaid all of its obligations on time and it always will.

News release, Office of the Comptroller, March 4, 1975:

For the truth is that from the time of the Revolutionary War, through the dark days of the Great Depression, and in every era of national economic uncertainty — New York City has compiled an unblemished record of full payment of bond principal and interest without a single default.

Investors in New York City securities are, therefore, absolutely protected.

News release, Office of the Comptroller, March 13, 1975:

We have experienced an insistent drumbeat of publicity on our budget problems, and this publicity has sometimes unfortunately failed to distinguish between balancing a budget, which *is* a problem; and meeting obligations to our creditors, which the City has never failed to do and which, it is my conviction, it never *will* fail to do, barring a complete collapse of our economic system and capital markets . . .

So the impact on New York of national and international inflation and recession which has affected all cities, is a separate issue, which should be of only marginal interest to investors.

NOTES

I am grateful to Amy Gutmann and Marion Smiley for helpful suggestions on an earlier version of this essay, and to Jeremy Paul for his valuable research on the fiscal crisis.

1. On the contrast between legal and moral responsibility see H. L. A. Hart, *Punishment and Responsibility* (Oxford: Oxford University Press, 1968), pp. 122-130; and Joel Feinberg, *Doing and Deserving* (Princeton: Princeton University Press, 1970), pp. 25-54. On the notion of excuse in ordinary language see the classic article by J. L. Austin, "A Plea for Excuses," *Proceedings of the Aristotelian Society*, 57 (1956-57), 1-30.

2. Feinberg, *Doing*, p. 245; H. L. A. Hart and A. M. Honoré, *Causa-*

tion in the Law (Oxford: Oxford University Press, 1959), pp. 338-339; and Federal Tort Claims Act, 1970, 28 U.S.C. SEC. 2680 (a).

3. See Richard A. Epstein, "Defenses and Subsequent Pleas in a System of Strict Liability," *Journal of Legal Studies*, 3 (January 1974), 165-216.

4. It is possible, of course, to understand political responsibility in a more substantive way — for example, as a judgment based on some normative principle, such as the public interest, but then political responsibility becomes a species of moral responsibility as I use it here. For a general discussion of the concept of political responsibility see J. Roland Pennock, *Democratic Political Theory* (Princeton: Princeton University Press, 1974), pp. 260-308.

5. J. L. Mackie, "Responsibility and Language," *Australasian Journal of Philosophy*, 33 (December 1955), 143-145. The example is discussed by Feinberg, *Doing*, pp. 200-201.

6. That causal responsibility depends on other noncausal criteria is even more evident with respect to omissions or negative actions, as in the following example presented by John Casey, "Actions and Consequences," in *Morality and Moral Reasoning*, ed. John Casey (London: Methuen, 1971), pp. 185-186. Imagine an execution of a criminal, attended by the executioners, a priest, a doctor, and the prison governor, each with his respective duties. If we believe that capital punishment is justified and that officials should fulfill their duties of office, we would object to describing the action of each official as "letting the criminal die." Their refraining from interference could not then be properly said to be the cause of the criminal's death. But if we believe that capital punishment is wrong, we might say that "because these officials ought to have prevented it, but did not, their non-intervention is a cause or even the cause of his death, and they bear some or full responsibility for it."

7. See John Stuart Mill, *A System of Logic*, bk. III, chap. V, sec. 4, in *Collected Works*, VII, ed. J. Robson (Toronto: University of Toronto Press, 1974), pp. 327-333.

8. Hart and Honoré argue for a stronger interpretation of the causal criterion, one that would allow us to say that the fact that a person caused a harm is a principal ground for ascribing (moral or legal) responsibility to him (*Causation*, pp. 61-62, 103-122). My interpretation more closely follows Feinberg, who maintains that on causal principles alone we can say only that a person's action is a "causal factor," not that it is "*the* cause of the harm." To establish the latter claim, we would have to appeal to "moral standards, policies and purposes" (*Doing*, pp. 201-207, 184). But Feinberg concedes that not all prior necessary conditions count as causal factors (p. 202n). On necessary conditions and sine qua non conditions see Hart and Honoré, *Causation*, pp. 103-122.

9. A. N. Prior, "The Consequences of Actions," *Proceedings of the Aristotelian Society*, suppl. vol. 30 (1956), 95.

10. We may still wish to criticize an official for remaining in office in a government even if the official can do nothing about the immoral policies

of that government, but such a criticism should be interpreted as a charge of complicity rather than of responsibility. That is, we should distinguish the claim that an official's association with this government is itself immoral or dishonorable from the claim that the official's acts or omissions in some way causally contributed to the policies we condemn. See Thomas E. Hill, Jr., "Symbolic Protest and Calculated Silence," *Philosophy and Public Affairs*, 9 (Fall 1979), 83-102.

11. Aristotle, *Ethica Nicomachea*, in *The Works of Aristotle*, ed. W. D. Ross (Oxford: Oxford University Press, 1963), 1109b-1111b. Some helpful recent discussions are Hart, *Punishment*, pp. 210-230; Jonathan Glover, *Responsibility* (London: Routledge and Kegan Paul, 1970), pp. 49-61; and Alan Donagan, *The Theory of Morality* (Chicago: University of Chicago Press, 1977), pp. 122-142. I plead both ignorance and compulsion in disregarding the difficult but relevant question of determinism. Some useful recent discussions of the topic are: Harry G. Frankfurt, "Freedom of the Will and the Concept of the Person," *Journal of Philosophy*, 68 (January 1971), 5-20; P. F. Strawson, "Freedom and Resentment," in *Studies in the Philosophy of Thought and Action*, ed. P. F. Strawson (Oxford: Oxford University Press, 1968); and Gary Watson, "Free Agency," *Journal of Philosophy*, 72 (April 1975), 205-220.

12. Glover, *Responsibility*, p. 61.

13. Aristotle, *Ethica*, 1110a 8-15.

14. On the concept of role responsibility see Hart, *Punishment*, pp. 212-214; R. S. Downie, *Roles and Values* (London: Methuen, 1971), pp. 121-145; Gerald Cohen, "Beliefs and Roles," *Proceedings of the Aristotelian Society*, 67 (1966-67), 17-34; and Bernard Williams, *Morality* (New York: Harper and Row, 1972), pp. 51-58.

15. John Ladd, "Policy Studies and Ethics," *Policy Studies Journal*, 21 (Autumn 1973), 41-42. See also Ladd, "Morality and the Ideal of Rationality in Formal Organizations," *Monist*, 54 (October 1970), 488-516. For a critique see Kenneth E. Goodpaster, "Morality and Organizations," in Thomas Donaldson and Patricia Werhane, eds., *Ethical Issues in Business* (Englewood Cliffs, N.J.: Prentice-Hall, 1979), pp. 114-122.

16. Cf. Downie, *Roles and Values*, p. 133.

17. Ladd, "Policy Studies," p. 42. On the idea of collective responsibility more generally see D. E. Cooper, "Collective Responsibility," *Philosophy*, 43 (July 1968), 258-268; Feinberg, *Doing*, pp. 222-251; Peter A. French, ed., *Individual and Collective Responsibility* (Cambridge, Mass.: Schenkman, 1972); and W. H. Walsh, "Pride, Shame and Responsibility," *Philosophical Quarterly*, 20 (January 1970), 1-13.

18. The documents are the *Securities and Exchange Commission Staff Report on Transactions in Securities of the City of New York*, published by the U.S. House of Representatives, Committee on Banking, Finance and Urban Affairs, Subcommittee on Economic Stabilization, 95th Congress, 1st Session (Washington, August 1977), issued less than two weeks before the primary election for mayor; and *Response of the City of New York to the Report of the Staff of the Securities and Exchange Commission on*

Transactions in Securities of the City of New York (New York, October 3, 1977), signed by W. Bernard Richland, Corporation Counsel to the City, and two law firms. The interviews with the principal participants were mostly conducted by Jeremy Paul, who under my supervision prepared a case study, "The New York Fiscal Crisis, 1974-75," Woodrow Wilson School, Princeton University, 1978, to which I am also indebted.

19. The most helpful general analyses of the fiscal crisis and its origins are: Congressional Budget Office, "The Causes of New York City's Fiscal Crisis," *Political Science Quarterly*, 90 (Winter 1975-76), 659-674; Martin Shefter, "New York City's Fiscal Crisis: The Politics of Inflation and Retrenchment," *Public Interest*, 48 (Summer 1977), 98-127; and Charles R. Morris, *The Cost of Good Intentions: New York City and the Liberal Experiment* (New York: W. W. Norton, 1980), pp. 215-240. Robert Lekachman reviews the SEC Staff Report in "How New York Went for Broke," *Nation* (December 31, 1977), pp. 715-720.

20. See "Book Finally Closed on City Fiscal Blame," *New York Times*, August 28, 1979, p. B1.

21. On deception for the public good and in a crisis see Sissela Bok, *Lying* (New York: Pantheon, 1978), pp. 165-181, 107-122.

22. Congressional Budget Office, "Causes," pp. 667-670. For historical comparisons and an interpretation that emphasizes political factors see Shefter, "Fiscal Crisis," pp. 101-127.

23. Congressional Budget Office, "Causes," pp. 661-664, 672-674.

24. See "Selected Public Statements of Mayor Beame and Comptroller Goldin," above.

25. *SEC Staff Report*, chap. 1, pp. 61ff., 260.

26. Interview with Goldin, July 18, 1978.

27. *SEC Staff Report*, chap. 2, pp. 66-70.

28. Ibid., chap. 2, pp. 9-17.

29. Ibid., chap. 2, p. 104.

30. Ibid., chap. 3, p. 26.

31. Interview with Jac Friedgut (Citibank), June 15, 1978.

32. *SEC Staff Report*, chap. 2, pp. 27-34; chap. 3, pp. 23, 26-27.

33. Interview with Beame, July 11, 1978.

34. See Hart and Honoré, *Causation*, pp. 66-76, 94; and Feinberg, *Doing*, pp. 153-155, 165-167.

35. See *Response of the City*, pp. 1-27; and *SEC Staff Report*, chap. 3, pp. 110-134.

36. *Response of the City*, p. 24.

37. Hart and Honoré, *Causation*, pp. 116-119.

38. Ibid., pp. 201-207; and Feinberg, *Doing*, esp. p. 165n. See also Robert Keeton, *Legal Cause in the Law of Torts* (Columbus, Ohio: State University Press, 1963).

39. Cf. *SEC Staff Report*, chap. 3, pp. 208, 43.

40. *Response of the City*, p. 27.

41. Immanuel Kant, *Critique of Practical Reason and Other Writings in Moral Philosophy*, ed. and trans. L. W. Beck (Chicago: University of

Chicago Press, 1949), pp. 346-350; and *The Doctrine of Virtue*, trans M. J. Gregor (New York: Harper and Row, 1965), pp. 92-96. Charles Fried defends a qualified version of this Kantian criterion of intention: we are "primarily" responsible for what we intend (in the sense that we may never do intentional harm to "ward off greater harm" that is not the result of intentional action). On Fried's view, we may still be held responsible for some foreseeable but unintended consequences of our actions. *Right and Wrong* (Cambridge, Mass.: Harvard University Press, 1978), pp. 21-28, 42, 80, 112-114, 168. On the relation between foresight and intention in ascribing responsibility see Thomas Baldwin, "Foresight and Responsibility," *Philosophy*, 54 (July 1979), 347-360. For a somewhat different version of the view that "each of us is specially responsible for what *he* does, rather than for what other people do" as a result of what each of us does, see Bernard Williams, "A Critique of Utilitarianism," in J. J. C. Smart and Bernard Williams, *Utilitarianism For and Against* (Cambridge, Eng.: Cambridge University Press, 1973), pp. 93-100, 108-118. For criticism of Williams see John Harris, "Williams on Negative Responsibility and Integrity," *Philosophical Quarterly*, 24 (July 1974), 265-273.

42. *Response of the City*, pp. 69-78.

43. Interview with Steven Clifford (a consultant to the comptroller), July 31, 1978; *SEC Staff Report*, chap. 3, pp. 28ff.; and *Response of the City*, pp. 66ff.

44. *Response of the City*, pp. 57-61 (which mentions some additional explanations); and *SEC Staff Report*, chap. 2, pp. 18-26, chap. 3, pp. 23-26.

45. Cf. *Response of the City*, p. 27.

46. *New York Times*, August 27, 1977, p. 1.

47. *SEC Staff Report*, chap. 3, p. 137.

48. But see *SEC Staff Report*, chap. 3, pp. 34-36, 135.

49. Elsewhere I have undertaken a more general analysis of such responsibility: "Moral Responsibility of Public Officials: The Problem of Many Hands," *American Political Science Review*, 74 (December 1980), pp. 905-916. The analysis there in large part provides the framework I apply here to the responsibility of officials in the fiscal crisis.

50. *SEC Staff Report*, pp. 116-118, and chap. 1, passim.

IV. Observations on Method

Peter G. Brown

12. Assessing Officials

Recent widespread concern about the behavior of public officials has been characterized by more heat than light. However valuable an intuitive sense of moral outrage may be, alone it is no substitute for understanding solidly based on careful analysis. Such understanding can arise only from an examination of the extent to which the behavior of officials conforms or fails to conform to appropriate moral rules. The purpose of what follows, therefore, is not to applaud or decry the behavior of officials, but to focus on a philosophical task: how one can decide what officeholding behavior is morally appropriate or inappropriate. In that context, there are three questions I wish to address: (1) How can we describe the circumstances under which problems of assessing the moral behavior of public officials arise? (2) How might we characterize the methods by which one can decide which standards are relevant to which kinds of behavior? and (3) How can we avoid unreasonable expectations about what such an analysis can accomplish?

We can raise moral (or, perhaps more accurately, "normative") questions about the conduct of public officials in at least three areas: (1) matters concerning their personal conduct (for example, when lying is justified); (2) the criteria they use in designing and evaluating public policies (for example, how income should be distributed); and (3) the analytical frameworks they employ in addressing policy problems (for example, welfare economics or cost-benefit analysis).[1] This essay is concerned primarily —though not exclusively—with the first of these sorts of issues.

A variety of philosophical approaches suggest themselves for these tasks. The most promising philosophical model for resolving practical moral problems, however, seems to me to be what John Rawls called "reflective equilibrium."[2] As I describe and make use of reflective equilibrium, I will also show how it differs from alternative approaches and explain why I believe it to be, for purposes of applied ethical analysis, superior to them. In so doing, I hope to fill in a conspicuous omission in the field of applied ethics—a direct focus on the strengths and weaknesses of its analytical tools.

Before turning to the analytical tasks themselves, let me make explicit a few preliminary assumptions. First of all, I take it for granted that much of human behavior is subject to rules of one kind or another. Two of the most important categories of such rules are legal and moral. Legal rules are embodied in positive law, and are enforced by compulsion of the state through such means as fines, imprisonment, or even death. Moral rules, on the other hand, generally have no formal governmental coercion behind them. Of course, most, if not all, legal rules are derived, directly or indirectly, from moral considerations.

I deal here with moral rules, whether or not embodied in law, rules which every society attempts to inculcate in every one of its individual members. That process, called socialization, is accomplished through habituation, or internalization in what Freud called the super ego, or in some other fashion, so that the behavior of individuals conforms to the society's rules by "second nature."

Moral rules, in turn, are of at least two types. General rules make claims on persons as human beings, such as that commanding "Thou shalt not kill!" Such rules state our obligations to all other persons, independent of any particular relation we may have to them. A second sort of rule is role-related. Such rules define the nature of duties attaching to particular roles —parent/child, employer/employee, professional/client, neighbor/neighbor, worker/coworker, and, of course, public official/member of the public. Each role carries with it its particular set of moral rules.

At least some role-related rules impose obligations that conflict with, and sometimes serve as excuses from, obedience to general moral rules.[3] For example, we have a general moral obligation to help those in need, but our role-related obligations to our children serve as at least partial excuses against the claims of humanity in general. Few question the primacy of a father's obligation to feed and clothe his own children over his more general obligation as a human being to send Care packages to the chronically malnourished.

In the context of his confirmation as attorney general in the Nixon administration Eliot Richardson made certain promises to the Senate about the latitude to be given to the special prosecutor, Archibald Cox. Richardson thus incurred perfectly general obligations—which apply to all persons

—concerning the keeping of promises. Nixon's later wish that Richardson fire Cox gave rise to another set of obligations which are role related: obedience to one's superiors.

Once we acknowledge that role-related rules can sometimes excuse one from obedience to obligations to humanity generally, we must move to the next step of examining when such excuses are permissible and when they are not. How ought we to decide what rules should govern the behavior of public officials when role-related obligations conflict with general obligations owed to all?

Before turning to the evaluation of excuses it will be useful to describe the circumstances in which problems of assessment arise.

MORAL PROBLEMS IN PUBLIC OFFICE

The moral dilemmas of public officials arise in a variety of circumstances, of which there are at least three principal categories. The first—simple moral deviance—is comprised of those situations where the moral issue is perfectly clear but the official acts immorally because of a failure of will or a wilful intention to place greater weight on some other value than on the moral imperatives. The second category is that of ambiguity, a class of circumstances where there is a genuine issue as to whether the moral rules apply to the act under consideration. The last embraces the most difficult problems of all—moral dilemmas—where the rules of morality that govern a particular action conflict.

SIMPLE MORAL DEVIANCE

Simple moral deviance occurs when a public official fails to observe some clear, relevant, and well-justified moral rule. This sort of behavior might arise where rules require the public official to tell the truth but where he or she fails to observe this rule for reasons of personal enrichment, convenience, or political advantage. Noncompliance of this sort, though very troubling in political life and crucial to our assessment of the character of public officials, is not of much philosophical interest. The conceptual tools at the disposal of the philosopher are of little use in such a context.

MORAL AMBIGUITIES

Another sort of moral problem arises when the general moral rules or the rules characterizing a particular role do not give adequate guidance about how to act. Moral ambiguities arise because the situation falls outside the available rules, or because a rule itself is unclear.

To prevent confusion, I will distinguish two different sorts of ambiguity. Where the problem confronting the public official is not covered by the seemingly applicable rule, we have an irrelevance of denotation. In other words, what the rule commands—what its subject matter denotes—is irrelevant to the particular problem confronting the official. Simply put, denotatively irrelevant rules enjoin or command actions that are different from and unrelated to the action under consideration. On the other hand, confusions of connotation occur because the words that state the rules have more than one possible meaning. They are subject to a variety of interpretations. The "richness" of the words, in other words, creates problems of understanding precisely what obligations are created by the rule.

When a public official confronts a genuinely or apparently novel situation, where there has been no chance for prescribed rules of behavior to evolve, he or she is faced with what I call an irrelevance of denotation. There usually is an established set of moral rules under which the public official normally acts, but none of these rules seem to cover the situation in question. There is, as it were, a blank space on the moral map according to which he or she normally charts the course. The situation in question falls between the chairs.

How an official should act in dealing with some of the moral questions about the long-term disposal of hazardous radioactive waste is such a case. Certain radioactive wastes resulting from the use of nuclear materials to generate electric power remain extremely hazardous to living organisms for periods of between 300,000 and 400,000 years. The various options for disposing of or storing this waste impose different patterns of benefits and burdens upon future generations, as well as ourselves and our contemporaries. While the reliability of those projections is weakened by a large number of uncertainties, it is not such uncertainties alone that make the choice among options morally problematical. Even without the uncertainties, we still require normative standards by which to judge which option is to be preferred. Certain technologies for handling such wastes may be fairly reliable in terms of protecting future generations. These technologies, however, may expose our contemporaries to higher levels of radiation than they would otherwise experience. We need moral standards in order to determine how we should evaluate who should bear such risks.

Nuclear waste disposal is a problem that has never been explicitly faced before, so we have had neither time nor occasion to develop reliable moral standards of guidance for such decisions. Theories of justice that govern the distribution of goods in a given society[4] would normally constitute one source of such standards. Unfortunately, however, such theories have almost exclusively focused on distribution of goods among living contemporaries (within a single society), with the consequence that they give us virtually no guidance in reasoning about justifications for the claims that might be advanced in behalf of future generations. Because it is future generations who may bear most of the burdens of today's decisions about disposal of nuclear wastes, we simply have no moral principles to which to turn in deciding what to do with such wastes.

The second sort of moral ambiguity — confusion of connotation — arises when there is uncertainty as to the exact meaning of key conceptual elements required for us to prescribe how one ought to behave. Such connotational ambiguities occur in rule ambiguity and factual ambiguity. In the former, it is unclear precisely what conduct the rule is intended to govern. The moral rule by which actions are to be judged is itself subject to a variety of interpretations. For instance, a rule requiring that an official always tell the "truth" is indefinite because "truth" may range from "the whole truth and nothing but the truth" to the avoidance of saying anything that is not consistent with what actually happened, with many stages between those two extremes. Consequently, the precise behavior required by a rule simply enjoining truth-telling can vary widely, depending on which definition of "truth" the rule is intended to embrace.

Another set of difficulties arises out of uncertainty as to the complex of facts faced by the official. Here it is not the content of the rule that is uncertain, the obligation to tell the truth, do what is right, honor one's promises. Rather, what is uncertain is the factual state of affairs to which the rule is to be applied. Different factual descriptions often imply different moral prescriptions. To borrow from medical ethics, for example, a rule forbidding physicians from terminating life support systems until a patient is dead contains factual uncertainty about whether the word "death" means the cessation of heart function, brain function, or something else. Yet how a physician is to behave toward a given individual will differ depending on how the factual circumstances are interpreted.

CONFLICTS AMONG COMPETING MORAL OBLIGATIONS

When obligations point in different directions, a third category of moral problems arises. An officeholder's obligations as a public official, for example, may conflict either with general moral precepts or with his or her obligations as a citizen. Frequently, there may be conflicts built into the several obligations of the role itself. Unlike the situation where there is a single rule prescribing conduct, which may be ambiguous either as to the content of the rule or the facts it is intended to cover, here the moral conduct is, as it were, codetermined. The official is under more obligations than he or she can respond to. The obligations of one role or set of roles simply cannot be fulfilled consistent with one's other obligations. Two or more sets of obligations overlap, one of which must be given greater weight.

Ambassador Richard Helms seems to have found himself in such a dilemma when he was called to testify before the Senate committee investigating CIA involvement in Chile. In falsely denying specific involvement by the CIA, Helms lied to the committee. He was convinced that telling the truth would undermine the effectiveness of the CIA, which in turn would pose a grave threat to the national security. From his perspective, the ordinary truth-telling rules that govern human relations, and which were embodied in his oath to the committee, were in conflict with the obligations he felt as a former director of the CIA and member of the intelligence community. He was convinced that those obligations required him to give greater weight to the national security, in some circumstances, than to his obligation to tell the truth to the committee.

APPLIED ETHICS: SOME PROCEDURAL SUGGESTIONS

Having examined a variety of different kinds of moral problems, let us now explore some ways of analyzing them. Before turning directly to the solution, a bit of background is required. The major method for analyzing problems in the field of applied ethics is akin to what John Rawls has called "reflective equilibrium." Although the latter two sorts of moral problems sketched above present different kinds of issues, their resolution will rely in one way or another on this method. Most scholars agree that it is, at least at present, the most useful method.

REFLECTIVE EQUILIBRIUM DESCRIBED

Reflective equilibrium is a process by which we refine and alter our moral principles by examining our considered intuitive sense of what is right in a given circumstance in light of principles or theories that grow out of those intuitions. (The important distinction between principles and theories can be ignored at this point.) The word "considered" signals that intuitions that are to count as evidence must pass certain minimal tests: they must be formulated on the basis of adequate information, under circumstances conducive to deliberation, and must not be mere rationalizations for self-interest, or based on misleading analogies.

Reflective equilibrium has two parts. It is reflective in that one moves from a series of considered intuitions to the principles or theories that seem to govern those intuitions; and one returns to the intuitions in order to alter them to fit the principles or theories most closely. The process *may* thus simultaneously require the modification of principles or theories so as to fit intuition, and/or altering our sense of what is intuitively appropriate in light of the principles or theories. Equilibrium is attained when the principles or theories fit the intuitions that fall under them. The key to the usefulness of equilibrium analysis, as Sissela Bok has pointed out, is the word "fit." It can be seen to serve two purposes: (1) to provide a boundary, a means of determining what falls under the principle and what does not; and (2) to conform the principle to that which is intended to fall under it.

Boundary establishment, the first purpose, is no different from the problem of determining whether a particular action is or is not intended to be part of the class of prohibited actions. The principle carries with it certain qualifiers. In other words, any principle concerning lying can be disaggregated into several subprinciples that specify what counts as a lie. These qualifiers will act as boundary conditions for determining what falls under a principle.

There is one important caveat, however. Insofar as how one's behavior in particular cases can affect one's own interest, we may have to take special precautions against rationalization and bias. It will be no surprise to note that how an act is classified may have an important bearing on one's own interest. Such precautions may take the form, for example, of testing one's willingness to classify similar actions on the part of others in the same way, or checking one's accuracy in classification by the views of others.

The second purpose — conforming the principle to those actions intended to fall under it — is checked by determining whether the principle authorizes actions that do violence to the intuitions. Such tests of the authority of the principle can, of course, be accomplished by means of either hypothetical or "real world" examples.[5] Twisting the principle to suit one's own interest can be guarded against in the same way one avoids a biased classification of which actions fall under it.

To understand the usefulness of this method it is very important to distinguish "narrow" from "wide" reflective equilibrium.[6] Consider the structure or moral reasoning. It has at least three levels — (1) intuitions about what to do in particular cases, (2) principles that systematize and account for those intuitions, and (3) theories that relate and justify those principles.

Narrow reflective equilibrium operates between levels (1) and (2), that is, between considered intuitions about particular cases and principles, without recourse to level (3)—theory. Narrow reflective equilibrium is fundamentally a method of arriving at justifications by applying a consistency test. Our intuitions must be "fitted" in such a manner as to make them consistent with the principle.

Perhaps a simple example of narrow reflective equilibrium will help to show how it works. Suppose we had an ambiguous rule that prohibited lying, and we have a great number of cases where the rule seems appropriate. We first formulate our principle: "Lying is wrong." But then we are confronted with a case where failure to lie will result in unwarranted harm to innocent individuals. In such a case, our intuition tells us that we are obligated to lie. So we return to the principle and alter it to say: "Lying is wrong, except to prevent unwarranted harm to innocent individuals." Suppose that next we are faced with a case where, if we lie, we may protect a person who is not innocent, but our intuition tells us that the degree of harm that will result from telling the truth is unwarranted; for example, it may mean a sentence of twenty years for possession of marijuana. We may then want to remove the word "innocent" from the principle formulated above. After many such modifications, we should have a principle that is finally formulated in such a way as to provide reliable guidance to us in solving troublesome cases. For instance, the principle should help us decide when one can justifiably lie to protect the national interest from potential adversaries who might, if told the truth, inflict unwarranted harm.

Narrow reflective equilibrium is essentially conservative. If, in our analysis of novel or unprecedented problems, we stop at narrow reflective equilibrium, our prescription will be substantively similar to our prescriptions for problems with which we have experience. Any given instance in which narrow reflective equilibrium is employed will not yield any particularly surprising prescriptions. Moreover, because it does not stand outside the spectrum of present practices, and does not invoke norms or values from the level of theory, narrow reflective equilibrium cannot, by the very nature of the case, be expected to give guidance on the moral acceptability of those practices.

Wide reflective equilibrium includes the narrow form but adds an important justificatory step. It provides a way of testing our principles so as to counter the conservative tendency of narrow reflective equilibrium. Our moral principles can thereby be accounted for by our theories in a manner similar to the way laws of physics are accounted for by theories about the physical world.

For the theories to play this role in justification, it is obvious that they have to be more than restatements of the principles or intuitions involved.[7] Otherwise they add nothing. To mirror something is not to justify it. Consequently, the theories must have either a different foundation, or at least a broader one, than whatever it is they are called upon to justify. They will be theories such as the theory of the nature of the person, or theories about the nature and purpose of democratic government, and the like.

While such theories often have moral aspects, they are not simply restatements of our moral principles or intuitions in a more abstract form. The evidence for them is eclectic. For instance, our theories about the nature of persons have more than one source of support. Some of these are philosophical in character, drawing on the philosophical literature of Aristotle, Kant, and Mill, as well as others. But the theories of the person also draw on knowledge from physiology, studies of man's place in evolution, therapeutic psychiatry, development psychology, and other fields. This is not to suggest for a moment that all such perspectives agree in detail or even in the main. It is to say that moral principles may not be inconsistent with suitably supported theories from these other domains.

The principles that we turn to for guidance will thus have two sources of justification. They must fit our intuitions about cases, and they must be consistent with the relevant theory or theories.

Informed consent, a principle of wide application in the field of medical ethics, enjoys these two sorts of justifications. It conforms to a variety of actual practices ranging from the law of contracts to our sense of what is right practice when involving persons in activities that contain risk. It is also consistent with at least two types of moral theories—those such as Kant's, which emphasize the importance of self-generated objectives, and those such as Mill's, which stress that, as a rule, the individual is the best protector of his or her own interest.

The foregoing description of wide reflective equilibrium enables us to see why this method is preferable to two alternative approaches which, on first examination, might seem more attractive. One would involve simply testing cases of ambiguity or conflicts by examining our settled intuitions about what to do in similar cases and then acting consistently in the case at hand. That, we have already seen, is narrow reflective equilibrium. The other approach is to try to argue directly from moral theory to a conclusion about what to do in the particular case at hand.

To employ narrow reflective equilibrium exclusively has at least two serious defects. First, it provides no external grounds for prescribing why we should behave in a given way other than the weak requirements that the intuitions be "settled" and that the behavior be consistent. These characteristics alone do not enable us to advance persuasive arguments as to why behavior in particular circumstances should be such and such. It fails to provide a reasoned basis for judgment. Second, and nearly as important, it offers no opportunity for re-examining or replacing present patterns of behavior or practice. Since narrow reflective equilibrium relies on an analogy between what we deem appropriate in related areas to the problem under consideration at the moment, it simply extends what we are already doing to the uncertain case. It thus offers little opportunity for providing a critique of established patterns of behavior.

Neither are we likely to make such progress trying to apply ethical theories—such as utilitarianism or Kant's views on the respect for persons—directly to particular cases. Since such theories are, by their very nature, abstract, they are usually compatible with a great variety of responses to particular situations. Abstract ideas about respect for persons in general shed little light on what our obligations are to our successors concerning nuclear waste disposal, since a great variety of options may all, in one sense or another, allow for the "respect" of persons. Only by testing plausible principles against settled intuitions about similar cases at the same time that we test them against relevant theories can we get the sort of principle with the appropriate level of specificity, as well as being suitably justified, for resolving this particular kind of case.

A simplified scheme of wide reflective equilibrium would thus look like this:

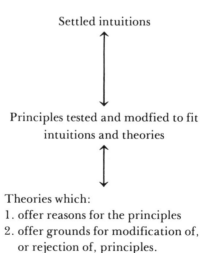

Settled intuitions

Principles tested and modfied to fit
intuitions and theories

Theories which:
1. offer reasons for the principles
2. offer grounds for modification of,
   or rejection of, principles.

Both narrow and wide reflective equilibrium can serve as means of resolving moral problems confronting public officials, once we have appropriately categorized the particular case with which we are confronted. Some problem cases can be resolved, at least in an ad hoc manner, by narrow reflective equilibrium, although we should have a lower level of confidence in our solutions since they will not have the added support of theoretical justification. Our analysis will have omitted the step of considering and invoking reasons in support of the principles.

In what follows I sketch how principles, which can be guides for behavior, may be developed. It goes without saying that formulating these principles is only a partial step in our overall determination of how we should behave. I do not, of course, try to set out the theoretical justification of any given principle. That is a complex task which for any given principle would require extensive argument.

CHOOSING PRINCIPLES AND MORAL AMBIGUITIES

Reflective equilibrium can assist in resolving an ambiguous situation in the following way. First, we should try to classify the ambiguous situation confronting the public official. Is it a problem of truth-telling, or of justice, or of particular rights? Such a classification supplies a criterion of relevance in selecting another example — an uncontroversial situation that is similar in relevant circumstances to the ambiguous one. We can then try to determine the nature of the principle that underlies our sense about what to do in the clear situation and apply it to the unclear problem case.

Formulating such a principle can have two consequences. The first is that the seemingly ambiguous problem can be demonstrated to be sufficiently similar to another situation with respect to which our intuitions are well settled that the ambiguity disappears. That is, the former can be shown to fall under an already clear and well-established principle about behavior. Alternatively, it may be that the problem in question will not lend itself to analogy with some settled situation. In that event, we can extend, and thereby modify, the principle that governs the well-settled case to make it cover the one about which we are uncertain.

For instance, using the tool of narrow reflective equilibrium, we may decide that the problems arising out of the disposal of radioactive wastes are really not different in kind from similar problems growing out of the handling of other hazardous materials. In the alternative, we can decide that the radioactive waste problem *is* different in kind, but that, by the method just described, we can modify the moral rules that govern our behavior in at least roughly similar circumstances so that they will give us guidance in the uncertain case at hand.

Suppose we decide, for example, that radioactive wastes are not different in kind from hazardous metals, such as mercury, which are by-products of industrial processes. We then could conclude that no additional criteria would be required for deciding on the appropriate measures regarding radioactive wastes. (I do not mean to imply by this example that other hazardous substances are properly handled.) If we were to conclude that radioactive wastes were different in kind, then we could try to modify the principles from related areas to take the difference into account. If the longevity of radioactive wastes were the distinguishing characteristic, then we could modify our principles concerning short-term risk to extend them to this different situation. However, as noted above, relying on narrow reflective equilibrium has serious defects which should be taken into account in deciding how much confidence to place in these modified principles.

In order to test a principle that might apply to a problem case by the mode of wide reflective equilibrium, one needs, of course, a theoretical structure. In a novel case such as nuclear waste disposal seems to be, the mere task of discovering appropriate theory can be an enormously difficult undertaking. Since we have no theory of intergenerational justice, we need to start one level further removed. One would want to examine the strengths and weaknesses of various traditional approaches to justification in order to know what approach is relevant. For example, we might examine whether attempts to justify moral principles on the basis of sympathy, such as Hume did, or mutual benefit, such as the contract theorists do, could serve as justifications for intuitively plausible principles. However difficult the search may be, we cannot afford to have much confidence in our principles until such a justification has been developed.[8]

Formulating relevant principles for addressing the second sort of moral ambiguity — those situations where the prescriptive force of the rule is unclear as a consequence of vague terminology (confusions of connotation) — can be approached in a two-stage manner. First, one should analyze the vague concept to determine the variety of meanings that could be given to it; for example, as noted above, the word "truth" is subject to a number of interpretations. The question then becomes: "Which sense is most applicable to the situation at hand?" We can employ narrow reflective equilibrium analysis, for instance, and attempt to fit the principle to the case. Such an analysis allows us to fill in the "vague spot" with the most applicable sense of the term in question. To continue the example of truth-telling: in the case of a subject involved in human experimentation, our considered intuitions would inform us that the applicable sense of truth-telling was "full disclosure of all relevant matters," or something of the sort.

If we wish to discover the normative assumptions that are buried in what appear to be straightforward empirical accounts, a similar method can be used to sort out various characterizations of the factual situation in which the policymaker is operating. For instance, we usually characterize our country's relationships with other nations in terms of two broad categories: allies and actual or potential adversaries. To those who are not philosophically inclined, this may appear to be a simple description of the facts of international relations. Yet, the terms "allies" and "adversaries" have very strong normative implications for the way we behave in a variety of situations, depending entirely upon which of them is employed. (Numerous intermediate characterizations may be possible.) If we use the term "ally," for instance, the moral rules that would govern our relations would be of a similar sort to those that pertain between friends. Designating a nation as an "adversary" carries with it at least implicit justifications for indifference or clandestine or overt aggression. (See Helms's views of relations with Chile above.)

Reflective equilibrium of both kinds can serve, along with relevant empirical information, to test the way we characterize the relations between nations. Certain ways of describing these relations can be shown to justify practices that will not stand up to the tests of reflective equilibrium. Either these practices may come into conflict with other settled practices, or they may be inconsistent with our theoretical conceptions concerning the purposes and functions of government.

For example, in the context of narrow reflective equilibrium, before characterizing our relations with Chile under the Allende regime as adversarial, it would be useful to take a clear case of such a relationship — Germany in 1942 — and then sort out the differences in the two cases. Such differences would obviously be actual belligerent conduct, ability to inflict harm, and so forth. This would serve to focus our attention on the question of whether justifications that could support the assassination of Hitler could properly be extended to Allende.

In the context of wide reflective equilibrium, the questions are, as usual, more difficult, both because we move beyond simply reasoning by analogy and because, in this case, there is no well-developed normative theory concerning the relations between nations. Nevertheless, at the theoretical level it is appropriate to ask whether it is a justifiable purpose of a government to protect its citizens by violent means against remote and speculative threats.[9] To answer such a question we need a theory concerning the proper limits on actions a government may take on behalf of its citizens.

The most difficult moral conflicts facing public officials arise because of conflicts among the various roles in which the same officials are required to act, or because of conflicts between role requirements and morality generally. One way to try to sort out the obligations that may exist in any circumstance is to examine the nature of the obligations that attach to the respective roles.

Some obligations that are attached to some roles may not permit any deviations. If we had available fully worked out, and hence consistent, theories to invoke for use when we employ wide reflective equilibrium, then such conflicts between competing obligations would presumably disappear. At least some obligations, however, are not binding in such strict fashion. In fact, many moral obligations are more similar to legal presumptions than to unambiguous and absolute rules of conduct. Moral obligation gives a direction to a course of action that may be shifted, either slightly or radically, if certain factors are present. The direction, in other words, is a presumption that admits of rebuttal. Reflective equilibrium can serve as a means of discovering what can serve as a rebuttal.

This is another way of saying that the obligations attaching to all roles do not have the same force. In *Discretion to Disobey*, Mortimer and Sanford Kadish develop the notion of what they call "a recourse role."[10] In a recourse role, an individual has a role that is so defined as to permit deviations from whatever the standards governing the role may be.

A recourse role is not to be confused with a simply discretionary role, such as that of a judge who can impose an indeterminate sentence, say one of from five to nine years for a given crime. An individual in a recourse role is not formally given any latitude in how he or she is to behave. Rather, he or she is held to a standard of behavior, but the standard constitutes a presumption that can be overridden by certain considerations that may be built into the role itself. To the extent that public officials serve in recourse roles, some of the moral dilemmas that are thought to confront them may be handled by perceiving of the role along this alternative model. For example, police officers may be presumed to arrest all lawbreakers, but since law enforcement resources will always be scarce, this presumption can be overridden; for example, so as to justify concentrating resources on more dangerous crimes, while overlooking other infractions.

Rebuttals may be of two types. The first simply call attention to the internal conflict of a seemingly obligatory course of action with the overall purposes of the role. Alternatively, the purposes of the role itself may, under certain circumstances, conflict with other more closely held moral imperatives. For pacifists the role requirements of soldiers conflict with more important general requirements.

How can we tell what constitutes a bona fide rebuttal as opposed to a specious one? Here again we use one or the other mode of reflective equilibrium. Either can serve as a means of determining whether the admission of a rebuttal would introduce morally counterintuitive consequences. Narrow reflective equilibrium would test the principles implicit in various rebuttals against considered practices. Wide reflective equilibrium would check those principles against relevant theories.

LIMITATIONS

The methods of applied ethics described above obviously are directed to the construction of criteria for judging behavior in particular contexts. Three limitations of this method should be noted.

First, the kind of applied ethics that is the subject matter of this essay can rarely offer an unambiguous rule of decision. In most circumstances, decisions will necessarily depend on judgments that are to be made in light of both the factual circumstances of the case and also the principles tested and confirmed by the method of reflective equilibrium. Since there is no a priori way to specify all the factual considerations that will need to be taken into account, clear prescriptions about how to behave will not be possible on the basis of this method alone.

Second, finding answers to the ambiguities and conflicts sketched above will not be easy. Since justification of moral principles is a technically difficult task, a great deal of patience will be required to outlast and overcome the many instances of academic obtuseness masquerading as subtlety, for example, the making of distinctions that do not in fact affect the course of the argument.

Third, and finally, we are seriously mistaken if we look to applied ethics as a cure-all for immoral behavior. Arjay Miller, formerly dean of the Stanford Business School, has said about the expanding study of ethics that: "I believe we ought to be doing more, but I am not sure exactly what. It's a problem of motivation and basic human values. There are a lot of people in jail today who have passed ethics courses."[11]

Ethics, even the sort of applied ethics I have focused on, is no substitute for moral character. It can serve two functions that will contribute to more acceptable moral behavior. It can provide assistance to persons of good character in resolving ambiguities or conflicts. In addition, practicing one or the other kind of reflective equilibrium analysis can help to mold character itself. Certain types of "instruction" can, in turn, be vehicles for the development of such capacities. We should no more expect all persons who take ethics courses to be moral, however, than we should expect all students of economics to be prudent investors.

NOTES

1. See my "Ethics and Public Policy: A Preliminary Agenda," *Policy Studies Journal*, 7 (Autumn 1978), 132-137, for a further discussion of these distinctions and their importance.

2. John Rawls, *A Theory of Justice* (Cambridge, Mass.: Harvard University Press, 1971), pp. 46-53. Approaches other than reflective equilibrium are: trying to derive principles for conduct directly from moral theories (for example, utilitarianism) or reasoning simply by analogy (a method very often employed in the law). Reflective equilibrium includes these methods but is not restricted to them.

3. See Richard Wasserstrom's "Lawyers as Professionals: Some Moral Issues," *Human Rights*, 5 (1975), 1, for a detailed discussion of the point. Thomas Nagel's "Ruthlessness in Public Life," in *Public and Private Morality* (Cambridge: Cambridge University Press, 1978), pp. 75-91, provides an interesting discussion of the characteristics of public roles and the manner in which individuals in them respond to somewhat different sets of considerations than do persons not so situated (see especially pp. 80-86).

4. I am indebted to Douglas MacLean, a colleague at the Center for Philosophy and Public Policy, the University of Maryland, for showing me why traditional sources of justification for moral principles are not readily suitable bases for principles to govern this case.

5. In formulating principles by using reflective equilibrium, philosophers will often have recourse to hypothetical examples. Here principles are tested against examples that may seem farfetched or even ludicrous, but the method is a familiar one to philosophers. Setting up a hypothetical example allows one to think away certain complications involved in any actual example. It can serve as an antidote to the conservative nature of narrow reflective equilibrium. We simply do not have to be constrained by present practice. But by ranging over hypothetical circumstances and resorting to ones that are implausible, one must formulate principles that will cover all these examples, often in such a weak form that they will offer little guidance. As hard cases make bad law, the philosophers' examples, as Henry Shue — also a colleague at the Center for Philosophy and Public Policy — has noted, will often make weak principles.

6. Norman Daniels makes this distinction between narrow and wide

reflective equilibrium in "Wide Reflective Equilibrium and Theory Acceptance in Ethics," *Journal of Philosophy*, 76 (May 1979), 256-282.

7. Ibid.

8. See Douglas MacLean, "Benefit-Cost Analysis, Future Generations and Energy Policy: A Survey of the Moral Issues," *Science, Technology and Human Values*, 31 (Spring 1980), 3-10.

9. See my ". . . in the National Interest," in *Human Rights and U.S. Foreign Policy: Principles and Applications*, ed. myself and Douglas MacLean (Lexington, Mass.: Lexington Books, 1979), pp. 161-172, for a discussion of national security and national interest.

10. Mortimer and Sanford Kadish, *Discretion to Disobey* (Stanford: Stanford University Press, 1973).

11. *New York Times*, February 1978.

Contributors

Sissela Bok, Lecturer in Medical Ethics at Harvard Medical School, is the author of *Lying: Moral Choice in Public and Private Life* (1978).

Peter G. Brown, Director, Center for Philosophy and Public Policy, University of Maryland, is coeditor of *Human Rights and U.S. Foreign Policy: Principles and Applications* (1979).

Joel L. Fleishman, Director, Institute of Policy Sciences and Public Affairs, Duke University, is coauthor of *Ethical Dilemmas and the Education of Policy Makers* (1980).

Lance Liebman, Professor of Law at Harvard University, is coeditor of *Race and Schooling in the City* (1981).

Mark H. Moore, Daniel and Florence Guggenheim Professor of Criminal Justice Policy and Management, Harvard University, is the author of *Buy and Bust: The Effective Regulation of an Illicit Market in Heroin* (1977).

Bruce L. Payne, Director of the Program in the Humanities, Policy, and the Arts, Institute of Policy Sciences and Public Affairs, Duke University, is coauthor of *Ethical Dilemmas and the Education of Policy Makers* (1980).

David E. Price, Professor of Political Science and Policy Sciences at Duke University, is the author of *Policymaking in Congressional Committees* (1979).

Dennis F. Thompson, Professor of Politics, Princeton University, is the author of *John Stuart Mill and Representative Government* (1976).

Donald P. Warwick, Institute Fellow in the Harvard Institute for International Development, is the author of *The Teaching of Ethics in the Social Sciences* (1980).

Charles Wolf, Jr., Dean of the Rand Graduate Institute, is coauthor of *The Demand for Oil and Energy in Developing Countries* (1980).

Douglas T. Yates, Jr., Associate Professor of Organization and Management and Political Science, Yale University, is the author of *The Ungovernable City* (1977).

Index